Contents

Great Excavations

Shaping the Archaeological Profession

edited by

John Schofield

Oxbow Books

Oxford and Oakville

Published by
Oxbow Books, Oxford, UK

© Oxbow Books and the individual authors 2011

ISBN 978-1-84217-409-8

This book is available direct from

Oxbow Books, Oxford, UK
(Phone: 01865-241249; Fax: 01865-794449)

and

The David Brown Book Company
PO Box 511, Oakville, CT 06779, USA
(Phone: 860-945-9329; Fax: 860-945-9468)

or from our website
www.oxbowbooks.com

A CIP record is available for this book from the British Library

Library of Congress Cataloging-in-Publication Data

Great excavations : shaping the archaeological profession / edited by John Schofield.
    p. cm.
Essays derived from a session at Institute for Archaeologists annual conference in 2007.
Includes bibliographical references.
ISBN 978-1-84217-409-8 (pbk.)
  1. Excavations (Archaeology)--Great Britain--Congresses. 2. Historic sites--Great Britain--Congresses. 3. Great Britain--Antiquities--Congresses. 4. Archaeologists--Great Britain--Congresses. 5. Archaeology--Great Britain--History--Congresses. 6. Archaeology--Social aspects--Great Britain--Congresses. I. Schofield, John, 1948-
  DA90.G773 2010
  930.1028'30941--dc22

2010031345

Font cover: Digging Deeper, *Mike Pitts.*

Printed in Great Britain by
Short Run Press, Exeter

List of Contributors

Evelyn Baker trained as a painter at Portsmouth College of Art and St Albans School of Art. She became involved in archaeology by working at Portchester Castle and Fishbourne Roman Palace with Barry Cunliffe and David Baker. With David Baker she co-directed major excavations with volunteer work forces at Elstow Abbey, Selborne Priory and Bedford Castle before excavating at Warden Abbey. She joined Bedfordshire County Council as a Field Officer on its first MSC training scheme, mainly directing at Grove Priory (La Grava), before becoming Manager of the County's Archaeological Service and Vice Chair of the IFA. She is now joint principal of Historic Environment Conservation. Contact: evelyn@suttons.org.uk.

Beverley Ballin Smith is an archaeological project manager at the University of Glasgow. She lived almost 13 years on Orkney, where she excavated and researched monuments of all periods including the broch of Howe, followed by several years digging in Scandinavia. Her research interests include later prehistoric ceramics, Northern Isles/Scandinavian links, Shetland and the island of Papa Stour, and stone buildings. She has published research papers as well as a few monographs and edited others. Contact: bbs@archaeology.gla.ac.uk.

Paul Barford, while studying at the Institute of Archaeology in London, worked on the excavation at Mucking for a number of seasons from 1975 until the end of the excavation. On leaving university he began work in Mucking Post Excavation followed by several years of freelance finds reporting, including work for the HBMC on material from Mucking. After a period teaching in the Institute of Archaeology, Warsaw University and a spell in the Office of the Chief Archaeologist in the State Service for the Protection of Historical Monuments, he is currently working freelance in Warsaw, living with his Polish wife (who he met in 1976 when she was camp cook at Mucking).

Now retired, **Dr C. Stephen Briggs** was sometime Head of Archaeology at the RCAHMW. He has a life-long interest in defining archaeological evidence, part of which demands an understanding of the history of archaeology. The present paper is a by-product of his chapter on Prehistory in the recent Society of Antiquaries Tercentenary History *Visions of Antiquity* (2007). Contact address: cstephenbriggs@yahoo.co.uk and Llwyn Deiniol, Llanddeiniol, Llanrhystud, Ceredigion SY23 5DT.

Martin Carver is Professor of Archaeology at the University of York and has directed research at Sutton Hoo since 1983. From 1996 he has directed excavation and research at the Pictish monastery at Portmahomack (published by EUP, 2008). He is currently editor of *Antiquity*. Contact: Kings Manor, York YO1 7EP, UK.

John Collis started digging as a schoolboy in his native city of Winchester in 1955, before studying archaeology at Cambridge, completing his doctorate on Iron Age Oppida in 1975. He supervised excavations in Winchester with Martin Biddle before directing his own large-scale excavations at Owslebury. He has studied and worked in several European countries, but has mainly been excavating in France on Late Iron Age sites. He retired as Professor of Archaeology at Sheffield University in 2004. Contact: j.r.collis@sheffield.ac.uk.

Bob Croft started his archaeological career in Northamptonshire and worked on the medieval village excavations at Lyveden sparking off a lifelong interest in deserted medieval villages. He first visited Wharram Percy as a schoolboy in 1972, went on to study Archaeology and Geography at Leeds University and later worked as a supervisor on the South Manor site from 1980 until 1990. He now works as the County Archaeologist in Somerset. Contact: racroft@somerset.gov.uk.

Barry Cunliffe is Emeritus Professor of European Archaeology at the University of Oxford. He has taught at the Universities of Bristol (1963–6), Southampton (1966–72) and Oxford (1972–2007). He has excavated extensively in Britain and in Spain and France and is currently working on the Isle of Wight and on Sark. He is a Trustee of the British Museum and a Commissioner for English Heritage. Contact: barry.cunliffe@arch. ox.ac.uk.

Christopher Evans is the Executive Director of the Cambridge Archaeological Unit of the University of Cambridge, which he co-founded together with Ian Hodder in 1990. He has directed a wide variety of major fieldwork projects, both abroad (Nepal, China & Cape Verde) and in UK, most recently publishing the results of the Haddenham Project in 2006. He was elected a member of the Society of Antiquaries of London in 2001. Contact: Cambridge Archaeological Unit, Dept of Archaeology, University of Cambridge, Downing St, Cambridge CB2 3DZ (e-mail: cje30@cam.ac.uk).

Dr Paul Everill completed his PhD in 2006 and now teaches applied archaeological techniques at the University of Winchester. His current research interests include the structure of British commercial archaeology; the teaching of field archaeology; training excavations; and the development of fieldwork techniques. His first proper experience of archaeology was at the 'Great Excavation' of Wroxeter in 1989. Contact: Paul.Everill@ winchester.ac.uk.

Dr Richard Hall directed 'The Viking Dig' in Coppergate, York, and is now Director of Archaeology at York Archaeological Trust, and Cathedral Archaeologist at York Minster and Ripon Cathedral. Sometime Chairman of the Institute of Field Archaeologists, President of the Society for Medieval Archaeology, and Secretary of the Council for British Archaeology, he is currently President of the Yorkshire Archaeological Society. He has been consultant to UNESCO and to major excavation projects in Sweden and Norway; his latest book, *Exploring the World of the Vikings*, is now available in Latvian.

Volunteer digger, pot-washer, small find 'specialist' etc turned professional, **Peter Hinton** worked for many years in London archaeology culminating as a senior manager for the Museum of London Archaeology Service responsible for specialist services and post-excavation. He has been Director then Chief Executive of the Institute for Archaeologists since 1997. Contact peter.hinton@archaeologists.net.

David Jennings' archaeological 'career' began as a school boy working on Philip Barker's excavations at Wroxeter, where he predominantly behaved as an insufferable youth tolerated by his elders and betters. He doubts whether his conduct has improved over the intervening 29 years. Working in professional archaeology since 1987 in a wide range of roles, he has been the Chief Executive Officer of Oxford Archaeology since 1999.

Chris Musson, born in 1935, originally trained and worked as an architect but in 1967 switched to archaeology to pursue his love of excavation. After work with the Rescue Archaeology Group and the Clwyd-Powys Archaeological Trust, until 1986, he turned to archaeological air photography with the Royal Commission in Wales. Following retirement in 1997 he has travelled Europe, occasionally digging but mainly urging other archaeologists to 'take to the air'.

Dominic Powlesland grew up in East Anglia. He first troweled at the age of 11, and attended Colchester Royal Grammar School, where he was taught archaeology (and greatly influenced) by Mike Corbishley. Early excavation experiences included roles as a senior site planner in 1971 in Winchester, and helping to set up the York Archaeological Trust drawing office in 1972. In 1973 he spent six months as a research assistant at the University of Manchester where he then undertook undergraduate and postgraduate studies. He was also acting as assistant director to Bill Hanson at Croy Hill on the Antonine Wall and directing excavations at Grove Priory in Bedfordshire. Since 1978 he has been directing excavations and other fieldwork at West Heslerton in the Vale of Pickering. In 1980 the Landscape Research Centre was established as a registered charity which later took on responsibility for the various research projects originally administered by the local authority. Dominic is internationally recognised on account of expertise in excavation techniques, remote-sensing, archaeological computing and landscape archaeology. He has held visiting or honorary lectureships in three fields, computing, geography and archaeology, at a number of British universities and is currently Visiting Professor at the Institute of Medieval Studies at the University of Leeds. Busman's holidays over many years have enabled him to assist, primarily in a training role, in projects abroad in Lebanon, Turkmenistan, Italy, Germany and the USA.

Following a degree and PhD at the University of Southampton (1981–8) **John Schofield** worked for English Heritage, in the Monuments Protection Programme and the Characterisation Team, until 2010. He is now Director of Studies in Cultural Heritage Management at the Univeristy of York. He recently completed his first excavation since Pontnewydd cave in 1983, on an old Ford Transit Van. Contact: js1032@york.ac.uk.

Niall Sharples was born in Glasgow and studied archaeology at the University of Glasgow from 1975–1980. After an initial period as a freelance excavator, he was appointed director of the Maiden Castle excavations. He subsequently published a general book on the hillfort and a detailed report on the excavations for English Heritage. Upon completing his work at Maiden Castle he was employed by Historic Scotland until 1995 when he acquired a position in the School of History and Archaeology at Cardiff University, where he is now a reader. Contact: sharples@cardiff.ac.uk.

Geoff Wainwright was, until recently President of the Society of Antiquaries. Born in Pembrokeshire, he studied in Cardiff and London and was a Professor of Archaeology in India before becoming Chief Archaeologist at English Heritage. He has undertaken many excavations in England and Wales and pioneered the large scale excavation of sites such as Durrington Walls (Wilts.) Gussage All Saints (Dorset) and Balksbury Camp (Hants.). Contact: Geoff@bluestone.eu.com.

Roger White is a Senior Lecturer at the Institute of Archaeology and Antiquity, University of Birmingham. He has for many years been involved in researching the archaeology of Western Britain in the Roman and Post-Roman periods and this has led to his long association to the site of Wroxeter Roman City. He is currently Academic Director at Ironbridge Institute where he has been exploring the varied and complex heritage of the industrial age. Contact: r.h.white@bham.ac.uk.

Tony Wilmott graduated from Newcastle University in 1977 and did post-graduate work at Birmingham. Following periods of work with Birmingham City Museum, Hereford and Worcester CC, the Museum of London and the West Yorkshire Archaeology Service, he joined English Heritage in 1987, where he now works as a Senior Archaeologist in the Archaeological Projects Department. During 21 years with EH he has directed excavations on many sites, principally on Hadrian's Wall, and including the four sites which are the subject of his paper.

Preface

Great Excavations began life, as things often do, in a bar over a drink. It seems appropriate somehow, especially now, realising how important pubs and beer really have been in the social history of archaeological practice. Editing this collection has been an enlightening and entertaining experience, not least given the vivid descriptions of projects characterised by harsh working conditions and toil, and people simply having the times of their lives. In editing this book I have become so closely familiar with these projects, many of which I must confess I knew little about previously, that I can almost begin to imagine I was there. Just imagine that – having worked on all nineteen of the twentieth-century excavations described in this collection. I haven't worked out how plausible that is, but if it were possible, that person could provide quite an overview. Accepting that no such archaeological super-hero exists, except in our imaginations, then this collection is hopefully the next best thing: a review of some of those excavations deemed to have achieved or attained greatness in retrospect for reasons of procedure, practice, publication, outreach or by virtue of their mythical status – it may have been great for more than one reason, maybe for all five, or maybe more.

But back to the pub. In fact it was in Tasmania of all places, talking to another English archaeologist (now expatriate) about our formative days on very different excavations, but with stories of hardship and humour in common. And it was the comment that these experiences shaped us, and made us the archaeologists we were to become, that caused me to think of the IfA (or IFA – Institute of Field Archaeologists – as it was then), and the possibility of a conference session on the subject. That session took place at the IFA's annual conference in Reading 2007. With two exceptions all of the speakers that day are represented in this collection, while numerous projects not included in the conference session are included here. In the discussion periods of the conference session, additional sites, projects and people were referred to, some repeatedly, so they naturally deserved invitations to participate in the published 'proceedings'. Also, for the publication, the contextual essays are extended. Of these, only Paul Everill's 'View from the Trenches' was included in the conference session. Here the views of a commercial unit (David Jennings), the IfA (Peter Hinton) and the Central Excavation Unit/English Heritage (Geoff Wainwright) are also included, as overview, commentary and reflective insight.

I want to thank everyone who has contributed to this book, and to the conference session from which it derives. I have been entertained by the process, and have learnt much about excavations which hold mythical status, and from which amazing stories are retold by younger archaeologists. I hope others will learn as I have learnt and know more about their profession as a result. I want also to thank Olwen Beazley, for it was her in the bar in Tasmania, as this was really a shared idea which I then developed for the UK. Maybe Olwen can follow up with a 'Great Excavations Down Under'? I hope so. I want to thank again (as I do in my Introduction) those that inspired me on my own great excavations. As Chapter 1 states, I was never really a great excavator, but I can recognise how the experiences with John and Bryony Coles on the Somerset Levels, Roger Mercer at Hambledon Hill and Stephen Green at Pontnewydd cave led me in a particular direction. Finally, I owe thanks to the staff at Oxbow who accepted the proposal to publish this volume with such immediate enthusiasm and for gently coaxing it to completion.

This project was intended not as a retelling of 'what Danebury taught us about the Iron Age' or 'what we learnt about the Vikings from Jorvik'. Rather it was always intended as a social history of archaeology, of how these projects shaped the profession we have today, the archaeologists who work within it, and who still want to join it in numbers. It is an 'archaeography', in Martin Carver's words, and an account of what it was like to be an archaeologist in the twentieth century, describing the passion and energy expended by so many in pursuit of understanding the past for the benefit of society. Finally, some of the chapters in this book recall archaeologists no longer with us, but whose participation, humour and energy are recalled in these pages. There are many absent friends in fact, and this book is dedicated to them all.

Wiveliscombe, Somerset
4 February 2009

Greatness in depth:
Why excavations matter

John Schofield

Great
    adj. 1 of an extent, amount, or intensity considerably above average; **2** of ability, quality or eminence considerably above average; **3** denoting the most important element of something. >particularly deserving a special description.

Excavate v.
    – DERIVATIVES **excavation** n. **1** make (a hole or channel) by digging. >extract material from the ground by digging. **2** carefully remove earth from (an area) in order to find buried remains.

(Source OED, 10th edn.)

A perfect moment

A hot summer's morning in August 1982, sitting on warm swept chalk in shorts, T-shirt and sunhat overlooking a wide, lush river valley in central Dorset. It was one of those perfect summer days – hot though not overly so, with a gentle breeze, sufficient to carry the sounds of industry and merriment from other diggers away on the hillside. I recall taking a short break from the close attention to the feature I was excavating, and looking out over the landscape below. The sound of a light aircraft came to my attention, and over the course of perhaps a minute or two I watched it fly up the valley, below me but some distance above the water-meadows beneath. I had barely a care in the world at this time. I was taking an archaeology degree at a good, local university, I had a circle of friends, a steady relationship, a place to live and no concerns over student debt, or employment prospects. I remember thinking: things can't get much better than this. It was a perfect moment. I had some bad moments on that excavation too. But this was perfect and one I will never forget. Whether it was the reason I became an archaeologist I have no idea, but it certainly didn't put me off.

Amongst stars, planets and dreams

Archaeology captures the public imagination in a way many disciplines can never hope to achieve. It is definitely up there as a popular branch of the academe, alongside geology (dinosaurs), astronomy (stars and planets) and ecology (plants and animals), and – to some extent – psychology and psychoanalysis (the brain, behaviour and our dreams). These are some of the things that captivate us, and they do this because there is an element of the unknown and the 'yet to be discovered' about them. There is also a measure of the 'isn't that interesting', and of being relevant, capturing an element of how we became the complex society and ever more complex individuals that we are today. These subjects captivate us also because they are things we can all do. We can all interpret our dreams; we can all take an interest in wildlife and the solar system; we can all look for fossils on beaches; and we can get involved in archaeology, either at a practical level, or on a more philosophical plane (as in, 'I know what those cave painters were up to', or 'I know why they turned to farming'). Perhaps I am biased, but one could suggest also that of these subjects archaeology stands out, because it is arguably the most sociable of these popular disciplines. Where else amongst this list of practices and disciplinary wanderings could we spend a month on a campsite, returning to nature, going native in some cases and living closely with like-minded people who share our passion for the past, and for life? And as most archaeologists (and very many others besides) are introduced to archaeology through an excavation, these unique experiences are obviously important. It also explains their importance for the future of the discipline (and the profession, as it has become). One of the clear messages of this book is the requirement for archaeology that great excavations continue in the future, to inspire another generation of archaeologists as they did us. The scope of our subject may have changed, and the methodologies with it, for example the increased emphasis on non-invasive, even remote, techniques of detection and recovery. The politics of excavation have changed too, with polluter-pays principles and a more commercially driven and professional endeavour. But it is still, typically, the direct physical engagement with earth, artefacts, place and people (of the past and the present) that draws us in. This is why excavations matter, and why they can be great.

This volume analyses some of the excavations deemed to have attained a degree of greatness, reassessing their contribution to the popularity of archaeology, its emerging professionalism, and its shape and state of health early in the twenty-first century. But claims of greatness are not to be made or taken lightly. We need some framework within which to make and assess such claims.

Greatness is ...

In the context of excavations, greatness can be determined by a combination of factors and considerations, as the chapters in this book illustrate: It may be about the contribution to understanding, to progressing knowledge about the past; it may be about innovation and developing new approaches, to aid that understanding, and to make the results and working methods transparent for future researchers; it may also be about publication and the dissemination of results through popular and academic reports, and increasingly now the broadcast media; and it is typically also about inspiration and social benefit. Arguably though it is ultimately about having fun; about enjoying oneself, and doing so in a context where emotional and intellectual stimulation exist side by side, or (sometimes literally) hand in hand.

This collection of essays considers what makes a 'great excavation', from the horses mouths, so to speak. The book, and the conference session from which it arose, asked specific questions of contributors: What does it mean to be great? What have great excavations in the past contributed to the archaeological profession that we have today? And, how have these events shaped us as archaeologists and as individuals, whether our role was as a volunteer, supervisor or director? To what extent do great excavations provide alternative histories of British archaeology? Is there a mythology somewhere here that could usefully be analysed or deconstructed? And is it important that the opportunities which these excavations provide exist in the future, to work not only on excavations that are important for telling us more about the past, but which inspire us and move us forward, as institutions, and as individuals?

The chapters that follow answer these questions directly, in the context of projects from different eras, separate regions and countries of the UK, various periods of study, and different institutional contexts and situations: Rescue is covered for example, as is the role and contribution of the Manpower Services Commission, large research excavations, and the emergence of developer funding. At the original session a speaker asked whether encouraging self indulgence had been a deliberate intention. I answered that yes, it had: this was an opportunity to reflect on past projects, and to describe what it was like to work on them, and how they influenced other excavation projects. How, in short, did these projects shape the profession we have today. Authors also allude to the various mythologies, folk histories and traditions that have accumulated around great excavations and their participants. All of the contributors discuss these points in various ways, and it is the variety of perspectives that makes this volume such an entertaining collection, as well as constituting an archaeography of the profession, to use Martin Carver's phrase.

Greatness can be a personal thing though, like holidays (though I hesitate to draw this particular comparison). The great excavations that I have worked on are not necessarily those that changed the way we thought about a particular period, or which introduced new approaches to recording, or the conservation of artefacts, or indeed new ways of digging. They are the ones that inspired me to become an archaeologist, and once there, to remain within the profession, even though at times that was quite hard to do. My great excavations are those that I enjoyed (for the camaraderie, the weather and the place), and those from which I learnt most – what I gained from the experience intellectually, and the skills I learnt which helped in other areas of life: patience for example; a degree of self-confidence; responsibility.

This book appears at a time of significant change within the UK heritage sector – the popularity of our subject has never been greater, heritage protection and the planning system are undergoing reform, while the higher education sector continues to promote innovative research now in a post-disciplinary world that exposes archaeologists increasingly to new theoretical ideas and to practitioners from other subject areas – artists for example. It is appropriate, then, that we address the influence of these great excavations at this time and coincident with the twenty-fifth anniversary of our professional institute – the IfA (Hinton, this volume).

I should explain briefly how the selection of great excavations in this collection was made. As a society we are obsessed with creating lists, Top 100s and so on. A journalist once said, 'There's only one thing in a newspaper or magazine that everybody will read – a Top 10 list. It can be the Top 10 of anything, they'll read it.' While this obsession was probably influential in shaping the session from which this book originates, I was anxious to avoid any sort of competitive element, yet to ensure the session reflected popular opinion. So I conducted an opinion poll on the internet forum Britarch in *c.* 2005–6. While responses were few, the excavations mentioned by respondants are mostly included here and were only excluded where authors were unavailable. Additional contributions resulted from a wider call for papers. So that's how the shape of the volume was produced. It is an indicative as opposed to definitive selection. Some major excavation projects are missing.

Three excavations, 1981–3

During the time that I worked on excavations I chose from the CBA calendar those that I thought I would: a) enjoy – an unfamiliar place perhaps; and b) learn something from – from an archaeologist I admired, or a site I had read about. The excavations I worked on certainly shaped my professional career, and my outlook. I worked on the Sweet Track for example, Hambledon Hill, and Pontnewydd cave. I once wrote an essay about the Cold War airbase at Greenham Common of which someone said, 'this could only have been written by someone grounded in early prehistoric archaeology!' Our early influences run deeper than we might expect, and can manifest themselves in the unlikeliest of situations.

At this point I will make a confession. I don't particularly like excavation. If we return to my perfect moment at Hambledon Hill (for it was there), you will recall my pulling away from the feature I was excavating to gaze out into the landscape. It is, and I think always has been, that wider landscape view that I prefer. That is the reason I undertook landscape-scale archaeological survey for my doctoral research and subsequently, and why I worked for the landscape characterisation team at English Heritage for as long. That is not to say, however, that I doubt in any way the value of excavations, and that I hope is made plain by my editing this book, and organising the conference session from which it derives. Excavation is fundamental to archaeology, and to the making and shaping of archaeologists. It is just that I prefer the wider view.

There is no question, though: my career was shaped by the three excavations on which I learnt to dig, and to be amongst archaeologists. Here I will describe briefly these early encounters, on the Somerset Levels, in the Sweet Track excavation, 1981; at Hambledon Hill 1982; and at Pontnewydd 1983. The narrative is probably typical of excavation experiences at that time. But they are also unique – they are my own experiences, filtered out over 20–30 years and assisted by the photographs I took. These are the things that shaped the archaeologist that I became, and which helped me to decide on my career path. This is what inspired me, for good or ill. But it is the ordinariness that is particularly relevant here. These are everyday encounters that I describe – nothing spectacular or unusual; nothing especially noteworthy, except to me, personally. On each site I was one of many archaeologists, and thus, for every year of excavation in the UK alone there could be hundreds, even thousands, of archaeologists producing accounts like these. Some projects require everyone on site to keep diaries now, so in some instances at least the personal becomes part of the formal record. But not here.

Sweet Track 1981

This was my first direct encounter with archaeologists. I had just completed an A level in Archaeology, was expecting grades sufficient to get me to university to study the subject, and decided to fill my summer with some relevant experience. A school friend thought it sounded fun, and we applied together for the Sweet Track, following a notice in the CBA Calendar of Excavations, and noting the provision of camp site and payment of subsistence. I had learnt about the Sweet Track during my A level course, and the Levels sounded fascinating, hence the (very deliberate) choice. I have the original notice, from the CBA archive:

It was in the May 1981 issue of the CBA Newsletter and Calendar (issue V/3). It read:

SOMERSET LEVELS

Excavation of the early neolithic wooden trackway (Sweet Track), north of previously examined areas, will be directed by Professor J. M. Coles and B. J. Orme. V(unspecified). CS. FH(full session). Preference given for volunteers staying for full session. Nearest station: Bridgwater, bus to Glastonbury. Apply to B. J. Orme, Dept of Archaeology & History, The Queen's Building, Queen's Drive, Exeter.   26.8.81–27.9.81

The Codes meant:

V – number of volunteers required
CS – Camping site available without equipment
FH – financial help offered, minimum qualifying period shown in brackets

This was what set my pace racing!

The journey involved my longest ever time spent on a bus. We left Saxmundham (Suffolk) early morning, and arrived at the cross in Glastonbury at about 2000 hrs. We had a map, sent to us with joining instructions, and headed off on foot across the Levels towards the village of Westhay heavily laden with rucksacks, tents, sleeping bags *etc*. We had walked about a mile, out into the flatland in evening sunlight, when a car approached from behind, slowing and pulling up just behind us. Out of one of those tiny (and in this case rather ancient and dicrepid) bubble-shaped fiats stepped two huge bearded men, one probably our age, and one slightly older. They wore tattered and dirty jeans, plimsolls and t-shirts, one with a waistcoat over. Both were long-haired, and ear-ringed. From the very sheltered existence of my private school and forces background, this felt like the start of something. These were precisely the types of people my parents had warned me against! A new world, brave or otherwise I was unsure. They were of course archaeologists on the way back to camp from a sojurn in Glastonbury, and rather to our surprise they offered us a lift. Not surprising in the sense that archaeologists would display generosity in this way, but there was simply no space. You know the joke about putting elephants in a mini ...? Yet somehow we were inserted into the car, and luggage strapped on. I remember nothing about the journey from that point on.

The excavation was, simply, great fun. About thirty people, many from the University of Exeter, and all of whom were delightful, and accommodating of us schoolboys (as we must have seemed). Bryony Orme (as she was then) and John Coles were both sociable and engaged with us, offering help and guidance for us novices, and creating an environment in which the work/play balance seemed exactly right, and the mood constantly upbeat and jovial. It was hard work, lying on planks all day, but it never seemed too onerous – no-one complained. Conversation flowed easily in the trench and at breaks. There were virtually no artefacts found that year (the jadeite axe came later I think), but a lesson I learnt was that palaeoenvironmental information also mattered, and that the structure of the trackway was itself the subject of our close attention. I excavated what was interpreted at the time as a bag of hazelnuts that had been dropped by someone walking along the track.

Site TG was the subject of our attention, part of a longer-term programme of survey and excavations along the Sweet Track to 'ascertain the precise position of the structure beneath the peat along the entire projected 1800 m, and to record the condition of the track and its likely future' (Coles and Orme 1984, 5). Site TG was then the largest stretch of track excavated as a single unit, allowing a view of over 50m of exposed trackway (Figures 1.1 and 1.2). As Coles and Orme described in their report, the excavation progressed in stages, the photographs of each emphasising the narrowness of track as it was originally conceived and used (*ibid.*, 24). They went on to describe the excavation as generally dry (though it didn't seem so!), but with the final two weeks 'dogged by incessant rain'. This I do remember, as each day on site was followed by an uncomfortable night in a waterlogged tent.

Summer 1981 was memorable for this excavation. The sun shone for the first two weeks at least, and we made good friends. The following term, my first at Southampton, my friend and I travelled to Exeter to stay with two people we met on the excavation. And from an archaeological

Figure 1.1. The Sweet Track excavations, summer 1981. (Photograph: Bryony Coles.)

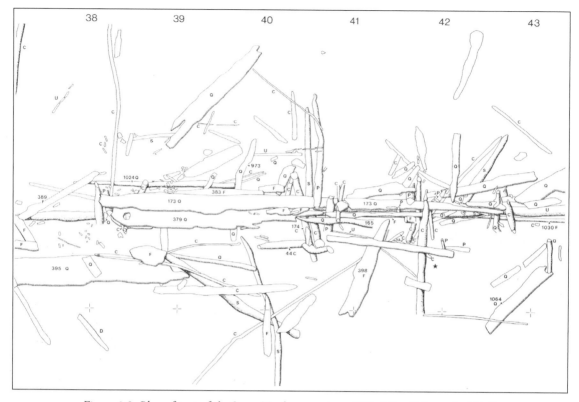

Figure 1.2. Plan of part of the Sweet Track excavations 1981 (after Coles et al. 1984).

perspective, the excavations and the experiences there helped me adapt to university and to my chosen subject with ease. I needed that excavation, to set me up and inspire me for what was to come. As I was to discover in 'Freshers' week', all of my peers had spent their summer on excavations too, many at Danebury and Wroxeter (this volume).

Hambledon Hill 1982

Hambledon was different! I knew it would be and wasn't disappointed to find it that way. There was little that could be described as refined or polite about Hambledon – this was archaeology and archaeologists in their raw and unrefined state, and it was wonderful for being so. Unlike the Somerset Levels I was now more familiar with archaeologists. Nothing would now surprise or unsettle me. Also, unlike the 'Levels I joined Hambledon for only a month of a much longer summer season. People were therefore bedded in when I arrived, and diggers came and went throughout. It was a more fluid existence, although many people knew each other from previous years or from their universities.

This was the year of the Hanford Spur (Figures 1.3 and 1.4), where I spent most of my time, on a quiet and unpopulated area of exposed chalk, typically alone and with small features to excavate. I found very little.

This was hard graft – far more so than the Sweet Track. The one mile level walk to site in Somerset

Figure 1.3. Hoeing chalk on Hambledon Hill, Summer 1982. (Photograph: Roger Mercer.)

compared very favourably to the much longer uphill climb onto Hambledon, meaning an earlier start to be on-site by (I think) 0830. There was the option of breakfast in the Child Okeford village hall, but I declined that and had my own, in the camp site. Tracing the walk now, in my forties, and having been desk-bound for some time, it does seem a daunting prospect, walking that walk every morning. Some people had gone native, and lived off the land – their walk to site was less direct, as they checked snares and traps set the evening before.

Proving that genuine hard work can often be the most fun, I did enjoy my time at Hambledon and wonder now why I never returned there. I recall systematically sweeping the chalk at the Stepleton Enclosure, preparing it for photographs, and working with the late Bob Smith, examining colluvial deposits in the dry valley north of the hill, admiring his sports car and discussing his switch of career, from RAF to archaeology (I had recently resigned my position in the university air squadron to concentrate on my degree course). I recall staff from my own university visiting the excavations, and a visit from the Prehistoric Society. The Prehistoric Society were fed and watered in style, with a seafood buffet, to which we had access after they left – eating cockles, mussels and the rest, and drinking wine in an old army marquee on an exposed hilltop was a rare moment of luxury and opulence in the early days of my archaeology career.

At the time of writing, the Hambledon report has been published, in the new Print on Demand format (Mercer and Healy 2008). No doubt this will be a great report, and cement Hambledon's

N

- ⌐⌐ Limit of excavation
- ▨ Protected chalk
- ⬤ Definite and probable Neolithic features
- ⬭ Possible Neolithic features and undated features
- ◉ Quarries
- ⬓ Galleries
- ☐

Inner Hanford Outwork
Outer Hanford Outwork

50m

Figure 1.4. Plan of excavations of Hanford Spur, Hambledon Hill 1982. (Drawing by permission of Roger Mercer.)

place as a great excavation. It is already deeply set within the mythology of modern archaeological excavations … and I would imagine most of the stories are true.

Pontnewydd Cave 1983

Another summer excavation, another long bus journey, this time from Southampton to the city of St Asaph, north Wales. I do recall a dilemma between choosing another year at Hambledon, and something new, and again very different to what had gone before. Clive Gamble's Palaeolithic classes had introduced me to Pontnewydd, and the thought of a cave appealed, as did north Wales.

Here I learnt the need for close attention to stratigraphic detail, and the significance of small finds that were often very small indeed. I found stone tools here, and excavated deep stratigraphic sequences (Figure 1.5). But if truth be told, I found the cave claustrophobic, and crowded, and much preferred my days at nearby Cefn Cave where small teams were sent for simpler less intensive excavation tasks.

Here the view was extensive and breathtaking; it was a peaceful spot, akin to my Dorset hillside the previous summer. At Pontnewydd the cave entrance was enclosed which I didn't like so much. My claustrophobic tendencies were not helped by being selected (as the thinnest person there) to head down a fissure with a tape measure, 'to see how far it went'. Squeezing gradually further down a very tight fissure was one thing, but having to remain there when the generator failed (the golden rule was to remain still until light returned) was almost too much to bear. I had to sing to relieve my tension, as I do now during injections! And then there was the tale of *Blue Peter* and the Neanderthal tooth.

This story seems unbelievable now, but on the day *Blue Peter* was due to visit I was scheduled to help at the finds hut, up the hill at the campsite. I was meticulous in the care and attention given to fragile and significant finds. Some key finds, including a hominid tooth, were to be put on display, outwith their boxes, for the presenter to handle and show to the camera and tens of thousands of young viewers. The finds officer returned to site as I completed this task. Having placed the hominid tooth prominently on its box, I looked around to see a Robin at the door of the finds hut. I know a bit about birds, and know how Robins can be inquisitive and brassneck creatures. But there is brassneck, and brassneck! In a flash the Robin had swept past me onto the table, picked up the tooth in its beak and flown for the entrance! I flapped and shouted as the bird escaped, thankfully dropping the tooth somewhere outside the hut entrance, in the grass. Closing the door behind me, I scrabbled for what seemed ages, eventually finding the tooth. With relief unimaginable, I returned it to its rightful place. *Blue Peter* was produced and aired without a hint of the drama that preceded it. No-one ever knew … until now. I have a feeling that at the time this was the only tooth to have been found there, and virtually the only evidence for a Neanderthal presence in Britain. May be it is no surprise that I have left prehistoric archaeology behind me!

Pontnewydd was the first excavation which involved me in logistical tasks: cooking and shopping (Figure 1.6). On the 'Levels and at Hambledon I was self-sufficient, with much of my subsistence money spent on food. Here things were more communal. The shopping trips to St Asaph were fun, as were visits to local sites on days off. Roger Mercer had organised this at Hambledon as well, taking us to Salisbury Plain for example, and to some Dorset hillforts. Pontnewydd also provided the opportunity to explore parts of Snowdonia, and the beaches of Llandudno.

It is funny how people easily forget who else was on these excavations. I remember, largely because I took lots of photographs. But meeting people at conferences, as happened recently, can sometimes lead to comments like, 'Yes, we worked together at X'. It may not be so common now, as the profession is so much larger and with greater student numbers. But for my generation, when there were fewer of us, the networks were smaller and contacts far more frequent.

Connections

Over the past decade or so we have become increasingly disconnected in many ways from the reality that previous generations experienced at first hand: and that can include archaeological endeavour. One can now watch an excavation unfold on television over the course of an hour (representing three days work for *Time Team*), or for some of their 'special' projects, over a weekend, live. One can also watch excavations online, and follow blogs of those involved. As onlookers we can participate wherever we are in the world: reading a blog that asks for advice on particular finds made earlier that day, for example, we can offer comment and suggest comparative material or sources. One might come to the view that one has witnessed (or is witnessing) a great excavation without ever having been there. One might reflect ten years later how, 'that was a great excavation', recalling one only viewed remotely.

Figure 1.5. Stratigraphy in the half-light of Pontnewydd, Summer 1983. (Photograph: Author.)

Figure 1.6. Shopping for provisions, St Asaph, Summer 1983. (Photograph: Author.)

One might even organise, run and participate in great excavations in 'Second Life' – as at Roma for example (http://slurl.com/secondlife/Roma%20Transtiberim/21/57/29/). As technologies and cultural values shift, not to mention the relative cultural benefits of commerce and conservation, so will the ways we engage with reality, and so will our views on greatness, in all aspects of life. Perhaps there will come a time when excavations of the type described in this collection will be organised as pieces of performance art, as social experiments (if they are not anyway), and even as re-enactments: I quite like the idea of recreating a 1950s or 60s excavation or a Mucking winter (Barford, this volume) but with the professionalized archaeologists of today, and especially those that have no experience of what went before. Maybe that is the future for reality TV and broadcast archaeology?

My purpose here has been to create a historiography for archaeology, but a historiography focused entirely on the practice of archaeology, and in particular the practice that really defines our discipline and gives it public recognition and support: excavation. It will be obvious that I personally prefer the wider landscape view to the view of/from the trench. But I also recognise that I wouldn't be the archaeologist I am without those experiences with Bryony and John Coles on the Somerset Levels, Roger Mercer at Hambledon and Stephen Green at Pontnewydd. And this is surely true for us all. We all owe debts of gratitude to those we have worked with, and who inspired us to follow a particular (some would say peculiar) career path. This collection is a recognition of that, and a documentation of some of the experiences, projects and people that made us who we are, as a profession and as individuals. Great excavations will continue for sure, with greatness perhaps judged by very different criteria in the future. What is certain is that those excavations will be very different in character to those that went before. That is progress, and that is change. And as archaeologists this is something we know all about.

References

Coles, J. C. and Orme, B. J. 1984. The excavations along the Sweet Track (3200 bc). *Somerset Levels Papers* 10, 5–45.
Green, H. S. 1984. *Pontnewydd Cave: a lower Palaeolithic hominid site in Wales: the first report.* Cardiff: National Museum of Wales.
Mercer, R. and Healy, F. 2008. *Hambledon Hill, Dorset, England. Excavation and Survey of a Neolithic Monument Complex and its Surrounding Landscape.* London: English Heritage.

Some notable British excavations before 1900

C. Stephen Briggs

Introduction

Nobody today questions the need for or value of methodical excavation techniques, though few of us ever have the time to ask how they evolved. Forgetting how far technique has advanced over the years, it can be easy to judge early excavators and their work by the yardstick of present day achievement.

Whereas a definitive account of the history of excavation in Britain is yet to be written, the purpose of this contribution is to draw attention to some significant, though largely forgotten digs and discoveries, which are probably landmarks, given the benefit of hindsight. This account is necessarily very selective, and attention is particularly focused on the adoption of novel approaches or inventive techniques and standards. The most significant questions arise from the adoption of stratigraphy and field survey strategy. To these should be added monument and artefact classification and interpretation, curation, illustration, presentation and publication. All make up the vital components of the portfolio carried by today's professional excavating archaeologists.

Beginnings in excavation: an outline from 1190

The excavation of early sites in Britain has a long history and became a particularly important component of medieval religious life (Wright 1846; 1860). One of the earliest archaeologists in the national psyche should be the Benedictine monk Adam of Damerham, who probably died in 1291. He sowed the seeds of the Arthurian legend in a chronicle of Glastonbury Abbey. In that, he (if indeed it was he) described the discovery of the alleged bones of Arthur and Guineveve around 1190. Apparently Abbot Henry de Soilli had ordered an excavation 'between two stone pyramids' in the cemetery at Glastonbury. As he investigated, the diggers were shielded from public gaze by a curtain. They found two coffins, one of 'amazing size', which contained 'incredibly large bones … one thigh bone reached from the ground to at least the middle of a tall man's leg'. They also found a lead cross inscribed, 'here lies the renowned King Arthur in the Isle of Avalon', and in the other coffin some beautiful golden hair skilfully arranged' (Gransden 2004). Such an imaginative account is almost worthy of a heritage lottery post-excavation grant application!

Proving the antiquity of the saints was central to the activity of exhumation, and Thomas Wright (1860, 284–5) reckoned to have found from 'fifty to a hundred examples in which barrows were opened for the sake of finding the bones of saints'. Other medieval investigations were more concerned with looting outside the net of Treasure Trove law (Hill 1936), as witness barrow openings on the Isle of Wight described by the late Leslie Grinsell (1967). In a slightly later historical context, William Camden incidentally mentioned all the excavations he knew of in his new descriptive *Britannia* of 1610. Thereafter, record keeping gathered pace only slowly, making the best-known seventeenth-century barrow-opening the one which figures in Thomas Browne's *Urn Burial* of 1643/56. Browne's engraving of Anglo-Saxon urns celebrated in that religious-literary work is well-known from many histories of archaeology (most recently re-printed as fig. 16 in Parry 2007, 35). It is well to be reminded that this clutch of urns was intended to represent neither treasure with obvious monetary value, nor saintly relic. It was among the first illustrations of artefacts probably excavated out of simple curiosity.

Another mid-seventeenth century excavator was George Villiers, first duke of Buckingham (1592–1628), who in 1620 sallied forth from his home, Wilton House, Wiltshire, to dig a couple of holes in Stonehenge apparently to impress James I who was due for a visit at the time (Chippendale 2004, 47, fn. 15, citing John Aubrey and other earlier sources). But like so many early digs, this one left no useful record, verbal or graphic.

Early measured surveys and excavation

Neither John Aubrey (1626–1697; Fox 2004) nor Edward Lhuyd (1659/60?–1709; Roberts 2004) was a digger, though each in his own way contributed to important developments in archaeological survey towards the end of the seventeenth century (Piggott 1965; 1978; Ucko *et al.* 1991). While Aubrey is credited with producing the first accurate survey of Avebury (Ucko *et al.* 1991), he may not have been its author. His real importance probably lies in a manuscript compilation, his *Monumenta Britannia*. This is actually a comprehensive assemblage of notes and plans of monuments in a variety of hands, particularly representative of England and Wales. It was for long known to antiquarian interests only from the manuscript in the Bodleian Library, but its full text, made available relatively recently in a rather idiosyncratic publishing venture (Fowles and Legge 1981–2) does suggest there was some contemporary excavation.

Towards the end of Aubrey's life, in the early 1690s Edward Lhuyd began undertaking scientific tours with a small group of helpers around Wales, then from 1699–1702 throughout the British Isles. Although his extensive field notes were subsequently decimated by fires at a country house and a printer's, a large corpus of plans remains unpublished at the British Library (Brit Lib Ms Stowe 1023–24). These demonstrate an unusual degree of accuracy and perception in field recording and survey (Briggs 1997). Whereas Lhuyd's correspondence mentions only an occasional contemporary excavation, the most notable so far published records how the great Neolithic passage grave of New Grange was partially cleared out and Roman coins found in what appears to have been a satellite tomb (Herity 1967).

Stratigraphic principles in excavation

Lhuyd and Aubrey belonged to the Royal Society of London, founded in 1660. It was a polymathic publishing community in which archaeology was only an incidental interest (Hunter 1971). The Society of Antiquaries of London was re-founded in 1708 (MacGregor 2007), but being at Oxford Lhuyd was not of its circle, and anyway died the following year. William Stukeley (Haycock 2004) soon became Secretary of the Society of Antiquaries (Piggott 1985). Interestingly, however, probably through access to Lhuyd's manuscript collections, important aspects of *his* intellectual mantle were soon taken up and developed by Stukeley. Stukeley was also a Fellow of the Royal Society, and through that he would have known the work of John Strachey, the Somerset geologist who published some of the first stratigraphic sections known to the history of British geology (Fuller 2004). Stukeley dug barrows around Stonehenge

Figure 2.1. Lincoln Hypocaust by Vertue (By permission of the Society of Antiquaries of London).

in 1723 and later published illustrations of his findings (Stukeley 1740). His graphics of artefacts and a section drawing are still capable of re-interpretation, and as such are today among the earliest images available for comparative Neolithic-Bronze Age studies (Chippendale 2004, fig. 51, p. 78).

George Vertue and Roman Lincoln in the eighteenth century

It seems likely that during the nineteenth century, important new techniques being employed abroad in the Classical and Biblical worlds (if not beyond) by European investigators were adopted by excavators in Britain. A similar situation probably obtained in the eighteenth century, though at the moment what actually did happen is still largely a matter of conjecture.

It is therefore of considerable interest that while preparing material for the Society of Antiquaries' catalogue for the British Academy *Making History Exhibition* in 2007, Bernard Nurse noticed a coloured engraving by George Vertue showing a superb three-dimensional illustration of a Roman hypocaust in Roman Lincoln (Smiles 2007, fig. 88, 127; here Figure 2.1). It is dated 1740, though the site may have been discovered earlier. Its caption explains how someone excavating cellars in the city had sent a young lad down a well. The illustration was drawn up from measurements he had taken underground.

Classical models initially spring to mind in considering the origins of such an accomplished technique: might this type of section owe its inspiration to Pompeii or Herculaneum? Interestingly, a search of the most obvious sources seems to render this unlikely, for Niccolo Marcello di Venuti's work on Herculaneum was not translated until at least 1740, and the English translation of 1750 included no graphics. Graphics do appear in Russell's *Letters to Young Painters*, but this was also published ten years after Vertue's print. And even then, the quality of Russell's seems hardly comparable to the maturity of Vertue's. It is clear that the Lincoln print precedes these and all other known three-dimensional images of Neapolitan ruins, which in the main date from the later eighteenth century. So although there is an unspoken assumption that British eighteenth-century archaeological technique may have been following that developed to deal with Mediterranean stratigraphies and structures, it now seems worth investigating how far the contrary may have been the case. In such an early antiquarian and excavation context this discovery quite unexpectedly puts a different gloss on the claim for Pitt-Rivers as introducer of three-dimensional graphics in British archaeology (Briggs 2007, 236), since Vertue anticipates the influential graphics of Cissbury by 120 years (cf. Bowden 1990, 80–81, fig. 19; Evans 2007, fig. 82, 285; Rowley-Conwy 2007, fig. 7.2, 244–5). In any case, there are many other three-dimensional reconstructions in the early antiquarian literature.

Cromwell Mortimer, Brian Faussett and James Douglas

Stukeley's initial delvings around Stonehenge were soon followed in 1729 by investigations into barrows on Swarling Down at Chartham to the West of Canterbury in Kent, the first of three major campaigns eventually spanning the eighteenth century that vastly expanded an understanding of Anglo Saxon burial and artefact types in Britain.

This first dig was sparked off when workmen encountered burials in a gravel pit. Sadly, Stukeley aside, digging activity at the recently re-established Society of Antiquaries of London were still hardly known at this time (MacGregor 2007) and it fell to Cromwell Mortimer, Secretary of the Royal Society (Courtney 2004) to take up the challenge of excavation. It is, however, unclear how far he considered this an affair exclusively for the Royal Society to sponsor.

Mortimer's unpublished account, preserved in the British Library, is accompanied by a plan of the barrows drawn up in 1730 (Figure 2.2) for its landowner, Charles Fagg. His account also includes

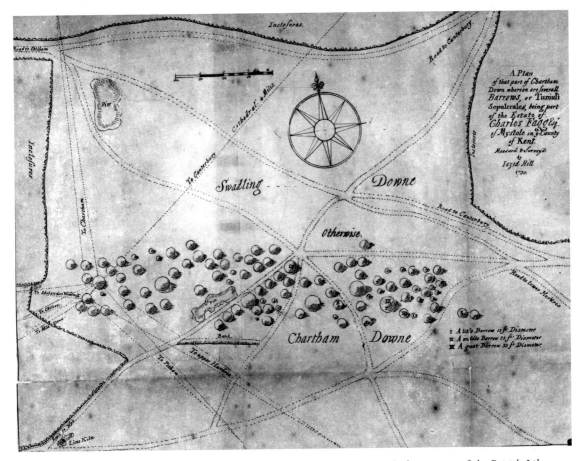

Fig 2.2. Plan of Chartham Down drawn 1730. Brit. Lib. Egerton MS 1041 by courtesy of the British Library.

polychrome drawings of the grave goods recovered, which are undoubtedly amongst the earliest such images of finds systematically excavated in Britain. Most are to scale and of a sufficiently high standard to permit both re-identification of the finds and enable informed discussion of them (Brit. Lib. Egerton MS 1041). As such, they themselves demand exhumation and would still repay detailed study by Anglo-Saxon finds specialists.

The history of excavation at Chartham after 1730 is complex. A young local lad named Bryan Faussett had been in attendance with Mortimer and Fagg, and as an adult he was to continue working across Kent in a second wave of investigations from 1757 opening 750 barrows in the next sixteen years (Ramsay 2004; Rhodes 1990). Excavations by a third enthusiast, James Douglas, followed, between 1779 and 1793 (Dean 2004; Jessop 1975). Douglas published his investigations under the title *Nenia Britannica* in 1793, but like Mortimer's, Faussett's account of his work, kept alongside the great artefact collection amassed from his excavations, remained unpublished for some time.

Douglas's avowed adherence to deductive interpretative principles helped give an almost immediate fillip to barrow investigation nationally (Jessop *idem* partic. 102–3: MacGregor 2003, 168), his followers being curious to discover the contents, if not also the ages, of the many burial mounds which then still populated much of the landscape.

Chartham and the Faussett collection assume an important place in both the history of archaeological interpretation and the development of museum collecting in Britain. Mortimer and Faussett pronounced their cemetery to have been the battleground where Ancient Britons were slain by Julius Caesar in his first battle for Britain. Later, his having recognised the bones of women and children amongst the graves which also contained many personal ornaments, Douglas argued that this must have been a local cemetery that had belonged to a working community from some nearby village or villages. Chartham is thus important because initial interpretation sparked off the next generation to offer an alternative explanation, while, in the intellectual climate of Enlightenment, it might be claimed that both narratives were argued from empirical principles.

In a later and entirely different, mid-nineteenth century antiquarian context, the first members of the British Archaeological Association were conveyed to Heppington in Kent to meet Brian Faussett's grandson, Godfrey on 11th September, 1844. A number of influential archaeologists thereby gained some appreciation of the truly national significance of the great Faussett family treasure which it vainly attempted to sell to the British Museum ten years later. The trustees' refusal to buy generated a public outcry, reflecting what was felt to be a general lack of interest in acquiring collections of British artefacts, as opposed to foreign *objets d'art* and *ethnographica*. Following Joseph Mayer's intervention and its acquisition for his collection, later to become the Liverpool Museum, the notion of retaining British *national antiquities* in a British Museum was thus strengthened to the better advantage of posterity under the able but modest guidance of A. W. Franks, who became an assistant keeper in 1851 (Wilson 2004).

Charles Roach Smith went on to publish Mortimer and Faussett's manuscript accounts in 1856 under Mayer's patronage (Rhodes 1990; Smith 1856). This is a tour-de-force of artefact description and high-quality illustration, setting an important standard for future excavation reports, even if by then almost a century overdue. This lapse of time carried with it at least one important penalty. By the time Roach Smith's transcription appeared, virtually all the topographical features depicted on Mortimer's 1729 plan (Figure 2.2) had gone, so none of the barrow sites could ever be re-located. Today the investigation area is occupied mainly by housing.

Colt Hoare and Cunnington

Some of the barrows excavated by Stukeley near Stonehenge were later re-excavated by William Cunnington and Sir Richard Colt Hoare. Traditionally, Colt Hoare is painted as one of the most iconic barrow excavators in the historical record, through his supposed promotion of exemplary excavation technique and high-quality publication. There can be no doubt about the quality of his publications, but his example in some excavation and even scholarly matters was far from exemplary. And anyway, William Cunnington initiated the Wiltshire barrow-digging project, while Colt Hoare bought him out and took much of the credit for that initiative. Cunnington was a practical man of geological bent who certainly tried to interest his rich patron in the mysteries of section drawing and of stratigraphy. But Colt Hoare, hardly enthusiastic about what went on inside the barrows, was more attracted to the splendour of their ancient artefactual contents and the kudos of publication.

Probably frustrated by this lack of interest in digging technique, Cunnington at one stage defected to Aylmer Lambert, a landowning botanist living nearby. Consequently Colt Hoare scolded Cunnington for disloyalty after he had published a couple of articles in *The Archaeologia* independent of his patronage. Colt Hoare's conservatism in the acceptance or adoption of new ideas was a major problem. He rejected Thomas Leman's Tripartite pre-Roman chronology of stone, bronze and iron, which, had Colt Hoare published it, could have been one of the really important outcomes of the Wiltshire digging campaigns, anticipating the Danes' publication of their Three Age System by up to 30 years. So although Colt Hoare's two volume work *Ancient Wiltshire* (of 1812 and 1819) was much acclaimed throughout the nineteenth century – and ever since – as *the* sourcebook on barrows and barrow-digging, and although prefaced by those well-worn pious words about *speaking from facts not theories*, the reality is that by publishing not a single barrow section or any accurate excavation plans, Colt Hoare's approach probably contributed to holding back the development of excavation methodology, if not also the scientific study of archaeology in Britain generally (Briggs 2007, 231).

Others were nonetheless to dabble in stratigraphic exercises over the next fifty years whilst the Society of Antiquaries went through a generally fallow, if not arid period, so far as archaeology was concerned (Pearce (ed.) 2007 *passim*). Some of it happened during the awakening of interest in improving investigation methods during the establishment of the British Archaeological Association (BAA) and the Archaeological Institute (AI). It might have been hoped that bringing together scholars of Roman archaeology and architect historians, both well-used to plans and sections, and mixing them with those who dug British and Anglo Saxon barrows, would have infected the latter with a greater interest in recording stratigraphies and spatial relationships.

Fig 2.3. Rankin's Thixendale barrows (by courtesy of the Yorkshire Philosophical Society and the Yorkshire Archaeological Society).

 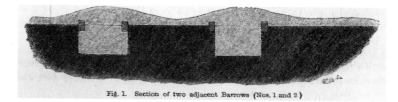

Fig. 1.   Section of two adjacent Barrows (Nos. 1 and 2)

Figure 2.4. Bourne Park. Plan and section of burials, from Wright 1845b.

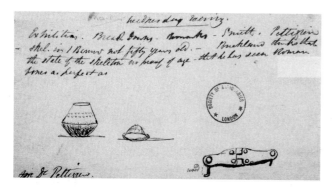 

SKELETON, AS IT APPEARED IN THE CIST.

Figure 2.5. Excavation notes on artefacts from Breach Down burials, author unknown, from SAL MS 877/1 Wright/Conyngham MS (By permission of the Society of Antiquaries of London).

Figure 2.6. Breach Down, barrow VII from Dunkin 1845 p. 95.

Whether or not raising investigational standards was in Lord Albert Conyngham's mind when he did a showpiece excavation on some barrows in his demesne at Bourne Park during the first Congress of the BAA at Canterbury in 1844 is unclear (Dunkin 1845, 97–100; Wright 1845b; here Figures 2.4 and 2.5). It is also unclear whether or not any plans or sections ever recorded his subsequent exhibition digging on nearby Breach Down (*idem*, 91–87; Wright 1845b; Figure 2.4). Printing the Bourne Park graphics alongside Thomas Wright's description demonstrated how the Anglo Saxon gravegoods were disposed and greatly helped understand the burials. The excavation record can still be enhanced somewhat from unpublished sketches of two further Breach Down Anglo-Saxon skeletons and their gravegoods (Figure 2.5), as well as by Dunkin's sketch of a further skeleton (Figure 2.6).

Although these brief records, and other basic graphics which appeared in the first volume of the *Archaeological Journal* (1845) and the *Journal of the British Archaeological Association* which often carried useful, if not even sophisticated images illustrating built or excavated structures, few, if any in the barrow digging fraternity were to follow Wright's example. He was probably not the best person to proselytise, for, rightly or wrongly, he was charged in the newspapers (and elsewhere) with being party to causing the split which resulted in the establishment of the AI in 1845. Furthermore, he was the scholar to stand against adopting the Scandinavian Three Age System (Rowley-Conwy 2007). So few were going to heed Wright's good example in excavation, particularly when he was not himself primarily an excavator.

Notable sections were being cut and illustrated nonetheless. As early as 1823 Rev Wm Rankine showed the stratigraphy of 'twin barrows' at Thixendale in East Yorkshire (Briggs 1981; here Figure 2.6). John

Yonge Akerman depicted his Iffins Wood dig of 1844 by 3–D section (Evans 2007, fig. 79, p. 279). And away from the conventions of London antiquarianism F. C. Lukis was observing the strata of Guernsey megaliths before 1843 (Briggs 2007, fig. 72, 234). Probably influenced by some of those he met at the BAA Canterbury Congress, from the mid-1840s Thomas Bateman drew competent cairn and barrow sections, mainly in Derbyshire, and later used to illustrate his popularising *Ten Year's Diggings* of 1861. One of them demonstrated a two-phase megalithic encisted structure on Balliden Moor (*idem* p. 60). Although such plans and sections put Colt Hoare to shame, contemporary excavators had no difficulty ignoring them, so only a tiny fraction of the excavated barrow resource was ever properly recorded.

The geological element in stratigraphic archaeology

Although most digging antiquaries were slow to realise the value of two-dimensional recording, a more practical approach came from those interested in the earth's structure. The first to bring geology into archaeology in an obvious way was John Frere, a Suffolk landowner. In 1797 he noted and described in detail the successive layers of the gravel pit at Hoxne, towards the lower end of which a Palaeolithic axe was found. Publishing it in *The Archaeologia* in 1800 was a visionary act on the part of the London Antiquaries, and it is interesting to speculate if the Geological Society would have had primacy had it then been in existence.

During the 1820s Dean William Buckland, a cleric and geologist teaching at Oxford, began to take an interest in the examination of cave sediments. Curious about finds of hyaena being taken from Kirkdale Cave near Helmsley in Yorkshire, he went hotfoot to describe the strata there in 1822, and in 1823 he tackled the Goat's Hole, Paviland in Gower.

Until recently, he was believed to have gone on and single-handedly tackled the cave. Recently published archive-based research has demonstrated how he actually saw little of the iconic excavation his *Reliquiae Diluvianae* of 1824 claims he undertook there. Most of the work had already been done by a group of local literati-landowners. Thus it now appears his famous stratigraphic section, long cited as one of the earliest exemplars to show a relationship between cave deposits and human occupation, was invented after the dig, so cannot be claimed an accurate record of it. This throws into doubt current beliefs about how the skeleton which became known as the 'Red Lady' burial was positioned and limits the value of its *c.* 20,000 year old radiocarbon dating. It also now emerges that two skeletons were excavated from the cave deposit and that Buckland failed to mention one of them (Weston 2008). As Weston observes (*idem*), these new findings are likely to invalidate much of the expensive scientific work already undertaken on the human bones, artefacts and accompanying faunal remains which are all now without proper context. These revelations could have far-reaching implications for British Quaternary studies. In common with other branches of science, archaeology clearly still has important lessons to learn about how old written texts are used in evidence outside their original social or intellectual contexts.

In this, we nonetheless see the serious beginnings of stratigraphic reasoning, a course soon followed in the Somme Valley by Jacques Boucher de Perthes (1849). It is well-known how his discoveries met great resistance from the French scientific community and that its scepticism was shared by the establishment in England. He had, nonetheless, certainly recognised Palaeolithic implements alongside a Pleistocene fauna. It is therefore curious that when John Evans and Joseph Prestwich visited and reported on the Somme gravel finds in 1859, neither published graphic explanations of a stratigraphic context for the Acheulean hand axes. It was as if they feared the very concept of stratigraphy would threaten the secure antiquarian ways of the establishment at a time when some were anticipating the Darwinian revolution (Briggs 2007, 244–8).

Some mid-nineteenth century plans and sections

This antiquarian psychology inhibiting archaeologists from producing archaeological sections obviously went back far beyond Wright and the Canterbury Congress. But not everyone was inhibited, as may be seen from what happened in the decades after 1835, when the foundations of London were being constantly explored in earth-moving construction for housing, business, docks and railways. This presented opportunities for archaeologists to collaborate in what was probably the largest development of its age. Unfortunately, London's past was left to be interpreted from artefact collections largely devoid of context, assisted only in rarer cases by sketched sections demonstrating relationships between soils, built structures and cultural debris.

Antiquaries like Charles Roach Smith, who collected and studied the city's artefacts, should have promoted better practice in site recording. But only one contemporary article he published in the 1840s carries plans or sections (1841a, pls XVII–XVIII; cf. Smith 1841b;1844), so his example was of limited value. In any case, he alienated the Corporation (Burton 2005, 170) and failed to cooperate with the Guildhall Museum, the most obvious repository for his collections, so his views would have carried little weight among those employed to undertake construction excavations.

London's stratigraphy was therefore left to others. Thus we have a remarkably detailed section of London's Roman wall in 1842 by William Devonshire Saull, an antiquary with strong geological leanings (Saull 1842; Figure 2.7). Similarly, a section of the gravel pit or pond that produced so many artefacts on the New Royal Exchange site in 1841, was drawn by the supervising architect (Sir) William Tite (Figure 2.8), whose thorough catalogue of those finds that eventually went to the Guildhall Museum was defensive of government policy in its record as

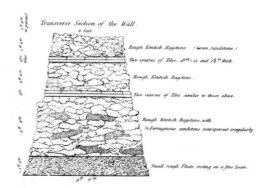

Figure 2.7. Section of London Roman Wall W. D. Saull (Archaeologia 30, 1841)

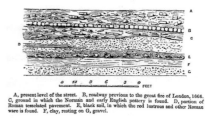

Figure 2.8. Section of Roman London recorded by Mr Chaffers in 1851. From fig. 27 p. 63 in Reeks and Rudler 1876.

Figure 2.9. William Tite's New Exchange Section: taken from Plan of the New Royal Exchange showing the situation in which the Roman Antiquities were found April 1841.

educator about the origins and history of the city. His text significantly mentions nothing of Roach Smith or others who had published work on the city excavations (Tite 1841). And by a similar token, during the recovery of pottery and other artefacts from the Cannon Street area, it was left to the ceramicist William Chaffers to provide a section of the deposits explaining the chronology of excavated structures and their accompanying pottery (Reeks and Rudler 1876, fig. 27, 63; Figure 2.9).

Canon Greenwell, General Pitt-Rivers and the Ganton burial

Although the one individual probably credited with most influence in the introduction of excavation techniques and section drawings from his work at Cranborne Chase in the 1880s, precisely when Augustus Lane Fox (later General Pitt-Rivers) became conscious of stratigraphy is unclear. What is certain is although he had attended many excavations before the 1870s, it took quite some time to appreciate the importance of the stratigraphic concept in graphic illustration. Realisation may have come during the 1860s, when he was drawn into the company of Sir John Evans, Sir John Lubbock, Augustus Wollaston Franks and last but certainly not least, Canon William Greenwell. All were well-versed in contextualising excavated artefacts, whether or not they themselves excavated.

Today best-known for his dry as dust *British Barrows* of 1878, it is now little appreciated just what a media man Greenwell really was. Yet between 1864 and 1880 he conducted one of the most high profile excavation projects in the history of British newspapers. He was to achieve greatest celebrity by bombarding *The Times* with around 60 individual accounts of the campaigns he was waging on burial mounds principally in North and East Yorkshire, Northumberland and Scotland (Briggs in press). Some regional newspapers also publicised his work.

Besides these newspaper descriptions of the barrow deposits' minutiae, Greenwell's accounts are remarkable for their unusual detail about the social life around his investigations. The great and the good were regularly invited to witness him at work, with attendees ranging from local clerics, landowners, nobility and farmers, as well as the aforementioned quartet of high-profile archaeologists. Unfortunately, his detailed descriptions of mounds and stratigraphies (where they were preserved), were never matched by graphic measured records, so neither digging techniques nor site interpretations were usefully advanced in his scholarly work until much later.

In attendance at Greenwell's excavations, though apparently not at that time generally advocating the adoption of graphic on-site recording, Pitt-Rivers sketched one of Greenwell's burials at Ganton Wold in 1866 (Kinnes 1977). This seems to have been his first attempt to achieve a recording standard in barrow excavation. And it may be significant that the Swedes had been recording excavated burials in a similar way on squared paper since the 1840s, and that Lubbock coincidentally entertained Sven Nilsson, the great Swedish prehistorian, in 1865. So Pitt-Rivers may have been influenced by this novel Scandinavian graphic methodology via Lubbock.

Discussion and conclusion

Rather than rehearse accounts of some better-known historical excavation campaigns, we have skirmished with a number of less well-known sites and some of the individuals associated with them. Even a cursory examination of this excavation history shows that our understanding of influences and fashions is only partial and at best dominated by studies of great names like Aubrey, Stukeley and Colt Hoare. We have almost forgotten some of the sites that emerge here as historically significant in technical or scholarly terms, or as touchstones to improving archaeological education or publicity. Yet it is possible to recognise how a great deal has been learned and has been absorbed by posterity, from several long-term investigations only retrospectively recognisable as excavation campaigns in their own right: Kentish Anglo Saxon barrow digging; Yorkshire prehistoric barrow investigation, and though a rather more fragmented activity, rescue archaeology as practised in nineteenth-century London.

Nothing better illustrates the neglected state and understanding of the history of archaeology, than to discover Mortimer Wheeler's biographer in the ODNB proclaiming one and a half centuries after the exemplar scholars of the 1840s, how he 'was almost alone in having adopted the excellent excavation principles of the pioneer, General Pitt-Rivers'. It view of the partial historical account we have sampled above, it is quite incredible that Wheeler should ever have been credited with beginning 'a crusade to introduce scientific techniques and rigour into the conduct and recording of excavations, notably by applying the principle of true stratification' (McIntosh 2004). Such a proclamation well illustrates how easy it can be to pronounce authoritatively, yet with only partial understanding, in a discipline that is and has been for many years populated by specialists with only limited time to read or write beyond their own expertise.

Finally, if anything, the limited examples presented here show how little is really understood about some of the most important influences that have affected the development of archaeological techniques. They also demonstrate how sometimes obscure printed texts and odd manuscript sketches can dramatically alter an understanding of site records. Some components of archaeological digging practice clearly have roots deep in a history populated by anonymous gentlemen and ladies who were rarely conscious of their contributions to science. It is therefore important to conclude by remembering that some of the really important advances in scientific study and scholarly practice are sometimes less easily recognised by peer groups than they may be retrospectively, by posterity.

Acknowledgments

This brief note is the product of a lifelong research interest informed knowingly by correspondents, or unwittingly by friends to all of whom I owe a considerable debt. The deductions drawn and views expressed are entirely my own. If it should move others to contribute to the story by addition or emendation, its purpose will not have been lost. The MSS illustrations appear courtesy of the Trustees of the British Library and of the Society of Antiquaries of London, where the assistance of Heather Rowlands, Bernard Nurse and Adrian James is gratefully acknowledged.

References

Bateman, T. 1861. *Ten years' Diggings on the Celtic and Saxon Grave Hills in the Counties of Derby, Stafford and York, from 1848–1858*, London: J. R. Smith.

Boucher de Perthes, J. 1849. *Antiquités Celtiques et Antédiluviennes*, vol. 1, Paris: Treuttel et Wurtz, Debache, Dumoulin et Didron [1847].

Bowden, M. C .B. 1991. *Pitt Rivers: the life and archaeological work of Lieutenant-General Augustus Henry Lane Fox Pitt Rivers, DCL, FRS, FSA*, Cambridge: Cambridge University Press.

Briggs, C. S. 1981. An early communication on a rusticated beaker from Flamborough and a description of two tumuli in Thixendale. *Yorkshire Archaeological Journal* 53, 1–6.

Briggs, C .S. 1997. A Megalithic Conundrum: The pedigree of some William Stukeley Illustrations, in W. Marx, (ed.), *The Founders' Library University of Wales, Lampeter, Bibliographical and Contextual Studies: Essays in Memory of Robin Rider, Trivium* 29 and 30, 195–214. Lampeter: SDUC.

Briggs, C. S. 2007. Prehistory in the Nineteenth Century, in S.M. Pearce, (ed.), 2007, 226–265.

Briggs, C. S. *in press.* From Antiquarianism to Archaeology in *The Times* 1785–1900: some preliminary observations, in H. Sebire, (ed.), *Pursuits and Joys, a conference to celebrate the Lukis Family,* Guernsey Museum 2006.

Buckland, W. 1824. *Reliquiae Diluvianae: or observations on the organic remains contained in caves, fissures, and diluvial gravel, and of other geological phenomena, affecting the action of an universal deluge,* second edition. London: John Murray.

Burton, A. 2005. London Museums in the 1850s. *London and Middlesex Archaeological Society* 56, 169–177.

Chartham Down: Investigation History, Novum Inventorium Sepulchrale: Kentish Anglo-Saxon Graves and Grave Goods in the Sonia Hawkes Archive, July 2007, 1st Edition, http://web.arch.ox.ac.uk/archives/ inventorium/siteoverview.php, Accessed: 14 June 2008.

Chippendale, C. 2004. *Stonehenge Complete.* London: Thames and Hudson.

Courtney, W. P. 2004. Mortimer, Cromwell (*c.*1693–1752), rev. Michael Bevan, *Oxford Dictionary of National Biography,* Oxford University Press [http://www.oxforddnb.com/view/article/19341, accessed 14 June 2008]

Dean, D. R. 2004. Douglas, James (1753–1819), *Oxford Dictionary of National Biography,* Oxford University Press, Sept 2004; online edn, Oct 2005 [http://www.oxforddnb.com/view/article/7902, accessed 14 June 2008]

Dunkin, A. J. 1845. *A Report of the Proceedings of the British Archaeological Association, at the First General Meeting held at Canterbury, in the month of September, 1844. Edited by Alfred John Dunkin, of Dartford, Kent, Member of the Association.* London: John Russell Smith, Old Compton Street, Soho; S. Prentice, Canterbury, MDCCCXLV. Only 150 copies printed.

Evans, C. 2007. Delineating objects: Nineteenth-Century Antiquarian Culture and the Project of Archaeology', 267–306 in S. M. Pearce (ed.).

Fowles, J. (ed.) and Legge, R. (annotater), 1981–82. John Aubrey's *Monumenta Britannica, or a miscellany of British Antiquities, illustrated with notes of Thomas Gale, D.D. and John Evelyn Esquire.* Sherborne, Dorset Publishing Co.

Fox, A. 2004. Aubrey, John (1626–1697), *Oxford Dictionary of National Biography,* Oxford University Press, Sept 2004; online edn, May 2008 [http://www.oxforddnb.com/view/article/886, accessed 13 June 2008]

Fuller, J. G. C. M. 2004. Strachey, John (1671–1743), *Oxford Dictionary of National Biography,* Oxford University Press, 2004 [http://www.oxforddnb.com/view/article/26622, accessed 14 June 2008].

Gaimster, D., McCarthy, S., and Nurse, B. (eds) 2007. *Making History: Antiquaries in Britain 1707–2007.* London: Royal Academy of Arts and Society of Antiquaries of London.

Gransden, A. 2004. Damerham, Adam of (*d.* in or after 1291?), *Oxford Dictionary of National Biography,* Oxford University Press, 2004 [http://www.oxforddnb.com/view/article/93, accessed 13 June 2008].

Grinsell, L. V. 1967. Barrow Treasure, in Fact, Tradition, and Legislation. *Folklore* 78, 1–38.

Haycock, D. B. 2004. Stukeley, William (1687–1765), *Oxford Dictionary of National Biography,* Oxford: University Press, 2004 [http://www.oxforddnb.com/view/article/26743, accessed 14 June 2008]

Herity, M. 1967. From Lhuyd to Coffey: New information from Unpublished Descriptions of Boyne Valley Tombs. *Studia Hibernica* 7, 135–145.

Hill, G. F. 1936. *Treasure Trove in Law and Practice from the earliest times to the present day.* The British Academy and Aalen Reprint 1980.

Hunter M. 1971. The Royal Society and the origins of British Archaeology. *Antiquity* 45, 113–21, 187–92.

Jessop. R. F. 1975. *Man of Many talents: An informal biography of James Douglas 1753–1819.* London and Chichester: Phillimore.

Kinnes, I. 1977. British barrows: a unique visual record? *Antiquity* 51, 52–3.

MacGregor, A .G. 2003. The Antiquary *en plein air*: eighteenth-century progress from topographical survey to the threshold of field archaeology, in R. G. W. Anderson, M. L. Caygill, A. G. MacGregor, and L. Syson, (eds), *Enlightening the British: Knowledge, discovery and the museum in the eighteenth century,* 164–75. London: British Museum Press.

MacGregor, A. G. 2007. Forming an Identity: The Early Society and Its Context, 1707–51, in S. M. Pearce, (ed.), 45–74.

McIntosh, J. 2004. Wheeler, Sir (Robert Eric) Mortimer (1890–1976), *Oxford Dictionary of National Biography*, Oxford University Press, 2004 [http://www.oxforddnb.com/view/article/31825, accessed 13 June 2008]

Parry, G. 2007. Mists of Time, in D. Gaimster *et al.* (eds), 17–35.

Pearce, S. M. (ed.), 2007. *Visions of Antiquity: The Society of Antiquaries 1707–2007*, *Archaeologia* 111. London: The Society of Antiquaries of London.

Piggott, S. 1965. Archaeological Draughtsmanship: Principles and Practice. Part 1, Principles and Retrospect. *Antiquity* 39, 165–176.

Piggott, S. 1978. *Antiquity Depicted*, Walter Neurath Lecture. London: Thames and Hudson.

Piggott, S. 1985. *William Stukeley, an Eighteenth-Century Antiquary*. Oxford: Oxford University Press. Revised and enlarged edition, London: Thames and Hudson.

Ramsay, N. 2004. Faussett, Bryan (1720–1776), *Oxford Dictionary of National Biography*, Oxford University Press, 2004. [http://www.oxforddnb.com/view/article/9214, accessed 14 June 2008]

Reeks, T. and Rudler, F. W. (eds). 1876. *Catalogue of specimens in the Museum of Practical Geology illustrative of the composition and manufacture of British Pottery and Porcelain*, (3rd ed; 1st ed: H. De la Beche and T. Reeks, 1855). London: Eyre and Spottiswoode for HMSO.

Rhodes, M. 1990. Faussett rediscovered: Charles Roach Smith, Joseph Mayer, and the publication of *Inventorium Sepulchrale*, in E. Southworth, (ed.), *Anglo-Saxon cemeteries: a reappraisal*, 25–64. Stroud: Sutton.

Rhodes, M. 2004. Smith, Charles Roach (1806–1890), *Oxford Dictionary of National Biography*, Oxford: University Press, 2004. [http://www.oxforddnb.com/view/article/25789, accessed 14 June 2008].

Roberts, B. F. 2004. Lhuyd , Edward (1659/60?–1709), *Oxford Dictionary of National Biography*, Oxford: University Press 2004. [http://www.oxforddnb.com/view/article/16633, accessed 13 June 2008].

Rowley-Conwy, P. 2007. *From Genesis to Prehistory*. Oxford: Oxford University Press.

Saull, W. D. 1842. On the foundations of the Roman Walls of London. *Archaeologia* 30, 522–4.

Smiles, S. 2007. The Art of Recording, in D. Gaimster *et al.* (eds), 122–141.

Smith, C. R. 1841a. Observations on Roman Remains discovered in London. *Archaeologia* 29 (1842), 145–166.

Smith, C. R. 1841b. Observations on further Roman Remains discovered in London. *Archaeologia* 29 (1842), 267–274.

Smith, C. R. 1844. Notice of a leaden coffin, of early fabric, discovered at Bow. *Archaeologia* 31 (1846), 308–11.

Smith, C. R. 1856. *Inventorium Sepulchrale*, privately printed.

Tite, W. 1848. *A Descriptive Catalogue of the Antiquities found in the Excavations at the New Royal Exchange, Preserved in the Museum of the Corporation of London*. London: Printed for the Use of the members of the Corporation of the City of London.

Ucko, P. J., Hunter, M., Clark, A. J and David. A. 1991. *Avebury Reconsidered*. London: Unwin Hyman (for The Institute of Archaeology).

Weston, R. 2008. John Traherne, FSA, and William Buckland's 'Red Lady'. *Antiquaries Journal* 88, 347–364.

Wilson, D. M. 2004. Franks, Sir (Augustus) Wollaston (1826–1897), *Oxford Dictionary of National Biography*, Oxford University Press, 2004 [http://www.oxforddnb.com/view/article/10093, accessed 15 June 2008.]

Wright, T. 1845. Account of the Opening of Barrows in Bourne Park, near Canterbury, the seat of Lord Albert Conynghan. *Archaeological Journal* 1, 253–56.

Wright, T. 1846. On antiquarian excavations and researches in the middle ages. *Archaeologia* 30, 438–457.

Wright, T. 1861. On antiquarian excavations and researches in the middle ages, in T. Wright (ed.), *Essays on Archaeological Subjects: and on various questions connected with the history of art, science, and literature in the middle ages*, 2 vols. London: John Russell Smith, Soho Square, vol 1, 268–304.

Wroth, W. W. 2004. Faussett, Thomas Godfrey Godfrey- (1829–1877), rev. Shirley Burgoyne Black, *Oxford Dictionary of National Biography*, Oxford: University Press, 2004. [http://www.oxforddnb.com/view/article/9215, accessed 14 June 2008].

Sutton Hoo –
an archaeography

Martin Carver

Introduction

Sutton Hoo is one of the great archaeological sites of Europe and pivotal for the understanding of how early Medieval kingdom-building and Christianisation were expressed. The latest campaign of excavation there was certainly great in size – almost a hectare was opened, but the estimation of quality (which probably lies behind our convenor's title) is something else. That needs a context. What I chose to do in this chapter was to describe not just the latest campaign, but the four that preceded it, and try to put each into the context of its day. My hope is that we may discover something useful about how the results of archaeological excavation relate to its objectives, its resources, its work-force and its contemporary situation. Everyone knows these things are relevant, but their influence is not always self-evident. I offer here an empirical description of how the excavations were done – giving this study the grand epithet 'archaeography', writing about the doing of archaeology, by analogy to historiography, writing about the writing of history.

Figure 3.1. The Sutton Hoo burial mounds, looking west in 1982 before the start of Campaign 5 (Photo: C. Hoppitt).

First Campaign, *c.* 1600

Sutton Hoo is a small group of burial mounds on the first gravel terrace on the east bank of the River Deben in Suffolk. The mounds, as we know now, were erected over a short period of about 60 years between 590 and 650 AD. They had stood during the Middle Ages in sheep pasture, rising to nearly their original height of 3–5m. Towards the end of the sixteenth century three things happened quickly: the mounds were exploited as warrens for farming rabbits, they were ploughed and they were explored by digging vertical shafts from above. These things may have been connected: in 1988 when rabbits were again rampant, they excavated a reticella bead from Mound 7, and something of the kind may have led an inquiring mind to investigate the source of a casual find in the late sixteenth century. Our own excavations showed that the technique of investigation employed was to dig a large pit from the summit of the mound, and go on digging until a treasure was sighted. Such a pit was documented in Mounds 2, 5, and 14, and is implied in Basil Brown's investigations of Mound 3, where the large depression in the top was referred to as a 'dew pond' (Carver 2005, 66–9).

Two mounds escaped: Mound 17 covered the grave of a young man in his coffin and, in another grave alongside, his horse. The merry shafters of Campaign 1 had begun as usual at the top of the extant mound and gone vertically downwards, with the result that they had arrived exactly between the two grave-pits (Carver 2005, 136). The shaft was continued into the subsoil and into the fill of a Neolithic ditch, not subsoil but apparently recognisable as not grave fill either. These excavators were not neat, but it would be a mistake to believe that they were not informed. The excavators also gave their attention to Mound 1, burial place of the celebrated Sutton Hoo treasure, which fortunately they did not find. Here medieval ploughing had so eroded and distorted the mound that its summit no longer lay directly above the burial chamber. The floor of the chamber was in any case some 3m below ground level, and the top of the mound 3m above that. The shaft gave up at 'about 10ft' from the high point of the mound in 1939. The sixteenth-century robber shaft thus missed the chamber to the east and ended about 3m short.

Evidence for the date of this first campaign, to around 1600, comes from Mound 2, where the shaft was cut by the trench of Campaign 2 and from tracks on dated maps which crossed the filled-in quarry ditches (Carver 2005, 465). Primary evidence came from Mound 1 where sherds of Bellarmine ware were found at the base of the shaft, along with the remains of a hearth. This assemblage was termed 'the lunch of the disappointed' by the 1939 excavators, who no doubt saw nothing strange in a group of robbers with a gin bottle cooking lunch at the bottom of a hole 1m across and 3m underground.

We can say rather little about the techniques of Campaign 1. That it was a campaign is implied by the number of shafts and the resemblance between them. One bonanza gives an appetite for more. Campaign 1 must have been a great success if the poor yield of Campaign 2 (which followed it) is anything to go by. The late sixteenth-century excavators must have hit the jackpot in at least Mound 2, Mound 14 and Mound 3, since the subsequent meagre remains of these burials suggest that they retrieved a deal of treasure. We can also deduce that the operation was fairly dangerous. The Sutton Hoo deposit does not stand easily more than about a metre high. Basil Brown brought the sides of his excavation down several times in both Mound 1 and Mound 2. Having said that, we found no evidence for the tragedy that a 3m shaft would seem to invite – no 'corpse of the disappointed'. One imagines long wooden ladders and small boys scrambling for anything bright and shiny.

This was a period known for a major redistribution of the nation's assets. It is my belief that as well as privatising the monasteries, the late sixteenth-century government felt it had a prerogative to license the digging of burial mounds, the contents of which would otherwise revert to the king

(Carver 2000, 25–7). We have some evidence that a systematic pillaging of mounds in Suffolk began around the time of the dissolution. In 1538 Thomas Toyser applied for a licence for a programme to finish off excavations at Brightwell that had been started by 'ill-doers,' that is, unlicensed diggers. The character of this type of archaeology is revealed by its local colloquial name 'gold mining'. John Dee (1527–1608), the great Elizabethan intellectual entrepreneur, may well have been involved with the Sutton Hoo Campaign 1, as he seems to have been an active treasure-hunter elsewhere. In 1574 he wrote to Lord Burghley saying that he would 'discover a mine of gold or silver in the Queen's dominions, which is to belong to her, on condition of his having a right to all treasure trove in her dominions' and somewhat unsubtly offered Burghley half the proceeds. 'Treasure trove' does not sound like an actual stratum of ore, and it seems more likely that we see here the tip of a highly lucrative portable antiquities scam, run by a gold-hungry cartel associated with the Tudor hierarchy.

From this we could also deduce that the Crown could licence landowners to quarry mounds on their own land. At Sutton Hoo, the landowners in the district were Sir Michael Stanhope, Sir Henry Wood and the Mather family, the latter being the most likely suspect. Sutton Hoo is labelled 'Mathershoe' on the early seventeenth-century Norden Map, and the Mathers lived in 'How farm', between Sutton Hoo and the river Deben. A study of the wills of the Mather family by A. M. Breen shows that while John Mather (dying 1567) and Thomas Mather (1592) are described as yeomen, Robert Mather (died 1639) and his son are styled as gentlemen (Carver 2005, 469). The Mathers had gone up in the world, then, not inconceivably as a result of the generous 'hoo' on their doorstep.

Second Campaign, *c.* 1860

The existence of a Campaign 2, as with Campaign 1, was discovered archaeologically by excavating and recording every recent disturbance with the same level of attention as the ancient features (Figure 3.2). No doubt we would have preferred to have found our burials intact (as Mound 17), but I would recommend this 'archaeology of archaeology' as a rewarding exercise in a league of its own. Certainly excavating an intact chamber is child's play in comparison: excavating earlier excavators requires navigation through a dozen random cuts and dumps amongst an explosive scatter of smashed artefacts and splintered bone.

Campaign 2 was identified during the excavation of Mound 2, which incidentally had been also visited by Campaign 1 and Campaigns 3 and 5, thus providing a sequence of intrusion which allowed us to characterise and order them (Figure 3.3). However, the clearest signature of Campaign 2 was offered by Mound 7. The excavators here dug a long trench running W–E straight through the mound at ground level. In one place at least a large block of mound make-up had become detached and was about to fall. The spoil was extracted on the east side along a barrow run which had become compact with traffic. At the west end a flight of steps had been cut into the mound make up and through the buried soil, so that a visitor could make their way gracefully down to the central pit. The bottom of this pit was round and about 1.5m below the old ground surface, and may have actually been the bottom of a Campaign 1 shaft. The scene is therefore fairly clear: workers excavated the dirt on one side and took the risks of collapse, while the gentleman antiquary descended the steps at intervals to see what interesting curiosities had been brought to light.

Similar trenches were cut through Mounds 2, 3, 4, 5, 6, 13 and 14. At Mounds 5 and 6, trial pits had been dug on the west side, apparently to establish the height of the subsoil. If there had been a trench through Mound 1 it did not reach the bottom and was not seen by the1939 excavators who used much the same technique themselves. Noting the W–E linear depressions in the top of many mounds,

Figure 3.2. The 19th century excavation through Mound 7, redefined in 1989 (Photo: Nigel Macbeth).

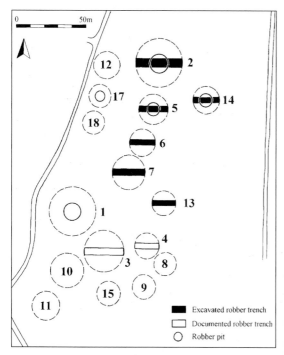

Figure 3.3. (left) Map showing located excavations of Campaign 1 (circular) and Campaign 2 (rectangular); (right) Visitations to Mound 2, Campaigns 1–3 and 5 (Photo: Nigel Macbeth).

Rupert Bruce-Mitford interpreted them as 'ship-dents,' that is, fill that had somehow collapsed along the line of a buried ship (1975, 159–60). This phenomenon was used to support the case for further excavation in the 1980s, but in reality argued against it: we know now that the 'ship-dents' were just the remains of the backfilled trenches of Campaign 2, and the mounds in question had already been excavated and contained no ships.

A possible date for this campaign was offered by the *Ipswich Journal* for 24 November 1860. This issue reported the excavation of a group of five Roman [*sic*] barrows about 500 yards from the banks of the Deben opposite Woodbridge on a farm occupied by Mr Barritt. The summary says: 'A considerable number (nearly two bushels) of iron screw-bolts were found, all of which were sent to the blacksmith to be converted into horseshoes! It is hoped, when leave is granted to open the others, some more important antiquities may be discovered'. The unimportant antiquities that were so usefully recycled were undoubtedly ship rivets, and the only known source of them would then have been Mound 2 (since Mound 1 remained undisturbed at this date). Disturbed ship rivets were found in the vicinity of Mound 5, 6 and 7, which implies that leave had been granted to open other mounds, and that the campaign had moved from north to south.

It seems reasonable to equate the set of W–E trenches of Campaign 2 with the entry in the *Ipswich Journal*, and date it to the mid nineteenth century. This was a period of barrow-digging of a new kind, the age of the antiquary. On the rising tide of archaeological curiosity the Archaeological Institute had been created in the 1840s and J. M. Kemble was publishing Anglo-Saxon objects in its proceedings throughout the 1850s. The cemetery at Snape a few miles north of Sutton Hoo had been investigated in 1827 by some 'gentlemen from London' but it was not until 1862 that a boat burial was found there. The great intact Scandinavian ships had not yet been found: the Gokstad burial was unearthed in 1880 and Oseberg in 1904 (Nicolaysen 1882; Brøgger *et al.* 1917). Thus the Sutton Hoo excavators of 1860 can perhaps be forgiven for failing to recognise their ship-rivets. All the same, the excavation team seems to have been somewhat isolated from the contemporary archaeological mainstream. The Suffolk Institute of Archaeology and Natural History held its meeting in Woodbridge in 1860, but makes no mention of the campaign; nor does the *Gentlemen's Magazine* in 1861, although it reported the Snape ship in 1863. Local historians Hele (1870) and Redstone (1897) seem unaware of any excavations at Sutton Hoo, although they knew the mounds well enough.

The explanation would seem to be that the excavators of Campaign 2 found very little, or recognised little of what they found; and the explanation for this would be that the excavators of Campaign 1 had already got away with the lion's share. The mounds had been ploughed again since the sixteenth century, so the shafts would not perhaps have been evident. In 1860 Robert Barrett was the tenant farmer and George Friston was the blacksmith. But there is no evidence that they, or any of the other associated farmers or landowners got rich. Besides, in this age when antiquities were regularly exhibited by the newly formed societies in village halls all over the country, the kudos would seem to lie in knowledge rather than wealth.

Third campaign, 1938–39

The circumstances of Campaign number 3 have been often retold. Mrs Edith Pretty was then the landowner, and her urge to investigate the mounds that were visible from the bow-windows of her twentieth-century pile is thought by many to have come through her propensity for the occult. It is true she had a medium, who was, incidentally, instrumental in her later decision to give the Mound 1 treasure to the nation. But she had also had previous archaeological experience in Vale Royal abbey

Figure 3.4. Excavations of 1939 (Campaign 3). (left) Basil Brown; (right) The Mound 1 team in action watched by Mrs Pretty and friends.

and in Egypt, and was no doubt able to imagine what the mounds might contain. All previous work having been consigned to oblivion, the expectation was that they would be Bronze Age like those on Martlesham Heath across the river. Mrs Pretty retained the services of Basil Brown, a self-taught professional excavator who worked free-lance for Ipswich Museum. His excavation technique was more or less identical to that of his nineteenth-century forerunners, although he himself considered it was state of the art, citing an article in *Norfolk Archaeology* by Rainbird Clarke and Apling (1935). Brown was eulogised by later generations of East Anglian archaeologists, so it is as well to remind ourselves that a contemporary viewed his on-site performance as 'just like a terrier after a rat.' He regularly collapsed trenches and his recording was bizarre. However, his recognition of ship rivets in Mound 2 and the subsequent definition of the ship in Mound 1 were strokes of genius. He had bicycled over to Snape and found the rivets of the 1862 excavation in a drawer. When confronted with the first rivet in Mound 1 he recognised it as being *in situ* – and, aided by the publication of the Oseberg ship burial which he had borrowed from Mr Maynard (of Ipswich Museum), was able to imagine the ghost of the ship laid out in its trench (Brown 1974, 166) (Figure 3.4).

In 1938 Brown drove trenches through Mounds 2, 3 and 4, having first found the level of the subsoil with a test pit: the one for Mound 2 contained an old bucket in its backfill. We know the Mound 2 trench very well since it was re-excavated in Campaign 5. His trenches were laid out on compass bearings, and this one is decidedly skew. He approached from the east, bumping along the surface of the buried soil as best he could, noting prehistoric material and hoping to find the brightly coloured splash of the burial pit towards the centre. In practice he did not, because Mound 2, like Mounds 3 and 4 had been excavated twice before, but he attempted to achieve definition within the fog of the disturbance by widening the trench at the centre of the mound into a square area, until he could define the original burial pit.

In 1939 he employed the same technique in Mound 1, starting the trench on the east side and driving it horizontally into the mound. In this case he hardly saw the buried soil or the subsoil, but happily had the rivets to guide him. The method of excavation was to slice the sand horizontally, using a shovel, or latterly, a coal shovel lashed to a long pole. When a red spot appeared, he recognised the iron of a rivet, and made the assumption that each rivet would be in situ, and must be left in situ, so he dusted it carefully with a pastry brush and moved forward. As he approached the centre, the mound got higher and the boat got lower, so the sides of the trench had to be continually cut back. The method did not give a standing section through the mound.

It is not commonly known that Basil Brown actually defined the whole length of the Mound 1 ship and the burial chamber at its centre, also having a poke at a few voids in the mat of decayed wood that covered it. Since the appointment of Charles Phillips, the Cambridge prehistorian who had got wind of the find, Brown had been repeatedly told to stop. But he continued to excavate without a pause for nearly four weeks, until he was finally dispossessed on 8 July by the Phillips team. At one time or another this team consisted of Stuart Piggott, W. F. Grimes and Peggy Guido (then Piggott) who did most of the work, with O. G. S. Crawford, Sir John Fosdyke, T. D. Kendrick, John Ward-Perkins, Graham Clarke, John Brailsford and Commander Hutchinson as visiting participants. In an incredible seventeen days, this team emptied the burial chamber of 263 objects which were then packed in moss in boxes, sweet bags and tobacco tins. An inquest held at Sutton village hall found that they belonged to the landowner, Mrs Pretty, and were not Treasure Trove because the seventh-century burial party had not planned to retrieve them. Mrs Pretty subsequently presented them to the British Museum and there they have been ever since.

Before taking leave of this well-known episode, we can note a number of things from a twenty-first century perspective. Mrs Pretty's motive was curiosity and there was no regulation to discourage her from satisfying it. The mounds were not scheduled, and unlike in the sixteenth century (when they were at the disposal of the crown), the contents were legally hers, as the inquest showed. Mrs Pretty has also been lavishly praised by posterity, so it is as well to remember that she provided very few resources for the excavation, other than some basins. She paid Basil Brown a labourer's wage, allowing him temporary accommodation in an upper room of the chauffeur's cottage, and the assistance of her gardener and game-keeper. It was this small team and their lack of money that, more than any supposed methodology, determined the course of the excavation. Three people can only move so much earth, and the best method is the one that maximises yield for the labour available. The required yield was objects, since the commissioning agent would know little of the broader scientific potential. Brown cannot be wholly blamed for being messy and inaccurate – because he was obviously in a great hurry. Fast digging is bad digging, and the reason, then as now, is usually money, and a lack of understanding that excavation of a disturbed site, done properly, takes just as long – and may take longer – than finding an intact treasure.

To begin with, it was also a cosy affair. Robert Pretty then aged 8 would be a regular face at the trench-side, and he buried his roller skates in the back fill of Mound 2 (where we found them). The atmosphere changed with the arrival of the upper echelon from Cambridge and London, for whom Brown became a labourer again. Now the voices on site were no longer broad Suffolk, but high pitched, point-scoring academics. This resulted in no immediate increase in quality – the coal shovel was still in use, and was augmented in the chamber by the pastry brush and the 'packer's needle', a long curved steel needle for sewing hessian. Although it was intended to erect a shelter (Brown 1974, 164), in the event there arrived only a tarpaulin and twelve scaffold poles 'for which little use could be found' as Phillips remarked (Sutton Hoo archive/vol 2/33). The excavators moved cheerfully about the chamber treading on everything. 'I have no doubt that we did in fact stand on quite a number of the objects a number of times' remarked W. F. Grimes, but 'you could have danced on that jewellery and you would not hurt it – not that we did! The amount of gold leaf that was blowing about was frightful.' (Carver 1998, 17) These excavators too pleaded shortage of time, but unlike Basil Brown, who had laid it out for them, they could not plead ignorance of the job in hand. In spite of the involvement of the British Museum, the University of Cambridge, the Office of Public Works and Mrs Pretty, herself a millionaire, the total expenditure for the excavation of Mound 1 was £250.

There was perhaps a spirit of make-do and mend that was seriously attractive to a generation brought up on Arthur Ransome and E. E. Nesbitt. Not just too proud to ask for money but even more proud of what can be achieved heroically without it, by a group of merry chaps (who anyway have plenty of their own), and whose resourcefulness and valour were about to be thoroughly tested by a world war.

Fourth Campaign 1964–1971

The objects from Mound 1 spent their war in the London underground, and in 1945 were to begin a long process of analysis culminating in their publication in 1983 (Bruce-Mitford 1975, 1978, 1983). One of the most detailed examinations of a grave assemblage ever achieved, this 2439 page book is monument to the diligence and persistence of Rupert Bruce-Mitford and his team. Those impressed with the Management of Archaeological Projects (MAP2) procedure might care to notice the ratio of effort here between excavation (3 months) and post-excavation (38 years). In addition to conserving and studying the objects, Bruce-Mitford, who had trained with Sune Lundqvist on the Uppland ship burials (Vendel and Valsgärde), was aware of several enigmas in the Sutton Hoo record. Should there not have been horses and dogs with the Mound 1 burial? Could there have been unconsidered fragments that would make sense of helmet or shield? What was Sutton Hoo's prehistoric predecessor, that Basil Brown had noted?

So, in addition to funding the study of the finds, the British Museum launched a return excavation of eight summer seasons. In contrast to the valiant pre-war adventure, here no expense was spared. The excavation crew was put up in hotels, and in addition to the contingent from the Medieval and Later department, included prehistorians: Paul Ashbee to study the mound, and Ian Longworth and Ian Kinnes (from Prehistoric and Roman) to study the earlier site. In pursuit of the varied agenda, there were eventually eleven interventions, five in the area of Mound 1 (including the excavation of the mound and the 1939 spoil heaps) and six in echelon across the north end of the site. The ship was reopened using 'area excavation', while the spoil heaps were excavated using the Wheeler system of parallel boxes (Figure 3.5). Area excavations were used in the northern sector to test for prehistoric settlement, and to verify the existence of Mound 5. Subsequently, trenches were used to chase the Neolithic ditch in the north and the Medieval lynchet in the south. The Mound 1 site, originally excavated in the open, was now covered by a vast shelter of scaffolding, and the ship was re-excavated, recorded again, rivet by rivet, and then lifted in a huge series of plaster of Paris casts, before being recast in fibreglass. Unfortunately the ship trench had been left open in 1939, shortly after which it had been included in a military training area and driven over by bren-gun carriers. The records made

Figure 3.5. Excavations of 1965–71 (Campaign 4) (left) A re-excavation of the Mound 1 ship under a shelter; (right) Excavation of the spoil-heaps, using box method (P. Ashbee).

Figure 3.6. The sutton Hoo site cleaned up for evaluation in 1983 (Photo: C. Hoppitt).

by Commander Hutchinson in Campaign 3 of the near perfect layout of the ship revealed by Brown had been lost in the war. But records of the highest precision were applied in Campaign 4 to the ship's mangled and distorted carcase. Meanwhile, the intensive sieving of the spoil heaps produced only 34 fragments of iron and pottery of which two objects may have been Anglo-Saxon (or Medieval) brooches (Bruce-Mitford 1975, 455).

Although it might appear lavish and disjointed, there could have been no question of *not* carrying out this campaign, and to the highest standards. The Sutton Hoo treasure had become famous both in scholarly and public circles, and its profile was raised further by the television film *The Million Pound Grave* made to celebrate the 1939 discovery. Just as the 1939 crew was anxious not to make too much fuss, the 1969 crew was anxious to show that they were pulling out all the stops. The world had changed, after all; this campaign was not powered by the idle curiosity of a landowner. It was led by the primary research project of a world class museum, with one eye on the Germanic continent which envied the find and another on the USA whose museums had rather greater resources. With these academic and social pressures in mind, Bruce-Mitford's achievement can be seen as remarkable.

Fifth Campaign 1983–2005

The fifth campaign came about partly through the agitation of Bruce-Mitford who wanted to see more mounds opened, and partly through the desire of the Society of Antiquaries to launch a flagship project. The matter was raised in public discussion at the Oxford conference entitled *Anglo-Saxon Cemeteries 1979*, which soon revealed the current tensions. Since the Sutton Hoo find had gone on display at the British Museum, the archaeology field profession had been born, grown up and become distinctly battle-weary. Margaret Thatcher had come to power and the long nurtured dream of a state archaeological service, in which respected practitioners could live out their days in peace, was looking decidedly shaky. The cold wind of competition blew through the caravans, and invited us to take up arms again, this time against each other. The sensibilities of such a field profession were never going to look kindly on a project which promised to spend a large amount of money on an unnecessary dig. Moreover, the deployment of this profession in county-based 'units' meant that they were given to zealous (or jealous) defence of their turf. On the other hand the academic profession was frustrated that its research agenda was continually being upstaged by the moralising of the rescue lobby.

Although I was a member of the field profession leading my own company, rather than an academic, I was invited to apply for the job of director when it was advertised in the London Gazette. And when offered it, I accepted, for a quite particular reason. Since 1973 I had been developing and promoting an approach to excavation which I thought ought to work in a formal research investigation, just as I believed I had made it work in the rescue theatre of the West Midlands. This was my big chance. I was also struck by how static was the excavation methodology of the 1970s, mostly but not exclusively owing to Phil Barker's unbending empiricism (Barker 1977, and White and Everill, this volume). A reasonably well-funded project ought to provide the opportunity to try new things – which might prove useful to the field profession. Similarly, the academic profession, notoriously cavalier in its treatment of sites and excavators alike, could only improve its attitude to fieldwork if caught sufficiently young as volunteers. These were some of the points I made to a meeting convened by the Society for Medieval Archaeology for all potential objectors in 1983, on which occasion I also presented a draft project design.

The project design for Campaign 5, the story of the project and its results have been published in some detail elsewhere, so I will use the space I have just to illuminate selected points and to compare and contrast with what had gone before. I will end by drawing what I hope you will accept as a general point of principle about the relationship between excavation and archaeological theory more broadly.

The first point I want to make is that Sutton Hoo was the first (and may prove to be the last) archaeological project to be awarded by design competition. Those who put in for the job had to submit a preliminary design for it and the winner then got to name the price. It was not won by preferment – the appointment of an acolyte by his deacon, nor the commissioning of a named academic by a grant-giving body, nor the result of pressure from a local authority. All these things we have seen many times before and since. Nor was it a result of competitive tender, as in the new Cultural Resource Management (CRM) profession. On this occasion, archaeological research was treated like a commissioned work of art and the archaeologist like an artist: the choice was made on the basis of an outline proposal defended at interview.

Before accepting the appointment, I was able to ask for, and obtain, a three-year period in which to prepare the programme (Figs 3.6, 3.7, 3.8). As I had in the West Midlands, I called this phase the 'design phase' and the preparatory process 'evaluation' and although the Sutton Hoo Trust was not apparently familiar with either they were supportive way beyond my expectations. During the design phase, every type of remote mapping was applied in order to try and anticipate more precisely what lay beneath the turf, and inquiries were made at home and abroad as to the expectations of the scholarly community. The funding of this phase was particularly far-sighted on the part of the sponsors, since all of them had committees to satisfy, and in the case of the BBC, had films to make. By contrast, English Heritage, which was founded at about the time that Campaign 5 began (in 1983), and required

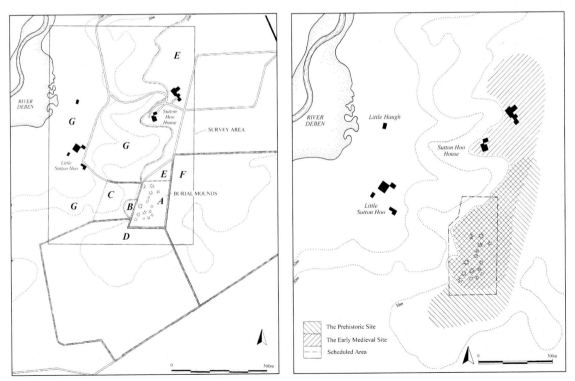

Figure 3.7. Campaign 5, evaluation stage (right) Zonation; (left) The main areas located.

Figure 3.8. Campaign 5: prototype ground penetrating radar, operated by Mike Gorman of the Scott Polar Institute, 1984.

us to apply for Scheduled Monument Consent, actively disliked my design-led procedure which they dubbed an attempt at 'creeping consent'. Curiously, in the light of their new branding, they also had no interest in acquiring the site. What a difference a decade makes! Although not owners of the site, English Heritage later helped in its protection and are now among the most ardent champions of evaluation and project design.

The evaluation had three parts to it: compiling the research objectives, creating the resource model and studying the social context. The research objectives were gathered through seminars and committees, where there soon emerged an obvious disjuncture between Sutton Hoo's various 'clients': the historians, who wanted more 'early kings'; the art historians, who wanted more treasures; the prehistorians who were most interested in the Beaker settlement; and the medieval archaeologists, who, being mainly processualists at that time, wanted some light thrown on the formation of the early kingdoms. Next came the resource model – the predictive modelling of the archaeology still underground, which would indicate how, and how far, the research objectives could actually be addressed at or around Sutton Hoo. The third arm of the evaluation was the social context, the assessment of the stake-holders, the interested parties, whose opinion and whose support was essential if the project was to survive and be productive (Figure 3.9). Among these, the state authorities were minor players, who at the time had washed their hands of the whole thing; but the County unit had a proprietorial attitude that needed to be mollified by acts of fealty and consultation. So had the treasure hunters, who considered their exclusion from the site to be 'elitist' since, as usual, no-one had bothered to explain the circumstances of their exclusion. As soon as I did, with an advanced copy of the project design, I was rewarded

Figure 3.9. The social context. (above) The newly formed Sutton Hoo Society, representing local residents; (below) a visit of the Sutton Hoo Research Committee, left to right: Tom Hassall, Martin Carver, Martin Biddle, Birthe Kolbye-Biddle, Rupert Bruce-Mitford, David Wilson (Photo: Nigel Macbeth).

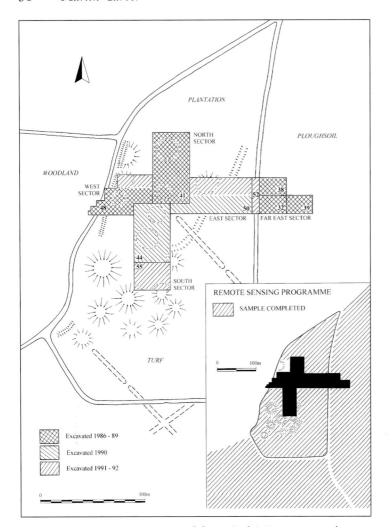

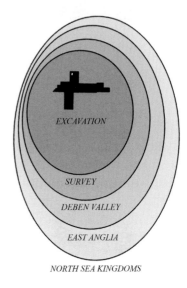

Figure 3.10. Campaign 5: Integrated design (right) Excavation and remote sensing; (left) nested surveys, local, regional, national and international.

with a friendly editorial in *Treasure Hunting Monthly* with the underlying message 'back off lads'. A third group, which was to prove invaluable in practical ways, was the cadre of local residents who had always considered Sutton Hoo their private property. As in much of England, your land is not what you own, it is where you can take your dog for a walk. Convened in a Woodbridge hotel, this group formed itself into the Sutton Hoo Society in 1984 and is still going strong.

The project design was constructed by putting these three sets of factors together: the research agenda, the deposit model and the current social context. The output was to be two programmes: the research programme, comprising a six year excavation, and a survey of the Deben Valley; and a management programme, comprising rabbit-proof fences, mowing, exhibitions and public access (Figure 3.10). Also, beginning then was a long negotiation that finally came to fruition when the landowners, the Tranmer family, bequeathed the entire Sutton Hoo estate to the National Trust.

Perhaps the most important point to make about the whole design process is what was done with

Figure 3.11 Recovery levels in operation in Int 50 (Photo: Nigel Macbeth).

Figure 3.12. Excavations at Sutton Hoo in 1989, looking north. The rain machine is on the baulk on the right (Photo: Nigel Macbeth).

it. Having assembled the materials for the design as the result of three years of fieldwork and many private consultations and public seminars, the proposed programmes of research, excavation, survey, conservation and display were then published before work began (Carver 1986). Anyone and everyone could have their say on what was about to happen at Sutton Hoo. Disappointingly, this procedure has not been adopted by large research projects that came later, like Tintagel or it must be said, like Çatal Hüyök. Hodder's version of multi-vocality can be seen as much more modest, relating only to people who work on the site, live near it or are already connected with it (Hodder 1999, 2000). Multi-vocality for me requires the publication of a proposed programme in detail and in advance – so as to argue for consensus between all parties. By the same principle, once the project design is agreed, a 'social contract' exists between the archaeological team and the many potential stake holders in the site, both in its home country and abroad, so the excavator is not at liberty to change it.

As for Sutton Hoo's subsequent history, I would like to pick out a few matters which I think are still pertinent, although much else has now become old hat. I would certainly urge the use of 'Recovery Levels' which predetermine the excavation techniques and records to be made (Figure 3.11). These proved invaluable for making comparisons and exercising quality control between one context and another (Carver 1999; 2005, 25). Technically, we strove to improve visibility using chemical mapping, but I cannot claim much of a break-through except on a small scale (*i.e.* in Mound 2) (Carver 2005, 49–50, 58–64) (Figure 3.13). Some progress was made in the surface mapping of the subsoil, which gives about 80 per cent of the total information in this kind of site (Carver 2005, 43). Everyone will agree that a sandy subsoil needs to be seen over a large area, but there are three requisites of which the modern profession seems to be dangerously shy: on-site water for spraying; a workforce of at least ten to prepare the surface by hand; and a tower from which to photograph the prepared surface (Figure 3.12). There is now clearly a problem in providing these things, since site after site appears without them, both on TV and in reality. Perhaps commercial companies cannot afford trowellers and find volunteers irksome; perhaps they are not allowed to use towers for safety reasons. I cannot see why they should have to do without water. However until someone comes up with something better (and I look forward to hearing about it) these ingredients are essential for the inspection and subsequent excavation of the majority of features on sand. You will not see them in a trench and especially not a dry one, and of course if you do not see them, as part of a field assessment or mitigation, no-one is ever the wiser.

The question of the work force seems especially relevant here since it is a natural concomitant of the tendering process that a work force should be small, even when the area to be excavated is large. High precision survey means that every anomaly can be quickly plotted and subsequently rediscovered with ease, but it must be seen in the first place. It is not only a question of scale and timing as suggested above, it is also a matter of experience: excavators must serve an apprenticeship. With all their faults, the use of students, volunteers and employment schemes (a Manpower Services Scheme did excellent work at Sutton Hoo) does provide a way in for newcomers to broad sandy sites. It also provides a way for stakeholders, whether local or from overseas universities, to take part. It seems wrong to me that our profession, and its clients apparently, are reluctant to make use of the voluntary labour which would so patently give their projects added value, technically and socially.

My last indulgence is to speak yet again in support of the multi-concept recording system, in which records additional to contexts are made on site (Carver 1999). In this system, contexts are sets of observable components, and themselves belong to groups or sets (defined as features), while features belong to sets which I define as structures. Contexts, features and structures are thus independent of each other, and their records run in parallel. Contexts, features and structures represent a hierarchy increasingly rich in interpretation. The profession ditched these things for a few decades in favour of single-context systems, especially in towns, but excavators working on the flat find they cannot manage without them, and I quite agree with them (Lowe 2006, 32). Hodder (1999) rightly talks of

Figure 3.13. Excavating burials (left) A 'Sandman'; (right) Andy Copp taking samples for ICP mapping from the base of the Mound 2 chamber (Photos: Nigel Macbeth).

on-site interpretation 'at the trowel's edge,' but like any other interpretation it needs recording in a disciplined manner, which is what feature and structure records are for. Similarly, there was no need to re-invent the site book and film monitoring since not only the excavators at Sutton Hoo, but the majority of research excavators in the twentieth century never abandoned them.

Conclusion

Are there messages here for the field archaeology of today and tomorrow? I believe so. Archaeological contexts have no idea whether they are being looked for by researchers or commercial mitigators. But our chances of finding them depend on the recovery level, the effort put in. For this reason there is a standard, a 'British Standard' if you will, that curators should insist on. Obviously it is easier to come up with a winning tender if you dig with a minimal workforce, no piped water and no tower. Moreover no-one will be able to prove there were things you did not see. But if well-funded full-time research excavations have a point (other than research), it is to discover how to see more, and having done so, share the knowledge widely. These procedures should then be built into the specifications recommended – no, *demanded* – by curators from developers.

Archaeological excavation is not like doing history in a library; without a proper evaluation you cannot know what you expect to do; you cannot even fill in an application form for a grant. Since the planning and building industry has known this for decades and rightly insisted on evaluation and submitted design as a concomitant of planning permission, it is a mystery that research excavations

Figure 3.14. The Sutton Hoo site on completion of Campaign 5 in 1991 (Photo: Justin Garner-Lahire).

can still get funding without it. I also do not understand how research excavations can get a permit either in this country, or any other, without a conservation plan. That plan should be part of the Project Design at its outset, and the Project Design needs to be published in advance of any permission or funding being awarded. The prior publication of project designs is rare in the commercial sector, which I suppose is not surprising given its propensity to hide behind commercial confidentiality. But it is hardly ever done in the research sector either – at least I have never seen one. Was Sutton Hoo really so exceptional that alone it has felt the need for a full evaluation, a research agenda, a deposit model, an appreciation of the social context, and the additional need to expose the plan for multi-vocal comment before it starts?

This 'archaeography' has shown something of how the agenda, the techniques and the resources of archaeological investigation have changed with the times. At one level this is simply part of the broad-brush history of archaeology: looting in the irreverent age of the late sixteenth century; curiosity and kudos in the age of the antiquarian in the mid nineteenth. The excavation just before the war was driven by an inquisitive (but not acquisitive) landowner. After the war, as archaeology donned its self-important mantle, we seemed to be striving for the greater good, as expressed in research and in conservation. This was not formalised until Campaign no. 5, but then its logic was inescapable. No known site should ever be dug in its entirety. Our task was to work out the key questions that could be addressed at that site, at that time: if they required the total excavation of the whole site, they were the wrong questions and we should think again, for in this matter the ethical takes precedence over the academic. For the same reason, a research excavation should never require more than five or six years to complete. Twenty five years separated Campaign 3 from Campaign 4, and 12 years separated Campaign 4 from Campaign 5. During these intervals the agenda, the approach and the techniques changed radically. To decide to excavate any site for more than 10 years risks being unethical as well as intellectually perilous (contra Cunliffe, this volume).

Students are often persuaded in their three years at university that excavation has something to do with theory – the Wheeler method pursues culture history, the random quadrat is the instrument of processualism and so on. But in my opinion excavation as a method of inquiry has its own theoretical basis. The objectives of excavation may arise from the research agenda, but its performance is rooted in its own contemporary society and has a lot more to do with people, methods and money than the gentle theorist might wish. Moreover fashions in theory change during the time that an excavation is in progress. When Campaign 5 began we were, by and large, processualists. By the time it ended we were post-structuralists, seeing each burial as an individual expression of its own knowledge and time, its message bearing more of poetry than history (Carver 2000). But the trajectory decided by the Project Design stayed on its rails. In practice the role of theory in fieldwork is advisory, and when it becomes something more overbearing – as with single context or reflexive approaches, the resource and its potential are at risk of being diminished. No-one wants an excavation in which the developer decides the objectives and methods. But an excavation driven by theory is little better – like a film made by a novellist or an aeroplane piloted by a travel agent. Field archaeology has its own logic and duties that lie beyond its clients, whether commercial or academic.

References

Barker P. A. 1977 *Techniques of Archaeological Excavation.* London: Batsford.

Brøgger, A. W., Falk H. J. and Schtelig, H. 1917. *Osebergfundet: Utgiv av den Norske Stat.* Kristiana: Universitetets Oldsakamlung.

Brown, Basil 1974. Basil Brown's Diary of the Excavations at Sutton Hoo in 1938 and 1939, in R. L. S. Bruce-Mitford, *Aspects of Anglo-Saxon Archaeology. Sutton Hoo and other discoveries*, 141–169. London: Gollancz.

Bruce-Mitford, R. L. S. 1975, 1978, 1983. *The Sutton Hoo Ship Burial.* Three volumes, London: British Museum.

Carver, M. O. H. 1986. Project Design. *Bulletin of the Sutton Hoo Research Committee*, 4, 1–89. Woodbridge: Boydell.

Carver, M. O. H. 1998. *Sutton Hoo. Burial Ground of Kings?* London: British Museum.

Carver, M. O. H. 1999 Field Archaeology, in G. Barker (ed.), *The Companion Encyclopaedia of Archaeology*, 128–81. London and New York: Routledge.

Carver, M. O. H. 2000. Burial as poetry: the context of treasure in Anglo-Saxon graves, in Elizabeth M Tyler (ed.) *Treasure in the Medieval West*, 25–48. York: York Medieval Press.

Carver, M. O. H. 2005. *Sutton Hoo. A Seventh-century princely burial ground and its context.* London: British Museum.

Hele, N. F. 1870. *Notes and jottings about Aldeburgh, Suffolk.* London: J. Russell Smith.

Hodder, I. 1999. *The Archaeological Process. An Introduction.* Oxford: Blackwell.

Hodder, I. (ed.) 2000. *Towards reflexive method in archaeology: the example at Çatalhöyük.* British Institute of Archaeology at Ankara: McDonald Institute Monograph.

Lowe, C. 2006. *Excavations at Hoddom, Dumfriesshire. An ecclesiastical site in south-west Scotland.* Edinburgh: Society of Antiquaries of Scotland.

Nicolaysen, N. 1882. *Langskibet frå Gokstad ved Sandefjord.* Kristiana: Alb. Cammermeyer.

Rainbird Clarke, R. and Apling H. 1935. An Iron Age tumulus on Warnborough Hill, Stiffkey, Norfolk. *Norfolk Archaeology* 25, 408–28.

Redstone, V. B. 1897. Woodbridge, its history and antiquity *Proceedings of the Suffolk Institute of Archaeology and History* 9, 345–58.

Sutton Hoo on-line archive: http://www.ahds.ads.ac.uk/downloads/suttonhoo (10 volumes).

Great excavations enhanced – Birdoswald, Richborough, Whitby and Chester amphitheatre

Tony Wilmott

Introduction

Great excavations can cast long shadows. Iconic excavations, which affect the archaeological views of generations, tend to be those that break new interpretative ground, and, most importantly, are rapidly published. All archaeologists are aware of the problems in advancing understanding caused by slow or non-existent publication. This problem is arguably not as great now as in the past thanks to the volume of archaeological work, the virtually universal application of the MAP2 (English Heritage 1992) assessment and analysis model, and several programmes of backlog publication. But during the 1970s, when I was an undergraduate, and early in my professional career, there were a surprisingly small number of major published reports. Of course at the same time, great excavations, or excavations which have since become seen as great, were taking place, among others the Brooks (Winchester), Philip Barker's excavation at Wroxeter, Mucking and Grimes Graves. All of these figured in the old CBA *Calender of Excavations*, which provided opportunities for subsistence paid volunteers. Reviews of several of these projects appear in this volume.

The subsistence-paid, voluntary diggers' circuit was key to my generation's development of experience, and was the place where opportunity existed in what we might term the proto-professional phase of archaeology in Britain. My most memorable experience of such a project was Catholme, the extensive early Saxon settlement in Staffordshire, excavated by the late Stuart Losco-Bradley, where I did a couple of months in 1974 as an unmemorable kak-handed volunteer, experiencing several of the (non-archaeological) rites of passage so important to an 18 year old in the mid 1970s. I also received my A-level results, via my parents, in a red telephone box – an excuse for a memorable evening in the pub. Unusually, the unique spirit and atmosphere of the Catholme experience, even including the site song penned by Simon Woodiwiss, is recalled in Hazel Salisbury's (2002) introduction to the site report. Catholme, like many of these excavations, was more than just a seminal early Saxon excavation; it was a social experience. Camping on site turned it into a community, with people coming and going, but with an identity and culture of its own, developed from the interaction of diverse people engaged in a communal endeavour. This tends to be true still on any large, long-running excavation, and this spirit was captured on the 2004 Chester amphitheatre excavation by the documentary artist Julia Midgley, in a series of action-packed drawings accompanied by commentary (Midgley 2005). In the introduction I reflected on the nature of this community:

> An archaeological excavation is … an event in the lives of the participants. Professional field archaeologists often have a precarious career. They are often highly experienced, all graduates, but they work on contracts for the duration of a project, usually for low pay, and then move on. In many cases they will be working away from their home base, and accommodation may be provided by a project. This was true at Chester. It means

that the team are thrown together, living and working together in very close proximity most of the time. The team is also the social group, as many may have no contacts in the area within which they are working. They have to come together as a working team, all aiming towards a common objective very quickly. All of this means that each project becomes a very intense experience, each formed by the mixture of characters of the staff; the team will develop its own rituals and in-jokes, which will be incomprehensible on the next project on which they work. (Wilmott 2005, 6.)

The impact of a project on the people participating in it, and the pride of having contributed to the results of a truly important excavation, is common to all who have been fortunate enough to work on a great excavation. This was brought home to me while working on the Chester amphitheatre over the last couple of years, as a number of colleagues have recollected to me their participation in the excavations directed on the site by Hugh Thompson in the 1960s, specifically John Williams, Blaise Vyner and Dai Morgan Evans. I am sure they will not mind me saying that for them the excavation was an important and memorable formative experience. Dai is actually singled out in Thompson's (1976) published report as the schoolboy volunteer whose careful trowelling revealed the traces of a timber amphitheatre. Later, of course Dai was to be Thompson's successor but one as General Secretary of the Society of Antiquaries, but he still proudly owns the trowel with which he found the amphitheatre.

Four excavations

The four sites in my title, all of which I have had the rare privilege of re-excavating while employed by English Heritage, are some of those that were obligatory reading during my undergraduate and post-graduate education. As an undergraduate at Newcastle University, taught by Charles Daniels and John Gillam, Hadrian's Wall loomed very large, not least through site visits and a training excavation at Housesteads. In a 1970's Hadrian's Wall education, the 1929 Birdoswald excavation loomed large. It had confirmed the four period system of Hadrian's Wall, holy writ for almost 50 years. For the Claudian invasion and the fortifications of the Saxon Shore, the excavations at Richborough by J. P. Bushe Fox in the early twentieth century, the final volume of which was published by Barry Cunliffe in 1968, were key to understanding, giving us the Claudian invasion fort, the history of the Saxon Shore fort, and, of course the great monumental arch. My teachers greeted the appearance of the report on the Chester amphitheatre in *Archaeologia* in 1975 with enthusiasm, and we were enjoined to read it closely. Later, as a post-graduate studying Medieval Archaeology at Birmingham under Phillip Rahtz, the site of Whitby Abbey was an important part of studies in early monasticism. The excavations by Sir Charles Peers, which were published by Ralegh Radford under incredibly difficult conditions during the London Blitz (Peers and Radford 1943), was required reading, along with the reconsiderations of the site which Phillip and Rosemary Cramp had produced in 1976 (Rahtz 1976; Cramp 1976a, 1976b).

Birdoswald

By any standards the famous photograph of the beginning of the 1929 Birdoswald excavation is an iconic image (Figure 4.1) (Richmond 1930), which says much about the practice of archaeology only eighty years ago, and the distance we have travelled as a profession, but also as a society since the interwar years. It is very familiar to those interested in Hadrian's Wall, but it, and the story that goes with it, are well worth revisiting for our theme. What immediately strikes one about this image is the difference between the foreground group of academics and archaeologists, and the people in the background, who are those who did the actual digging work. The only thing the two groups have in

Figure 4.1. The offering to fortune at the opening of the excavation at Birdoswald in 1929.

common is that all are male. Even their clothing is different. The workers, standing back, showing social deference to those in the foreground, and clearly posed in position, wear waistcoats and flat caps. One wears overalls, and one is bare-headed. The supervisor, Tommy Hepple, shown near the foreground to the left, wearing plus-fours, is the only one not either holding, or standing by, a shovel and stands nearest the foreground group. This is a social and hierarchical division that is simply unthinkable on a modern excavation photograph. In the photographic archive of this excavation there are two other telling pictures in this respect, Richmond is in both, surrounded by the academics and students in one, and by the workers in the other. Both were taken in the same place, and Richmond wears the same clothes in each. They were clearly taken on the same day, but the prevailing social apartheid applied.

Fortunately John Charlton, seen on the far left of the central group, a student at the time, and a regular visitor to the Birdoswald excavations of 1987–92, gave me the authoritative who's who on the picture. John died only a couple of years ago, and was the last surviving individual present. The

Figure 4.2. Telegram from Birley to Collingwood recording the discovery of the two inscriptions at Birdoswald in 1929 (by kind permission of the Birley family).

picture of an offering to Fortune was taken by Sir Ian Richmond as the 1929 season got under way. Facing the camera in the centre is F. G. Simpson, the great Wall scholar. In the hat with the pipe to the left, next to John Charlton is Eric Birley, later, of course professor at Durham. Simpson is flanked by two un-named students, then on the right of Simpson are Kurt Stade later Professor at Freiburg-im-Breisgau, and co-initiator with Birley of the International Roman Frontier Congress, and its first meeting in Durham in 1949 (The twenty-first of this series of congresses was held in Newcastle in September 2009), Shimon Applebaum, later Professor at Tel Aviv, and finally R. G. Collingwood, the archaeologist, epigraphist and philosopher, on a visit from Oxford.

The day after the photograph was taken, Collingwood returned to Oxford, and work began on the flagstone floor. The two slabs on which Collingwood, Applebaum and the altar are standing turned out to have major inscriptions. One had been face down, the other, on which Collingwood was standing was actually face up but unrecognised. One of the two texts was Severan, commemorating the erection of a granary; the other belonged to the period of the Tetrarchy, after the Carausian usurpation, and recorded restoration work. News of the find was immediately telegraphed to Collingwood, and the telegram arrived in Oxford before he did (showing the efficiency of telegraphic communication at the time: Figure 4.2). There are several telegraphic errors: 'Sugustis' for 'Augusti', 'blab' for 'slab', even 'Bollingwood'.

Four Wall periods had already been proposed following the 1911 work on Milecastle 48, by Simpson and Gibson, but at Birdoswald four stratigraphic periods of the building excavated in 1929 were identified (Figure 4.3). These were interpreted and dated with heavy reference to the texts and to historical evidence to produce the Hadrianic, Severan, Constantian and Theodosian Wall Periods 1–4, later added to by splitting Period 1 into Hadrianic and Antonine. This remained the basis for interpretation of the chronology of the Wall for virtually fifty years and was one of the reasons Mortimer Wheeler opined that all major questions on Hadrian's Wall were answered and all that was

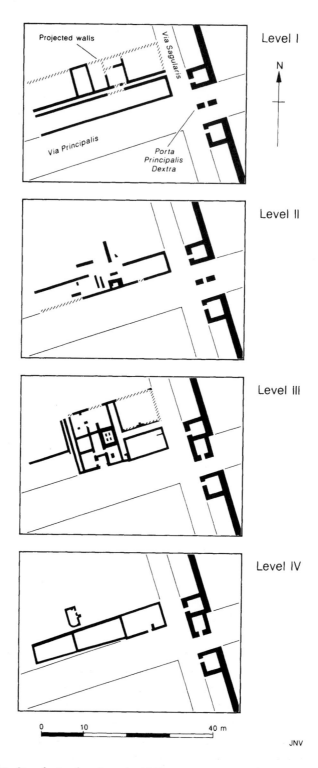

Figure 4.3. Site phasing based on the 1929 excavation at Birdoswald.

left was to dot the i's and cross the t's. I am still today asked what the point of working on the Wall is – surely we know everything about it.

The subsequent excavations on the site from 1987–92 (Wilmott 1997) showed that this simple period framework was not even secure for the site of Birdoswald. It was based on a single building in a single fort, and the other buildings around it had different chronologies. The Hadrianic period, culminating in the final construction of stone buildings in the fort, had five broad sub-phases, each of which reflected changes in the plan and vision for Hadrian's Wall. Even these were nuanced – it was possible to identify seven significant plan changes all told belonging to the period from the start of construction in 122 to the move to the Antonine Wall around 138. This was actually foreshadowed by the 1929 excavators, who included an early Hadrianic 'Period zero', which never made it as a full Wall period. The 1987–92 excavations were centred on the granaries, which were shown to date to the Severan period of the 1929 excavations, and the main west and minor east gates , both of which proved key to phasing the fort. Ironically, when we revisited the site in 1998/9 and looked at the same sort of buildings as the 1929 excavators, barracks, we found that for these at least, the Hadrianic and Severan Wall periods actually worked perfectly, enabling draft phase plans for the Hadrianic and Severan *praetentura* to be drawn up.

At the end of the sequence came the archaeology for which these excavations will be best remembered: a series of early post-Roman, surface built, timber buildings reaching into the fifth century - basically three full post-Theodosian structural phases before the abandonment of the site at a date unknown. The methodology I chose to use on the site was a thorough examination of the uppermost surviving surface. This comprised a rubble patchwork of robbed wall-tops, internal building floors and external road surfaces, and it was in this surface that the patterns of surface-built structures could be seen. They were revealed by those drawing the surface, who began to see and record what appeared to be lines. Prompted by their comments I climbed to the top of the tower on the end of Birdoswald farmhouse to get an aerial view of the site, and there was the imprint of a large rectangular building. The method employed at Birdoswald was the direct result of a visit to a truly Great Excavation, that conducted in the Baths Basilica at Wroxeter (see White and Everill, this volume), where Philip Barker found a range of surface built sub-Roman structures (Barker *et al.* 1997). Philip visited the site and it was a great moment when he confirmed the Birdoswald structures as the best parallel he had yet seen to the Wroxeter evidence. The difficulty was in photographing the building. The most effective photograph was the one in which site staff in white t-shirts are seen standing on the post-positions of the main timber structure (Wilmott 1997; Figure 4.4). Though most of the people in this picture have left the archaeological profession since 1988, those with who I am in touch are still very proud of featuring in a photograph that has been much-reproduced since, and is perhaps the iconic Birdoswald image for a new generation.

When the excavations of 1929 took place, the exploration of sites like Birdoswald concentrated on the forts. Emphasis was on the military archaeology and the big questions of the phasing of the Roman frontier. Life on the frontier was a secondary issue, and was a secondary consideration even in the excavation of the barrack. Civilian settlements, or *vici*, were known, though the extent of the civil settlements of Hadrian's Wall was unappreciated. It was not until the work of Alan Biggins and David Taylor (1999, 2004) in geophysical survey around forts, that our eyes were opened to the amazing archaeological resource represented by these settlements, even with the hitherto unsuspected presence of Roman structures to the north of the Wall line. In enhancing what we know of the great excavations of the past, while more rigorous stratigraphic methods are undoubtedly of great importance, what really stands out is the idea of contextualisation within the historic landscape, and, as at Birdoswald,

Figure 4.4. *The 1987 Birdoswald excavation. The site staff stand on the post positions for a major, surface-built, post-Roman timber building.*

demonstrating the actual extent of the site, often by the use of extensive geophysics. This has shown its value to a remarkable extent at Richborough.

Richborough

The site of Richborough was excavated over many years between the wars by J. P. Bushe-Fox (Figure 4.5). The work was published in four volumes by Bushe-Fox himself (1926, 1928, 1932, 1949), with a fifth volume by Barry Cunliffe (1968). Richborough has largely remained in archaeological perception as a military site, because of its two well known military phases. The first of these is the double ditch and gateway of a Claudian fortification, thought to be a bridgehead fort during the invasion of AD 43. This was commemorated by the erection of a great quadrifons arch, one of the largest in the Roman Empire, which was finally correctly identified by Donald Strong (1968). The second military phase was the Saxon Shore Fort in its third century earthwork and fourth century stone phases. These are the features emphasised in the modern display. However, it has always been clear that between the military phases was a good century of civil port development around the great monument. Buildings were excavated by Bushe Fox within the walls of the Saxon Shore fort, truncated by the later military ditches. In the 1968 report, the extent of knowledge of the area beyond the walls was a single building identified by aerial photography, a small area of possible buildings and graves,

Figure 4.5. Richborough 'castle' The interior of the Saxon Shore fort is laid out to show the different occupation phases recorded by J. P. Bushe-Fox.

and two excavated temples and the earthworks of the amphitheatre to the south of the fort (Figure 4.6). Recent aerial photographic transcription and geophysics now reveals a different picture, showing a thriving settlement of 21ha with the late fort inserted in the waterfront area after the demolition of half a dozen *insulae* (Millett and Wilmott 2004; Figure 4.7). The edge of this settlement was examined by excavation in 2001. More detailed stratigraphic excavation in the area of the temples showed that occupation took place within an active process of colluviation, and that the temple precinct had been abandoned by the late third century, contributing to the picture of a settlement in decline from an early date, possibly due to competition from the rival ports of Dover and London. Further evidence began to indicate that ideas of Roman period and later coastal morphology were not secure, and at the time of writing a further piece of work is planned to examine the putative Roman coastline for patterns of terracing, silting and erosion. This was not a large scale excavation, but there was certainly a general consciousness of working on a site which had been part of the archaeological education of most of the participants. Continuity from the past came in the form of a visit from John Charlton, who we have already encountered on the 1929 Birdoswald photograph. As a young man he had visited the Bushe-Fox excavations in the 1920s, and regaled the site staff with an anecdote which he had from the great man himself (whether apocryphal one does not know), concerning a student on a previous site who had been fonder of talking to the female staff than getting on with his pottery work. Bushe-Fox had purchased a padlock and chain, and locked this young man, one Mortimer Wheeler, to his workbench. Those on the 2001 work will remember the excavation for one salutary moment, however; afternoon tea-break on 11 September, and the news, heard on the radio in the finds shed, of the attack on the World Trade Centre in New York. The security guard's portable TV allowed us the grim sight of the impact of the second plane.

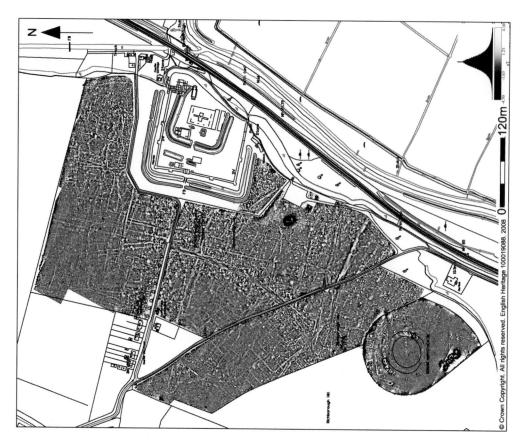

Figure 4.7. The 2001 magnetometry survey of the area around the Shore fort showing the real extent of Roman occupation (English Heritage).

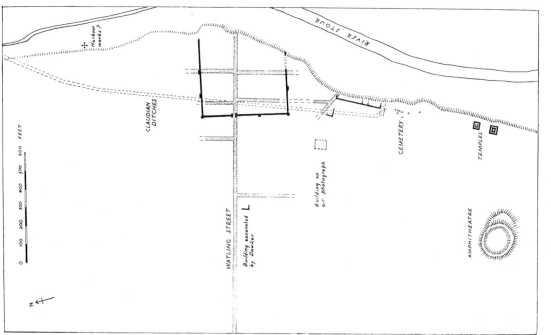

Figure 4.6. Roman occupation around the Saxon Shore fort at Richborough as understood in 1968 (Cunliffe 1968).

Whitby

The excavations of the 1920s at Whitby took place in an area in the immediate vicinity of the thirteenth-century Abbey church, and revealed the structures of the Anglian period identified as monastic cells of the type known from isolated sites of Celtic monasticism, a smithy, a guesthouse (or storehouse or refectory) (Peers and Radford 1943). The interpretation of small cells suggested a monastery placed, like others in a solitary and wild cliff-top location by monks escaping from the world. Rahtz's (1976) re-interpretation of the plan evidence identified that Peers' 'cells' were rooms in larger buildings, though the function of these buildings was unclear. Rahtz also recognised that not all the walls excavated by Peers were necessarily contemporary, and showed that the settlement was larger than allowed by Peers. Despite this, the idea of Whitby as a windswept and isolated monastery inhabited by ascetics largely remained. Unlike Birdoswald and Richborough, the subsequent contextualisation of the earlier work was the result not of geophysics, but of a series of excavations undertaken for purposes of evaluation, mitigation and research on the headland (Figure 4.8). This work was undertaken by my colleagues the late Sarah Jennings, Buzz Busby, Kath Buxton and myself. It has shown an enormous area to the north and south of the Abbey to have been occupied during the Anglian period. To the north, a catastrophic cliff collapse prompted salvage excavation, which revealed the back-land of Anglian houses which had long fallen into the sea. The extent of this settlement was probably great. Map regression has shown that this cliff has receded quite rapidly, and It has been convincingly argued (Bell 1998) that the Roman signal station which almost certainly existed on this site was sited about 500m further north than the current cliff edge. Bede called Whitby the haven of the watchtower, suggesting that this tower existed in his day, and that all of this land, probably intensively settled, has been lost since then. An Anglian inhumation cemetery was identified 500m south of the Abbey. There is now also clear evidence that the settlement was zoned. This work has concluded that the Whitby Anglian settlement was not a small collection of monastic cells, but a major settlement probably clustering around a royal abbey (its founder St Hild was a King's daughter), and on a good deep-water harbour suitable for North sea trade. This view makes more sense of the fact that the site was selected to host the Synod of 664.

Figure 4.8. The Whitby Abbey headland has been the subject of a number of excavations from 1993–2007. The whole of the area in this photograph saw occupation in the Anglian period (English Heritage).

Chester

Finally, we return to where we began, at the Chester amphitheatre. Work on the site by Keith Matthews had already shown that Thompson's conclusions on the nature of the structure might not be safe, but in spite of this I fell firmly into the Great Excavations trap, namely the assumption that it had all been done, that there was only a little surviving, and that it would be a relatively simple exercise of t-crossing and i-dotting. Here, surely the enhancement would be chronological

Figure 4.9. The 2005 area excavation of the Chester amphitheatre (English Heritage/Chester City Council).

Figure 4.10. Timber frames for seating at the Chester amphitheatre (English Heritage/Chester City Council).

and not to do with the actual structural phasing of the Roman amphitheatre. The main aim would be to understand the post-Roman archaeology which was removed by machine in the 1960s to get to Roman levels. The influence of the amphitheatre and the adjacent church of St John on the urban landscape would also be traced, largely through a series of non-invasive techniques such as geophysics, building survey and historical research. Sure enough, within the excavated post-Roman sequence were

Figure 4.11. The 2005 Chester Amphitheatre excavation team (English Heritage/Chester City Council).

elements of garden archaeology, battlefield archaeology, and the pits and post-holes of a post-Roman occupation in the very centre of the arena; further evidence to add to that from Wroxeter, Birdoswald and elsewhere for changes in the immediate post-Roman period.

What I had not expected was the changes we made to the received Thompson version of the phasing and structure of the building. Thompson had not in fact fully removed the Roman stratigraphy in his excavations. His trenches were difficult to locate, as they had been backfilled with the excavated spoil. They were often revealed only by artefactual evidence, memorably the interface marked by the plastic wrapper from a loaf of Tiger Bread. Area excavation (Figure 4.9) showed that his interpretation of the structures was wrong. The timber amphitheatre did not exist. The first amphitheatre comprised timber seating constructed within a stone shell. The excavation methodology was informed by Thompson's report. Where he excavated the traces of timber uprights as post-holes, we built on his methods and results by exposing timber frames in section, an approach that paid dividends in terms of the volume of new information recovered. The timber frames (Figure 4.10) were mineralised and retained nails demonstrating that the frames were pre-fabricated. It was even shown that the structure was built in an anti-clockwise direction. This primary building was dated to *c.* AD 100. Stratigraphy around this structure, later cut by the walls of the second amphitheatre provided evidence for activities associated with the use of the amphitheatre including latrines, sand disposed of from the arena, temporary stalls, a shrine, the consumption of snack food and the purchase of souvenir pottery. This is the first such evidence to be excavated anywhere in the Roman empire. The second amphitheatre, as yet undated, was a structure of imperial pretensions. With its external classically ornamented façade and *vomitoria* entrances, this was by far the most elaborate such building in Britain (Wilmott *et al.* 2006).

Conclusion

The message of all of these projects is surely that however iconic the site, however key the text produced by a past great excavation, there is always more to be learned by new approaches, and there will always be new questions to be asked of these sites. New archaeological questions will always emerge, and where such questions are asked of an entire period or a whole class of monuments it should be self-evident that the most appropriate places to ask such questions are on such sites where we already know a great deal. No individual and no archaeological generation can claim to have the last word, and, generation by generation we can re-invent and enhance our understanding of such sites.

Figure 4.11 was taken at Chester in 2005, only 76 years, a single lifetime, since that Birdoswald site photograph (Figure 4.1). The contrast is enough itself to show how things have changed for the better. I hope that for the team of professionals and student trainees the amphitheatre site has been one of those important and memorable formative experiences, but was it a Great Excavation? – that is for them to say.

References

Barker, P., White, R., Pretty, K., Bird, H. and Corbishley, M. 1997. *The Baths basilica, Wroxeter; excavations 1966–90*. London: English Heritage Archaeological Report, 8.

Bell, T. W. 1998. A Roman signal station at Whitby. *Archaeological Journal* 155, 302–22.

Biggins, J. A. and Taylor, D. J. A. 1999. A survey of the Roman fort and settlement at Birdoswald, Cumbria. *Britannia* 30, 91–110.

Biggins, J. A. and Taylor, D. J. A. 2004. Geophysical survey of the *vicus* at Birdoswald Roman fort, Cumbria. *Britannia* 35, 159–77.

Bushe-Fox, J. P. 1926. *First report on the Excavation at the Roman Fort at Richborough, Kent*. London: Reports of the Research Committee of the Society of Antiquaries of London, 6.

Bushe-Fox, J. P. 1928. *Second report on the Excavation at the Roman Fort at Richborough, Kent*. London: Reports of the Research Committee of the Society of Antiquaries of London, 7.

Bushe-Fox, J. P. 1932. *Third report on the Excavation at the Roman Fort at Richborough, Kent*. London: Reports of the Research Committee of the Society of Antiquaries of London, 10.

Bushe-Fox, J. P. 1949. *Fourth report on the Excavation at the Roman Fort at Richborough, Kent*. London: Reports of the Research Committee of the Society of Antiquaries of London, 16.

Cramp, R. J. 1976a. Monastic Sites, in D. M. Wilson (ed.), *The Archaeology of Anglo-Saxon England*, 201–52. Cambridge: Cambridge University Press.

Cramp, R. J. 1976b. Analysis of the finds register and location plan of Whitby Abbey, in D. M. Wilson (ed.), *The Archaeology of Anglo-Saxon England*, 453–8. Cambridge: Cambridge University Press.

Cunliffe, B. W. 1968. *Fifth report on the Excavation at the Roman Fort at Richborough, Kent*. London: Reports of the Research Committee of the Society of Antiquaries of London, 23.

Martin, L. 2001a. *Richborough Amphitheatre, Kent: Report on Geophysical Surveys, February 2001*. Portsmouth: Centre for Archaeology Reports 30/2001.

Martin, L. 2001b. *Richborough, Kent: Report on Geophysical Surveys, Septembery 2001*. Portsmouth: Centre for Archaeology Reports, 35/2001.

Midgley, J. 2005. *Amphitheatre*. Chester: Chester City Council.

Millett, M. and Wilmott, T. 2004. Rethinking Richborough, in P. Wilson (ed.), *The Archaeology of Roman Towns; studies in honour of John S Wacher*, 184–194. Oxford: Oxbow Books.

Peers, C. R. and Radford, C. A. R. 1943. The Saxon monastery at Whitby. *Archaeologia* 89, 27–88.

Rahtz, P. A. 1976. The building plan of the Anglo-Saxon monastery of Whitby Abbey, in D. M. Wilson (ed.), *The Archaeology of Anglo-Saxon England*, 459–62. Cambridge: Cambridge University Press.

Richmond, I. A. 1930. The university excavations on Hadrian's Wall 1929. *Durham University Journal*, March, 1–7.

Salisbury, H. 2002. Preface, in S. Losco-Bradley and G. Kinsley, *Catholme: an Anglo-Saxon settlement on the Trent gravels in Staffordshire*, xi–xii. Nottingham: University of Nottingham.

Small, F. 2002. *Richborough environs Project, Kent*. English Heritage Aerial Survey Report Series, AER/12/2002.

Strong, D. E. 1968. The Monument, in B. W. Cunliffe, *Fifth report on the Excavation at the Roman Fort at Richborough, Kent*, 40–73. London: Reports of the Research Committee of the Society of Antiquaries of London, 23.

Thompson, F. H. 1976. Excavation of the Roman Amphitheatre at Chester. *Archaeologia* 105, 127–239.

Wilmott, T. 1997. *Birdoswald: Excavations of a Roman Fort on Hadrian's Wall and its Successor Settlements: 1987–92*. London: English Heritage Archaeological Report 14.

Wilmott, T. 2005. Excavation: event and art, in J. Midgley, *Amphitheatre*, 6–7. Chester: Chester City Council.

Wilmott, T., Garner, D. and Ainsworth, S. 2006. The Chester amphitheatre; an interim statement. *English Heritage Historical Review* 1, 7–23.

Wilson. D. M. (ed.) 1976. *The Archaeology of Anglo-Saxon England*. Cambridge: Cambridge University Press.

Aspiring to greatness:
The recent excavations at Maiden Castle

Niall Sharples

Greatness seems to be fashionable these days: not so long ago I wrote an article for a book on great archaeologists (Sharples 1999); there are great archaeological sites/monuments (now officially recognised as World Heritage Sites, and the subject of a series in the magazine British Archaeology a few years back) and great excavations (see also Romer 2000). To this triumvirate of greatness I would also like to add great excavation *reports*. In many of these lists of greatness, the hillfort of Maiden Castle is singled out as worthy of mention and I wish to begin this chapter by briefly enumerating its claims for greatness.

Maiden Castle is a great archaeological site; one of the few prehistoric earthworks in Britain, or Europe, that even the most jaded member of the public can appreciate as a demonstration of the abilities of prehistoric society. The size and complexity of the earthwork fortifications are unsurpassed by any other prehistoric settlement in Europe. They were an inspiration to one of England's greatest novelists, Thomas Hardy (Sharples 1991b, 11–12),[1] and played a prominent part in one of the best film adaptations of his work, *Far From The Madding Crowd* directed by John Schlesinger. I would consider it a serious and worthy candidate for World Heritage status.

The original excavator of Maiden Castle, Sir Mortimer Wheeler, is one of the pre-eminent British archaeologists of the first half of the twentieth century. He is written into the history of archaeology as the second major figure in the development of a scientific archaeology, after Lt. Gen. Pitt Rivers (Trigger 1989; Lucas 2001). He was Director General of Archaeology in India and had key administrative roles in the development of the National Museum of Wales, the Institute of Archaeology in London, the London Museum and the British Academy that placed him at the centre of the development of British archaeology in the twentieth century. He is one of the few archaeologists to have written not only an autobiography (Wheeler 1955), but also to be the subject of a popular biography (Hawkes 1982).

Wheeler's excavations at Maiden Castle were of immense importance for a number of reasons. Academically they provide a framework for Iron Age studies and to a lesser, but still significant degree, Neolithic studies. Wheeler took a tentative proposal for a sequential structure for Iron Age studies (Hawkes 1931) and transformed it into a series of chronologically fixed invasions. The excavation also provided the most detailed picture of the internal occupation of a large hillfort until excavations at South Cadbury and Danebury in the late 1960s and 1970s (Alcock 1972; Cunliffe 1983b and this volume), and provided an evocative, if probably inaccurate, picture of the Roman invasion (Sharples 1991b, 124–5). These excavations were also the key site in demonstrating the 'Wheeler' method of stratigraphic excavation, and the use of the box grid (Wheeler 1955). This technique became the accepted way to dig complex stratified sites, until the development of the single context recording system at Winchester and London, and was used throughout the world.

M Collingridge, xxx xxx Tony Stirling, Betsy, Mrs Wheeler, Dr Wheeler, Col Drew, Peter McKay, Carruthers, Conway, Canon ? Molly Cotton, Veronic Seton-Williams Stewart Birkett
Doreen de Labillieve, Ann Robertson, Margot Eates Pru Dimdale, Leslie Scott Mrgt Freeman Rachel Clay
'Miss Orient' Kathleen xxx, Eric Gee, Janet Crawford; Miss Smith

Figure 5.1. Photograph from the late Ann Robertson's Maiden Castle album currently held by the The Dorset Natural History and Archaeological Society at the Dorset County Museum.

Wheeler's innovative techniques spread across the world because he used the excavations at Maiden Castle as a training camp for an emerging group of young and enthusiastic archaeologists (Figure 5.1). It was acknowledged at the time that if you wanted to get a good training in field archaeology you went and dug at Maiden Castle. The size of the excavations and the efficiency and professionalism of the team assembled by Wheeler, and his wife Tessa, meant the excavations could train a large number of people and there was nothing comparable elsewhere in Britain at the time. An enormous number of archaeologists who went on to have impressive careers in the discipline were involved in the excavations at Maiden Castle. These include B. di Cardi, J. D. Clark, M. Cotton, J. S. Kirkman, D. Marshall, Xia Nai, J. Du Plat Taylor, K. Richardson, A. Robertson, V. Seton Williams and J. Waechter. This was the training dig *par excellence* and the practices undertaken at Maiden Castle were influential not just for Britain, but also for the archaeology of the Middle and Near East, China and Africa.

The greatness of Maiden Castle is enhanced by the publication of the excavations. A full and handsome volume, *Maiden Castle, Dorset*, was published by the Society of Antiquaries of London in 1943, six years after the excavation had ceased and in the middle of a war in which Wheeler was directly involved. It was an amazing feat of scholarship, and despite the doubts of Wheeler who claimed 'The following pages are less a report than the salvage of the report that should have been' (Wheeler 1943, xvii), this is one of the best excavation reports to appear in the middle of the twentieth century.

New work

So Maiden Castle as a place, an associated person, an event and a product all meet the general criteria of greatness. It is not therefore surprising that there was some controversy when an announcement was made in 1984 that further work would be undertaken at the site. I will use this chapter to revisit the circumstances and reaction to that decision, and to review the success of the excavations - as they provide an insight into the difficulties involved in undertaking a 'great' archaeological excavation in the later part of the twentieth century.

The decision to dig Maiden Castle arose because of two events and a process. The first event was a visit by the landowner, His Royal Highness the Prince of Wales, to Maiden Castle which resulted in a meeting at Kensington Palace in July 1984, between Lord Montague, newly appointed as Chairman of English Heritage, Peter Rumble, Chief Executive of English Heritage, John Higgs, secretary of the Duchy of Cornwall and the Prince of Wales. At this meeting it was recorded that:

The Duchy felt strongly that an improvement in the care for Maiden Castle and its presentation ought to take place. It seemed desirable to consider:

  a) repair to the monument itself
  b) ongoing maintenance
  c) presentation

and English Heritage agreed that something should be done soon.

At roughly the same time English Heritage were being sounded out about the possibility that they might support the forthcoming World Archaeology Congress at Southampton. According to Peter Ucko (1987, 40), Lord Montague came up with the idea that they would undertake a major excavation to coincide with the conference. Ucko wrote to English Heritage proposing a list of sites that would be suitable for excavation and insisted that the excavation must be funded using 'non-rescue funding'. The sites on this letter were Stonehenge, Durrington Walls, Hengistbury Head, Danebury, Beacon Hill and Old Sarum, but not Maiden Castle. Stonehenge and Beacon Hill were ruled out almost immediately, but the rest were considered as possibilities.

The matter was raised at the AMAC (Ancient Monuments Advisory Committee) meeting in August 1984 when it was suggested that it would be a good thing because it would be 'demonstrating archaeological techniques and methods both to professionals and the public' and it was at this point that Andrew Saunders (then Chief Inspector) and Geoff Wainwright added another suggestion, Maiden Castle. 'The advantages of the choice of this site lay in the fact that additional funds would not have to be found as the repairs to the earthworks, scarred by large numbers of visitors and the effects of erosion, would be taking place during the Congress anyway, and the erection of an interpretive centre for the public was also planned. Dr Wainwright drew attention to the exciting possibilities which the site offered.' (AMAC Minutes 5/8/84 11.2). The suggestion was generally 'applauded' and the Committee approved the choice of site and told them to 'make the appropriate arrangements with Professor Ucko'. Ucko publicised the news and almost immediately had '… to deny any WAC responsibility for this highly contentious decision' (Ucko 1987, 42).

A package was swiftly put together by English Heritage that included:

- A major programme to refurbish the eroding ramparts
- A programme to enhance the presentation of the monument, which included noticeboards on the site and the creation of a new visitor centre
- A fieldwork programme that would include
  - a new topographic and geophysical survey of the monument
  - a landscape survey to explore the setting of the monument
  - limited excavations to bring Wheeler's work up to date

These events should be understood in the historical context of the creation of English Heritage in 1984 (Hunter and Ralston 1993, 31–32). The organisation was brand new and full of enthusiasm. It had been nominally separated from Civil Service control and was being encouraged to be entrepreneurial, to set up new projects that would stimulate public interest and enthusiasm for the past and, it was hoped, generate an income stream that would replace its dependence on public funding. The chairman Lord Montague was interested in prehistoric archaeology and regarded monuments as an important part of his remit. Maiden Castle could be seen as a demonstration of what English Heritage could do in the new climate of proactive heritage management.

Opposition

It seems from a distance that English Heritage did not anticipate the opposition that a pro-active approach could generate, and the proposed work at Maiden Castle soon came under attack from three different groups of people:

1) The local inhabitants of Dorchester
2) The local archaeological institutions
3) National archaeologists

The announcement of the project incited considerable press interest from both the local and national media and several meetings had to be hastily arranged to present the proposal to the press and the public, particularly in Dorset. The principal local fear was centred on the belief that access to the hilltop of Maiden Castle would become restricted and that a fee might eventually be charged to obtain access. This was never a serious consideration for English Heritage, but it was a perfectly reasonable worry to have; this was the mid 1980s, privatisation of public assets was becoming a political issue and Prime Minister Margaret Thatcher was soon to be accused of 'selling the family silver' by Harold MacMillan.[2]

Another concern was that Maiden Castle would be inundated with tourists and that this would ruin the rural atmosphere of the hilltop. English Heritage would certainly have liked to increase visitor numbers on the hilltop, which was after all one of their principal roles, and it is clear that to make the proposed visitor centre viable numbers would almost certainly have to rise. However, I say almost certainly, because no one actually knew how many people visited the site. As an unmanned site, visitor numbers were not available and the best estimates were based on the numbers at Battle Abbey (East Sussex).[3]

The local archaeological response was expressed in a letter to English Heritage by the Dorchester Association (Excavation Committee) that concentrated on the fieldwork programme. They were quite supportive of the proposal for a survey of the monument and its landscape, but when it came to excavations:

2.1   The Association does not consider that further excavations of Maiden Castle at this time are necessary
2.2   It is suggested that funds allocated for the excavations should be used to finance rescue excavations in the area affected by the line of the [Dorchester] by pass
2.3   In the event of Trust for Wessex Archaeology (TWA) carrying out excavations at Maiden Castle, while the broad objectives outlined in the English Heritage brochure are acceptable, the reopening of Wheelers excavations is considered to be of doubtful value.[4]

There were also worries that the proposed visitor centre would undermine visitor numbers at the County Museum. The archaeology display in the museum had only recently been restructured and the evidence from Maiden Castle was used as a narrative thread linking prehistory and the Romans.[5]

The response of the wider archaeological profession was mixed and several letters were written to the Times, which seemed to worry Peter Ucko (1987, 42). The debate was initiated by a letter from Tim Tatton-Brown as chairman of the British Archaeological Trust, better known as Rescue. He wanted to know

... why re-excavate Maiden Castle. If congress members (or the general public) want to see a hill fort excavation, why shouldn't they visit Professor Cunliffe's unique excavations at Danebury....

If, however, it is really felt necessary to carry out a special excavation for the 1986 congress, it would surely be much more appropriate for the excavation to be either a 'rescue' excavation .... or at the very least the digging of a major site that really does need re-excavation before it can be displayed. (*The Times*, 13 October 1984)

This letter was followed by letters from archaeologists F. H. Thompson, Professor Christopher Hawkes, Andrew Selkirk (editor of Current Archaeology) and Roger Peers (curator of Dorset County Museum). Apart from the letter from Hawkes they were all essentially critical of the decision to excavate an unthreatened site. Other establishment figures such as Professor Colin Renfrew and Professor Glyn Daniel, then the Duchy of Cornwall's advisor and the editor of antiquity, were in favour of the excavation. Rescue News gave the announcement of the project front-page billing but for a campaigning organisation it was relatively constrained in its comments, following the line that the survey of the hilltop was fully justified but that excavations were not.

There was also a critical response from a younger generation of more politically committed archaeologists. A group (Archaeologists Communicate and Transform) based in Southampton were agitating for better working conditions and proper wages for digging archaeologists. At this time excavations were still operating with volunteers who were taken on for the time span of the excavation and let go when it was completed. They were paid cash in hand, were responsible for their tax and national insurance, and there was no consideration of pensions or holiday pay. ACT were deeply critical of English Heritage's approach to excavation funding, which relied on a large 'volunteer' labour force to keep costs low, and regarded the excavations at Maiden Castle as a good excuse to publicise their argument.[6]

Appointments and research objectives

This criticism had very little effect on the organisation of the Maiden Castle project. An English Heritage minute dismisses these criticisms as what one would expect from the archaeological world; they clearly assumed archaeology was a perpetually fractious discipline, which is probably correct. When I turned up in Dorchester to direct the excavations everyone was very polite, though several cars were driving around with windscreen stickers proclaiming 'Hands off the Maiden', 'Don't rape the Maiden' 'Preservation not exploitation' and I have recently found out these were printed and distributed by the (then) County Archaeologist.

It is perhaps relevant that it was I who turned up in Dorchester as the Director of the excavations at Maiden Castle. Four people were interviewed for the post in the month before the dig was due to start: Peter Woodward, John Hedges, Claire Halpin and myself. Peter Woodward was offered the job, and though he initially accepted it he eventually turned it down, and I was offered the post. Peter already had a complicated series of commitments to the archaeology of Dorchester and decided that adding the excavation of Maiden Castle would restrict his capacity to complete these projects.

My appointment came as a great shock to some people, and some were extremely put out that a Scot had been appointed to dig England's premier monument, perhaps forgetting that Wheeler was a Scot by birth. It was perhaps more relevant that I had very little directorial experience, very little experience of digging chalk and my publications, which were all forthcoming, were largely concerned with the Neolithic. However, there were very few people to choose from; rumour has it there were roughly 12 applicants – only 12 people were interested in being director of one of the most famous archaeological sites in Europe. This is quite astonishing and deserves further thought.

One of the reasons was the conditions of employment: the post was poorly paid,[7] it was only a two-year appointment, and it was limited to directing the excavations with no guarantee that the appointee would write the report, and no permanent position once the job was done. This was not going to attract anyone who was already in a secure post, and many insecure posts were paid more. Either English Heritage had a very limited budget that restricted their ability to appoint a senior professional, or they specifically wanted to appoint at a relatively junior level to retain control of the project. I suspect both these conjectures were relevant.

However, despite the salary, one would still have expected more people to apply for this post. There were after all a large number of experienced archaeologists working in units on very short term contracts, who would have been more qualified and more experienced than me. These people may not have applied because of the fear factor; they did not think they would get the job and did not want to be rejected.[8] Despite this possibility I think the main reason for the small number of applicants was the hostile attitude towards the project from the junior members of the profession. The excavations were felt to be an inappropriate use of state funds.

The late appointment of the director of excavations meant that I had no input into the research plan created by Wainwright and Cunliffe (1985). When Wainwright originally suggested the project he clearly envisaged a substantial excavation of the interior that would expose the plan of the settlement. By the time of the published research plan (Wainwright and Cunliffe 1985), this had been refined and revised and the approach to the hillfort occupation had been reduced to an examination of two areas: one in the south west corner of the hillfort, and the other a larger area behind the east entrance that would include the reopening of the northern gateway. The trench in the southwest corner would provide a sequence of deposits covering the last 400 years of the fort's life, which would enable the detailed examination of chronological change. The entrance excavations were designed to find a substantial gateway that had not been found by Wheeler and which was believed to lie to the west of his excavated area at the end of a long tunnel-like entrance.

The early incorporation of John G. Evans onto the excavation sub-committee also led to the addition of a research strategy directed towards the earlier Neolithic occupation of the hilltop. Evans was interested in acquiring samples to interpret the long-term history of the environment on the hilltop, and this required the re-excavation of Wheeler's trenches in the centre of the hillfort where the causewayed enclosure, bank barrow and hillfort overlapped. Richard Bradley also suggested the re-opening of another small trench to examine the construction of the bank barrow.

The excavations in 1985

The relatively limited interventions required to obtain environmental samples from the Neolithic levels provided an opportunity to undertake a preliminary season in 1985. This was planned to be a relatively low-key introduction that would resolve problems prior to the major Iron Age excavations laid out for the World Archaeological Congress in 1986.

Three trenches were opened up. The original intention had been to dig out Wheeler's backfill by machine, clean and record the sections, and then take samples from these for environmental analysis. However, on arrival I successfully argued that we needed to excavate undisturbed deposits adjacent to the original trench that would be large enough to understand the context of the samples for radiocarbon dating. The excavation would also recover reasonably large samples of animal bones, crop remains, pottery and flint that would enable a thorough discussion of the Neolithic economy as well as the environment.

The 1985 excavations were undoubtedly successful; the sequence of monuments was exceptional and looked spectacular even with all the ugly shoring. The deposits present in the causewayed enclosure ditch were exceptionally rich and large assemblages of pottery and flint were recovered, as well as a substantial assemblage of animal bone, and carbonised plant remains. The samples dated provided a chronology that was one of the best available for a causewayed enclosure at this time.[9]

One of the trenches involved the re-excavation of the Early Iron Age ditch and rampart. This was a spectacular boundary over 8.4m from the base of the ditch to the top of the rampart and provided a very impressive sight for visitors (Figure 5.2).[10] The principal reason for excavating this ditch was to recover a long sequence of environmental samples that should have provided a detailed environmental history of the Iron Age settlement. Unfortunately this proved to be unsuccessful as the soils were too acidic to preserve snails.[11]

The success of the 1985 excavations and the recovery of a substantial assemblage of Neolithic material had implications. This preliminary season had cost more money than was anticipated, and the post excavation analysis of an assemblage of Neolithic pot and flint had not been anticipated in the initial budget. There was no chance of an increase in funding so the cost of this had to be met by redirecting the budget internally. Further budgetary problems were to arise that winter.

Winter developments

The Maiden Castle landscape survey had been designed by Peter Woodward to enable detailed fieldwalking and analysis of an area from the South Dorset Ridgeway to the River Frome. It complemented work undertaken on the South Dorset Ridgeway (Woodward 1991) and was designed to include the area of the proposed Dorchester by-pass (Smith *et al.* 1997). The decision to proceed with the by-pass was made in March 1986, and the remaining threatened area was quickly incorporated into the Maiden Castle survey. The Maiden Castle project was therefore important in providing cash, outside of the rescue budget, for the initial analysis of the by-pass landscape prior to the Department of

Figure 5.2. The Maiden Castle committee view the excavation of the Early Iron Age ditch in 1985. From left to right John Hinchcliffe, Geoff Wainwright, Andrew Lawson, Nick Balaam, Niall Sharples (in the ditch), Andrew Saunders, Professor Barry Cunliffe and Peter Donaldson The Dorset Natural History and Archaeological Society at the Dorset County Museum

Figure 5.3. The Maiden Castle team in 1986. The Dorset Natural History and Archaeological Society at the Dorset County Museum.

Figure 5.4. Panoramic view of the excavation of the south west corner of the hillfort in 1986.

Transport decision to proceed. This survey enabled the identification of potential sites well in advance of the rescue funded excavations in 1987, and provided a context that was superior to the restricted linear survey that the by-pass would have financed. However, funding for the Maiden Castle survey was inadequate to undertake the amount of work that was now required, and an important source of additional financing was the Dorchester Manpower Services Programme.

Peter Woodward had established a Manpower Services Programme in Dorchester to undertake the excavations at Greyhound Yard (Woodward *et al.* 1993). This had been extended in 1985 to undertake the excavations at Alington Avenue (Davies *et al.* 2002) and a further renewal was due in the winter of 1985 to run a programme in 1986. As no large excavations were planned in 1986, other than Maiden Castle, it was decided that the tasks to be undertaken in 1986 would include the Maiden Castle project, and that in the summer the labour force would be split between the landscape survey and the excavations.

This injection of resources proved essential, as in the winter of 1985/6 English Heritage decided that the budget allocated to the Maiden Castle project had to be cut by between £50–100,000.[12] All aspects of the project were cut and eventually we managed to make a saving of over £70,000, a substantial part of which came from the excavation budget. The most significant consequence of these cuts was the abandonment of the area excavations behind the eastern entrance[13] but it also undermined the post excavation process.[14]

The excavations in 1986

The excavations in the summer of 1986 consisted of a large trench in the south west corner of the extended hillfort and two small trenches in the eastern entrance. The former was provided with a massive gantry that enabled constant supervision of the site by the public, but restricted person-to-person interaction.[15] The workforce was varied in origin and fluctuated in numbers (Figure 5.3). The core of the labour force was the MSC contingent[16] and the freelance excavators, many of whom had worked on the recent Dorchester excavations; these were supplemented by students, including a reasonable number from the Universities of Glasgow, Cardiff and Southampton.[17]

The area excavation in the south west corner proved to be problematic as what had not been fully appreciated from the reading of Wheeler's report was that the natural geology of this area was not chalk but clay with flints. This is a much more difficult substrate to work on than chalk and caused a number of problems. The intractable nature of the clayey soils slowed down the work, it made the recognition of stratigraphy more difficult and it made the archaeology much less clear to the viewing public. These problems seriously undermined the spectacle of the excavations and our ability to progress quickly through the quarry stratigraphy. Despite working for most of the summer, we were unable to excavate all the features in the area opened up. Nevertheless, the excavations were able to record the sequence of settlement activity in this area, and the presence of a large number of storage pits and numerous houses provided an invaluable collection of data for the interpretation of the occupation of the hillfort in the Middle to Late Iron Age (Figure 5.4). The quantity of the material culture from the site was actually greater than had been expected, and it was possible to demonstrate that material densities increase as one moves westwards in Iron Age Wessex.

Despite the relatively restricted area of the excavations it was possible to provide a substantial and significantly different picture of the occupation because of the new surveys of the hillfort. A detailed survey of the earthworks by the Royal Commission on the Historical Monuments of England (RCHME) revealed a number of interesting features that allowed a new and more complex interpretation of the development of the monument that placed it within the developing landscape. Even more spectacular was the result of the geophysical survey. The Maiden Castle survey was one of the first to use 'digital data recording and computerised plotting of the data' (Payne *et al.* 2006, 18); this enabled the complete survey and display of a large hillfort in detail that had hitherto not been possible. It emphatically demonstrated the total occupation of the interior and a density of settlement comparable to that exposed by the excavations at Danebury (Cunliffe, this volume). The density actually inhibited any subtle interpretation of the occupation, but it was possible to identify roads traversing the interior and most surprisingly the presence of a large internal enclosure. This new discovery is undated but it was argued that it could represent a pre-hillfort enclosure of later Bronze Age date (Sharples 1991a, fig. 33).

Post Excavation

The successful completion of the excavation led to a two year extension to my original contract to undertake the post excavation analysis and publication of the Maiden Castle project. The management of the post excavation process had been planned and budgeted before the excavation began as the previous excavations provided a detailed understanding of what was likely to be found and the work at Danebury provided an example of the timescales required for analysis and report writing on these materials.

The original plan had allocated all the finds analysis to the team working with Barry Cunliffe on the Danebury excavation,[18] though conservation would take place in London. However, the recovery of large quantities of early prehistoric flint and pottery required a set of specialists not available in the Danebury team. Appropriate specialists were therefore recruited from researchers working with Richard Bradley and Peter Woodward.[19] The mollusc, animal bone analysis and carbonised plant remains were studied as postgraduate studentships based in the universities of Cardiff, London and Durham respectively.[20] Data entry was undertaken by the Central Excavation Unit at Fort Cumberland, Portsmouth, publication drawing by the Trust for Wessex Archaeology at Salisbury and contextual analysis, archive drawing and various other tasks at the Maiden Castle base in Dorchester, Dorset.

The relationship between all the different specialists and particularly the coordination of the data entry and analysis was difficult. One of the most significant transformations in archaeological fieldwork in the last thirty years has been the development of computerised databases and this has undoubtedly radically altered the way archaeologists work. When I arrived at Maiden Castle my knowledge of computers was limited to viewing a Commodore Pet that was almost completely unusable. The Central Excavation Unit in contrast had developed one of the most advanced computerised database systems used in archaeology at this time: Delilah. Nevertheless computer use was still very different to today, data input was a laborious and complex process, and the production of reports and analysis was the responsibility of specialists at Fort Cumberland. In Dorchester we had access to an early word processing package but at the beginning of the project the decision was made to use an operating system, Concurrent CPM, that soon became obsolete. By the end of the project most of the specialists were submitting electronic text[21] that was unreadable by the project computers and had to be sent to Devon to be translated to discs and software that our computers could understand.

In retrospect, given the dispersed nature of the specialists and the complex and time-consuming features of the technology, it seems miraculous we were able to meet any of the deadlines set. This is possibly a good indication that technology is always subservient to people. All of the specialists were aware that this project was of considerable importance to English Heritage and the pressure to meet deadlines and deliver text was always present. The report was completed, and published in 1991 only five years after the excavations were completed.

Publication

The excavation and field survey were to appear as an English Heritage Archaeological Report. This was a relatively new series[22] that emerged with the creation of English Heritage. It represented a substantial commitment to the publication of archaeological monographs, which reflected the belief that a lack of publication outlets was restricting the publication of backlog projects.

My original publication plan for Maiden Castle envisaged two monographs, one for the landscape

Figure 5.5. David Collison filming Tony Clark, sampling a hearth to obtain an archaeomagnetic date, for an English Heritage video on the hillfort.

survey and early prehistoric deposits, and the other for the earthwork survey and later prehistoric deposits. When the proposal was submitted, I did not really believe it was going to be acceptable and it was no surprise when I was encouraged to produce one volume (Sharples 1991a).[23] However, the proposal drew attention to the amount of information the project had produced and the decision was taken that much of the descriptive data would have to be presented in microfiche.[24] Fiche was not a popular medium (Manning 1985) and though it was a cheap and compact means for the dissemination of data (Lavell 1981) it is cumbersome to read and to reprint. The unpopularity of fiche may have influenced the publication department to try to renege on their commitment to produce the fiche immediately before the publication was due to take place. Only a letter writing campaign by the specialists managed to have it reinstated, though it was not attached to the volume but had to be requested separately from the Trust for Wessex Archaeology. The desire to compress the report into one volume also resulted in the use of two font sizes, one for general synthetic statements and one for more detailed descriptive comments. This is unattractive and caused problems; many of the illustrations referenced in the detailed descriptive text were separated from their text reference by several pages and makes it difficult to follow the discussion of the stratigraphy.[25]

The presentation of the excavation data (Sharples 1991a) was designed to follow the format of the Danebury reports. The description of the excavation begins with an outline of the historic sequence as determined by Wheeler's excavation, and leads through a description of the trenches excavated in 1985 and 1986 and a discussion of the historic sequence provided by the modern excavations, to conclude with the results of the scientific dating programmes (Figure 5.5).[26] This is followed by a chapter on the evidence for the environment and agricultural economy of the site, and comprised separate specialist reports on the soils, land mollusca, charcoal, plant resources, animal bones and human remains, in that order. The next chapter presented the finds and was comprised of separate specialist reports on copper alloy objects, copper alloy metallurgy, iron objects, iron working debris, glass, early prehistoric pottery, later prehistoric pottery, Roman pottery, briquetage, structural daub, objects of daub, objects of chalk, flaked stone, foreign stone, shale, worked bone and antler, in that order.[27] These reports were bracketed by a brief introduction that discussed the recovery processes and the problems of differential preservation and a conclusion that examined the taphonomy, chronology, function and distribution of the finds assemblage, and provided a quantified comparison with other assemblages from southern England.[28] The final chapter provided a discussion that integrated the landscape and monument surveys with the excavations to provide an overall narrative.

I do not think the structure used for the Maiden Castle report was satisfactory and since then I have written/edited two major excavation monographs (Sharples 1998; 2005) using a completely different structure.[29] There are two major problems with the traditional format of excavation reports; they separate finds and archaeological context and they fail to integrate specialist reports.[30] The association between contexts and the materials, finds and environmental evidence, recovered from them is important and it is essential to make this relationship visible in the publication. It is amazing that so much time on excavations is spent defining and cataloguing material from contexts, which are then amalgamated into blocks or phases, and never appear in the publication (see Hill 1995 for an extended discussion of this problem). Understanding the nature of the site and the assemblage depends on an interpretation of the formation processes and as this can only be examined at the level of a context there must be some presentation of the evidence by context for this to be possible.

I also took against the inviolate nature of the specialist report. Why were individuals reports always presented as discrete entities when they clearly provided information and discussion which was relevant to different research problems and which could be closely linked to information and debate presented in other specialist reports? This seems completely illogical to me and since Maiden Castle I have always attempted to breakdown specialist reports into themes which can be amalgamated or combined with similar themes in other reports. This approach certainly annoys the specialists and several have indicated to me that they do not like integrated reports because it forces them to read extraneous information about archaeological sites when all they want is to extract the data relevant to their specialist interest. This is not an unreasonable request, but I don't believe that specialists should ignore the peculiarities of taphonomic, sampling, cultural and behavioural practice that influence what is recovered on each site.

The print run for the Maiden Castle report was 500 volumes. These were sold out by 1999 and it is almost impossible to obtain second-hand copies, which suggests it is a valued report. An examination of 20 British and Irish university libraries revealed that Maiden Castle was present in all of them.[31] A further 16 important later prehistoric monographs were examined and only two of these were present in all of the university libraries examined.[32] An analysis of the borrowing patterns of a more limited number of reports in 18 libraries (Jones *et al.* 2001) enables a comparison of the borrowing patterns of the Danebury (volumes 1 and 2) and Maiden Castle volumes. This indicated that Maiden Castle was borrowed more often at 11 libraries, whereas Danebury was borrowed more often at four libraries. The accompanying citation survey showed that Danebury was cited ten times whereas the Maiden Castle report was cited only four times. It would appear therefore that the Maiden Castle report is regarded as an important source for interpretation and discussion.

Conclusion

I will conclude this chapter by considering whether the Maiden Castle excavations were successful and have contributed to the 'greatness' of the monument. In many respects the excavations of the 1980s cannot be compared to the work undertaken by Wheeler, as the latter was much more extensive and revealed many striking new discoveries that were completely unexpected (such as the 'war cemetery' and the Neolithic enclosure). New discoveries were not expected in the 1980s excavations, which was designed to develop the original work.

The work undertaken by Wheeler had undoubtedly a considerable impact on Neolithic and Iron Age studies in the middle of the twentieth century, but by the end of the 1970s the report was much more problematic. The interpretive framework used by Wheeler seriously constrained how people understood the site and the data collection, whilst excellent for the period, made it difficult to make quantitative comparisons with contemporary excavations and provided almost no understanding of the economic and environmental occupation of the settlement. These problems had reduced the prominence of Maiden Castle in the archaeological literature; Danebury, and to a lesser extent South Cadbury, were now regarded as representative examples of developed hillforts.

The recent excavations have transformed this situation and have enabled a contemporary reading of Maiden Castle that places it back at the centre of the archaeological discourse. Maiden Castle provides the only sizeable assemblage of plant remains, animal bones and artefacts from a developed hillfort that can be compared to the assemblages from Danebury. The survey of the hillfort, and the surrounding landscape, provide not only an essential management tool but a research archive of considerable significance and give the hillfort a context which is as good as any in southern Britain. These must be seen as the most tangible results of the work, and have made Maiden Castle relevant to contemporary debate in both Iron Age and Neolithic studies.

On a more negative side the redisplay of the monument has not been as successful as planned. The new visitor centre has not been built and the facilities provided at the site are not much different to what they were in the 1980s. The most significant change has been the erection of notice boards at various significant spots on the hilltop that provide detailed information on the complex history of the site. The main areas of erosion that so blighted the monument in the 1980s have been stabilised and stock levels seem to have a reasonably harmonious relationship with the monument, though this has resulted in the re-erection of fences that were removed in the 1980s. Perhaps the greatest failure of the project however was not persuading English Heritage that high profile research excavations are an important part of their remit. Since the excavations at Maiden Castle there have been no equivalent excavations funded by English Heritage on prehistoric monuments solely to find out more about the past. I personally believe innovative research is part of the role of English Heritage and that 'great (and state-funded) excavations' would have enormous benefits for the public understanding of the past.

Acknowledgements

I would like to thank John Schofield for inviting me to give the paper from which this chapter derives; it brought back many happy memories. Danny Parker was invaluable in helping me locate the English Heritage files on the excavations and I am grateful to Peter Woodward for access to the archive in the Dorset County Museum. Peter Woodward, Ian Barnes, Hal Dalwood and Duncan Brown were also happy to reminisce about days gone by and helped stir some forgotten memories. Mary Davis provided many helpful comments on the finished text.

References

Alcock, L. 1972. *'By South Cadbury, is that Camelot....' Excavations at Cadbury Castle 1966–6–70*. London: Thames and Hudson.

Barrett, J. C., Freeman, P. W. M. and Woodward, A. 2000. *Cadbury Castle Somerset. The later prehistory and early historic archaeology*. London: English Heritage.

Bidwell, P. T. 1985. *The Roman fort of Vindolanda at Chesterholm, Northumberland*. London: English Heritage.

Cunliffe, B. W. 1983a. *The publication of archaeological excavations. Report of the joint working party of the Council for British Archaeology and the Department of the Environment*. London: Department of the Environment.

Cunliffe, B. W. 1983b. *Danebury: anatomy of an Iron Age hillfort*. London: Batsford.

Cunliffe, B. W. 1984. *Danebury: an Iron Age hillfort in Hampshire. Volumes 1 and 2*. London: Council for British Archaeology.

Davies, S. M., Bellamy, P. S., Heaton, M. J. and Woodward, P. J. 2002. *Excavations at Alington Avenue, Fordington, Dorchester, Dorset, 198–87*. Dorchester: Dorset Natural History and Archaeological Society Monograph 15.

English Heritage 1991. *Management of archaeological projects*. London: English Heritage.

Hawkes, C. F. C. 1931. Hillforts. *Antiquity* 5, 60–97.

Hawkes, J. 1982. *Mortimer Wheeler: adventurer in archaeology*. London: Weidenfeld and Nicolson Ltd.

Hill, J. D. 1995. *Ritual and Rubbish in the Iron Age of Wessex: a study in the formation of a specific archaeological record*. Oxford: British Archaeological Report (British Series 242).

Hunter, J. and Ralston, I. 1993. *Archaeological resource management in the UK: an introduction*. Stroud: Sutton.

Jones, S., MacSween, A., Jeffrey, S., Morris, R. and Heyworth, M. 2001. *From The Ground Up. The publication of archaeological projects: a user needs survey*. York: Council for British Archaeology.

Lavell, C. 1981. Publication: an obligation. Archaeological documentation in Britain today. *Bulletin of the Institute of Archaeology* 18, 91–125.

Lucas, G. 2001. *Critical approaches to fieldwork. Contemporary and historical archaeological practice*. London: Routledge.

Manning, W. H. 1985. Microfiche and archaeological publication. *Scottish Archaeological Review* 3, 70–72.

Payne, A., Corney, M. and Cunliffe, B. 2006. *The Wessex Hillforts Project: Extensive survey of hillfort interiors in central southern England*. London: English Heritage.

Powys, J. C. 2001. *Maiden Castle*. Woodstock, New York: the Overlook Press.

Romer, J. 2000. *Great excavations: John Romer's history of archaeology*. London: Weidenfeld Nicolson.

Sharples, N. M. 1991a. *Maiden Castle: excavations and field survey 1985–86*. London: English Heritage Archaeological Report 19.

Sharples, N. M. 1991b. *English Heritage book of Maiden Castle*. London: English Heritage.

Sharples, N. M. 1998. *Scalloway: A Broch, Late Iron Age settlement and Medieval cemetery in Shetland*. Oxford: Oxbow Monograph 82.

Sharples, N. M. 1999. Stuart Piggott (1910–1996), in T. Murray (ed.) *Encyclopedea of Archaeology: the great archaeologists volume II*. ABC–CLIO: Oxford, 615–634.

Sharples, N. M. 2005. *A Norse farmstead in the Outer Hebrides: excavations at Mound 3, Bornais, South Uist*. Oxford: Oxbow Books.

Smith, R. J. C. Healy, F., Allen, M. J., Morris, E. L., Barnes, I. and Woodward P. J. 1997. *Excavations along the route of the Dorchester Bypass, Dorset, 1986–8*. Salisbury: Wessex Archaeology.

Trigger, B. G. 1989. *A history of archaeological thought*. Cambridge: Cambridge University Press.

Ucko, P. 1987. *Academic freedom and apartheid: the story of the World Archaeological Congress*. London: Duckworth.

Wainwright, G. J. and Cunliffe, B. W. 1985. Maiden Castle: excavation, education, entertainment? *Antiquity* 59, 97–100.

Watkins, A. 1992. *A Conservative Coup*. London: Duckworth.

Wheeler, R. E. M. 1943. *Maiden Castle*. London: Society of Antiquaries of London.

Wheeler, R. E. M. 1955. *Still digging: interleaves from an antiquary's notebook*. London: Readers Union.

Whittle, A. Healy, F. and Bayliss, A. (in prep.) Gathering time: dating the early Neolithic enclosures of southern Britain and Ireland.

Woodward, P. J. 1991. *The South Dorset Ridgeway: survey and excavations 1977–84*. Dorchester: Dorset Natural History and Archaeological Society Monograph 8.

Woodward, P. J., Davies, S. M. and Graham, A. H. 1993. *Excavations at Old Methodist Chapel and Greyhound Yard, Dorchester 1981–84*. Dorchester: Dorset Natural History and Archaeological Society Monograph 12.

Notes

1 The site and excavations also inspired the John Cowper Powys novel, Maiden Castle, which is set in Dorchester at the time of the excavations.

2 The quote is routinely attributed to Harold MacMillan but is not an accurate precis of what he said (Watkins 1992, 105).

3 A visitor survey was quickly commissioned.

4 Professor B. W. Cunliffe was President of the Dorchester Association at this time and his name was prominently displayed on the letter but he had not been able to attend the meeting and had no knowledge of this communication. He quickly dispatched a letter to the chairman T. Hearing, copied to English Heritage, in which he makes it clear that he 'unreservedly supports the [English Heritage] proposals'.

5 It is ironic to note that the there are now several 'museums' in Dorchester competing with the County Museum: the Teddy Bear House Exhibition, the Keep Military Museum, the Tutankamen Museum and the Dinosaur Museum. All presumably make money and on that basis it seems quite possible that the visitor centre at Maiden Castle would have been successful. The preferred location would have been well placed to take advantage of the development of the Poundbury estate on the west side of Dorchester. The number of museums reflects the general expansion of tourism related activities and the decline in the importance of farming and light industry in the local economy.

6 They had an opportunity to ambush Lord Montague when he attended the Young Archaeologists Conference in Southampton in 1985 but this seemed to have little influence on policy or practice.

7 The post was advertised with a salary of between £7524 and £8262. It was based in the Trust for Wessex Archaeology, even though the Central Excavation Unit provided most of the post excavation analysis and equipment. This was a sign of things to come. The role of the state excavation service was beginning to decline. The CEU under Wainwright had been responsible for many of the 'great' excavations of the 1960s and 1970s, but they were not able to maintain their role in the 1980s and 1990s when the state service was limited to undertaking small excavations and first the Trusts and then the commercial units began to dominate rescue excavation.

8 This is something I can identify with and it would probably be my normal reaction. However, I had just seen my marriage collapse and my job opportunities in Edinburgh were minimal. I needed to leave and if I did not get the Maiden Castle job I was intending to move to Holland.

9 In recent years a new programme exploring the date of causewayed enclosures has obtained a much larger quantity of radiocarbon dates using samples collected during the recent excavations (Whittle *et al.* forthcoming). By using Bayesian statistics these have provided a very accurate chronology for the Neolithic enclosure and Bank Barrow.

10 The excavation of the Early Iron Age ditch demonstrated that Wheeler was fallible, as he had failed to locate the bottom of the ditch. The ditch was so deep that as his trench neared the bottom the battered edges meant it was less than a metre wide. As a consequence, he mistook the primary fill for solid chalk and missed a major recut that was associated with the refurbishment of the rampart.

11 A large number of soil samples were taken from the ditch fills and processed to recover carbonised plant remains and radiocarbon samples but due to the budget cuts these were not studied and remain in the archive for future analysis.

12 The original budget was £386,508 for three years.

13 It was possible to undertake small scale excavations to examine the outer ditch of the Neolithic enclosure and a Late Iron Age metalworking site outside the eastern gateway.

14 The examination of the animal bones and the carbonised plant remains was restricted to a sample of the assemblages recovered, and detailed examination of Wheeler's archive and the assemblages held by Dorchester Museum was curtailed.

15 The importance of the public presence on the hill meant that the excavation was underway seven days a week, with different excavators and supervisors working weekdays and weekends. My memory is a little hazy but I think I had a single half day off during the 1986 season. By September I was exhausted and had no desire to prolong the excavation.

16 The MSC labour force was very variable comprising individuals who were completely useless and some who were exceptionally gifted. However, the process created links with the local community that were very valuable.

17 The non-residents were accommodated in a terrace of three houses in the centre of Dorchester. These were owned by Dorset County Council and were unoccupied, awaiting development when funds became available. Apart from service costs the accommodation was free and the houses were subsequently used for the Dorchester by-pass excavators. One of the perks of the Maiden Castle job was to equip these houses with furniture and fittings and I spent many enjoyable mornings at the auction in the Dorchester Cattle Market, and even managed to turn a profit on a few items. The houses had a small yard behind them, and they provided a good venue for parties that attracted a number of archaeological teams working in the south of England at the time.

18 Cynthia Poole looked at the daub and baked clay; Lisa Brown looked at the pottery; and Cathy Laws examined a variety of finds categories including the worked bone and antler.

19 Peter Bellamy and Mark Edmonds undertook the analysis of the flint: the latter concurrent with his PhD on axe production at Great Langdale. Ros Cleal examined the pottery.

20 The molluscs were examined by Amanda Rouse under the supervision of John Evans at the University of Cardiff. The animal bone was undertaken by Miranda Armour Chelu who was largely supervised by Juliet Clutton-Brock at the Museum of Natural History, South Kensington, London. The plant remains were examined by Carol Palmer under the supervision of Martin Jones, then at the University of Durham.

21 On disc by post, this was before the internet.

22 The first volume was published in 1985 and was a report on the excavations at Vindolanda (Bidwell 1985). Maiden Castle was report number 19.

23 The English Heritage monograph series superficially appeared to be based on the principal that you could produce as much, or as little, data as you deemed necessary so long as it all fitted into one A4 sized monograph.

24 This revised proposal followed the 'Cunliffe report' (1983a) in providing the detailed structural, artefactual and environmental evidence in microfiche with only an interpretive synthesis published. However, the amount of detail published in the interpretive synthesis was clearly substantial, and reflected the prestige of the project and the resources available.

25 These design problems reflect my inexperience and distance from the publication department in English Heritage. In the final stages of the publication process, I was working as a freelance contractor and in the winter of 1990 to 1991 I travelled from France to Edinburgh and on to Shetland, which made contacting me quite difficult.

26 For example, the Neolithic sequence, phase 2, described the definition of the enclosure, the nature of the inner ditch fills, the outer ditch fills and pits associated with the use of the enclosure. Discussion of the extended hillfort, phase 6, started with a description of the defining earthworks then moved on to describe the occupation, concentrating on the sequence exposed by the excavation of the quarry in the south west corner. This was followed by a detailed discussion of the houses, hearths, oven, pits and 4-posters.

27 The arrangement of the finds reports was based on the Danebury report (Cunliffe 1984) and I was assured this followed a natural order of how material categories should be arranged. The argument presented to me was that it is better to follow a customary format in the structure of these reports as then people know where to look to find a particular piece of information that they may require. This has a certain logic to it but it fails to acknowledge the unique identity of a site and places a structure onto the data which is not necessarily appropriate or helpful.

28 All of the specialist reports could have been divided into early prehistoric and later prehistoric sections and this would have helped the presentation of the report, and the understanding of the site.

29 I was also closely involved in setting up the post excavation programme for the Cadbury Castle excavations and the general structure of the final report (Barrett *et al.* 2000), which I had nothing to do with, reflects the original proposal, though the text is not as integrated as I would have liked.

30 The lack of integration of specialist reports was highlighted as one of the principal problems of excavation reports in the recent CBA survey of publication use (Jones *et al.* 2001).

31 The catalogues examined were for the universities in Belfast, Birmingham, Bradford, Bristol, Cardiff, Cork, Dublin (Trinity College), Durham, Edinburgh, Glasgow, Leicester, Liverpool, London (University College), Manchester, Newcastle, Nottingham, Reading, Sheffield and Southampton. All of these universities have well established departments of archaeology.

32 The reports searched for were the monographs on the excavations of Breiddin; Bu, Gurness and the Brochs of Orkney; Cadbury Castle; Cranborne Chase (Landscape, monuments and society); Danebury; Flag Fen; Gussage All Saints; Haddenham (volume 2); Howe; Iron Age Cemeteries in Yorkshire; Mingies Ditch; Segsbury Camp; Thorpe Thewles; Uffington Castle and the White Horse; and Winnal Down. Only the reports on Danebury and Cranborne Chase were available in all the libraries. Only three of these volumes were present in fewer than 75% of the libraries, the Haddenham, Uffington and Segsbury reports, and this probably represents their recent publication dates.

The urban revolution: Martin Biddle's excavations in Winchester, 1961–1971

John Collis

No one excavation had a greater impact on archaeology in Britain in the later twentieth century than Martin Biddle's project in Winchester in the 1960s. It brought a new diachronic vision to urban archaeology, treating the city as an organic whole, from its Iron Age origins to the modern day, using archaeological, historical, topographical and architectural evidence in conjunction rather than as separate disciplines. It developed new approaches to excavation such as open area, metrication, and the matrix approach to stratigraphical analysis. Finally, in the 1970s, its Research Unit became the model for the professional 'units' which developed initially within local government, but later within national agencies such as English Heritage, and which finally evolved into the commercial units which, in financial terms and in the quantity of survey and excavation, now dominate British archaeology.

Background

Though Hampshire was among the pioneer areas of British archaeology in the 1930s, notably Christopher Hawkes' series of campaigns on Iron Age hill-forts, this had largely happened in a rural context. Observations in Winchester by the honorary curators of the museum were only of an antiquarian nature, and it was not until the arrival of Frank Cottrill in 1947 that the museum display was modernised and stratigraphical excavation commenced with the first trenches across the Roman and medieval city wall in 1951 (Cunliffe 1962). Cottrill had had experience working in urban contexts in both London and Leicester, and, as part of the Wheeler team, had specialised in pottery drawing. Faced with developments in the town, especially the plans to widen St George's Street to remove traffic from the High Street, Cottrill organised summer excavations directed by archaeologists who were usually invited in for a single season (Cunliffe 1964; Collis 1978, forthcoming). This was the pattern of work from 1953 to 1961, with museum staff, usually Cottrill himself, carrying out more ad hoc work where planned excavations were impossible. During this time the officers and elected members of the City Council as well as the public became sensitised to the history of the city and the potential of archaeology to expand that knowledge.

In 1961 the major project was the building of the Wessex Hotel adjacent to the Cathedral precincts. The person asked to direct it was Martin Biddle, and though he initially had reservations due to other commitments, he was impressed by the potential of Winchester for multi-period research, and especially by Roger Quirk's paper on the Old Minster (Quirk 1957). His background, unusually for the time, was mainly in medieval archaeology, having, as a schoolboy at Merchant Taylors' directed with Lawrence Barfield and Alan Millard the excavations of the Manor of the More (Biddle, Millard and Barfield 1959). But he too was a product of the Wheeler school, and was especially influenced as a schoolboy attending the evening lectures which Wheeler was giving in London to the London and Middlesex Archaeological Society at the Bishopsgate Institute; he also worked for him at Stanwick in 1952 (Biddle 2008). He had had experience working for Molly Cotton at Verulamium in 1949 and Shepherd Frere at Canterbury in 1953. While doing his National Service in Berlin, his tank unit was disbanded, giving him the opportunity of carrying out other work, and he wrote to Wheeler for advice; this led to a secondment to work for Kathleen Kenyon at Jericho. His lessons from working for two of the outstanding excavators of the time impressed on him the need for site discipline, for example the detailed description of layers, systematic labelling (two labels for each finds tray), and the necessity for a continual overview of the finds as they were excavated to inform excavation strategy and identify problems such as contamination, disciplines which he finds sadly lacking in most modern excavations.

After National Service, he studied Archaeology and Anthropology at Pembroke College, Cambridge, and as for many students who studied there in the late 1950s and 1960s, the economic approaches of Grahame Clark and especially Eric Higgs were a major influence, and he even published a joint bone report with Higgs (Higgs and Biddle 1960). So, unlike most traditional archaeologists working at the time in urban contexts who generally just discarded animal bones, at Winchester Biddle accorded them great importance. Like a number of undergraduates at that time at Cambridge, he was already directing major excavations, and this continued in the period when he worked for the Ministry of Works, and later as a lecturer in the Department of History at Exeter University. Chronologically these excavations covered a wide range of periods from Roman to post-medieval: the deserted medieval village at Seacourt in Berkshire in 1958 (Biddle 1962b); and in the same year the Roman villa at Twyford, where I first dug for him, and I also dug with him for the first season on Henry VIII's palace at Nonsuch in 1959 (the largest excavation in Britain that year). He later dug Dover Castle in 1961–3.

Thus, by the time he undertook the first of his Winchester excavations, Biddle's experience was exceptionally wide, from the Neolithic to the post-medieval. He was also familiar with the difficulties and potentials of excavating multi-period sites, including urban excavations at Jericho and Canterbury, but also in London – the work of W. F. Grimes based in the London Museum, especially at Cripplegate and the temple of Mithras which he visited regularly as a schoolboy in 1953–4. At that time the study of medieval towns was considered the almost exclusive territory of historians, which archaeologists could only supplement or illustrate (archaeology as the 'handmaiden of history') despite the results of, for instance, Frere's excavations at Canterbury. Among archaeologists there was still a tradition of largely ignoring the medieval and especially the later deposits. In 1967 Biddle was to provoke a sharp exchange of views in *Antiquity* when he accused some archaeologists of simply machining off later deposits to expose the Roman levels (Biddle 1968a, 1969a). Again he considers his inspiration in this multi-period approach to have been the lectures he had attended given by Wheeler on topics such as the Harappan civilisation, and especially the description of the city of Balkh on the Oxus.

The evolution of the project

The area now occupied by the Wessex Hotel had been a cemetery up to the mid nineteenth century, but the monuments had been cleared in the 1930s to provide a tarmacadam car park. Thus, with the top two metres heavily disturbed by intensive grave digging and vaults, the site was ideal for the removal of the overburden by machine to expose the archaeology (an early example of mechanical excavation in an urban context for archaeological purposes), with the bones from the eighteenth and nineteenth century burials collected for re-burial; it was not realised until later in the excavation that some of these burials were late Saxon, from a cemetery which underlay what is interpreted as the mausoleum

Figure 6.1. Rescue excavations on the Wessex Hotel site, Winchester, 1961.

for the Norman bishops of the New Minster. Initially trenches were dug the length of the car park, then selected areas opened up for more extensive excavation, of both the early medieval features, but also the Roman levels – a north-south street with a courtyard house to the east and what proved to be part of the forum to the west (Figure 6.1).

The areas opened up were much larger than the trenches and boxes then largely used on British excavations; this had already happened on several sites in Winchester in St George's Street (*e.g.* the Middle Brook Street site in 1953), though there the recording methods had not been adequate to deal with the complex features encountered. Previously techniques had been developed by Frere at Verulamium to deal with large area trenches, and Biddle had visited Verulamium and discussed the methods with him; similar methods were employed at Nonsuch, and now applied to Winchester. On an essentially straight-forward site such as the Wessex Hotel this was relatively easy with each area being given a number as though it were a trench, and the deposits within each area given discrete 'layer numbers'. Each layer number was entered into a 'site book' (with alternating pages of lined and graph paper to allow drawings and sketches of plans and sections to be made), and the relationships of each layer to deposits above and below were also recorded. Major plans were drawn on graph paper using triangulation from fixed points, though drawing frames made an early appearance. An important feature of the recording were sections showing the overall sequence of deposits over the whole or large parts of the site using the edges of trenches or of the excavated areas.

These methods were to form the basis of the increasingly sophisticated recording methods used in

Winchester, though briefly in 1962 and 1963 a more traditional 'grid' or 'box' method was used on the Assize Courts site and sites on Lower Brook Street. For sampling linear features such as roads or the defences of the Iron Age (Figure 6.2), Roman and Medieval cities (*e.g.* Tower Street, Oram's Arbour) relatively narrow trenches were employed. The trench / layer system worked well where buildings and other features were fairly substantial (*e.g.* the Castle Yard, Wolvesey Palace), and even on a site such as Cathedral Green with its complicated sequence of intersecting graves, walls and robber trenches (Figure 6.3).

The medieval domestic buildings on Lower Brook Street, however, presented a major problem. Though some buildings had stone phases, most, especially in the early phases, were wooden with various methods of construction (post holes, sleeper-beams, *etc.*), and rather than having substantial floor surfaces as in Roman or higher status medieval buildings, they mainly consisted of overlapping lenses which might suddenly disappear as they abutted ephemeral walls or other structures. In these cases features might be difficult to define, and baulks to provide sections, however narrow, might mask important junctions. Though initially the area had been divided up into a series of separate large 'trenches', these were gradually abandoned in favour of one large area, and all baulks removed (Figure 6.4). However, overall master sections were still recorded by setting up temporary baulks on predetermined lines, which could be drawn and demolished when only a few centimetres high, and the drawing added to the master drawing ('cumulative sections'). Much greater emphasis than before was now placed on the plan, drawn in considerable detail with the use of colour (something common on Dutch excavations, but rare in Britain at this time), with both coding for certain prescribed stone types and artefacts such as pottery, but with more naturalistic representation of layers. These plans needed to be overlain to establish some relationships which both required much greater accuracy (within a few centimetres) and also a drawing medium which was both transparent and stable, which neither the traditional graph paper or tracing paper were. From 1965 standard size sheets of plastic drawing film with a printed grid were introduced, a major innovation which has become standard on all British excavations. The physical relationship of the plans was further fixed by extensive use of levelling using a dumpy level or a theodolite which would be set up on arrival on the site each morning.

Horizontally the plans also needed to be accurately fixed, using fixed points around the site from which a grid could be laid out over the whole site. This was linked to another major change which started in 1965, the shift from imperial to metric measurements, and the introduction of a metric grid, innovations due to Birthe Kjølbye, based on her Danish experience (Biddle and Kjølbye Biddle 1969). This allowed the much simpler method of recording using co-ordinates, which, at a later date, facilitated the computerisation of data, and allowed the easier linking together of plans and recorded finds. At Winchester local grids were used for each site, rather than attempting to use the Ordnance Survey's national grid.

The recording methods for finds are described in detail in Biddle (1990, 9–18). A strict discipline was maintained on site with each worker excavating one deposit (layer) at a time with a single 'finds tray' which would be given two labels for bulk finds. 'Small finds' (special or fragile finds such as glass or copper alloy objects) would be separately bagged and numbered, and perhaps removed from the bulk finds on site. 'Recorded finds' were objects such as coins whose precise position might be important for interpretation and dating, and these were given their own unique number and usually three-dimensional co-ordinates. Finds from linear features such as the defences were separately numbered and their position projected on to the section by affixing a label which could be recorded when the section was drawn. All finds were taken to the 'finds shed' at the end of the day for washing and marking, one label being kept with the processed and one with the unprocessed finds during operations such as pot-washing so that no finds would be left unlabelled at any point. Two or three times a week finds

Figure 6.2. Excavation of the Iron Age defences on Oram's Arbour, Winchester, 1967.

Figure 6.3. Cathedral Green, Winchester, excavations.

would be inspected, identified and dated by the director prior to bagging, allowing a running check to be kept on site interpretation and allowing an exchange of ideas between site supervisors, finds supervisors and director.

Strategic and organisational developments

From the start, and especially as the late Saxon – early Norman cemetery and buildings started to emerge on the Wessex Hotel site, the potential of archaeology for understanding something more of two of the major buildings of Late Saxon England, the Old and the New Minsters, become apparent, especially in collaboration with an historian familiar with the documentary sources. In the case of the New Minster, this was Roger Quirk (Quirk 1957; Biddle and Quirk 1962), but Winchester possesses an exceptionally rich written documentation, and this co-operation was soon expanded into a more ambitious programme to locate the individual tenements and their history using both the legal documents, and also the topography of the city, working back from the earliest accurately surveyed plans and maps. The first part of this project was an analysis of a unique document, the *Winton Domesday*. At Biddle's invitation, the text was edited and translated by Frank Barlow, Head of the History Department in Exeter, with the personal names analysed by the Swede, Olof von Feilitzen, and discussion of every aspect by Biddle and Derek Keene (Barlow *et al.* 1976). This volume set the interdisciplinary character of the *Winchester Studies* series. To exploit the more extensive later documentary evidence, Keene, then a research student, was recruited, and he later became a permanent member of the Research Unit, not only publishing his

Figure 6.4. Open area excavation of medieval houses and St. Pancras Church on Lower Brook Street, Winchester.

own research (Keene 1985), but also providing historical information on other sites in the City such as those excavated in the 1950s (*e.g.* in Collis, forthcoming).

Once the decision had been made to develop a long term research strategy, the model used was that developed in the 1930s of setting up an academic 'Winchester Excavations Committee' to advise, and to raise funds, with Dilys Neate, then Mayor of Winchester, as it first Chairman, and with representation of major archaeological and historical organisations in Britain. The role of the museum from now on would be as eventual recipient of the finds and documentation of the excavations, but with a more restricted role dealing with rescue needs in the City which fell outside the scope of the Research Unit, and to this end a full-time archaeologist was appointed in 1966 (a post which this author failed to get!). With the end of the Research Unit's excavations, in 1972 a City Archaeologist was appointed initially under the Unit, but in 1977 this role was transferred to the museum, with the Research Unit concentrating on the publication of the 1960s excavations. Initially the major source of funding was the Ministry of Works for rescue excavations and for research excavations on sites under the Ministry's care, such as Wolvesey Palace. There was also substantial local financial support, especially from the City Council; the then Mayor Dilys Neate, and the Town Clerk, Robin McCall, were strong supporters of the project. These sources provided initially enough to employ permanent members of staff to help with administrative work, but more substantial funding was needed, beyond the usual sources such as the British Academy and the Society of Antiquaries. A major break-through from 1964 came with funding and the participation of staff and students from American universities (North Carolina and Duke Universities). Subsequently in 1967, with funding from the Ministry of Public Building and Works, local government and various trusts, Biddle himself became full-time director of the Unit, and part-time and full-time excavators and specialists were employed. The Unit was thus independent, though working under the general aegis of the City Council which helped provide work space and accommodation.

Up to the 1950s the normal model for the staffing of excavations was to employ unskilled workmen for the heavy digging, with students or people with private incomes to do the recording and fine digging, a structure also used at Nonsuch, though with more volunteer input (Figure 6.5; Collis 2001, figs 2–14 a–d). In the late 1950s under excavators such as Shepherd Frere and John Wacher a new model came in under which the diggers were volunteers, recruited mainly through the Council for British Archaeology's *Calendar of Excavations*; from these volunteers more skilled ones were selected to act as paid student-labourers, and the best of these subsequently became site supervisors and eventually site directors in their own right (female site supervisors missed out the labouring stage!). The Winchester model was slightly different, with no paid labourers, and volunteers staying for a minimum of three weeks and were paid a basic subsistence of 10 shillings a day. Initially, in the early 1960s, there was no body of workers to draw on, and for 1961 it was too late to raise many volunteers through the *Calendar*. So the initial labour force was drawn from student friends of the director (*e.g.* Robert Soper) and local volunteers from schools, some of whom were to become supervisors (myself, Ffiona Gilmore), and we in turn invited our friends – I wrote to one friend I had met at Verulamium, Alan Carter, who was eventually to direct the Lower Brook Street site, and to become Assistant Director of the Winchester excavations (1965–1971); later Derek Keene became Deputy Director of the Unit. Initially other supervisors were brought in on other people's recommendation (not always a success!), but from 1964 a system of internal promotion from among the volunteers was the rule. Volunteers came from all over the world (Scandinavian ladies proved particularly attractive to some senior members of the staff!). However, though some such as myself were to employ this model well into the 1980s, and it is again coming back into fashion with community projects, the model for the rescue excavations from the 1970s was that used by Ministry excavators such as Geoff Wainwright,

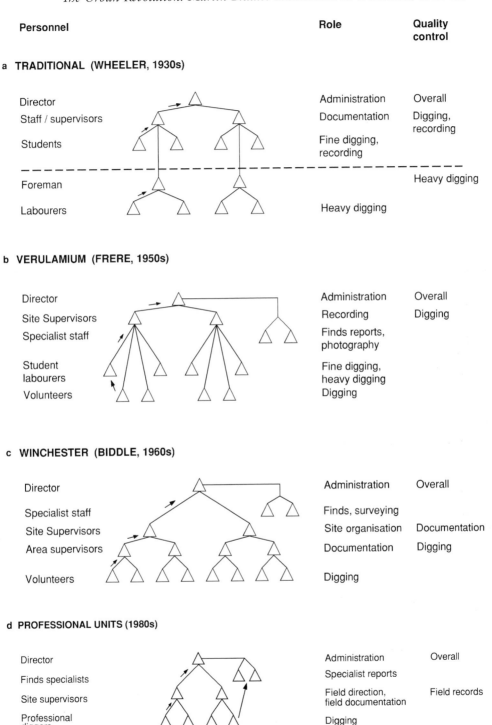

Figure 6.5. Team structures, after Collis 2001, figs 2–14 a–d.

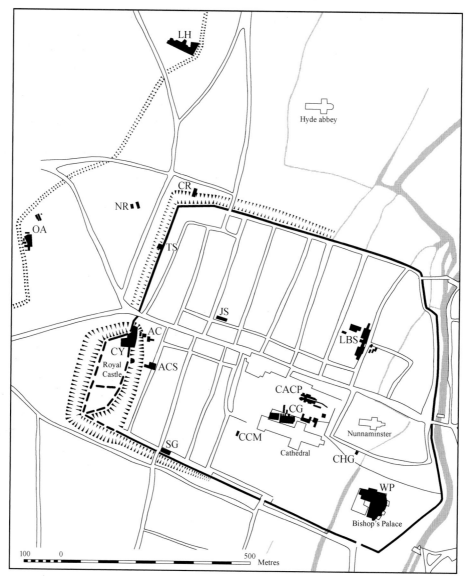

Figure 6.6. Location of sites excavated in Winchester 1961–1971.

using paid itinerant excavators from whom the developing class of professional archaeologists was largely drawn.

Sampling strategies in urban contexts to decide which sites to excavate is, for rescue excavation, largely opportunistic – which sites are under threat, and for which funding is available (Figure 6.6). This was partly true in Winchester in the 1960s (*e.g.* the Lower Brook Street and Assize Court sites). But the possibility of external funding for research excavations gave much wider choice. In the 1960s relatively little was known of the defended Iron Age site and the Roman civitas capital, and though opportunities were taken, for instance, to investigate the nature and date of the defences, sampling in the Roman town was dictated by the choice of medieval structures to be excavated. In part the research interests incorporated traditional interests of medieval archaeology; the history and development of major buildings, especially the architecture, and so the excavations included the Bishop's castle (Wolvesey Palace), the Royal Castle, and the Old Minster. However, socially and economically this was balanced by the Lower Brook Street excavation, and also the excavations around the Cathedral produced a large sample of skeletons, allowing a study of the human population of the Saxon and medieval town. The excavations also investigated the structure and planning of the town, such as the street layout; one major discovery of the excavations was that the modern rectilinear layout of the streets owed virtually nothing to the Roman grid as had been assumed (only the main axes were dictated by the siting of the Roman gates), but was due to the planned establishment of the Saxon burh in the later ninth century, a phenomenon subsequently recognised at a number of Wessex sites (Biddle and Hill 1971). The diachronic nature of the excavations, ignoring the normal period specialisations (Iron Age, Roman, Medieval), also meant that detailed study could be made of the periods of 'transition': how the Iron Age defences affected the layout of the early Roman town, and especially the evolution from the late Roman town to the Saxon burh.

The impact and legacy of Winchester

The impact of the excavations was immediate during the 1960s, chiefly because the results of each season were published as interim reports usually within a year, mainly in the *Antiquaries Journal* (Biddle and Quirk 1962; Biddle 1963, 1964. 1965, 1966, 1967, 1968a, 1969a, 1970, 1972,), a tradition which was normal in the 1950s and 1960s for major excavations such as Verulamium and Cirencester. It was clear that similar approaches were needed in other major cities where rescue excavations still tended to be haphazard; indeed threatened sites were often destroyed without any meaningful archaeological excavation. The first city to start to emulate the Winchester organisation was York where the York Archaeological Trust was set up by Peter Addyman, who had been a fellow student and close friend of Biddle's at Cambridge, and who likewise had strong medieval credentials. Biddle himself was involved in the survey of the problems in London (Biddle and Hudson 1973), which led to the setting up of the Museum of London's Department of Urban Archaeology, later to become the Archaeological Service (MoLAS). The threat to urban sites was one of the main themes which led to the founding of Rescue (of which Biddle was the first chairman), and in the 1970s rescue excavation and the establishment of archaeological units on the Winchester model to deal with those threats became a major concern for local government at both a city and at a county level.

In the late 1950s and early 1960s medieval archaeologists led the way in developing new methods of excavation: John Hurst at Wharram Percy; Brian Hope-Taylor at Yeavering; Philip Barker at Hen Domen and Wroxeter; the first issue of *World Archaeology* in 1969 contained two articles on excavation methods, that by Martin and Birthe Kjølbye-Biddle mainly about the methods used on the excavations of the Old Minster, and by Philip Barker on Hen Domen and Wroxeter; eventually it was Barker's *Techniques of Archaeological Excavation* (1977) which was to prove the bible for the new generation of excavators. From these techniques pioneered in urban contexts the new orthodoxy of excavation, 'single context recording' was to develop which has been propagated in the Museum of London's *Manual of Excavation* (MoLAS 1980), though this was never part of the Winchester recording system where there was (and Biddle would argue should still be) a strong emphasis on the traditional overall section; my own version has involved a greater emphasis on temporary baulks and dividing up areas using a grid to allow detailed density plots of finds (Collis 2001; Deberge *et al.* 2007). But one of the best known legacies of Winchester bears the name of one of the unit's employees in the early 1970s, the Harris Matrix (Harris 1979). Ed Harris was one of the people employed to help publish the Lower Brook

Street excavation, and his matrix was developed to try to systematise the mass of stratigraphical data recorded in the site note books and drawings. He also advocated the use of *pro forma* recording in the form of context sheets, something now disseminated via the MoLAS manual through many countries in Europe and elsewhere: the US (*unité stratigraphique*) numbers of French archaeology; and *schedi*, the forms officially used on Italian sites.

In Britain the new methods of excavation were not always welcomed, as I found when I introduced them to Exeter in 1971, along with the structure of volunteers and my team of supervisors; I was criticised for not digging small trial trenches, but going straight to open area excavation, and for spending too much time on the medieval and post-medieval deposits (Allan 1984). When the early Roman levels were reached after some three months, and evidence of the Roman military foundation was found in the form of timber barrack blocks, even the most stern critics realised that, with the extensive later disturbance leaving only small islands of undisturbed deposits, trenching would never have identified the timber buildings for what they were. As a spin off of what was a deliberate emulation of Winchester, the animal bones were studied in detail by Mark Maltby (1979), the first major multi-period study of the fauna from a town in Britain, supervised by Graeme Barker and myself, and so an application of the economic approaches of the Cambridge school.

There was also a major impact on French archaeology, under bizarre circumstances. A French student was visiting a girl-friend in Winchester, but as she was working during the day, he brought a colleague as company. When this friend, one night, broke his leg falling off a fence and had to return to France, the student decided to respond to the advertisement for volunteers on the Cathedral Green site as a way to pass the time. His encounter with the site director, a pipe-smoking Danish lady, caused him to decide this was the life for him, and Henri Galinié eventually became a senior supervisor of the Wolvesey Palace excavation. He later obtained a lecturing post in Tours, and, though his only archaeological training had been in Winchester, he decided that something similar could be tried in France (Jason Wood recalls his introduction at Tours to 'la méthode Winchester'). At the time urban archaeology in France was very undeveloped, but the influence of Tours quickly inspired teams working in Orléans and Chartres, and later St. Denis. My own attempt at introducing open area methods in France in 1973, on the Iron Age site at Aulnat near Clermont-Ferrand were met with bemusement by my French co-director who had been brought up on the Palaeolithic tradition of working in spits in two-metre squares, and could not understand why I was digging holes all over the site (emptying pits and ditches!). Sadly despite the highly detailed plans he made, people working on our finds from the 1970s have tended to treat his material as 'unstratified' as it is almost impossible to assign finds with assurance to specific features and so reconstruct closed groups of finds. An evolved version of the recording methods we developed in the Auvergne based on Winchester methods has now become the norm at the influential training and research excavation at Bibracte / Mont Beuvray (Stephenson forthcoming). The other major influence on French archaeology was Bohumil Soudský's large scale rescue excavations on the gravels of the Aisne valley, though these lacked the complex stratigraphy of the urban sites. This pioneering work in the 1970s has resulted in a total revolution in French archaeology, in which Winchester clearly played a major part.

If in many ways the 1960s were a golden era for archaeology, when young excavators were able to introduce new ideas and methods, and run major projects, it also had its drawbacks as much of the infrastructure which we now take for granted simply did not exist: no specialists to work on the great mass of finds which excavations such as Winchester produce; no methodology or computers capable of manipulating the complex data a site such as Lower Brook Street produced. The 1960s also saw major changes in the theoretical basis of, especially, prehistoric, archaeology, but I have argued elsewhere that the revolution in excavation techniques and the paradigm shift of the 'New Archaeology' were processes which, in the 1960s at least, ran parallel courses, hardly influencing one another (Collis 2004). The Winchester excavations owe their origin to a traditional approach in Medieval Archaeology through History, which at this time was being profoundly affected by the socio-economic approaches of scholars such as Maurice Beresford. Though the main results of the excavations were disseminated extremely quickly, the more detailed publication is slower, especially if one is unwilling to cut corners. The handsome series of *Winchester Studies* under Biddle's editorship has seen publication of the very highest order, and has been expanded to include sites or projects which were not directly under the control of the Research Unit, *e.g.* Giles Clarke's excavation of the Late Roman cemetery at Lankhills (1979) or Michael Lapidge's study (2003) of the cult of St Swithin who was so intimately linked with the Old Minster, and even in their uncompleted form already represent one of the finest records of the history of any city in Britain. Other studies which do not fit within the remit have been published elsewhere, for instance the Research Unit's investigation of the Round Table (Biddle 2000).

In summary, the Winchester excavations, though themselves building on traditional structures and methodologies, represented a major departure in British archaeology as it evolved both during the period of fieldwork and during the post-excavation phase. This chapter has dealt with the more general impact rather than the detailed results of the excavations for the archaeology of Winchester. Its concerns, both the theoretical approach, the need for an overall research plan which can be easily adjusted as the situation changes, the need for strong site discipline, and also the involvement of the wider community, are matters still as relevant today as they were in the 1960s.

Acknowledgements

My thanks especially to Martin Biddle who has been a major influence on my own excavation techniques and my career as a professional archaeologist in general; our recent discussion on the development of Winchester was most illuminating; both he and Birthe Kjølbye Biddle commented on and corrected the first draft. My thanks too to Henri Galinié for his amusing reminiscences of his days in Winchester.

In memoriam: Birthe Kjølbye Biddle, Alan Carter and Sissel Sødring Collis who dug at Winchester.

References

Allan, J. P. 1984. *Medieval and Post-Medieval Finds from Exeter*. Exeter Archaeological Reports. Exeter: Exeter University Press.

Alexander, J. 1960. Report on the investigation of a round barrow on Arreton Down, Isle of Wight. *Proceedings of the Prehistoric Society* 26, 276–296.

Barker, P. 1969. Some aspects of the excavation of timber buildings. *World Archaeology* I–2, 220–235.

Barker, P. 1977. *Techniques of Archaeological Excavation*. London, Batsford. First edition.

Barlow, F., Biddle, M., von Feilitzen, O. and Keene, D. J. 1976. *Winchester in the Early Medieval Ages: an edition and discussion of the Winton Domesday*. Winchester Studies 1. Oxford: Clarendon Press.

Biddle, M. 1962. The deserted medieval village of Seacourt, Berks. *Oxoniensia* 26/27, 70–203.

Biddle, M. 1964. Excavations at Winchester 1964: second interim report. *Antiquaries Journal* 44, 188–219.

Biddle, M. 1965. Excavations at Winchester 1964: third interim report. *Antiquaries Journal* 45, 230–264.

Biddle, M. 1966. Excavations at Winchester 1965: fourth interim report. *Antiquaries Journal* 46, 308–32.

Biddle, M. 1967. Excavations at Winchester 1966: fifth interim report. *Antiquaries Journal* 47, 224–250.

Biddle, M. 1968a. Excavations at Winchester 1967: sixth interim report. *Antiquaries Journal* 48, 250–284.

Biddle, M. 1968b. Archaeology and the History of British towns. *Antiquity* 42, 109–116.

Biddle, M. 1969a. Excavations at Winchester 1968: seventh interim report. *Antiquaries Journal* 49, 295–329.

Biddle, M. 1969b. Reply to discussion of 'Archaeology and the History of British towns'. *Antiquity* 43, 42–43.

Biddle, M. 1970. Excavations at Winchester 1969: eighth interim report. *Antiquaries Journal* 50, 277–236.

Biddle, M. 1972. Excavations at Winchester 1970: ninth interim report. *Antiquaries Journal* 52, 93–131.

Biddle, M. 1973. Winchester: the development of an early capital. In J. Jankuhn, W. Schlesinger and H. Stewer (eds), *Vor- und Frühformen der europäischer Stadt im Mittelalter*, 229–61. Gottingen.

Biddle, M. 1975. Excavations at Winchester 1971: tenth interim report. *Antiquaries Journal* 55, 96–126, 295–337.

Biddle, M. 1990. *Object and Economy in Medieval Winchester*. Winchester Studies 7–ii (volumes I and II). Oxford: Clarendon Press.

Biddle, M. 2000. *King Arthur's Round Table*. Woodbridge: The Boydell Press.

Biddle, M. 2008. Recollections of a student archaeologist. *Pembroke College Cambridge Gazette* 82, 51–55.

Biddle, M. and Hill, D. 1971. Late Saxon planned towns. *Antiquaries Journal* 51, 70–85.

Biddle, M. and Hudson, D. 1973. *The future of London's Past: a survey of the archaeological implications of planning and development in the nation's capital*. Worcester.

Biddle, M. and Kjølbye-Biddle, B. 1969. Metres, areas and robbing. *World Archaeology* 1–2, 208–219.

Biddle, M, Millard, A. and Barfield, L. H. 1959. The excavation of the Manor of the More, Rickmansworth. *Archaeological Journal* 116, 136–199.

Biddle, M. and Quirk, R. N. 1962. Excavations near Winchester Cathedral 1961. *Archaeological Journal* 119, 150–194.

Clarke, G. 1979. *The Roman Cemetery at Lankhills*. Winchester Studies 3–ii. Oxford: Clarendon Press.

Collis, J. R. 1972. *Exeter Excavations: the Guildhall Site*. Exeter: University of Exeter.

Collis, J. R. 1978. *Winchester Excavations 1949–1960. 2: excavations in the suburbs and western parts of the town*. Winchester: Winchester City Museum.

Collis, J. R. 2001. *Digging up the Past*. Stroud: Sutton Publishing.

Collis, J. R. 2004. Paradigms and excavation, in G. Carver (ed.), *Excavation Techniques in Europe: excavation in a new millennium*, 31–43. Oxford: British Archaeological Reports International Series 1256.

Collis, J. R. forthcoming. *Excavations in Winchester, 1949–1960; 3: excavations in the High Street and St. George's Street*. Winchester: Winchester City Museum, and J. R. Collis Publications. Typescript in Winchester Museum.

Cunliffe, B. W. 1962. The Winchester city wall. *Proceedings of the Hampshire Field Club and Archaeological Society* 22, pt.3, 51–81.

Cunliffe, B. W. 1964. *Winchester Excavations 1949–1960, Vol. 1*. Winchester: Winchester City Museum.

Deberge, Y., Collis, J. and Dunkley, J. 2007. *Clermont-Ferrand – Le Pâtural (Puy-de-Dôme). Evolution d'un établissement agricole gaulois (IIIe–IIe s. avant J.-C.) en Limagne d'Auvergne*. Lyon: Documents d'Archéologie en Rhône-Alpes et en Auvergne 30.

Harris, E. 1979. *Principles of Archaeological Stratigraphy*. London: Academic Press, first edition.

Higgs, E. S. and Biddle, M. 1960. The animal bones, in J. Alexander 1960, 301–2.

Keene, D. 1985. *Survey of Medieval Winchester*. Winchester Studies 3–ii (volumes I and II). Oxford: Clarendon Press.

Lapidge, M. 2003. *The Cult of St. Swithin*. Winchester Studies 4–ii. Oxford: Clarendon Press.

Maltby, M. 1979. *Faunal Studies on Urban Sites: the animal bones from Exeter*. Exeter Archaeological Reports 2, Sheffield: Department of Prehistory and Archaeology.

MoLAS, 1994. *Archaeological Site Manual*. London: Museum of London Department of Urban Archaeology, 1st edn.

Quirk, R. 1957. Winchester Cathedral in the tenth century. *Archaeological Journal* 114, 28–68.

Stephenson, P. forthcoming. *Bibracte: site manual*. Glux-en-Glenne: Bibracte.

The rural revolution: Excavation of the Iron Age and Roman farming settlement at Owslebury, Hampshire, 1961–1972

John Collis

Gerhard Bersu's excavations at Little Woodbury in 1938–9 formed a major watershed in Iron Age studies in Britain (Bersu 1940). Though there was an underlying recognition that the circular stone 'huts' in highland areas of Britain were prehistoric in date, the people in the lowlands still lived in 'pit dwellings', and even as late as 1943 Wheeler was suggesting that burnt areas in pits were hearths around which people had huddled while eating their food (Wheeler 1943, 52, plate CVIII). The biggest shock of Bersu's discoveries was the large round house which at last suggested a sophistication in the standards of living which matched the high level of art and technology demonstrated by Late Bronze Age and Iron Age metalwork. Alongside the round houses, Bersu recognised two-post structures which he interpreted as perhaps hay-drying racks, and four-post structures which ever since have been mainly interpreted as raised granaries, he thought for the storage of seed grain. Many of the pits he interpreted as silos for the storage of grain for consumption, by humans and by animals, on the assumption that grain stored in this way would not maintain its fertility. A large area of pits he suggested might be a 'working hollow'. Bersu went on to attempt a reconstruction of the farming economy based on calculations of the capacity of the storage pits; in the chaos of the outbreak of war, the animal bones were unfortunately lost before they could be studied.

For the next 30 years Little Woodbury remained virtually the sole point of reference for Iron Age farming settlements in Lowland Britain. Caesar's characterisation of Britain as being divided into a coastal area where agriculture predominated, and an inland pastoral economy still had a major influence on interpretation, and even where major excavations took place in northern or western areas, such as Hamilton's work at Jarlshof and Clickhimin (Hamilton 1956, 1968), or Mackie's work on brochs (Mackie 1965), the emphasis was on architectural history rather than the economy. Some major excavations had taken place in the war years on sites such as Draughton (Grimes 1961), or rescue excavation on the Thames gravels as at Langford Downs (Williams 1947), or research excavations like Sonia and Christopher Hawkes' excavation of Longbridge Deverill (Hawkes 1994), or Dennis Harding at Pimperne (Harding and Blake 1963; Harding *et al.* 1993), but these largely confirmed rather than challenged the results at Little Woodbury (*e.g.* the large round houses, storage pits, bones of domestic animals). The main driving force for academic research was still mainly the 'Culture-Historical' paradigm as epitomised by Hawkes' (1959/1960) classification of the Iron Age based on putative invasions, and even the study of the pottery from Little Woodbury was couched in similar terms (Brailsford 1948).

To answer these cultural questions excavations were biased towards the excavation of hill-fort ramparts, and especially entrances, as these provided both chronological sequences and distinctive types of architecture which could be interpreted in cultural / invasionist terms. There was a similar bias in Roman rural archaeology with a heavy emphasis on the excavation of Roman villas, both because of a special interest in architectural history, and because it was assumed that villas were the driving force in production and innovation, while 'native settlements' were assumed to be conservative and not fully integrated into the Roman economy. Even on villa excavations concentrated on the living quarters of the villa, with their mosaic pavements, heating systems and baths, rather than on aspects of production such as barns and middens. Interpretation in the Roman period aimed at writing political and military history rather than social and economic.

New approaches to the Iron Age

The shift in Iron Age studies in Britain came from two main sources. The first was from landscape studies, which had been developing in Britain during the wars, for instance in the Curwens' identification of 'Celtic Fields' (Curwen and Curwen 1923), or of Hawkes' (1939) study of the Late Bronze Age 'ranch boundaries' at Quarley Hill. In the 1950s these approaches were raised to a higher level mainly through the work of the Salisbury Office of the Royal Commission on Historical Monuments under H. C. (Collin) Bowen, with studies of whole landscapes on the chalk downlands, and an interest in the agricultural systems which had produced them; the seminal work in this development was Bowen's book *Ancient Fields* (1961). The recognition of many enclosures from the air as crop-marks but occasionally as earthworks, encouraged an increasing concern for Iron Age and Roman rural settlements, but even for the latter, discussion in Wessex still had to rely on Pitt Rivers' excavations from the 1890s (Hawkes and Piggott 1947)!

The second major input came from the theoretical approaches especially associated with the Department of Archaeology at Cambridge. Under the influence of Scandinavian archaeology's approach to prehistory with its strong environmental and economic basis, the professor at Cambridge, Grahame Clark introduced into British archaeology methodologies such as pollen analysis, and all students were expected to attend classes given by Eric Higgs on the identification of animal bones. Clark himself attacked the traditional invasionist basis of Iron Age studies in his controversial paper 'The Invasion Hypothesis', as epitomised by the Oxford School under Hawkes (Clark 1966), but perhaps more controversy had been caused by a Cambridge graduate, Roy Hodson, who in a series of papers had attacked and effectively demolished the theoretical and factual basis of the Hawkes scheme (Hodson 1962, 1964, 1968). His approach was still 'cultural' in the Childe sense of the term, referring to an indigenous 'Woodbury Culture', while accepting possible foreign cultural intrusions ('Hallstatt', 'Arras' and 'Aylesford'). He considered that in the then state of knowledge, only a simple division into 'Early' and 'Late' was possible in contrast to the minute divisions of Hawkes' ABC. As a direct result of his critique, another Cambridge graduate, Barry Cunliffe, for his PhD carried out a survey of assemblages of pottery in southern and eastern England, allowing a more detailed chronology than Hodson, but he too emphasised the need for extensive excavations to provide good stratified closed groups and stratigraphies on which to base local and regional chronologies (Cunliffe 1974).

From the mid 1960s there was further theoretical development in Cambridge, what was later to be termed the 'New Archaeology' (I avoid the term 'Processual' as I consider it as largely irrelevant to what was actually going on), a movement in Britain especially associated with David Clarke, though it was not until the 1970s that he himself turned to Iron Age problems with his paper on Glastonbury (Clarke 1972; Coles and Minnitt 1995). The new approaches were derived from a number of varied sources, from the Sciences (especially statistical methods of classification), economic anthropology (*e.g.* gift exchange, market economies, social evolution) and geography (location analysis, least effort models, central places). After his brief flurry of papers on British archaeology, Hodson turned to more continental matters, such as the chronology of the Münsingen cemetery (Hodson 1968), so by the late 1960s and into the 1970s the main protagonists of the new approaches were myself and Barry Cunliffe, though we disagreed on the best methodologies to achieve our aims. However, there was a stinging backlash from 'traditionalists' especially, though not exclusively students of Hawkes at Oxford, (*e.g.* Rodwell 1976; Collis 1981b), while Alcock (1972, 108) dismissed the criticisms of the migrationist interpretation as 'a flight from history', part of a violent riposte to myself when I objected to his extending the discredited Hawkes methodology to Wales and Ireland (Collis 1994a). What was required were substantial new data from fieldwork and excavation to demonstrate how the new ideas could function in practice. This, then, was the academic background to the Owslebury excavation.

The excavation at Owslebury

Work on the site started modestly: the tenant farmer, Philip Hellard, had been sensitised to the archaeological remains on his farm by a local amateur, Mr. A. R. Edwardson (later Honorary Curator of Bury St. Edmunds Museum), who had walked the field picking up flints. During deep ploughing in 1961 Mr Hellard had hit a 2nd century AD cremation burial, and he informed Winchester City Museum who sent a member of staff to record it, though no proper records were kept (no plan, no photographs). A similar problem emerged the following year when further deep ploughing in a neighbouring field produced a Late Roman corn-drying oven; this time the museum requested me to take over the excavation and recording. This field had not previously been ploughed, and there were visible earthworks in it, including a rectangular ditched enclosure. Having completed my A- and S-level examinations, I returned to school to obtain a university place, but this was achieved within a few days of the school year, and the headmaster gave me permission to take up to three days a week off school to excavate, as long as I had completed my duties as Head Prefect. I trenched two sites: an Iron Age and Roman settlement at Borough Farm, Micheldever (Fasham and Collis 1980); and Owslebury where I investigated the visible earthworks. In the autumn of 1963 with a small group of friends and local schoolchildren I continued the work at Owslebury, concentrating on the rectangular enclosure, showing that it was early Roman, but with an earlier Late Iron Age phase. I finished the surveying of the trenches (which has never fully made sense!) late in the evening of the day before I went to Cambridge to start my degree course.

Late Iron Age finds from Hampshire were, at that time, rare, so I contacted Christopher Hawkes with whom I had dug at Longbridge Deverill, and he put me in touch with Collin Bowen who arranged for a local amateur flier, John Boyden, to take aerial photographs (Figure 7.1). The first, taken in the summer of 1964, revealed extensive cropmarks in a field to the east of where I had been working. While following this up on foot, I located what was clearly a series of Late Iron Age and Roman cremation burials which had been disturbed by the deep ploughing. Iron Age burials in Hampshire also were rare, and for the Late Iron Age virtually confined to the tumulus burial from Hurstbourne Tarrant (Hawkes and Dunning 1930), but a cemetery associated with a settlement was totally unique. On the advice of Martin Biddle I contacted the Ministry of Works for funds to carry out a rescue excavation, and for the years 1965 to 1970, and 1972, this was the major source of funding, with grants of up to £1000 a year, which were administered by the Hampshire Field Club. In 1965 this allowed me to employ some fellow students as labourers to clear by hand a small area on the settlement and on the cemetery and the first trench to investigate the wider environment (Figure 7.2). With income now virtually assured, I was able to contemplate the mechanical stripping of large areas, which happened every year between 1966 and 1970, and I could employ site supervisors and pay subsistence to volunteers.

Figure 7.1. Owslebury. Aerial photograph of the farming settlement at Owslebury in 1964 (John Boyden)

Figure 7.2. Owslebury. Trench cut across a mid-1st century BC trackway, showing the build-up of colluvium and location of the column sample taken by John Evans.

Large-scale stripping of a site with a mechanical excavator was still something relatively new, though I was familiar with it first hand in Winchester, on the Slaughter House site in 1957 (Collis forthcoming) and the Wessex Hotel site in 1961 (this volume), as well as, from the literature, on

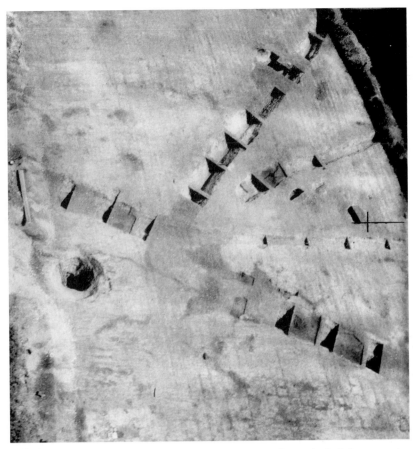

Figure 7.3. Owslebury. Aerial photograph of site Q, 1967, showing the method of the excavation of ditches.

Bandkeramik sites in the Netherlands, and the Czech site of Bylany (Soudský 1966) which I visited in 1967. Nor was it new on Iron Age sites in Britain, at Grimthorpe in 1961–2 (Stead 1968), and Tollard Royal in 1965, though in the latter case it was in the form of trenches, with the site criss-crossed with baulks, rather than complete clearance (Wainwright 1968, plate II). Sites on the gravels in the valleys of the Thames and Nene had also been subject to stripping on various scales. At Owslebury the plan was to completely clear individual enclosures, using a Drott rather than the more normal JCB, as the caterpillar tracks were less prone to sink into features than the rubber-tyred JCB, and by finishing with a back scrape a more even surface could be obtained, if slightly compacted, but which could easily be cleaned with shovel and trowel; it was also cheaper!

What we had to develop ourselves were methods of excavating the features. With pits and post-holes the usual method was to take out half the filling, draw the section, and then excavate the other half (though in the case of post-holes I would now recommend greater emphasis on the plan than the section – Collis 2003, 114–119). Our experience of ditches in 1965 led us to divide each ditch into 10-foot lengths, in each of which a 3-foot wide trench was dug to check the stratigraphy, before removing a 6-foot section, leaving a one-foot baulk for section drawing purposes – most were left intact at the end of the excavation (Figure 7.3). We learnt quickly that there were often disturbances in the ditches, from quarrying the sides to extract chalk, or from later burials. We could also identity in the initial cut the presence of recutting or deliberate infill, though these varied in their visibility from one section to another. Finally, when we felt we understood the ditches and their phases, we would investigate the often complex intersections. As far as possible ditches were excavated stratigraphically, but this was not easy where there were multiple recuts, and in ditch fills completely different deposits can be forming at the same time (*e.g.* fine grained soil on the edge of the ditch, coarse rubble in the centre), so the normal rules of stratigraphy did not apply. At this time the full complexity of how ditches filled in was being documented by the experimental earthwork on Overton Down (Jewell 1963), and it became clear that, unlike deep defensive ditches or shallow gullies, there was no simple way of excavating the medium sized ditches 1–2m deep with which we were dealing (Collis 2001). We tried various techniques, but none produced the detailed chronological divisions we wished for.

From 1963 onwards the fields were divided into areas, H, P, Q, S, *etc.* (Figure 7.4). Where there were trenches these were individually numbered (I, II, III, *etc.*) and each layer numbered (1, 2, 3, *etc.*), and a description entered into a site book. For the larger areas where there were no trenches, the finds were assigned the area letter and a layer number, as though they were large trenches. This was also done for the linear features, but the 10-foot lengths were distinguished by a letter of the alphabet (12A, 12B, 12C, *etc.*). All finds were double labelled with small luggage labels with site code year (*e.g.* OW68) and area, and layer number which could be marked on the pottery and animal bones, and also a brief mnemonic in case of mistakes ('Top 3" IADE', that is the disturbed top fill of the Iron Age Ditch East); pits and post-holes were assigned letters of the alphabet (Pit A, Pit AB, PH BBB, *etc.*), and these were also listed in the site book with a comment on the fill, stratigraphy, *etc.* Labels with the layer number were pinned in the sections so that these could be entered on the drawn sections. Finds were washed and marked on site, and bagged in polythene bags, and/or shoe boxes from a local shop, separated into major categories such as pottery, bone, sea shells, *etc.* The finds were mainly stored in a barn on the farm lent to us by Mr. Hellard, where we also set up a small exhibition for the volunteers and visitors.

The areas were divided up with a grid of 25-foot squares, marked by nails dipped in red paint and banged through tin lids to make them visible. The site was then given a 'pre-excavation' plan, on which all features natural and man-made were marked (*e.g.* patches of clay with flint, tree-throws), though the site was regularly inspected after light rain which could reveal features not immediately apparent after the first scraping. The plans at this stage were done in the 'pictorial' style championed by Bersu, but in black and white rather than colour; it quickly became clear that the symbolic method used by Wheeler was not adequate to show the subtleties of infill of ditches and pits. Sections of ditches were drawn every 20 feet, if not more closely, according to the complexity of the fill; the layer numbers on the labels were then entered on the drawings, which were recorded on graph paper or in the site note book. Finally, after excavation a simple line drawing of features was made showing the top and bottoms of features with hachures and the positions of baulks and sections, with numerous spot heights to show depth and slope. Detailed plans were made of features such as burials and ovens, along with photographs of assemblages of bones, sections, *etc.*

My undergraduate studies had a major influence on the project. I had been largely trained in urban contexts in which it was normal to discard animal bones; it was more obvious in a rural context that these threw light on a major aspect of the site's economy, and the impact of the Higgs' training at Cambridge was to invert the normal value placed on different classes of finds. It become a mantra on site that animal bones were more important than pottery, and when possible we organised training sessions on site in bone identification to encourage a high standard of recovery and care in excavation, including the recovery of microfauna such as rodents and amphibians. One failing is that we carried out minimal

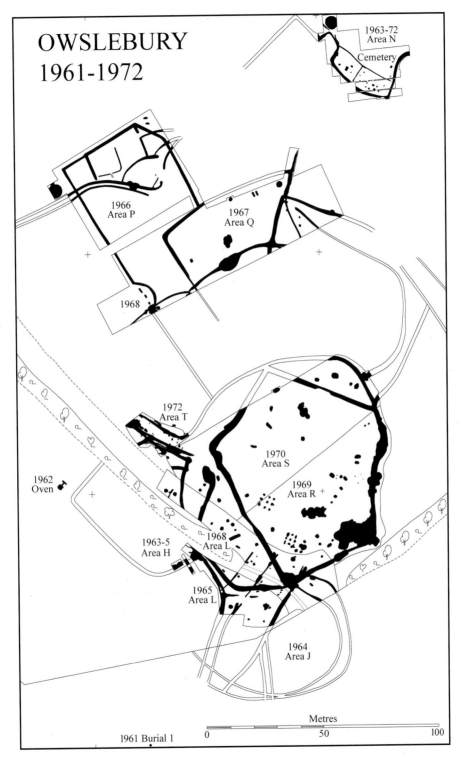

Figure 7.4. Owslebury. Plan of the areas excavated.

Figure 7.5. Owslebury 1969. Work in progress with flotation in the background.

sieving, and that very coarse grained. A major aim was to obtain as large a sample of bones as possible which led to the systematic clearing out of ditches, and so contrasts with excavations with a more cultural than economic paradigm where trenches were normally only trenched to give the sequence and dating evidence, for example at Gussage All Saints (Wainwright 1979, fig. 3). The success of this policy can be demonstrated numerically: 735 bones identified at Grimthorpe; 315 at Tollard Royal; 15,500 at Gussage; 110,000 at Owslebury. It is still the second largest assemblage from an Iron Age/Roman farming settlement in Britain (Maltby, pers. comm.).

The recovery of plant remains was less successful, and we encountered no deposits of burnt grain such as was normally used to study crops. But in 1967 Jane Renfrew suggested we try flotation, and this became a regular activity on the site using a water carrier in which to dump the soil and a plastic strainer to scoop off the flot (Figure 7.5). Our sampling strategy was non-existent ('haphazard'), and the methodology falls a long way below modern standards. It was good enough however to form the basis of Peter Murphy's Masters thesis on crops in Wessex in the Iron Age and Roman period (1977) and in this respect it was a pioneer survey which was not superseded for a number of years.

Environmental studies too were only partially successful. Owslebury was one of the first sites sampled in 1964 by John Evans in his revolutionary studies of snails on the chalklands, mainly from the ditches and pits which were under excavation at that time. But, with one exception, our first trench dug in 1964 on the line of a trackway where it crossed the bottom of a coombe where we had about a metre of colluvium (Figure 7.1), our trenches across visible lynchets produced a minimum of deposits, and our other two trenches dug in the valley bottom were equally unsuccessful, one hitting an area of relatively recent quarrying and the other mainly containing natural clay with flints with no artefacts and a minimal amount of evidence of deposition or geological structure.

Rethinking Little Woodbury

We had, however, begun to question some of Bersu's interpretations. Sadly, centuries of ploughing and erosion meant we identified no obvious buildings on the site other than two 9-post structures, presumably granaries. The 'working hollows' of Bersu seemed to us to be merely quarries for chalk, presumably for building and perhaps for marling, and all the Iron Age and Early Roman ditches and many pits had been subject to secondary quarrying. In the Late Roman period these small delvings were replaced by the more systematic digging of large open pits 3–4m deep, of which two were excavated. The site produced a range of ovens and corn-drying ovens, mainly late Roman in date, but more enigmatically four late Roman cess-pits whose presence on an unsophisticated rural settlement still requires explanation (some sort of collection for intensive cultivation, or a slave population whose movements were restricted?).

The major shift in interpretation was for the storage pits. It had seemed to me illogical to use grain stored in them for food as it would involve the continuous breaking of the seal; in other words, if a pit was opened, it was logical to use the contents in one go, and the obvious time to do this would be at sowing time. Independently experimental work by Bowen and Woods (1968), and later, by Peter Reynolds (1974), had demonstrated firstly that Bersu's calculations of capacity were wrong, and that corn stored in this way would retain a high level of fertility, contrary to what Bersu had assumed, and so his interpretation was turned on its head, with grain for food stored above ground where it was easily accessible on a daily basis, and seed grain underground. We also found in some cases evidence of continuous clearing out of the pits for re-use over a number of years (Collis 1970, 253). A more recent suggestion by Reynolds, that the grain might be stored for export seems unlikely, as the period in which the pits were used at Owslebury corresponds to a period when the evidence of trade is relatively slight, but they disappear when we have clear evidence of long-distance trade in the form of the Italian wine amphorae. I am also sceptical on a site such as Owslebury that the contents were used for feasting, as recently suggested by van der Veen and Jones (2007), though the deliberate concealment of surplus in case of emergency might be another possibility.

The settlement in its geographical and social context

After the initial phase of rescue and small-scale excavation, our ambition was to excavate a 'typical' farming settlement, and study its evolution over 800 years, something that had not really been attempted since the time of Pitt Rivers. Initially I conceived of the site as a self-sufficient entity, at least in its earlier phases, and I devised some simple models of the likely exploitation using least effort principles, and concepts such as 'maximising' and 'satisfising' locations as used by geographers such as Chisholm (1962) to consider why the farm may not have developed into a villa (Figure 7.6). From the start, however, it was clear that this was not true for the Roman period with the establishment of the civitas capital of Winchester (Venta Belgarum) some 20 kilometres away, and already in pre-conquest times, from the end of the Middle Iron Age, a surplus was being produced which allowed the import of luxury goods such as wine, presumably through the port of Hengistbury Head, and later fine pottery, probably via Colchester and Silchester, and in my doctoral thesis I explored the relationship of Owslebury to these sites in terms of core-periphery models (Collis 1984).

As a subsidiary part of my doctoral research I had collected information about rural settlements in Hampshire, using especially evidence from aerial photographs from John Boyden's collection, and also working systematically through the Cambridge collection which was not readily accessible to non-university researchers. It became clear that the number of Iron Age and Roman 'native settlements' far out-numbered villa sites, and it became another mantra of the Owslebury excavation that it was more important than villa sites as it was more representative of the rural population (Collis 1968, fig. 1), or indeed than Fishbourne which was unique! In reality I envisaged Owslebury as part of a settlement system, or rather of a number of changing systems throughout the 800 years in which it was occupied, with the trading links with ports such as Hengistbury Head and Colchester, and later with the network of civitas capitals and small towns of Roman Britain. For the Middle Iron Age there was the relationship with the hill-forts such as St. Catharine's Hill, which led to the two contrasting models propounded by myself based on Owslebury, and by Cunliffe based on Danebury. For Cunliffe,

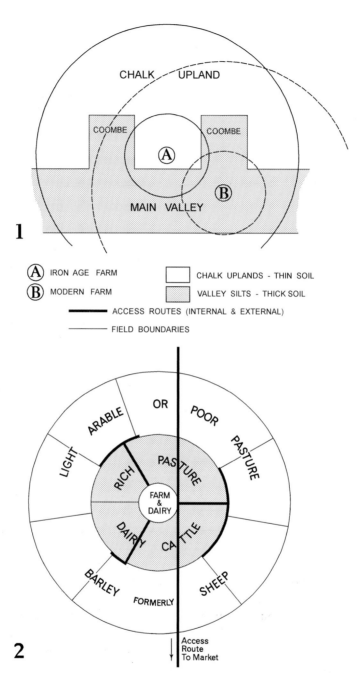

Figure 7.6. Owslebury. Simplified models of land use and a least effort model of exploitation of the modern farm which contrast with that assumed for the Iron Age farm, after Collis 1970. A first, and last for the Antiquaries Journal?

Danebury was a 'central place' co-ordinating trade and production under the control of a resident 'king' or 'chief' who redistributed goods to subsidiary settlements such as Owslebury, and coupled with a rise to dominance of 'developed hill-forts' at the expense of others.

In contrast I suggested a 'crisis' model (Collis 1981a) with the farming population agglomerating at times of need, but then either staying nucleated, or dispersing after the 'crisis'. The hill-fort was a focus of activity and population with only a few special roles such as defence, perhaps central storage and possibly ritual, but not of trade and production, and I could see nothing at Danebury which might indicate individuals of higher social status. Rather, I argued that over-nucleation could lead to inefficiency in agricultural production, whereas small settlements such as Owslebury were potentially more efficient and so could produce surpluses for trade more easily, as suggested by the presence of wine amphorae, gold and silver coins, fancy wagon fittings, *etc*. The contrasting settlement patterns around Danebury (nucleated) and St Catharine's Hill (dispersed) fit my model better, and most scholars have subsequently tended to follow my more egalitarian interpretation (*e.g.* Stopford 1988; Hill 1989, 1993a, 1993b).

The longevity of the site allowed us to look at the long-term trends as they affected an individual farming settlement, and so, for instance, contribute to the debate on the significance of single and multiple enclosures and access points (Figure 7.7; Collis 1970, 1993, 1996, 2006; Hingley 1984) in relationship to population size and social evolution. The burial evidence provided supporting evidence, especially with Calvin Wells' innovative approaches to skeletal analysis (Collis 1977; Morris 1992). The Iron Age and Roman coins gave a good idea of loss patterns on a rural settlement and their significance and meaning, an important topic of discussion in the 1970s (Allen 1965; Collis 1969, 1981c; Casey and Reece 1974/1988), while the querns provided a major input into David Peacock's ground-breaking study of the quern production at Lodsworth (Peacock 1987). Our policy of almost complete excavation of features and recording methods also led to pioneer studies of the deposition of pottery (Pierpoint 1981) and animal bones (Maltby 1989; Albarella 2007), though in a functional way following the ideas of Schiffer (1975) rather than the more ideologically based interpretations of the 1990s (*e.g.* Hill 1995; Poole 1995).

Owslebury and the development of rural archaeology

The excavation was helped by a number of senior archaeologists who provided moral support and help in obtaining grants: Christopher Hawkes, Collin Bowen, Martin Biddle, John Brailsford, Derek Allen, Graham Webster; but it lacked any institutional support. The Hampshire Field Club which oversaw the finances was itself going through an internal crisis from which it did not recover until the 1970s. There was no museum interested in the finds; the policy of Winchester Museum was only to take finds from the city, and it was another decade before the Hampshire Museum Service was established and agreed to take the finds. As a temporary measure we sold three of the grave groups to the British Museum which provided us with funds to carry out conservation work on finds from the cemetery, notably the Iron Age sword and shield boss from Burial 39 (Collis 1973, 1994b). Though we had a close relationship with the village (*e.g.* a rota of bath nights for the diggers), the site on a working farm was not one where we could encourage visitors, especially during an outbreak of foot and mouth disease, and there was nothing much visible on the site outside the excavation season. Hampshire County Council was more interested in funding the Butser Ancient Farm, and the excavation of Danebury which it owned, and which had great potential for tourism and recreation. The training school set up at Owslebury in 1966 and 1967 by Alan Aberg did not survive his move from Southampton Extra Mural Studies to Leeds.

What the long-term impact of the excavation has been is difficult to judge. Information about the excavation was disseminated, at least within the archaeological world, though interim reports (Collis

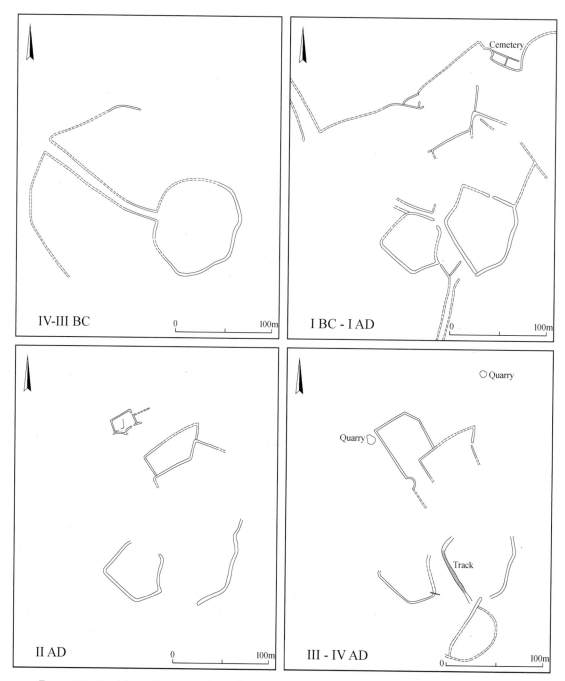

Figure 7.7. Owslebury. Phasing of the settlement, contrasting single access with multiple access layouts.

1968, 1970) and through *Current Archaeology* 25 (1971) – Andrew Selkirk was the nephew of the farmer, so was a regular visitor – and through lectures, even if the one at the Society of Antiquaries was delivered in candlelight without slides due to an national electricians' strike! As a site paying subsistence to volunteers, it was on the circuit for students looking for excavation experience, several of whom went on to archaeological careers: Ian Kinnes, Dave Whipp, Gill Huxley (Varndell), Roger Palmer, Jude Plouviez, Graham Black, Alison Taylor, John Bintliff. Through the Association for Cultural Exchange we had connections with Poland and Czechoslovakia, and among their American students were some who continued in the profession: John Cole, John Jameson, and Joan Gero for whom Owslebury was an influence in her feminist critique of American archaeology (positively, as an example of a non-sexist field project!). Through the Association Française pour l'Étude de l'Âge du Fer, Owslebury has also had some influence on the upsurge of the study of Iron Age rural settlements in France (Collis 1990, 1993, 2001).

One piece of advice I did not take was from Sir Mortimer Wheeler, in giving me a small grant from the British Academy to prepare the first interim report, that I should not dig more than I could publish. Though I had originally planned to work on the animal bones and pottery myself, the sheer scale of the excavation and the quantity of finds made this impossible, and at that time there were no funds or facilities available. Owslebury was typical of the sites which were building up pressure in the 1960s and 1970s of unstudied and unpublished material, a problem which was fortunately addressed by English Heritage in the 1980s with the establishment of the Faunal Units and grants from the British Academy and the Leverhulme Trust for the study of pottery and other finds, initiatives from which Owslebury benefited. Work is now going on towards the final publication of the site, which I hope will include a fundamentally new way of constructing a chronology for the Iron Age using a concept of horizons and attributes rather than the usual phases and type fossils (cf. Collis 2008; 2009), especially given the failure of the Danebury project to progress much beyond Cunliffe's original 'ceramic phases' developed in the 1960s.

More recent public exposure of the site has been less fortunate. The Winchester treasure, of gold brooches, necklaces and bracelets (Hill *et al.* 2004) dating to the mid 1st century BC was found 5–6 kilometres from the site, and Owslebury appeared (anonymously) in the disastrous BBC series *Hidden Treasure*. My connections with the programme-makers broke down when their researcher left, so I had no input whatsoever in the subsequent programme. On the basis of the size of the banjo enclosure (which they claimed they had discovered!), there are now suggestions that this may be some sort of 'royal' site. The banjo enclosure had been levelled 200 years before the treasure was buried, and the film makers completely failed to realise that I had excavated burials contemporary with the treasure, notably burial 39 with its weapons which provided the closest parallels in Europe for those found on the battlefield of Alesia (Figure 7.8; Collis 1973, 1994b; Sievers, in Reddé and von Schnurbein 2001). Though I have belatedly received a half apology from Mark Thompson, the Director General of the BBC, it does leave unresolved questions about quality control of television 'documentaries'. The programme did however initiate a geophysical survey of the site by Pre-Construct Geophysics, which we were able to continue in 2008 (at the time of the excavation Tony Clarke had advised me that, in the then state of the art, the mechanical excavator would be quicker and more effective!), but the new evidence has changed our perspective of, for instance, the location of the cemetery and problems of access to the site (Figure 7.9).

In 1972, with diminishing returns, and no resolution about the future of the finds or publication, the Ministry of Public Building and Works decided to halt further funding, and that last season was used to finish off final pressing problems like completing the excavation of the cemetery and the entrance to the banjo enclosure. The site shed and excavation equipment were handed over to the Butser Farm Project, and I left to work in France. In many ways Owslebury was the predecessor of

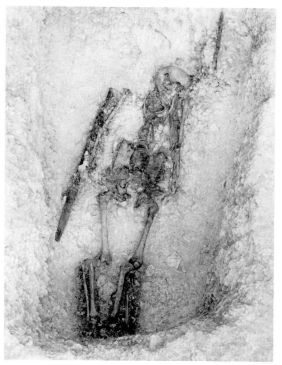

Figure 7.8 (left). Owslebury. Burial 39, an inhumation with weapons dated to the mid-1st century BC.

Figure 7.9 (below). Owslebury. The geophysical survey of the settlement by Pre-Construct Geophysics, 2008.

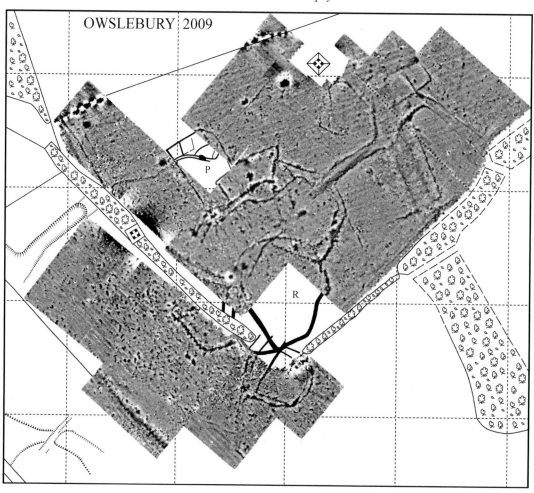

the Danebury and Danebury Environs projects, though their evolution was parallel rather than a direct descendant from our project, and simply reflected the changing attitudes and methodologies at the time. By the 1970s a new consensus had appeared about the excavation of rural settlements, for instance between excavators such as myself and Geoff Wainwright, even though our backgrounds and academic training were very different. It may not be clear what influence, if any, Owslebury had on the long term trends in Iron Age and Roman archaeology, but it stands as an exemplar of the changes which were happening in the 1960s both in theory and methodology, and their inter-relationship.

References

Albarella, U. 2007. The end of the Sheep Age: people and animals in the Late Iron Age, in C. Haselgrove and T. Moore (eds), *The Later Iron Age in Britain and Beyond*, 389–402. Oxford: Oxbow Books.

Alcock, L. 1972. The Irish Sea Province in the Pre-Roman Iron Age, in A. C. Thomas (ed.), *The Iron Age in the Irish Sea Province*, 99–112. Council for British Archaeology, Research Report 9.

Allen, D. F. 1965. A Celtic miscellany. *The British Numismatic Journal* 34, 1–7.

Bowen, H. C. 1961. *Ancient Fields: a tentative analysis of vanishing earthworks and landscapes.* London: British Association for the Advancement of Science.

Bowen, H. C. and Woods, P. D. 1968. Experimental storage of corn underground and its implications for Iron Age settlements. *Bulletin of the Institute of Archaeology* 7, 1–14.

Brailsford, J. 1948. Excavations at Little Woodbury. Part II: the pottery. *Proceedings of the Prehistoric Society* 14, 1–18.

Casey, J. and Reece, R. (eds) 1974. *Coins and the Archaeologist.* Oxford: British Archaeological Reports 4. (Second edition, 1988. London: Seaby).

Chisholm, M. 1962. *Rural Settlement and Land Use.* London: Hutchinson.

Clark, J. G. D. 1966. British prehistory: the invasion hypothesis. *Antiquity* 40, 197–299.

Clarke, D. L. 1972. A provisional model of an Iron Age society and its settlement system, in D. L. Clarke (ed.) *Models in Archaeology*, 801–69. London: Methuen.

Coles, J. M. and Minnitt, S. 1995. *Industrious and Fairly Civilised: the Glastonbury Lake Village.* Exeter: Somerset Levels Project and Somerset County Museums Service.

Collis, J. R. 1968. Excavations at Owslebury, Hants: an interim report. *Antiquaries Journal* 48, 18–31.

Collis, J. R. 1970. Excavations at Owslebury, Hants: a second interim report. *Antiquaries Journal* 50, 246–261.

Collis, J. R. 1971. Functional and theoretical interpretations of British coinage. *World Archaeology* 3, 71–84.

Collis, J. R. 1973. Burials with weapons in Iron Age Britain. *Germania* 51, 121–133.

Collis, J. R. 1977. Owslebury (Hants) and the problem of burials on rural settlements, in R. M. Reece (ed.) 1977, 26–34.

Collis, J. R. 1981a. A theoretical study of hill-forts, in G. Guilbert (ed.) *Hill-fort Studies: papers presented to A. H. A. Hogg*, 66–76. Leicester: Leicester University Press.

Collis, J. R. 1981b. Coinage, oppida, and the rise of Belgic power: a reply, in B. W. Cunliffe (ed.) 1981, 53–55.

Collis, J. R. 1981c. A typology of coin distributions. *World Archaeology* 13, 122–28.

Collis, J. R. 1984. *Oppida: earliest towns north of the Alps.* Sheffield: Department of Prehistory and Archaeology.

Collis, J. R 1985. Review of Cunliffe 1984. *Proceedings of the Prehistoric Society* 51, 348–349.

Collis, J. R. 1990. L'impact des processus d'urbanisation sur les sites ruraux: le cas d'Owslebury, Hants. Angleterre, in A. Duval, J. P. le Bihan and Y. Menez (eds), *Les Gaulois d'Armorique. La fin de l'Âge du Fer en Europe Tempérée*, 209–22. Revue Archéologique de l'Ouest, Supplément 3.

Collis, J. R. 1993. Structures d'habitat et enceintes de l'Âge du Fer, in A. Daubigney (ed.), *Fonctionnement Social de l'Âge du Fer; opérateurs et hypothèses pour la France*, 231–38. Table Ronde Internationale de Lons-le-Saunier (Jura) 24–26 Octobre 1990. Lons-Le-Saunier.

Collis, J. R. 1994a. The Iron Age, in B. Vyner (ed.), *Building on the Past: a celebration of 150 years of the Royal Archaeological Institute*, 123–48. Royal Archaeological Institute.

Collis, J. R. 1994b. An Iron Age and Roman Settlement at Owslebury, Hants, in A. Fitzpatrick and E. Morris (eds), *The Iron Age in Wessex: recent work*, 106–8. Salisbury: Trust for Wessex Archaeology.

Collis, J. R. 1996. Hill-forts, enclosures and boundaries, in T. Champion and J. Collis (eds), *The Iron Age in Britain and Ireland: recent trends*, 87–94. Sheffield: J.R. Collis Publications.

Collis, J. R. 2001. *Society and Settlement in Iron Age Europe; L'Habitat et l'Occupation du Sol en Europe*. Actes du XVIIIe Colloque de l'AFEAF, Winchester – Avril 1994. Sheffield: J. R. Collis Publications.

Collis, J. R. 2002. Danebury, its environs and the Iron Age in Hampshire. *Landscape Archaeology*, 91–94.

Collis, J. R. 2006. Enclosure in an open landscape: Iron Age Wessex and modern Amblés Valley, in A. Harding, N. Venclová and S. Sievers (eds), *Enclosing the Past: inside and outside in prehistory*, 155–62. Sheffield: J.R. Collis Publications.

Collis, J. R. 2008. Constructing chronologies: lessons from the Iron Age, in A. Lehoërff (ed.) *Constuire le temps*, 85–104. Glux-en-Glenne: Bibracte, Collection Bibracte 16.

Collis, J. R. 2009. Die konstruktion von Chronologien, in R. Karl and J. Leskovar (eds) *Interpretierte Eisenzeiten: Fallstudien, Methoden, Theorie. Tagungsbericht der 3. Linzer Gespräche zur interpretativen Eisenzeitarchäeologie*. Studien zur Kulturgeschichte von Oberosterreich 22, 373–421.

Cunliffe, B. W. (ed.) 1981. *Coinage and Society in Britain and Gaul: some current problems*. London: Council for British Archaeology, Research Report 38.

Cunliffe, B. W. 1978a. *Iron Age Communities in Britain*. (2nd edition). London: Routledge and Kegan Paul.

Curwen, E. and Curwen, E. C. 1923. Sussex lynchets and their associated field-ways. *Sussex Archaeological Collections* 64, 1–65.

Fasham, P. and Collis, J. 1980. Excavations and field survey at Borough Farm, Micheldever, Hants. *Proceedings of the Hampshire Field Club and Archaeological Society* 36, 145–52.

Grimes, W. F. 1960. Some smaller settlements: a symposium (Draughton, Colsterworth, Heathrow), in S. S. Frere, *Problems of the Iron Age in Southern Britain*, 17–28. London: Institute of Archaeology, Occasional Papers 11.

Hamilton, J. R. C. 1956. *Excavations at Jarlshof, Shetland*. Edinburgh: HMSO.

Hamilton, J. R. C. 1968. *Excavations at Clickhimin, Shetland*. Edinburgh: HMSO.

Harding, D. W. and Blake, I. M. 1963. An Early Iron Age settlement in Dorset. *Antiquity* 37, 63–64.

Harding, D. W., Blake, I. M. and Reynolds, P. J. 1993. *An Iron Age Settlement in Dorset; excavation and reconstruction*. University of Edinburgh: Department of Archaeology, Monograph Series no. 1.

Hawkes, C. F. C. 1939. The excavations at Quarley Hill, 1938. *Proceedings of the Hampshire Field Club and Archaeological Society* 14, 136–194.

Hawkes, C. F. C. 1959. The ABC of the British Iron Age. *Antiquity* 33, 170–182.

Hawkes, C. F. C. 1960. The ABC of the British Iron Age, in S. S. Frere, *Problems of the Iron Age in Southern Britain*, 1–16. London: Institute of Archaeology, Occasional Papers 11.

Hawkes, C. F. C. and Dunning, G. C. 1931. The Belgae of Gaul and Britain. *Archaeological Journal* 87, 150–335.

Hawkes, C. F. C. and Piggott, S. 1947. Britons, Romans and Saxons around Salisbury Plain and in Cranborne Chase. *Antiquaries Journal* 104, 150–335.

Hawkes, S. C. 1994. Longbridge Down, Cow Down, Wiltshire, House 3: a major roundhouse of the Early Iron Age. *Oxford Journal of Archaeology* 13, 49–70.

Hill, J. D. 1989. Rethinking the Iron Age. *Scottish Archaeological Review* 6, 16–23.

Hill, J. D. 1993a. Danebury and the hillforts of Iron Age Wessex, in T. C. Champion and J. R. Collis (eds), *The Iron Age in Britain and Ireland: recent trends*, 95–116. Sheffield: J. R. Collis Publications.

Hill, J. D. 1993b. Can we identify a different European past? A contrastive archaeology of later prehistoric settlements in southern England. *Journal of European Archaeology* 1, 57–76.

Hill, J. D. 1995. *Ritual and Rubbish in the Iron Age of Wessex: a study on the formation of a specific archaeological record*. British Archaeological Reports, British Series 242. Oxford: Tempus Reperatum.

Hill, J. D., Spence, A. J., La Niece, S. and Worrell, S. 2004. The Winchester Hoard: a find of unique Iron Age gold jewellery. *Antiquaries Journal* 84,1–22.

Hingley, R. 1984. Towards social analysis in archaeology: Celtic society in the Iron Age of the Upper Thames Valley, in B. Cunliffe and D. Miles (eds), *Aspects of the Iron Age in Central Southern Britain*, 72–88. Oxford: University of Oxford Committee for Archaeology, Monograph 2.

Hodson, F. R. 1960. Some reflections on the 'ABC' of the British Iron Age. *Antiquity* 34, 138–140.

Hodson, F. R. 1962. Some pottery from Eastbourne, the 'Marnians' and the pre-Roman Iron Age. *Proceedings of the Prehistoric Society* 28, 140–155.

Hodson, F. R. 1964. Cultural groupings within the British pre-Roman Iron Age. *Proceedings of the Prehistoric Society* 30, 99–110.

Hodson, F. R. 1968. *The La Tène Cemetery of Münsingen–Rain.* Acta Bernensia 5.

Jewell, P. 1963. *The Experimental Earthwork on Overton Down Project 1960.* London: British Association for the Advancement of Science.

Mackie, E. W. 1965. The origin and development of the broch and wheelhouse building cultures of the Scottish Iron Age. *Proceedings of the Prehistoric Society* 33, 93–146.

Maltby, M. 1987. *The Animal Bones from the Excavation at Owslebury: an Iron Age and Early Romano-British settlement.* London: English Heritage Ancient Monuments Laboratory, Report 6/67.

Morris, I. 1992. *Death-Ritual and Social Structure in Classical Antiquity.* Cambridge and New York: Cambridge University Press.

Murphy, P. 1977. *Early Agriculture and Environment on the Hampshire Chalklands circa 800 BC–400 AD.* Unpublished M.Phil. Thesis, University of Southampton.

Peacock, D. P. S. 1987. Iron Age and Roman quern production at Lodsworth, West Sussex. *Antiquaries Journal* 67, 61–85.

Pierpoint, S. J. 1981. *Report on the Iron Age and Roman pottery from Owslebury, Hampshire.* Unpublished report.

Poole, C. 1995. Pits and propitiation, in B. W. Cunliffe, *Danebury: an Iron Age hillfort in Hampshire. 6: a hillfort community in perspective*, 249–75. London: Council for British Archaeology, Research Report 102.

Reddé, M. and von Schnurbein, S. (eds) 2001. *Alésia: fouilles et recherches franco-allemandes sur les travaux militaires autour de Mont Auxois (1991–1997).* Mémoires de l'Académie des Inscriptions et Belles Lettres 21. Paris: Diffusion de Boccard, 2 vols.

Reece, R. M. (ed.) 1977. *Burial in the Roman World.* London: Council for British Archaeology Research Report no 22.

Reynolds, P. J. 1974. Experimental Iron Age storage pits. *Proceedings of the Prehistoric Society* 40, 118–131.

Rodwell, W. J. 1976. Coinage, oppida, and the rise of Belgic power in south-eastern Britain, in B. W. Cunliffe and T. Rowley (eds), *Oppida in Barbarian Europe*, 181–367. Oxford: British Archaeological Reports, Supplementary Series 11.

Schiffer, M. B. 1975. *Behavioral Archeology.* New York: Academic Press.

Soudský, B. 1966. *Bylany: osada nejstarších zemědělců z mladší kamenné (Bylany: a settlement of the earliest agriculturists from the late stone age).* Prague: Academia.

Stead, I. M. 1968. An Iron Age hill-fort at Grimthorpe, Yorkshire, England. *Proceedings of the Prehistoric Society* 34, 148–190.

Stopford, J. 1988. Danebury: an alternative view. *Scottish Archaeological Review* 4.2, 70–75.

Wainwright, G. J. 1968. The excavation of a Durotrigian farmstead at Tollard Royal in Cranbourne Chase, southern England. *Proceedings of the Prehistoric Society* 34, 102–147.

Wainwright, G. J. 1979. *Gussage All Saints: an Iron Age settlement in Dorset.* London: Department of the Environment, Archaeological Reports No. 10.

Williams, A. 1947. Excavations at Langford Downs, Oxon (near Lechlade) in 1943. *Oxoniensia* 11–12, 44–64.

The Danebury decades

Barry Cunliffe

At the end of July 1969 a small group, having just completed the season's excavation at Portchester Castle, descended on the unsuspecting hillfort of Danebury, then largely hidden in a dense beechwood, crowning a prominent hilltop in the gently undulating chalk downland of eastern Hampshire (Figure 8.1). The team, about 20 strong, was made up of trench-hardened volunteers who had been digging for some years at Fishbourne and Portchester, leavened by undergraduates from the recently-created Department of Archaeology at Southampton University. None of us, arriving on the hill for the first time that July morning, could have guessed that the Danebury project, in its various manifestations, would last for 40 years. As I write these words the last set of excavation reports are going through their proof stage and are due to be published in July 2008.

The 1969 excavation at the hillfort came about as the result of two wish-lists colliding. A year or so earlier Hampshire County Council had purchased the hillfort at the instigation of its energetic and far-sighted County Land Agent, Colin Bonsey, with the intention of making it a countryside open space for people to visit and enjoy. The intention was to enliven it with a trail giving information about the natural history and archaeology of the site. Bonsey realized that to do this required a programme of investigation and he turned to Professor Christopher Hawkes of Oxford University for advice – an obvious choice since Hawkes had carried out limited trial excavations in the nearby hillforts of Quarley Hill, Bury Hill and Balksbury in the years immediately before the Second World War.

The second wish-list was my own. I had been appointed to the newly-created Chair of Archaeology at the University of Southampton in 1966 – the first student intake arriving in the autumn of 1967. It was highly desirable to set up a Wessex-based excavation which could provide training and a research focus for them. Since I was at the time working on a book on the Iron Age of Britain, in which the problem of hillforts necessarily featured large, a Wessex hillfort was the obvious choice. Christopher Hawkes, knowing this, put me in contact with Colin Bonsey – and the rest is history.

The excavation on the hillfort of Danebury lasted 20 seasons (1969–88) and was published in five volumes (Cunliffe 1984a and b; Cunliffe and Poole 1991a and b; Cunliffe 1995). This was immediately followed by an eight-year programme of excavations on other Iron Age sites in the region, including the hillforts of Woolbury and Bury Hill. The Danebury Environs Programme (1989–96) as it became known was published in two volumes (the second comprising seven separate parts) (Cunliffe 2000; Cunliffe and Poole 2000a–g). A third programme followed – the Danebury Environs Roman Programme (1997–2006) – which examined seven Iron Age and Roman sites in the region: it too was published in two volumes, the second similarly divided into seven parts (Cunliffe 2008; Cunliffe and Poole 2008a–g).

It is not possible, in the space of this short chapter, to give even a summary overview of all 38 seasons of excavation. Some general background to the first 24 seasons has already been published (Cunliffe 1993b). Here we will restrict ourselves to a few specific themes of general relevance to archaeology today.

Figure 8.1. Aerial view of Danebury after many of the trees in the interior had been removed.

Why dig at all?

The Danebury programmes were carefully structured to meet a series of research objectives but it would be nonsense to suggest that we set out, in 1969, to plan for the next 38 years of digging! The research structure was constantly being modified as the work progressed and results were fed back to generate a more nuanced understanding of the issues, and as new questions were being framed within the discipline.

We began at a time when Iron Age studies were in their infancy. The old invasionist model had only recently been discredited and it seemed to be time to draw together what was known of the British Iron Age and to set some guidelines for future advances. Reviewing the evidence for the whole country showed, quite starkly, just how anecdotal our knowledge base was and how small scale had been most of the excavations – with a few notable exceptions like Mortimer Wheeler's work at Maiden Castle. I summed up that review by writing:

> The questions which we are asking of our material today are far more complex than those posed in the past: they concern change and equilibrium. The methods of study are necessarily more arduous and lengthy, but if the subject is to progress, rather than accrete, we must not be afraid to undertake projects requiring broader vision and rigorous discipline. (Cunliffe 1974, 313)

Those words were written early in 1971 after we had completed the first stage of the excavation at Danebury, which had focused on the defences, and were now contemplating the possibility of large-scale excavations within the interior of the fort. We could easily have stopped at that point – there was a story to tell which served the County Council's educational needs – but had we done so comparatively little would have been added to our understanding of the Iron Age apart from another rampart section and a gate sequence – accretion rather than advance. Danebury offered a rare opportunity to revolutionize our understanding of hillforts. Thus two decisions were made – to invest a high level of resource in examining the interior of the hillfort over a number of years and, in parallel, to make a study of the broader Danebury region in order to provide the context within which to attempt to understand the social and economic functions of the fort. The resulting survey, which began in 1971 (Bowen and Cunliffe 1973), was subsequently taken over, to our great relief, by the Royal Commission on the Historic Monuments of England (RCHME) and resulted in a ground-breaking publication (Palmer 1984) which has served as a vital reference for all subsequent work in the Danebury landscape. The area excavations within the fort lasted for a further 18 seasons at the end of which over 50% of the interior had been examined (Figure 8.2).

The progress of the excavation was guided by a number of factors. The overriding aim was to acquire

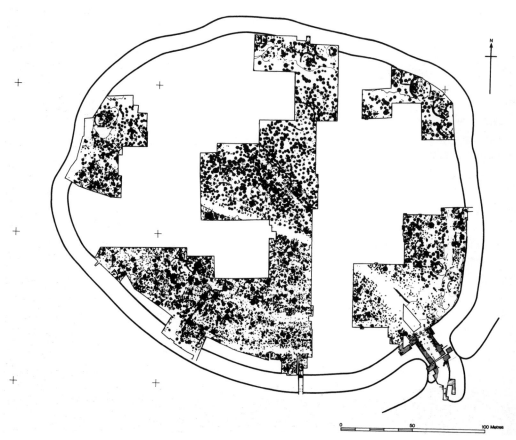

Figure 8.2. The excavated area within Danebury. About 50% of the enclosed 2.5ha was excavated.

a large body of data that would be susceptible to statistical analysis reflecting, insofar as possible, the different zones within the defences. The hill was tree-covered when the project began but the trees were rapidly dying of beech bark necrosis and were being cut down in the interests of public safety. This meant that we could not apply a rigorous statistical sampling methodology and, at least in the early years, had to be opportunist in choosing the areas for digging. A further restraint to the siting of excavations was that we had decided at the outset to excavate large contiguous areas, rather than to dissipate effort in smaller more scattered excavations, hoping in this way to better understand the overall plan of the settlement.

It soon became clear that the enclosed area divided into two broad zones: the interior where the topsoil lay directly on the natural chalk with no surviving stratigraphy except that preserved in features cut into the chalk (Figure 8.3), and the peripheral zone extending for 10–15m immediately inside the rampart where stratified deposits up to a metre and a half in depth survived. Clearly the potential of this peripheral zone was considerable in that it provided a tight stratigraphical sequence and, as we were to find out, the conditions here were such that the structural evidence of timber buildings was remarkably well preserved allowing successive contemporary ground surfaces to be exposed in a detail seldom before seen (Figure 8.4). The excavation strategy aimed to examine both the central and

Figure 8.3. Area excavation within Danebury showing the work of one season.

Figure 8.4. Well stratified houses in the zone immediately behind the rampart at Danebury.

peripheral zones in large area excavations, the peripheral zone being sampled at several places around the circumference of the fort.

Since the aim was to maximize the data recovered we adopted a policy of total excavation within each chosen area, except for three seasons (1979–81) when a sampling strategy was adopted. The area chosen for this experiment lay in the central zone where no superficial stratigraphy survived, the archaeological evidence being restricted to pits, post-holes and other small features like gullies and stake-holes cut into the natural chalk. The policy for these three years was to strip a large area and to totally excavate all features except the pits. The pits would be examined selectively based on a 10% sample (later increased to 20%) chosen randomly. The reasoning behind this sampling policy was that whilst we needed to understand the site in plan we had already excavated about a thousand pits and the results were becoming repetitive. The advantage of sampling was that a much larger area could be examined for the same resource. In the event, the sampling was found to so inhibit interpretation that it was quickly abandoned.

Another approach to sampling was to retrospectively sample the large areas already totally excavated, using various sampling strategies, to assess the usefulness and validity of results that would have been obtained had the site been excavated using these constraints. The results showed that most sampling strategies, while valid at certain levels, would have greatly inhibited the more detailed interpretation of the site (Lock and Cunliffe 1995, 111–17). In other words if the research strategy required a high resolution of social, chronological and spatial issues it was necessary to excavate large areas totally.

The excavation of the hillfort of Danebury was one element in the broader research framework. The publication of the Danebury survey (Palmer 1984), covering an area of 450km² around the hillfort, provided the necessary database upon which to plan the next stage of the work – *The Danebury Environs Programme* (1989–96) – the aim of which was to sample the range of Iron Age sites in the region so that the social and economic trajectories within the study area could be identified and explained (Figure 8.5). Fortunately a number of Iron Age sites in the Danebury region had been examined on a small scale in the 1930s and more were currently being excavated under rescue conditions (Cunliffe 2000, 10–13). The sites we chose, therefore, were selected to augment the existing database but had the added value that since they were dug to the standards adopted at Danebury, the datasets could be directly compared. The list included the neighbouring hillforts of Woolbury and Bury Hill, the multiple ditched enclosure of Suddern Farm, the small banjo enclosure of Nettlebank Copse (Figure 8.6), two rectilinear enclosures attached to linear boundaries at New Buildings and linear boundaries related to field systems in two locations, one near Quarley Hill, the other to the east of Danebury.

The results of the excavations and analyses were to show just how complex the Iron Age really was. The simple model we had developed in the early stages of the programme had to be scrapped and replaced by a far more intricate narrative allowing each individual site its own place in the story (Cunliffe 2000, 149–96). The broader implication is that each region of Britain is likely to have followed its own trajectories and until more intensive regional surveys have been undertaken our understanding of the Iron Age of the country as a whole is unlikely to advance significantly.

One of the follow-ups to the Danebury Environs Programme was *The Wessex Hillforts Project* carried out by a partnership between English Heritage and the Institute of Archaeology at Oxford (Payne, Corney and Cunliffe 2006). Its aim was to examine 18 hillforts in Wessex, using detailed ground survey and geophysics in order to characterize the sites and thus to display their similarities and their differences. The results showed that, while there is a very considerable variety among the hillforts of this comparatively restricted region, the patterns which emerged could be built into a narrative, compatible to that constructed on the basis of the Danebury study, to give a far more subtle appreciation of the place of hillforts in Iron Age society in central southern Britain. The project also demonstrated, with great clarity, the immense potential of geophysical survey.

As the Danebury Environs Programme proceeded it became increasingly apparent that the Roman invasion, which began in AD 43, had had comparatively little effect on the settlement development of the Hampshire downland and that ending the study at the beginning of the Roman interlude would thus be unnecessarily arbitrary. Extending the project to include sites of the Roman age would allow a full cycle of agrarian development to be studied from its inception in the Mid Bronze Age to its demise with the collapse of the Roman economic system – in broad chronological terms, from 1500 BC to AD 500. Thus it was that in 1997 *The Danebury Environs Roman Project* was initiated – a programme which was to last for ten seasons during which time five Roman villas (Figure 8.7) and two non-villa

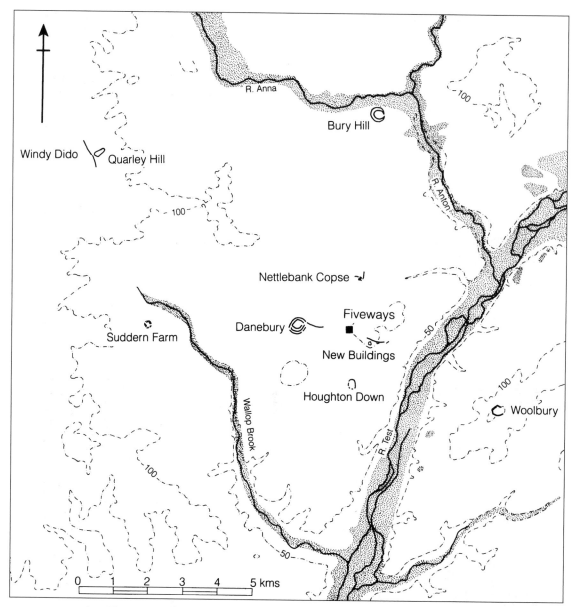

Figure 8.5. The sites examined during the Danebury Environs Programme.

settlements (one of which turned out to have been wholly Iron Age!) were excavated. The objectives were to examine the effects of romanization on an established rural community focusing on such themes as land-holding, economy and technology transfer in an attempt to identify patterns of continuity and discontinuity. By keeping landscape as a constant it was easier to contain and explain the variables.

So it was that the Danebury project developed from its very modest beginnings in 1969. The 38 seasons of comparatively large-scale excavation (*c.* 1500m² per year) have generated a considerable database which has enabled us to achieve our major objectives. The work has also allowed us to pursue many other themes. For example, it has provided a fascinating insight into the aims and aspirations

Figure 8.6. The excavation of the banjo enclosure at Nettlebank Copse in progress.

Figure 8.7. The aisled hall at Grateley. One of the major buildings within a Roman villa complex.

of nineteenth and early twentieth century antiquarians and has generated much sobering evidence vividly displaying the destructive effects of modern agriculture. These are among the many outputs that feed into other research initiatives. But perhaps most important is that a massive database now exists to be worked and reworked by researchers with their own agendas to explore.

Making it all work

In terms of organization I have always pursued a minimalist policy – a minimum amount of infrastructure to achieve the maximum research output. The Danebury projects were under the auspices of the Danebury Trust which soon came into existence to replace an initial organizing committee. The Trust, composed of elected representatives of Hampshire County Council and attended by the relevant County Officers and by representatives of English Heritage, met once a year on site to inspect the work and to discuss and agree the next year's programme. The Trust was one of the three strengths on which the project was founded (the other two being English Heritage and the Institute of Archaeology at Oxford). It provided a direct link to the county's archaeological services in the Planning Office and to the County Museums Service, responsible for curating the finds and archive, and whose education officers helped to communicate the excitement of the excavation to the county's schools. English Heritage's involvement ensured that the projects were guided by national agendas and standards and offered financial help (when rescue work was undertaken) as well as valuable technical assistance throughout. The Institute of Archaeology (where I was based) provided the research infrastructure of the operation and the academic input so essential in maintaining the relevance of the research thrust. This firm tripod of underpinning, involving a local authority, the national heritage body and a university, has very much to recommend it. It has ensured that the project has remained firmly bedded in local needs and aspirations while being continually informed by national and international agendas.

Throughout, the Danebury excavations have been run in the British tradition of the volunteer dig, initiated by Wheeler in the 1930s, involving a small core staff employed for the duration, leading a large volunteer force made up of local people and students from Britain and abroad. Crucial to the success of the project has been the continuity of the core team and the maintenance of a strict work ethic, inherited from the earlier projects of Fishbourne and Portchester, which has meant that new volunteers have known exactly what was expected of them from the moment of their arrival. I strongly believe that directors should be present on site throughout and should lead from the front – there is no better way of making clear what is expected and instilling standards than by working alongside the digging force.

The Danebury projects have been particularly fortunate in having had a high percentage of staff and volunteers return year after year bringing with them not only their increasing knowledge but also their dedication: several of the more mature diggers present during the last season in 2006 first joined the project as bright-eyed youngsters in the mid-1970s. Danebury has also provided a training ground for young people who have gone on to become professionals in universities, museums, heritage management and the units. Although we have never set out to provide formal training, our volunteers have learned the essentials by being creative members of a hard-working team.

Perhaps the most difficult aspect of the whole project has been maintaining an income stream year on year to fund the 38 successive seasons. A degree of stability was provided by a level of core funding from the County Council while a contribution from English Heritage for the rescue aspects of part of the work meant that a few short-term contracts were available to underpin some of the post-excavation work, but each year it was necessary to raise grants from trusts and other research sponsors.

We managed but not without some difficulty. The way funding is organized in Britain makes it very difficult to set up a long-term field programme with any degree of assurance. This places a serious limitation on research and encourages short-termism which is not good for the discipline.

Ideals and aspirations

All field projects have operational ideals to which they aspire and most are shared in common by us all. What follows is a brief comment on a few of the drivers which have been given particular emphasis during the Danebury programmes.

High on our list of priorities was to work at the scale appropriate to the research aims of the project. This required designing the excavations to explore large contiguous areas and, as far as possible, to excavate totally, except in the case of extensive linear features, like ditches, which were usually sampled on a 25% basis. Experiments with other types of sampling, as we have seen above, showed that too much is lost if the scale of the sampling is increased, the resulting narrative becoming the poorer. It is, I believe, a regrettable consequence of much developer-funded excavation that contractors are encouraged to sample at much too small a fraction. In some instances one might wonder if the results of this kind of work have any value at all.

Our second aspiration was to record at a high degree of detail in the field and in particular to invest time and skill in drawing plans and sections by hand at an appropriate scale. A good site drawing can encapsulate an immense amount of careful observation but it must be executed by a practitioner with considerable experience and cannot be hurried. All this might seem self-evident but it is a sad fact that the constraints of competitive tendering are having an adverse effect on the quality of field recording, as is now all too evident in an increasing number of published reports. As one experienced unit manager said when he saw the detail in which we were recording the post-holes of an Iron Age house at Flint Farm, 'We just could not afford to do it in that detail.'

Our third imperative has been to publish our results efficiently and in the appropriate degree of detail. There has been some debate in the past about how much data should be presented in hard copy and how much should be made available in another media. Fiche was favoured for some years, DVDs had a brief innings, but now most are turning to web sites. Various different strategies have been adopted but there must always be the lingering doubt about how robust the non-book media will prove to be. While we can be reasonably sure that some copies of our published reports will still linger in the depths of at least a few libraries in 50 years' time, can we be equally confident that web managers will have bothered to keep our interminable screeds of data compatible with current retrieval systems? It is this uncomfortable doubt that has encouraged us to publish in hard copy as much data as is necessary to support the interpretations inherent in the site narrative. By some standards it will be thought to be too much but time will tell.

We have always believed that our responsibility to the discipline is to publish full reports within a short period following the end of the final field season – we have worked hard to put this belief into practice. The first ten years' work at Danebury was published within six years, the second ten years within three years with the overview appearing four years later. The Danebury Environs Programme was published within four years of its end and the Danebury Environs Roman Programme within two. This has meant that the data from each of the programmes have been put quickly into the public domain so that it can be available to researchers to inform new projects. It is, I believe, inexcusable that some major excavations remain unpublished after more than 20 years.

Alongside the production of the specialists' reports we have been concerned to communicate the project to the wider audiences through popular books, exhibitions and television programmes. Throughout we have worked closely with the County Museums Service and with its Countryside Open Spaces Officers in an attempt to make the results of the work widely available. In 1986 a museum dedicated to Danebury – The Museum of the Iron Age – was opened by the Museums Service at Andover supported by a guidebook (Cunliffe 1987). This replaced a guidebook produced a decade earlier for the Open University as part of its Arts and Environment Course (Cunliffe 1976). We also contributed teaching notes for an educational pack published by Oxford University Press (Cunliffe 1973). In more recent years, to ensure that up-to-date information was constantly being fed into the educational system, staff from the Museums Service's Education section regularly took part in the excavations. The educational programme was further advanced in 2005–6 when, in partnership with the Museums Service, we received a grant from the Local Heritage Initiative to involve the local community, and in particular its schools, in the excavation at Dunkirt Barn. During that time *c.*1000 children from 24 schools visited the site.

Media coverage has been constant throughout – I forget the number of times I have walked around the ramparts with television crews, speculating about what Iron Age life was like. Over the years successive producers have chosen the same routes and much the same camera angles – only the speculations have changed. One serious full length programme, *Decoding Danebury*, was made by Horizon in 1984, filming the excavation in progress and involving the various specialists in discussion on site. It gave a fair impression of the pace and complexities of a long-term research excavation countering the media-inspired view that archaeologists are always in a rush!

Another contribution to outreach has been a popular book first published under the title of *Danebury: Anatomy of an Iron Age Hillfort* in 1983 and revised and reprinted under variant titles each decade (Cunliffe 1993a, 2003). Across the full range of output from the specialist monographs to the television interviews this little book has had the greatest impact on communicating the project to the public. Through short popular books of this kind, written by the experts in charge, archaeology will, I believe, continue to make its most long-lasting impression on public consciousness.

So, what have we learnt?

The short answer is humility. In 1969 it all seemed comparatively easy. A few seasons of excavating producing a decent-sized dataset would be sufficient to answer the main questions posed and would enable us to characterize Iron Age life in a neat and contained way. How naïve! Even at the end of the first season the few pits excavated just behind the rampart had begun to hint at intricate patterns of behaviour enacted during their filling and as the project progressed the complexity of the archaeological record began to dawn. But it was the first area excavation within the fort in 1971 that really sharpened the focus on the task ahead. At the end of the season I remember giving the last site talk summing up the year's results. Three things stood out – the remarkable degree of planning and consistency of use over time that was revealed in the sample; the patterns of deposition in the pits which we had begun to refer to as 'special burials'; and the quantity of human remains that were found in different contexts throughout the area. In the following years these three themes became the *leitmotifs* running through the project.

The spatial theme was developed as each year more areas were uncovered and it became possible to appreciate the degree of control that had been exerted over the internal layout dominated by a through road, later truncated when one of the gates was blocked, and dendritic patterns of side roads branching off from the main axis. Within this framework areas had been set aside for religious structures, pit storage, storage in above-ground 'granaries' and houses. The authority which controlled the fort was able to maintain order over many generations. This was vividly demonstrated by the houses in the north-western peripheral zone which had undergone six successive phases of rebuilding. By the end of the project we were able to suggest that lying behind the internal arrangements there was not only a coercive power but also some agreed notion of the appropriate use of space conceived in terms of the bilateral symmetry of the site – that is control over what it was proper to do on the left hand and the right hand when viewing the interior from the main entrance (Cunliffe 1995, 19–42).

From 1971 the special burials in pits featured large in our study of the site. During that year I vividly remember the realization dawning that the recurrence of articulated horse legs, found on pit bottoms, reflected deliberate behaviour conditioned by belief. To begin with the study focused on Annie Grant's work on the animal bones but it soon became evident that other classes of material culture were being treated in this way culminating in Cynthia Poole's thorough study (Cunliffe 1995, 80–6). Meanwhile these issues were presented in a popular account in the American journal *Archaeology* (Cunliffe 1988) and were further developed, together with an explanatory model, in papers published a few years later (Cunliffe 1992, 1993c). Since then the theme has become widely explored by others (e.g. Hill 1995).

The variety of contexts in which human skeletal material was found scattered throughout the hillfort (Figure 8.8) reflected something of the complexity of attitudes towards the human body and led us to argue that the normative means of disposal of the dead was excarnation (Cunliffe 1995, 72–9). This was further

supported by the discovery, in 1996, of a cemetery at Suddern Farm where we were able to argue that the tightly bound and wrapped bodies had probably been exposed for a long period before being interred as bundles in small pits just large enough to contain them. Excarnation is now generally accepted as having been widely practised in prehistoric Britain.

When the excavation of Danebury began it was normal to consider hillforts as structures geared to defence and the language used to discuss the enclosing earthworks was that of military architecture. But fashions changed and by the 1990s some writers were

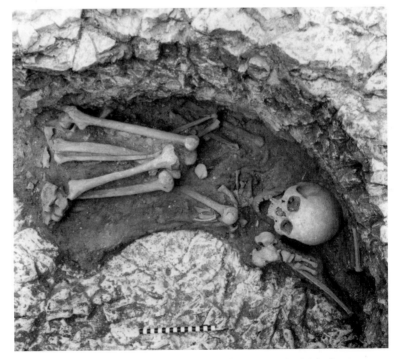

Figure 8.8. Human burial found in a pit at Danebury. The body appears to have been tightly bound.

arguing that the military/defensive interpretation was entirely untenable. More recently the pendulum has swung again with the defensive nature of hillforts being once more broadly accepted (Armit 2007).

Danebury has much to contribute to the debate. The excavation of the main entrance in 1970 showed, with some clarity, how the entrance earthworks were carefully designed with sling warfare in mind (Figures 8.9 and 8.10), and the discovery of large quantities of sling stones in and around the entrance provided strong supporting evidence that the defences had been put to practical use. It remains a possibility that the destruction of the entrance by fire and the abandonment of the fort may have resulted from an act of aggression.

But that said the enclosing earthworks and the gates were more than simply defences: they were statements of the power of the community and there can be little doubt that they were also imbued with power as boundaries separating 'outside' from 'inside' and thus, through taboo, controlling behaviour. One insight into the function of the ramparts and ditches comes from the way in which they were refurbished. The ditch was cleared out on a number of occasions, on each the spoil being thrown on the downhill side building up the 'counterscarp' bank by the addition of a thin increment. The removal of such small amounts of silt would have had little effect on the defensive capability of the ditch but the event may be interpreted as an act of redefinition rather like the annual 'beating of the bounds' in medieval towns. The rampart was also refurbished but on less frequent occasions. The refurbishments added little to the strength of the bank but the new coating of bright white chalk would have been a startling symbol of a 'rebirth'. What controlled these acts of redefinition we cannot say. It may have been a periodicity controlled by time but it could have reflected social events like the passing of a dynasty. However explained, these acts represent the history of the community.

But then we must ask – can more dramatic events be recognized? In the 1930s it was customary to explain hillfort archaeology in terms of major events, a tradition culminating in the publication of the Maiden Castle report (Wheeler 1943). Subsequently archaeologists have become more reticent. Reviewing the totality of the Danebury data, including that derived from the Environs programmes, I believe that it is possible to recognize two major events within the region, the first at the end of the fourth century BC, the second at the beginning of the first century when the gate was burnt and the settlement largely abandoned.

At the end of the fourth century the hillfort appears to have been attacked and was extensively burnt. Then followed the massive rebuilding of the rampart and main gate and the blocking of the second gate. Before these events the community was sharing pottery styles and fabrics in common use within what is now Wiltshire. After the rebuilding the pottery in use was characteristic of the Hampshire/West Sussex region. Given these observations it is tempting to suggest a major political realignment, with Danebury perhaps becoming a frontier establishment belonging to the Hampshire/West Sussex polity, behind a political boundary which may have followed the valleys of the Bourne and lower Avon. There is no space to develop the arguments further here. The possibility is introduced simply to suggest that, given a sufficient database, it may well be possible to return to issues of political geography of the kind that we have been so reticent to face in the last 40 years. Iron Age communities each enjoyed a history – it is incumbent on us to try to tease it out.

After the major phase of rebuilding at the end of the fourth century Danebury enjoyed more than two centuries of continuous occupation during which time huge quantities of material – pottery, animal bones and small objects – were brought into the fort and eventually deposited there. The question which arises is what function did the hillfort perform at that time? Reviewing the evidence in 1984 we suggested that

Figure 8.9. The first exploratory trench at Danebury in 1969 explored the structure of the defences.

Figure 8.10. The main entrance of Danebury.

the fort served as a central-place where, mitigated by a complex of social obligations, commodities were exchanged. In this way locally produced surpluses like wool and grain were exchanged for exotics, like quernstones, metals, salt, glass and amber, brought in from outside the region. The suggestion did not meet with universal approval, some arguing that the range of items found on the hillfort was similar to that found on settlement sites. The argument is not, however, solely based on type but on sheer quantity of material. The activity leading to deposition on the hilltop was many times greater than that observed on neighbouring settlements, a fact made even clearer by the excavation of a number of settlements during the Danebury Environs Programme. Reviewing the evidence once again we reiterated our conclusion that during the Middle Iron Age the hillfort served as a central-place in a broader region (Cunliffe 1995, 91–5). The social and religious practices which took place on the hilltop provided mechanisms for the exchange of commodities, for storage of surpluses and for limited manufacture, and probably for much else, feasting, the sealing of marriage alliances, competitions and the many practices which reinforce coherence and give a degree of stability to the community.

The first century BC was a time of readjustment within the region caused, in no small part, by the growing impact of the Roman world. When eventually Britain became part of the Empire, life in the Danebury region continued much as before. Most of the settlements continued in occupation and even after 300 years of Roman rule the agro-pastoral economy remained very little changed. It was not until the end of the third century AD that the attributes of Roman style – masonry buildings encapsulating private space, mosaics and baths – became at all widespread, but that each of the settlements investigated showed its own individual trajectory of development hints at a series of local decisions taken by the land-holding lineages constrained by the productivity of their estates and motivated by their desire to embrace *romanitas*. One suspects that little had changed: in 300 BC a tithe of surplus would have been transferred to the elite to redistribute in the form of patronage, feasting and the like: in AD 200 surplus was paid through taxes to the state who in turn maintained an infrastructure and ensured peace. The *longue durée* of rural life controlled by the seasons and the rhythm of the agricultural cycle continued.

The Danebury programme has continued year on year through a period of massive change in archaeology. When we began professional contractors were a glint in the eyes of a few and computers were in their ungainly infancy. The discipline was still in a state of comparative theoretical innocence before the waves of successive 'isms' flowed over it and, for a while, the divide between theoretical archaeology and the realities of fieldwork seemed unbridgeable. But now even the most ardent of theoreticians find solace in excavation while diehard diggers enjoy the intellectual spice of a dash of theory. Embedded within the Danebury debates and publications one can glimpse this process of coming-of-age in action.

And where next? There is so much to be done and so little space left to discuss it. At the local level there is broad agreement among many of the specialists involved in the Danebury programmes that the effect of man on the late prehistoric and early historic environment is a theme worthy of more detailed study. This would involve chemical analyses of grain, animal bones and human skeletal remains together with limited excavation and core boring to study soil micromorphology and chemistry, colluviation and peat formation. Such a study, using the existing database as a resource, would, we hope, provide a wholly new context against which to examine human history.

On a broader front I hope that the Danebury programmes have shown some of the advantages of working on a large scale over an extended period of time. The difficulties of funding and sustaining the energy of projects of this scale cannot be denied but in the end, I think, it has been worth it.

References

Publications generated directly by the Danebury programmes.

Monographs

Cunliffe, B. 1984a. *Danebury: an Iron Age Hillfort in Hampshire. Vol. 1 The excavations 1969–1978: the site.* London: Council for British Archaeology Research Report 52.

Cunliffe, B. 1984b. *Danebury: an Iron Age Hillfort in Hampshire. Vol. 2 The excavations 1969–1978: the finds.* London: Council for British Archaeology Research Report 52.

Cunliffe, B. 1995. *Danebury: an Iron Age Hillfort in Hampshire. Vol. 6 A hillfort community in perspective.* York: Council for British Archaeology Research Report 102.

Cunliffe, B. 2000. *The Danebury Environs Programme. The Prehistory of a Wessex Landscape. Vol. 1 Introduction.* Oxford: English Heritage and Oxford University Committee for Archaeology Monograph 48.

Cunliffe, B. 2008. *The Danebury Environs Roman Programme. A Wessex Landscape During the Roman Era. Vol. 1 Overview.* Oxford: English Heritage and Oxford University School of Archaeology Monograph 70.

Cunliffe, B. and Poole, C. 1991a. *Danebury: an Iron Age Hillfort in Hampshire. Vol. 4 The excavations 1979–1988: the site.* London: Council for British Archaeology Research Report 73.

Cunliffe, B. and Poole, C. 1991b. *Danebury: an Iron Age Hillfort in Hampshire. Vol. 5 The excavations 1979–1988: the finds.* London: Council for British Archaeology Research Report 73.

Cunliffe, B. and Poole, C. 2000a. *The Danebury Environs Programme. The Prehistory of a Wessex Landscape. Vol. 2 – Part 1 Woolbury and Stockbridge Down, Stockbridge, Hants, 1989.* Oxford: English Heritage and Oxford University Committee for Archaeology Monograph 49.

Cunliffe, B. and Poole, C. 2000b. *The Danebury Environs Programme. The Prehistory of a Wessex Landscape. Vol. 2 – Part 2 Bury Hill, Upper Clatford, Hants, 1990.* Oxford: English Heritage and Oxford University Committee for Archaeology Monograph 49.

Cunliffe, B. and Poole, C. 2000c. *The Danebury Environs Programme. The Prehistory of a Wessex Landscape. Vol. 2 – Part 3 Suddern Farm, Middle Wallop, Hants, 1991 and 1996.* Oxford: English Heritage and Oxford University Committee for Archaeology Monograph 49.

Cunliffe, B. and Poole, C. 2000d. *The Danebury Environs Programme. The Prehistory of a Wessex Landscape. Vol. 2 – Part 4 New Buildings, Longstock, Hants, 1992 and Fiveways, Longstock, Hants, 1996.* Oxford: English Heritage and Oxford University Committee for Archaeology Monograph 49.

Cunliffe, B. and Poole, C. 2000e. *The Danebury Environs Programme. The Prehistory of a Wessex Landscape. Vol. 2 – Part 5 Nettlebank Copse, Wherwell, Hants, 1993.* Oxford: English Heritage and Oxford University Committee for Archaeology Monograph 49.

Cunliffe, B. and Poole, C. 2000f. *The Danebury Environs Programme. The Prehistory of a Wessex Landscape. Vol. 2 – Part 6 Houghton Down, Stockbridge, Hants, 1994.* Oxford: English Heritage and Oxford University Committee for Archaeology Monograph 49.

Cunliffe, B. and Poole, C. 2000g. *The Danebury Environs Programme. The Prehistory of a Wessex Landscape. Vol. 2 – Part 7 Windy Dido, Cholderton, Hants, 1995.* Oxford: English Heritage and Oxford University Committee for Archaeology Monograph 49.

Cunliffe, B. and Poole, C. 2008a. *The Danebury Environs Roman Programme. A Wessex Landscape During the Roman Era. Vol. 2 – Part 1 Houghton Down, Longstock, Hants, 1997.* Oxford: English Heritage and Oxford University School of Archaeology Monograph 71.

Cunliffe, B. and Poole, C. 2008b. *The Danebury Environs Roman Programme. A Wessex Landscape During the Roman Era. Vol. 2 – Part 2 Grateley South, Grateley, Hants, 1998 and 1999.* Oxford: English Heritage and Oxford University School of Archaeology Monograph 71.

Cunliffe, B. and Poole, C. 2008c. *The Danebury Environs Roman Programme. A Wessex Landscape During the Roman Era. Vol. 2 – Part 3 Fullerton, Hants, 2000 and 2001.* Oxford: English Heritage and Oxford University School of Archaeology Monograph 71.

Cunliffe, B. and Poole, C. 2008d. *The Danebury Environs Roman Programme. A Wessex Landscape During the*

Roman Era. Vol. 2 – Part 4 Thruxton, Hants, 2002. Oxford: English Heritage and Oxford University School of Archaeology Monograph 71.

Cunliffe, B. and Poole, C. 2008e. *The Danebury Environs Roman Programme. A Wessex Landscape During the Roman Era. Vol. 2 – Part 5 Rowbury Farm, Wherwell, Hants, 2003*. Oxford: English Heritage and Oxford University School of Archaeology Monograph 71.

Cunliffe, B. and Poole, C. 2008f. *The Danebury Environs Roman Programme. A Wessex Landscape During the Roman Era. Vol. 2 – Part 6 Flint Farm, Goodworth Clatford, Hants, 2004*. Oxford: English Heritage and Oxford University School of Archaeology Monograph 71.

Cunliffe, B. and Poole, C. 2008g. *The Danebury Environs Roman Programme. A Wessex Landscape During the Roman Era. Vol. 2 – Part 7 Dunkirt Barn, Abbotts Ann, Hants, 2005 and 2006*. Oxford: English Heritage and Oxford University School of Archaeology Monograph 71.

Palmer, R. 1984. *Danebury: an Iron Age Hillfort in Hampshire. [Vol. 3] An aerial photographic interpretation of its environs*. London: Royal Commission on the Historical Monuments of England Supplementary Series 6.

Popular works

Cunliffe, B. 1973. *Exploring Man. 4 Iron Age Fort*. Oxford: Oxford University Press.

Cunliffe, B. 1976. *Danebury. The Story of a Hampshire Hillfort*. Milton Keynes: Open University Press.

Cunliffe, B. 1983. *Danebury. Anatomy of an Iron Age Hillfort*. London: B. T. Batsford.

Cunliffe, B. 1987. *Danebury. The Story of an Iron Age Hillfort*. Winchester: Hampshire County Council.

Cunliffe, B. 1993a. *Danebury*. London: English Heritage.

Cunliffe, B. 2003. *Danebury Hillfort*. Stroud: Tempus.

Other works

Armit, I. 2007. Hillforts at War: from Maiden Castle to Taniwaha Pā. *Proceedings of the Prehistoric Society* 73, 25–37.

Bowen, C. and Cunliffe, B. 1973. The evolution of the landscape. *Antiquaries Journal* 53, 9–15.

Cunliffe, B. 1974. *Iron Age Communities of Britain*. 1st edn. London: Routledge & K. Paul.

Cunliffe, B. 1988. Celtic Death Rituals. *Archaeology* March/April, 39–43.

Cunliffe, B. 1992. Pits, preconceptions and propitiation in the British Iron Age. *Oxford Journal of Archaeology* 11, 69–83.

Cunliffe, B. 1993b. Danebury: the anatomy of a hillfort re-exposed, in P. Bogucki (ed.) *Case Studies in European Prehistory*, 259–86. Boca Raton: CRC Press.

Cunliffe, B. 1993c. *Fertility, propitiation and the gods in the British Iron Age*. Amsterdam: The Kroon Lecture, Universiteit van Amsterdam, Albert Egges van Giffen Instituut voor Prae- en Protohistorie.

Fletcher, M. and Lock, G. 1984. Post built structures at Danebury hillfort. An analytical search method with statistical discussion. *Oxford Journal of Archaeology* 3, 175–96.

Hill, J. D. 1995. *Ritual and rubbish in the Iron Age of Wessex: a study on the formation of a specific archaeological record*. Oxford: British Archaeological Reports British Series 242.

Lock, G. and Cunliffe, B. 1995. Spatial sampling at Danebury, in B. Cunliffe, *Danebury: an Iron Age Hillfort in Hampshire. Vol. 6 A hillfort community in perspective*, 111–17. York: Council for British Archaeology Research Report 102.

Payne, A., Corney, M. and Cunliffe, B. 2006. *The Wessex Hillforts Project. Extensive survey of hillfort interiors in central southern Britain*. London: English Heritage.

Wheeler, R. E. M. 1943. *Maiden Castle, Dorset*. London: Reports of the Research Committee of the Society of Antiquaries of London, no. 12.

South Cadbury, the Breiddin, the Rescue Archaeology Group ... and then respectibility

Chris Musson

As the editor of this volume said, when trying to coax contributions from the unwilling and perhaps unreliable memories of his contributors, the aim is not to say that "these were the great excavations of the late twentieth century" but to recall projects, personalities and ideas that in one way or another might have influenced the very different realities of the present day. Hence this light-hearted and cliché-ridden memoir, looking back through the mists of time to events that happened half a lifetime ago. My aim has not been to summarise any particular project but to reflect something of the 'pioneering spirit' that began for a small group of us with the Breiddin excavations and the formation of the Rescue Archaeology Group in 1969–70 and ended (or perhaps began again?) five years later when we attained respectability as salaried staff at the newly-formed Clwyd-Powys Archaeological Trust. The situations and events may seem very different from the structured but rather less 'heroic' world of excavation archaeology in the early years of the new millennium, but the two are not entirely unrelated.

Pre-history

To go back to the beginning, then, and to the Breiddin (one of those strange Welsh place-names, pronounced *bri* as in Brian, *th* as in the, and *in*, as in Talbot, Fir Tree, Red Lion and many other ale-houses that have enlivened archaeological debate over the years). In the late 1960s the southern end of the 28ha Breiddin hillfort, crowning a striking dolerite ridge above the River Severn on the central Borderland of Wales, came under threat from quarrying for roadstone. ... But no, that wasn't really the beginning at all. Instead, we must go back to the 1950s, to the revolutionary impact on excavation technique and public presentation (= enlightened self-publicity) that Wheeler brought to Britain and the Indian subcontinent in the decades either side of World War II. One of Wheeler's post-war protégé's, Leslie Alcock – far smaller in stature but no less inspiring as excavator and teacher – was then the newly-appointed lecturer in archaeology at what is now the University of Cardiff. It was there in Cardiff that I began my training as an architect in the early 1950s. Before starting my five years of designing improbable buildings in the Welsh School of Architecture I was required to do a preliminary year of 'academic' study at the University. I chose Ancient History, Latin and – almost by chance – Archaeology (it was reputed, quite falsely, to be a 'snip' for undergraduate work, rather like media studies or blancmange technology in the present day).

In the course of that preliminary year I became irrevocably infected by the excavating 'bug' during undergraduate weekends in the company of a handful of others (including not one but *two* Pembrokeshire Wainwrights) on Alcock's excavations at the Iron Age, Dark Age and later settlement at Dinas Powys, near Cardiff. The results of those root-infested investigations were strikingly described by Alcock in a volume that set an important but often-neglected precedent in discussing the *way* the excavations were carried out and the effect that site-conditions might have had on the reliability or otherwise of some of the observations (Alcock 1963, especially Chapter 2). The lessons learned at Dinas Powys were still with me when I came to undertake, and then to write up, the excavations at the Breiddin in the 1970s and later (Musson *et al.* 1991, in particular pages 11–14; see also Musson 1971).

From Dinas Powys I went on to supervisory duties at the Roman fort of Castell Collen, in central Wales, where I bought my first pint of beer (for the present-day equivalent of 11p) and taught the young Geoff Wainwright how to draw a section (well, *tried* to). In the following years the seed planted on these excavations grew into a spare-time passion, indulged during progressively more sporadic escapes from architectural duties in London. On the windswept hilltops of North Wales, the physical and intellectual challenges of excavation (and of excavation-*technique*, Wheeler-inspired but Alcock-adapted) became indelibly imprinted on my archaeological consciousness.

Some years later, during what seemed like a temporary impasse in my architectural and sporting career in London, I answered Alcock's unexpected call to work as his Assistant (later Deputy) Director on the first season of excavations at Cadbury Castle in Somerset. On a supposedly 'Arthurian' site the early discovery of a gilt-bronze letter 'A' (probably from a Roman temple-offering of some kind) caused some hilarity, along with a degree of professional heart-searching about the way it should be presented in the Sunday newspaper that was one of the project's financial sponsors at the time. But Alcock, like Wheeler before him, found the right kind of words to feed popular interest in the pursuit of legitimate research aims. His popular account of the excavations (Alcock 1972) was a magnificent and beautifully written illustration of archaeology's responsibility to explain itself to the general public, all the more so in the light of a scribbled note by Wheeler on a draft for one of his efforts: "I fear Leslie is no litterateur" (Leslie told me this himself, so it *must* be true!). For the 'academic' publications on

Figure 9.1. The Breddin 1969; trial excavations on the rampart. Site photographs can be enlivened by the inclusion of human figures. John Daw caught unawares while adjusting ranging poles on the outer slope of the Iron Age rampart.

Figure 9.2. The Breiddin 1969: trial excavations on the rampart. Jeff Coppen burning off leaves and tree roots with a flame-thrower. It seemed a good idea at the time, but it didn't really work and the radiocarbon samples might not have liked it.

the Cadbury site see Alcock *et al.* 1995 (the Early Medieval archaeology) and Barrett *et al.* 2000 (the later prehistoric and early historic periods, discussed in a way that mystified some of us who saw the excavation evidence at first hand. Sorry chaps, only joking!).

South Cadbury

Anyway, in those first three weeks at South Cadbury in 1966 I fell once again in love with excavation, to such an extent that soon after I abandoned architecture in favour of penurious but state-funded PhD research at Cardiff. The research, on prehistoric timber roundhouses in Southern Britain produced (I flatter myself) a small but perfectly formed contribution to the discussion of archaeological 'reconstruction' (Musson 1970). It was never completed, however, because the Breiddin excavations and the events that followed gave me the entré into full-time archaeology that had always been the main aim of that second stint as a student at Cardiff – in the 1960s a doctorate was more or less a pre-requisite for securing any of the few jobs available in the academic, museum or civil service world. By the mid-1970s, of course, the rescue revolution had changed all that, creating numerous

Figure 9.3. The Breiddin 1969: trial excavations in the interior. Roundhouse wall-gullies and individual stake-holes in the damp soil after rain. Earlier in the trial work, when the soil was dry, these structural details had been virtually invisible.

posts for 'practicing' archaeologists and preparing the ground for the other changes that have created the very different situation of the present day.

At times the three years of my supposed research work at Cardiff were dominated by preparations for the next season's work at South Cadbury, a typical volunteer-based summer excavation of the 1960s. The experience of that project, and of its hoard of up to a hundred dedicated but largely unskilled volunteer excavators, was crucial to what happened next – to myself, to the Breiddin and to the small group of fellow-spirits who later made up the Rescue Archaeology Group, or RAG (Peter Fowler, in a letter to me at the time, found the name a little presumptuous; in retrospect I suppose he had a point).

To be more specific, the Cadbury experience took the form of supervising (or observing) small groups of conscientious but painfully slow and uncertain volunteers, working at a pace which those of us with greater skill and confidence *knew* we could exceed more or less on our own. But that was how things *were* in the 1960s. Excavations, whether research-based or (tentatively at first) responding to rescue needs, were supervised almost exclusively by university staff and students. These, for entirely understandable reasons, were only available at Easter or in the (sometimes mythical) heat of summer, when sun-baked deposits, whatever their original colour, texture and stratigraphical significance, tended to merge imperceptibly into one another. They certainly did so from time to time at South Cadbury, where the meagre watering that we devised through the use of watering can and bowsers hauled laboriously up the hill from the village below only rarely restored colour and intelligibility to deposits that *had* to be excavated before the season's money and manpower ran out (I can hear my friend and mentor, Philip Barker, turning in his grave at such a statement, but it seemed a necessity at the time). Occasionally, of course, the summer rain revived the colours but brought with it the contrasting risk of damaging the site by trying to work in conditions that were *too* wet for realistic operation by any other than experienced and very disciplined excavators (like us skilled supervisors, that is!).

During evenings at the (very) minor public school which served as our off-site head-quarters during one (or was it two?) of the later years of the project, a group of us talked about the possibility of setting up a small team of highly-skilled 'professional' diggers, to work on site all year round, or at least at times (and in soil-conditions) that were more favourable to decent archaeological visibility. Those late-night musings, against the background noise of Dave Clarke's weighing and numeration of a sling-stone hoard and my own labours in hand-created dot-density representation of geophysical survey data, eventually gave birth to the Rescue Archaeology Group, though it took time and other events to bring the idea to fruition at the Breiddin in 1970.

The Breiddin and RAG

By that time, it should be said, a few intrepid excavators were already 'digging all the time', as at Mucking on the benighted Essex gravels, under the direction of Margaret and Tom Jones (Jones and Jones 1975; Clark 1993; Hamerow 1993; Barford, this volume). A few others had made similar moves, if for shorter periods, on other rescue sites. The Breiddin, however, provided the test-bed for our much-discussed theory, when trial excavations were required to see if useful results could be achieved in the heavily weathered and stony soil above the growing quarry that already disfigured the western flanks of the hill. A small team of half a dozen of us, from Cardiff and elsewhere, showed in the un-naturally dry autumn of 1969 that this was indeed possible, though the sudden appearance after rain of otherwise barely visible stake-holes and roundhouse gullies reinforced our conviction that digging in the wrong conditions could destroy at least as much as it revealed.

The upshot, with the help of unflinching and highly inventive support from Dai Morgan Evans, later General Secretary at the Society of Antiquaries of London but then Inspector of Ancient Monuments in the Cardiff office of the Ministry of Public Building and Works, was the formation of the Rescue Archaeology Group, to continue work at the Breiddin and on other rescue sites in the following years. The character and results of the Breiddin excavations, along with the objectives, preconceptions and working methods that underpinned them, were fully described in the long-delayed excavation report (Musson *et al.* 1991), brought to completion only through the unremitting persistence of Bill Britnell, the author's successor as Director of the Clwyd-Powys Archaeological Trust. Figures 9.1 to 9.9 will give readers at least a taste of the peculiarities of the site and of the way it was excavated – over and above the fact that the work was done in the 'damper' months of the year and (for the most part) by a team of no more than six or so highly-skilled and confident full-time excavators (Musson 1972 and 1991).

In those days 'digging all the time' and the use of a small but highly skilled team of 'professional' excavators represented relatively new ideas, though the first at least is now widely accepted (by necessity if nothing else) in the present-day workings of archaeological units and commercial practices across the country. Looking back, I feel that we were in some senses more 'heroic' then, more inclined to see archaeology as the ruling aspect of our lives rather than as an absorbing but probably temporary way of earning a living, or as 'a job to be done' (however conscientiously). I don't mean that as an insult to present-day staff in archaeological units and commercial firms; it is just a mild and regrettably realistic observation on the infinitely better supported and more advanced rescue work (and workers) of the present day.

In the Rescue Archaeology Group we aimed to rotate directorial responsibility for successive excavations around the members of the team. We achieved our productivity through keenly-honed inherent skills, strength, endurance and unremitting commitment to an activity which for us bordered on an obsession. We were paid (or paid ourselves) £30 a week, whether directing or simply being one of the members of the team. ('Ah', said some beardless youth to me recently, '£30 was quite a lot of money in those days'. Well, so it was, so long as you didn't have to *live* on it!). For our £30 we worked six or more days a week, in all sorts of weather, sometimes for ten or more hours a day, followed by evenings spent on drawing and record work etc. Fortunately we were not encumbered with worrying distractions about holiday pay or pension provision – we had neither. We knew even then, I guess, that this could not last in the longer term. Inevitably, we would pick up family and publication commitments. And we, just like our academic colleagues before us, completely misjudged the amount of time and effort that either of these would take to bring to fruition.

Other aspects of what we did at the Brieddin were (more or less) developments or refinements from our previous experience at South Cadbury, York Minster, Usk and elsewhere. In the pre-computer (and for most of us pre-matrix) days of the early 1970s we worked hard at refining stone-by-stone and profusely annotated recording of excavation surfaces, on standard-sized pieces of then-expensive drafting plastic, and at trying to be as objective and systematic as possible in our on-site recording and post excavation reporting. The question of 'objectivity' was at that time, and remains today, a matter of some contention. We felt then, and still believe today, that the single-context recording and abnegation of on-site 'interpretation' espoused by some of our London contemporaries flew in the face of an essential archaeological truth – that excavation evidence is by its nature fragmentary, often imprecise and only recordable within the powers of observation and interpretation of the excavator *at the time of excavation*, as distinct from post-fieldwork attempts at analysis through re-examination of inevitably inadequate site records. Personally, I maintained then, and still maintain now, that if you cannot hold in your head, concurrently, half a dozen hypothetical interpretations, revising, discarding or replacing each in turn as new evidence is revealed by excavation, you should not be in a position of responsibility on an archaeological site. Better to confine yourself to office-based cogitation and theorizing (in this and other comments, of course, I have attempted to avoid any hint of moderation.)

We felt, too, that we were being mildly innovative in our progressively greater use of open-area excavation and in our meticulous recording of successive slope-adjusted 'excavation surfaces' when our well-trained eyes could make out no perceptible stratification. When colour variations *did* show, of course, we followed them. But in the friable, uniformly-coloured and stone-littered soil that typified the interior of the site (and some of the rear-of-rampart deposits too) we could think of no other way of working. Some of the stones, or stone-concentrations, that we recorded quite close to the present turf-line could later be seen (through re-examination of the earlier drawings) to coincide with features that became identifiable with clarity only at a much lower level, as packing or lining-stones in post-holes or furnaces cut into the underlying 'natural'. In those days any kind of 'spit-digging' was reviled by most British archaeologists as a Continental abomination, not least by the magisterial Martin Biddle when I explained our methods to him on a fleeting visit to Winchester (Collis, this volume). 'I have

Figure 9.4. The Breiddin 1970: action painting and pocket billiards. Above the white line tumbled stone has been replaced to represent the original face of the Iron Age rampart, the base of which lies at about the level of Chris Musson's demonstration of pocket billiards. The underlying stone and postholes belong to the Bronze Age defence.

Figure 9.5. The Breiddin 1970: painting a good picture. Graeme Guilbert using water and a paint-brush to improve postholes of the Bronze Age defence, excavated in 1979 in advance of the main body of the rampart on the right.

Figure 9.6. The Breiddin 1970: digging in difficult conditions – winter. Snow did not always improve the diggers' enjoyment of the crisp winter air. The single-layer plastic sheets were later replaced by 'blankets' of straw between two layers of plastic. But the rain got in … granulated polystyrene might have been better.

Figure 9.7. The Breiddin 1975: digging in difficult conditions – summer. In dry summer conditions the level of natural was reached without a single feature being detected. When rain restored colour to the soil more than 100 postholes were detected in the previously 'blank' area.

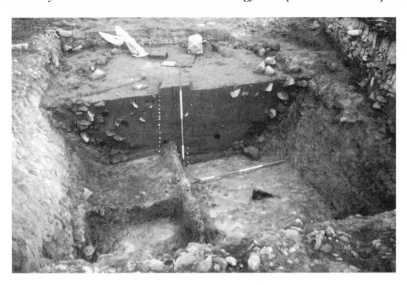

Figure 9.8. The Breiddin 1975: Iron Age water cistern in the interior. The remarkable shape of the cistern's floor, with upstanding ridges of clay between sections dug to variable depths, may represent an attempt to control the inflow of water during its initial construction.

been dreading for years', he said, 'someone saying this kind of thing would come along'. Well, never mind Martin, we all have our little weaknesses.

So, what happened to the Rescue Archaeology Group? Excavations of note were done at Llanstephan Castle on the South Wales coast, Beckford in Worcestershire, and Moel y Gaer and the Brenig Valley in North Wales (Guilbert and Schweiso 1972; Guilbert 1974; Britnell 1975; Guilbert 1973, 1975a, 1975b; Allen 1979). Several of us worked, too, as guest supervisors with Geoff Wainwright's incipient Central Excavation Unit at Gussage All Saints in Dorset, surely one of the great excavations of the early 1970s (Wainwright and Spratling 1973, Wainwright 1979). It was at Gussage that my future wife tried to entice me down a storage pit to examine her skeleton (of a dog, as it happens). It was here, too, that Jo Jefferies, later the creator of archaeological computer programmes with mildly scatological names such as DELILAH (still in use until recently in the Dyfed Archaeological Trust), called over the supervisor of an adjacent area and said, 'George, have a cup of tea and a tranquiliser and look at this'. A window of finely-layered stratification had opened up (under George's area) after a fall of chalk from a 'window' in the side-wall of an already excavated storage pit. The hand-trowelled surface above this strange phenomenon seemed absolutely un-disturbed. In time, however, we learned to recognise the barely perceptible signs of re-deposited chalk where it had been rammed back into an abandoned storage pit during the digging of a new pit alongside it. Experiences of this kind, on a 'black-and-white' site like Gussage, should encourage budding excavators to be cautious about their capacity to detect archaeological features in contexts (such as those of the Breiddin) where there is little differentiation between the features themselves and the deposits through which they were dug.

This was all hard work, fun, fulfilling, and worthwhile of course, in terms of the information saved from unthinking destruction. But in the end, time ran out for us – the time that we needed, and did not grant ourselves, for post-excavation processing and publication, the time that saw the maturing

Figure 9.9. The Breiddin 1975: wooden objects from the cistern. A wooden bowl from the base of the cistern and a votive or toy sword from the upper levels. The sword measures just over 40cm long.

of the rescue archaeology revolution of the early 1970s, progressively formalising the archaeological fraternity's principled response to the needs of threatened sites, as distinct from delving into sites that were threatened by no-one other than archaeologists themselves. In Wales, again through the initiative of Dai Morgan Evans, joined now by his admirable assistant and successor the late Richard Avent (in time the first Chief Inspector at Cadw) we saw the creation, by degrees, of the Wales-wide system of regional archaeological Trusts that has achieved so much in the following decades.

The realisation that the formation of a Trust for 'our' part of Wales would isolate us if we did not get in on the act persuaded us, after much heart-searching, to exchange our treasured independence for the relative comfort of state-funded research and rescue work amid the hills and valleys and moors of central and north-eastern Wales. In retrospect, for all the failings, both then and since, the initial experiments with RAG and our later years of respectability as salaried staff at the Clwyd-Powys Archaeological Trust, seem to have been worthwhile. Whether the Breiddin, or any of our other projects, should be classified as 'great excavations' remains an open question, but we perhaps made our own little mark on history (to end with a suitably pompous final cliché).

Acknowledgements and amusements

For the title and general structure of this little memoir I am indebted to St Augustine, for his words 'Good Lord .... grant me the gift of chastity .... but not yet' (or something like that). I am grateful, too, for having survived several decades of archaeological stimulation and good company with a host of friends and colleagues. While still extant I can be contacted at Tanyffordd, Pisgah, Aberystwyth, SY23 4NE. The idea of a small but highly skilled digging team arose from conversations with Graeme

Guilbert, Mansel Spratling, Dai Morgan Evans, Bill Britnell and (I think) John Casey. In addition to myself, the founding members of the Rescue Archaeology Group were Graeme Guilbert, Bill Britnell and Dave Allen. Others who served personfully with the Group were Penny Guilbert, Jenny Britnell, Denise Allen, Josh Schweiso, Tim O'Leary and Brian Williams (to name but a few). John Barrett, then a student at Cardiff, was invited to join the Breiddin team, on condition that he cut his hair in deference to the hill's winter wind and rain. Well, no success there, either with the invitation or the hair. A stalwart of the first year's work at the Breiddin, and of later seasons too, was the un-schooled but fiercely intelligent and musically gifted Jeff Coppen – to use his real name rather than one of the alternatives that eased his eventual release from a fate worse than death as a squaddie in the HM forces. Jeff tended, in those days, to oscillate between the Rescue Archaeology Group and Geoff Wainwright's incipient full-time digging team. He remains an ever-diverting source of recollections about those times, including the totally unenclosed 'loo with a view' from which we contemplated the pine-wooded slopes of the Breiddin Hills. All of those who worked with RAG, or with the Clwyd-Powys Archaeological Trust in later years, owe a deep debt of gratitude to Dai Morgan Evans for his support in the early years, and to the late Richard Avent and his colleagues in Cadw, the equivalent of English Heritage, on the more fortunate side of Offa's Dyke (note the important final comma).

References

Alcock, L. 1963 *Dinas Powys: an Iron Age, Dark Age and Early Medieval settlement in Glamorgan.* Cardiff: University of Wales Press.

Alcock, L. 1972. *'By South Cadbury is that Camelot ...'. The Excavation of Cadbury Castle, 1966–70.* London: Thames & Hudson.

Alcock L. with Stevenson, S. J. and Musson, C. R. 1995. *Cadbury Castle, Somerset: the Early Medieval archaeology.* Cardiff: University of Wales Press.

Allen, D. W. H. 1979. Excavations at Hafod y Nant Criafolen, Brenig Valley, Clwyd, 1972–1974. *Post-Mediaeval Archaeology* 13, 1–59.

Barrett, J., Woodward, A., Freeman, P. W. M., Stevenson, S. and Speller, K. 2000. *Cadbury Castle, Somerset: the later prehistoric and early historic archaeology.* London: English Heritage.

Britnell, W. J. 1975. An interim report upon excavations at Beckford, 1972–4, *Vale of Evesham Historical Society Research Papers* 5, 1–12.

Clark, A. 1993. *Excavations at Mucking, Volume 1: The Site Atlas.* London: English Heritage Archaeological Report 20.

Guilbert, G. C. 1973. Moel y Gaer, Rhosesmor: a progress report. *Current Archaeology* 37, 38–44.

Guilbert, G. C. 1974. Llanstephan Castle: 1973 Interim Report. *Carmarthenshire Antiquary* 10, 37–48.

Guilbert, G. C. 1975a. Moel y Gaer, Rhosesmor: an area excavation on the defences. *Antiquity* 49, 109–117.

Guilbert, G. C. 1975b. Moel y Gaer (Rhosesmor) 1972–3: an area excavation in the interior, in D. W. Harding (ed.), *Hillforts: later prehistoric earthworks in Britain and Ireland*, 303–317. London: Academic Press.

Guilbert, G. C. and Schweiso, J. J. 1972. Llanstephan Castle: an Interim discussion of the 1971 Excavation. *Carmarthenshire Antiquary* 8, 75–90.

Hamerow, H. 1993. *Excavations at Mucking, Volume 2: The Anglo-Saxon Settlement.* London: English Heritage Archaeological Report 21.

Jones, M. U. and Jones, W. T. 1975. The crop-mark sites at Mucking, Essex, England, in R. L. S. Bruce-Mitford (ed.), *Recent archaeological excavations in Europe*, 133–187. London: Routledge and Kegan Paul.

Musson, C. R. 1970. House-plans and prehistory. *Current Archaeology* 21, 267–277.

Musson, C. R. 1971. Settlement patterns and excavation methods in Iron Age hillforts, in M. Jesson and D. Hill (eds), *The Iron Age and its hill-forts*, 85–90. University of Southampton Monograph Series 1.

Musson, C. R. 1972. Two winters at the Breiddin. *Current Archaeology* 33, 263–267.

Musson, C. R., with Britnell, W. J. and Smith, A. G. 1991. *The Breiddin Hillfort: a later prehistoric settlement in the Welsh Marches*. London: CBA Research Report No 76.

Wainwright, G. J. 1979. *Gussage All Saints: an Iron Age settlement in Dorset*. London: HMSO.

Wainwright, G. and Spratling, M. 1973. The Iron Age settlement of Gussage All Saints. Part 1. The settlement. *Antiquity* 47 (186), 109–130.

The legacy of Howe,
thirty years after

Beverley Ballin Smith

Preamble

When you arrive off the Stromness ferry in Orkney take the old road to Kirkwall. As you drive over the brae enjoy the vistas towards Scapa Flow and the lochs of Stenness and Harray. Slow down as you drive downhill towards the Brig of Waithe in front of you and glance to the right as you pass Howe Farm. In the second field beyond the road somewhere in front of the electricity poles was originally a large grass-covered mound (see Ballin Smith 1994, fig. 2). That mound was the site of one of the great Scottish excavations, arguably one of the great British excavations – and is the subject of this chapter.

Introduction

Travel back with me to a summer at the end of the 1970s where the volunteers who came to dig at Howe hardly knew where Orkney was before setting out on their adventures, and had no idea what awaited them. Orkney was the *ultima thule* – the end of the world: there were no supermarkets; sweet peppers and curries were unknown; the nearest public telephone was a good half hour walk from the accommodation; there were no mobile phones; national daily newspapers arrived a day late depending on the weather; and if the weather stopped the ferries running that was very bad news. Punk rock had been and gone, so too had flared jeans and long skirts, and personal computers were some years off replacing typewriters. Thatcherism was in its infancy and Scotland did not yet have a devolved government. Very few archaeologists or volunteers had cars or could drive, and some hitched up to Scotland from the south because they could not afford the rail fare. For most it was their first visit to Scotland.

The North of Scotland Archaeological Service (NoSAS), under the direction of John W. Hedges, rented a large country house in the middle of the mainland which was the base of operations and the accommodation for most of the archaeologists and volunteers. NoSAS had developed into a locally based unit, one of the first in Scotland, to encourage archaeologists to come to and stay on Orkney and deal with the archaeology there. Apart from seasonal training and research excavations conducted by the archaeology departments at Durham and Birmingham universities, there were only occasional small scale excavations funded by the Scottish Development Department at known monuments or at specific areas of coastal erosion. But all that was to change.

The volunteers who came to work at Howe knew that there was work for them, and that they were to be housed and fed and given a little pocket money. Unknown to them were the facts that they were to encounter some of the most arduous, spectacular and exciting archaeology of their lives. It was an experience that would be hard to repeat, and the memories of that time would never leave them. As they approached Howe on the mainland of Orkney little did they know that they would give their enthusiasm, energy and ultimately dedication to the excavation of a two-thousand year old settlement that had lain virtually undisturbed for more than a millennium.

Some volunteers only got as far as the quayside in Stromness, took a quick look around and returned home on the next boat, but others stayed for several six-month long digging seasons and some put their roots down in the islands. Orkney is like that: it enfolds you in its rolling landscape, and you become part of the community. Leaving the islands was difficult but even now, a generation after Howe was levelled and backfilled, when I return I still glance at the site as I drive past and acknowledge my debt as an archaeologist to what it gave me.

The history of the excavation 1978–1982

The excavation of Howe took place because the farmer wanted to level a field that was close to his steading by removing the large mound which dominated it. The mound was full of stone and it was a hazard for the dairy cows that grazed it. According to the Inventory of Ancient Monuments of Scotland: Orkney (RCAHMS 1946, 324), the mound was a possible *broch*. A simplified definition of a broch is a defensive Iron Age dry-stone-built round building or tower, with or without external buildings and usually surrounded by defences. The atypical but well-preserved tower of Mousa on Shetland is often portrayed as the classic broch. Brochs were largely, but not exclusively, confined to the Atlantic seaboard of Scotland.

The mound at Howe and a Viking grave that was found close to the top of it had been disturbed by Victorian investigations. In 1978 the Scottish Development Department (Historic Buildings and Monuments) funded a short season of work to explore and investigate the mound. This was the beginning of a further four years of intensive fieldwork that ended in 1982.

At the end of the excavation eight major phases of occupation had been examined in detail and removed. The history of the site, a 'tell', spanned four millennia and at the time was the most costly excavation ever to have been undertaken in Scotland (Figure 10.1). It was the first excavation in Scotland where the Inspectorate of Ancient Monuments had to approach the Treasury to ask for funding to continue the excavation. Howe was not a Scheduled Ancient Monument and it is debatable whether a similar excavation could take place today with such large sums of government money. The excavation of Old Scatness, a similar site in Shetland, has been undertaken with a number of funding bodies including the European Union, and was largely a research and training excavation. Howe was a rescue excavation and dug largely by a volunteer workforce. In fact, Howe was one of the last big volunteer excavations in Scotland, before the onset of commercial funding.

The archaeological development of the Howe 'tell'

The formation of the mound at Howe Farm was complex and of long duration. It began as a Late Neolithic stalled tomb with an adjacent mortuary house and possibly a standing stone (Phase 1) (Figure 10.2). The funerary monument was later remodelled as a Maeshowe-type chambered tomb with a long paved entranceway, possibly three side chambers and an underground compartment. The structure was covered with a mound of clay dug from its surrounding ditch (Phase 2). The next couple

Figure 10.1. Aerial view of Howe during the excavation. The settlement lies within its rampart and ditch with the Phase 7 broch encasing that of Phase 6, with three houses and yards lying to either side of the village entranceway. The Phase 2 Neolithic passage is visible just below the entrance to the broch. Note the barrow runs and trailers used for moving stone off the site, the photographic tower, the tea hut, tool shed, toilets and the office (the caravan). Photograph: copyright Charles Tait.

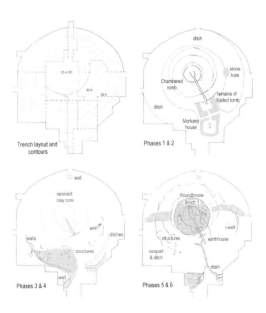

Figure 10.2. Howe Archaeological Phases 1 to 6 Neolithic to Middle Iron Age (after Ballin Smith (ed.) 1994).

of developmental phases are not comprehensively understood due to the paucity of surviving evidence. Nevertheless, enough features survived to indicate that an enclosed settlement with an entrance and adjacent rock-cut well of sixth to fifth centuries BC built largely within the arms of the Neolithic ditch (Phase 3), was established in front of the tomb. The settlement was reorganised during the fifth to fourth centuries BC to include a new well within the re-cut enclosing ditch, an enclosure wall, and at least three domestic buildings (Phase 4). The Phase 3 causeway through the ditch was maintained.

The best preserved phase of this early history of the site was Phase 5, which included the construction of a roundhouse within and over the remains of the mound of the Phase 2 chambered tomb. This took place some time between the fourth and third centuries BC. The entrance passage of the Neolithic tomb was used for aligning the entrance of the roundhouse and all subsequent monumental buildings on the site. Although little remained of its internal structure, what did survive was a formalised shaft that led down under the floor to an earthhouse which was built into, and enlarged, the underground compartment of the Phase 2 Neolithic tomb (Figure 10.3). The earlier buildings across the forecourt were levelled and the enclosure ditch and wall replaced by a rock-cut ditch and stone-faced, clay-cored revetment which abutted the remains of the Phase 2 mound. Although no other buildings

Figure 10.3. After the removal of the Iron Age stonework of the Phase 6 and Phase 7 brochs, the Phase 5 roundhouse was found beneath. Part of it can be seen as the single faced wall above the archaeologist's head. The penannular clay mound is Neolithic in origin, belonging to the Phase 2 Maeshowe-type chambered tomb. The entrance passage to the tomb can be seen in front of the archaeologist, where it was used later as a drain for the roundhouse. The boarding beneath the staging within the clay bank covered the entrance to the underground earthhouse or chamber.

were confidently assigned to this phase, building remains (Phase 5/6) were found lying within the apron of the defences, and the entrance way into the settlement was altered but retained.

The position and architecture of the thick-walled Phase 5 roundhouse began a trend that influenced the two subsequent buildings on the site. It was replaced by another round structure or broch, probably due to subsidence and collapse sometime during the second and first centuries BC. This Phase 6 building incorporated within its comparatively thinner walls architectural features such as opposed intra-mural staircases (one is normal for the majority of brochs), entrance cells, and an interior which had a central hearth and radial partitions (Figure 10.2). The defences were also modified several times to enlarge the enclosed area and take in the Phase 2 tomb mound. Additional buildings were built within the defences and evidence of them survived to either side of the broch entrance.

Sometime between the end of the first century BC and the first century AD a two-part remodelling of the site took place (Phase 7) (Figure 10.4). The

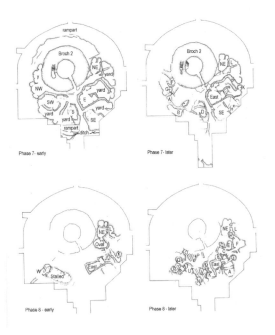

Figure 10.4. Howe Archaeological Phases 7 to 8 Middle Iron Age to Later Iron Age (after Ballin Smith (ed.) 1994).

significance of these events is that the buildings survived largely in a remarkable state of preservation. The Phase 6 broch was cleared out and partly demolished, and replaced with a much thicker-walled, heavier and more monumental version, but without entrance cells (Figure 10.5). One of the first floor intra-mural staircases and landings was retained as was the access to the earthhouse. The interior gained a radial arrangement of features and upper level cupboards survived (Figure 10.6). An intra-mural cell was constructed in the broch wall behind the earthhouse shaft and the entrance passage doorway gained bar holes. During its construction, or not long after its completion, the broch suffered a major collapse and it had to be partly rebuilt and underpinned.

The defensive appearance of the site was maintained for a while but with modifications, and six sophisticated buildings with yards were designed and built to replace those constructed in Phase 6 within the arms of the rampart: three to either side of the settlement entrance and passageway to the broch. Cells in two of the buildings survived to their corbelled roofs which were over 2m high (Figure 10.7). These buildings had a succession of hearths and floors, and exhibited repairs, alterations and also changes of use (Figure 10.8). How long these structures were occupied is not known but they were drastically levelled on the western side of the settlement because of the threat of collapse of the broch walls due to a major fire.

A new plan was initiated for the remodelling and rebuilding of part of the settlement. The defences which had been gradually filled in were now built over as reconstruction began at a safe distance from the broch tower. However, this did not last long as a significant portion of the broch wall collapsed. A retaining wall was constructed in an attempt to hold back the collapse, and once the rubble had

Figure 10.5 (above). In dismantling the walls of the Phase 7 broch the remains of the Phase 6 broch wall were visible (under the archaeologist in blue). Large stone was put in the wheelbarrows and taken along the barrow run to the trailer. Smaller stone and soil was put in buckets and then emptied into a separate barrow and dumped on the spoil heap. There was much manual handling of heavy stones, buckets and wheelbarrows.

Figure 10.6 (left). In excavating the upper rubble fills of the broch tower this archaeologist had to explore the stratigraphy around a surviving vertical stone slab that formed the side of an upper cupboard resting against the broch wall. The vertical slab was held in place by a modern metal strut, but otherwise was unsupported. Even the archaeologist's hard hat would not have protected him had the slab slipped or fallen!

Figure 10.7 (above). The best surviving corbelled chamber on the site stood to 2m in height and opened into the centre of the North-East building which was contemporary with the Phase 7 broch. This building and cell were used, with modifications, for approximately 600 years to the end of Phase 8, the later Iron Age settlement. No shoring was used throughout the excavation of this structure.

Figure 10.8 (right). In the initial stages of excavating the Phase 7 buildings in front of the broch, the stratigraphic events were hard to tease out. Walls of buildings were easy to follow, especially with their othostats (upright stones), but floors of houses (where the archaeologists are working) and of the surrounding yards were difficult to disentangle. It did not help that part of the building being excavated (the South-West) lay beneath a massive rubble collapse from the broch and also partly within a separate trench where at least a metre depth of rubble had to be excavated before everything was down to the same stratigraphic level.

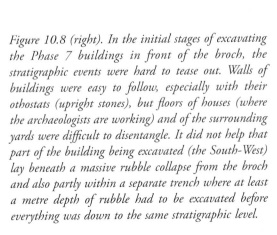

stabilised an earthhouse was built within it. The broch collapsed again, and this was such a significant event that it prevented any further rebuilding attempts on the southern and western sides of the settlement (Figure 10.9). The buildings on the east continued in use after this collapse but they also endured changes of use, alterations and expansion across the former defences. Access to the interior of the broch was still possible by means of its collapsed walls, and new floors were established and replaced four times. Due to its increasing instability the broch was finally abandoned during the fourth century AD.

Phase 7 structures on the eastern side of the site were sheltered from the collapse of the broch and continued to be used as the centre of an unenclosed post-broch settlement or farmstead(s) (Phase 8) (Figure 10.4). Over the next three centuries numerous ephemeral stone structures, with a variety of designs and uses shifted spatially across the lower slopes of the mound. The conglomeration of buildings expanded and contracted, but throughout this phase, which lasted until about the seventh century AD, they were continually modified. Finally, the single nucleus that was left was abandoned to gradual decay and become part of the mound. The final events (Phase 9) were minor in comparison to what had gone before but included a possible Norse burial, and Victorian intrusions.

An expanded narrative record of the structures by phase, along with the environmental account, the material cultural evidence, the details of the remains of the inhabitants of Howe and the dating of the settlement was published in Ballin Smith (1994).

The archaeological achievements of the excavation of Howe

During the excavation we were conscious of breaking boundaries that had been set some forty years previously in Scottish Iron Age studies. Our excavation approaches and techniques were completely different to what had gone before. Howe caused archaeologists to re-examine the origins and developments of roundhouses and brochs, and informed in great detail our cultural, social and architectural understanding of these elaborate monuments. It also pushed back (with Bu, see Hedges 1987a) the construction of roundhouses into the early Iron Age between 800 and 400 BC. Howe was a particularly local development in stone of a common British theme of round buildings that did not require foreign architectural influences. Instead of the technological developments pointing from the south of Britain to the north, the pattern has changed completely around and become far more complex.

In the north of Scotland no complex Iron Age settlement had been systematically excavated and documented since the 'clearance' of the brochs of Gurness (Hedges 1987b) and Midhowe (Callander and Grant 1934) both on Orkney, and the excavation of the settlements of Jarlshof and Clickhimin (Hamilton 1956 and 1968) in Shetland. Although Hedges (1987a) excavated the enigmatic roundhouse at Bu in the late 1970s situated close by Howe, it did not have the structural extent or complexities of the latter site. The broch and settlement at Crosskirk on the north Caithness coast was partly excavated in the late 1960s but its results were not published until after the fieldwork at Howe had been completed (Fairhurst 1984).

Howe was therefore the first broch tower with its surrounding village to be excavated on Orkney since the 1930s. It was also the largest excavation for almost fifty years on the islands. From the moment the turf was cut the problems of working on a mound of stone were apparent. Separating out structural features, often of only a few courses high from the rubble that surrounded them, and trying to make sense of the patterns of stonework were extremely difficult. This was a problem that had beset the excavators of the Broch of Gurness (Hedges 1987b, 65–71) who had recognised a few of the better preserved post-broch structures, but not the remainder. By the use of techniques not used by previous 'broch' excavators, such as context sheets, matrices, regular photographic recording and photogrammetry, it was possible to disentangle the intricate structural details from the rubble and establish the close relationship of the Late Iron Age buildings at Howe to each other and to the Middle Iron Age broch and village. We demonstrated the continuity of settlement at the site and its decline from monumental architecture to the vernacular.

The evolution of broch studies has been a long one and Howe has contributed enormously to the development of our understanding of these unique Atlantic round houses. On Orkney, complicated structures surrounding brochs had been noted during Victorian excavations (see Petrie at Lingro, St Ola in Hedges 1987c, 81, pl. 3.9). Buildings external to, and most likely contemporary with, the use of the broch tower were exposed and preserved during the excavations at Gurness and Midhowe but their stratigraphic relationship to the tower was, and is still, disputed (see MacKie 1998, 23). At Howe the development of broch and village as a planned and contemporary unit was recognised for what it was. The relationship between the structures was proven not once, but several times, from Phases 5 and 6 through to 7. We excavated from the top of the Iron Age stratigraphic sequence down to the bottom and below it, not only in the broch but also in the surrounding village, and this had not been achieved previously. Very few brochs have been demonstrated to have been excavated down to their primary levels on Orkney. There were rare exceptions elsewhere such as the Broch of Skitten, Kilmster in Caithness excavated in the 1940s (Calder 1948), and Dun Mor Vaul (MacKie 1974) excavated in the 1960s in Tiree. The results of our work at Howe have become a benchmark for the reinterpretation of other similar complex broch sites and they established a dataset for others to confirm or challenge (see current work on brochs in Caithness and Old Scatness Broch, Shetland).

The thorough examination of the broch and its village extended also to the surrounding rampart and ditch. These were features which had not been entirely satisfactorily explored or understood on other sites and in earlier excavations, especially in their stratigraphic relationship with the broch tower and other structures. The links between these features (rampart and ditch) and the roundhouse and brochs at Howe were complicated. The excavation demonstrated that the defensive elements of these settlements had developed earlier than previously thought, and that they had changed considerably over time. The rampart and ditch during Phase 7 were already several centuries old when the last broch, the most monumental (and defensive) in appearance, was built. They had been much altered and the characteristics which made them defensive had degenerated to such an extent that they performed no valuable function, other than for rubbish disposal in the final stages of that phase.

Another first for the excavators of Howe was the recognition that buildings contemporary with the latter stages of the Middle Iron Age broch and village (Phase 7) existed beyond the rampart and ditch. Although these were poorly preserved they are important in helping us broaden our concepts of settlement, defence and the use of sites of this period.

I believe that today the excavation of Howe is still extremely important for the very reason that we excavated it to modern professional standards, and to destruction. There had been no question of preserving the latest broch and its houses for public display as the exposed stonework crumbled under the Orcadian sun, wind and rain. Without removing those structures the entire stratigraphic sequence of the site would not have been revealed. By manually removing an estimated 1500 tonnes of stone (David Lynn pers. comm.) the complex evolution of the roundhouse to broch on this site was exposed, as was their placing on top of Neolithic structures.

Figure 10.9. To appreciate the architecture and geometry of the site it had to be viewed from above. The photographic tower was dismantled and re-erected regularly as it was moved about the site. This image shows how it had to be positioned on the broch walls for the inside of the structure to be photographed. While recording was happening in one part of the site, a small band of archaeologists were 'enjoying' shifting heavy rubble!

The excavation of Howe is important also because of the survival of Neolithic structures beneath those of Iron Age date. The demolition of a stalled tomb and the construction of a Maeshowe-type tomb on top of it was a sequence of events that had not previously been recorded. The influence the Neolithic ritual structures had on those of the domestic Iron Age was enormous. Many of the fundamental elements (and problems) of the roundhouse and broch, their location, orientation, their architecture, and their instability, amongst others, were due largely to their construction within and around the clay mound of the Phase 2 Neolithic chambered tomb. As archaeologists we were excavating Iron Age structures that were two thousand years old, and that the time gap between the end of the Neolithic and the utilisation of the site by Iron Age 'developers' was about the same. We often wondered if our Iron Age ancestors sited their buildings on top of an older burial site by chance or whether it was a deliberate choice.

Important archaeological lessons were learnt from Howe: what you think you have may not be all you have, or it may not be what you think it is. Only by systematically dismantling the buildings and brochs could the evidence and facts of the whole site be teased out. We revealed information that pushed the origins of brochs further back in time. We found evidence about the architectural and design problems of building round monumental structures, and the people who built these structures came alive with these problems.

For the first time in forty years a complex Iron Age site was recorded in detail. This in itself was no minor archaeological achievement and was accomplished without the aid of a computer. No highly technical equipment was used on the site and all the recording was done by hand. On a three dimensional site such as this, surveying was tricky, matching up plans and structures was difficult, sorting out stratigraphy and matrices was a major feat of logic and deduction. But we kept track of everything and published the results after twelve years of work!

What we could have done better

This is not the place to review the quality of the archaeological evidence and the publication (see MacKie 1998 and Cowley 2003 amongst others). However, when experiencing recent excavations with their wide range of digital equipment and new scientific techniques, I often think that if this technology had been available in the late 1970s could so much more information have been recovered from Howe. Would these tools simply have made our lives much easier and would our results have been any different? Newer dating techniques such as thermo-luminescence could have been useful in providing dates from stratigraphy where we were struggling to get radiocarbon samples. Geophysical surveying could have been used in the fields surrounding Howe to test the full extent of the settlement and to perhaps locate contemporary field boundaries and other isolated structures. In spite of the visual documentation of the site that was made, many more photographs could have been taken. Trying to find photographs and slides of people who dug at Howe to illustrate this chapter was extremely difficult!

Video, time-lapse photography and monthly aerial shots would have been useful tools. Recording the structures using modern standing building methods would have added considerable detailed information to the site record, to the publication and to the archive. EDMs, Total Stations and sub-metre GPSs would have saved so much time and frustration during the surveying and drawing of curved and circular three dimensional buildings. What CAD drawing and computers could have done in producing wire frames, 3D imaging, and artefact distribution mapping would have been beyond our wildest dreams in the early 1980s. For ease of data handling and recording stratigraphy, finds and samples, a computer would have been a godsend. But none of this equipment was available on Orkney at the time of excavation, and many of the tools we take for granted now were still in their developmental stages. The fact that Howe was excavated, and to a high standard, was perhaps by today's criteria, quite remarkable and a major achievement.

When I occasionally look back over images from the site there are times when I take a sharp intake of breath. This is because I am now looking at the excavation with different eyes attuned to a whole barrage of Health and Safety legislation and equipment. Risk Assessments were not part of the site's procedures and hard hats were rarely worn. We cared about site safety and did what we could to minimise accidents, but compared to today there was very little safety gear on this site of stone. A few people wore hiking boots or wellingtons, others wore lightweight trainers, but we drew the line about volunteers wearing sandals in good weather. It was rare that goggles were worn when breaking large boulders and the amount of manual handling of large stone would have caused serious problems for the site director and Health and Safety officials today. How different it was then when the guys, and some of the girls, would manfully lift and remove large and heavy stones out of the excavation area. Other than using rather battered wheelbarrows to facilitate this, no other techniques were used for removing large stone (Figure 10.10)!

Gantry systems with planks were also used for taking stony spoil to farm trailers. These were used with caution, but mainly when the weather was wet or when the planks were muddy! We considered that some of the built stonework across the site was loose or could have been potentially dangerous, but we were never particularly worried about working at the base of 2m high, corbelled flagstone walls that were unsupported by anything other than their own weight. There was great pleasure in working within the walls of buildings that remained as their previous occupants left them, and uncluttered by scaffolding and supports. The construction, the colour, design and texture of these walls could be enjoyed without encumbrances. By today's normal archaeological experience of two dimensional developer-funded excavations, working at a three dimensional Howe was an absolute revelation.

The only time our on-site safety procedures caused concern was with our light-weight scaffolding photographic tower (Figure 10.9). We had hauled it around the site from the beginning of the excavation. It frequently had been positioned close to the interior edge of the broch from on top of its wall, but usually it was erected on level ground outside the excavated area but in front of the broch entrance. During our last digging season a gentleman from a Scottish power company had spied us from his car whilst driving past the site. He stopped and with his binoculars checked the position of our tower in relation to the live overhead power cables, and came to tell us in rather firm words to take the tower down. He reckoned it was too close to the cables. ... (In researching this chapter, one of my colleagues told me that someone had actually fallen off the photo tower. This was a secret that had been kept for nearly thirty years!)

By the end of the fieldwork, in spite of the lack of risk assessments, the lack of training in safety techniques, the lack of safety gear, and the lack of site safety procedures, we did not have any serious accidents to my knowledge. There were no broken bones, no other visible damage to personnel apart from bruises, scrapes, cuts and blisters: and yes, we were lucky, very lucky.

Two major aspects of the whole excavation experience that could have been dealt with in a better way were visitor experience and publicity. Many visitors came to see us: mainly local residents who came not just to see what we were doing, but one suspects to empathise with the disruption to the workings of the farm and be grateful it was not their land that we were on. The site was difficult to explain and show to people who could not necessarily pick out structures from the rubble. Sometimes there was such a regular stream of visitors that their appearance hindered progress and the sheer enjoyment of digging. Showing people around was not everyone's favourite job, but occasionally an unexpected visitor would turn up who we would afterwards learn was some renowned archaeologist!

We could have done much more for visitors and during the last season or two we produced a small booklet for them (and for our new crop of volunteers), to explain some of the major complexities of the site. We often had good finds in our site caravan that were shown to visitors but we did not have a seasonal display of artefacts, photographs or information. In fact, I do not believe we ever had a formal open day. Some of our most interesting finds were put on temporary display in the Orkney Museum in Tankerness House, Kirkwall, and many of those objects are now displayed in a permanent Iron Age exhibition there.

At the time we were excavating there was almost no publicity about Howe, either locally or nationally. Amongst the copious local newspaper cuttings collected of other Orcadian excavations over the years, there was not a single dedicated article concerning Howe during the time that we were digging there. There may have been the occasional local radio interview but the lack of media coverage would now be seen as a tremendous loss of opportunity. Howe was a most visually spectacular site with an extraordinary story, and we should have attracted local and national media interest. I speculate that the greatness of excavations can be measured to some extent by the number of newspaper column inches and photographs, and also by television programmes made about them. We deliberately kept a low public profile but by writing this chapter Howe can be gently pushed towards the limelight it should have had.

The public and social benefits of Howe

The excavation at Howe brought people to Orkney to gain archaeological fieldwork experience who would not normally have travelled so far north in Britain. Some of the volunteers came from within Orkney and other parts of Scotland, but many more travelled greater distances from England and America. Most stayed a few weeks but others became temporary residents for a few years, while others still have become long term residents on Orkney. People from all walks of life came to dig: many were archaeology students fulfilling their fieldwork requirements, while others went on to become archaeologists after their experience of working at Howe. From the list of volunteers, one became a doctor, one a clergyman, one a dry stone waller, one is a well-respected writer, another an artist and yet another a musician, but the vast majority are unfortunately now just names on a page.

Reviewing the names of staff gives a different picture from that of the volunteers as the excavation started many archaeologists on their careers. Many of them are still working in archaeology or in related professions even after all this time. Some run their own archaeological businesses, others work in commercial or university-based archaeological units or in university departments; at least one works for a local council planning department; another publishes archaeological books; another became a teacher of archaeology; and one is a museums officer.

I asked one of my archaeological colleagues what she remembered of working at Howe: 'It was like the bloody Somme! I arrived in the dark and I left in the dark and it rained all day, and there were lots of stones! I even had to hitch to site and back again because there was no money for public transport!'(Heather James, pers. comm.). Heather worked on the site during the month of November and had no sense then that it was a great excavation. She came early to the project and it was her first job after finishing university. She told me that working there reinforced how little she knew about archaeology. The experience and training she got at the site thrust her into the real world of archaeology and encouraged her to pursue her career.

Heather stayed at the unit's headquarters where local people thought there were parties every night. When they came to visit, somewhat apprehensively, they were disappointed to learn that that was not the case. I remember one party where formal dress was required, and certainly one top hat made its appearance around the mahogany dining table. There were some pretensions to follow the life of gentry in a house with an enormous kitchen and servants' quarters.

Volunteers also stayed in another large house near Stromness, and for some coming to Orkney this was a period of growing up. Being part of a social unit, making and evolving rules and systems by which to live, and making friends were all part of the new experience of being on a dig. Another archaeological colleague remembered:

In the spring of 1979, I reached my 21st birthday and realised that I wanted to do more with my life than work in a supermarket. In those days, archaeological digs were often advertised in the personal column of *The Guardian*, so when I saw the small ad for the Howe dig, I wrote off, thinking that I might have an adventure for a month. I wasn't interested then in archaeology but despite never having been to Scotland before, I was fascinated by its remote islands. My months volunteering became five years of archaeological digging. The Howe excavation changed my life and the lives of many folk who were involved (Dave Lynn pers. comm.).

Dave continued by adding:

Nothing now has the open-door recruitment style of thirty years ago, when virtually anybody could sign up to try an archaeological adventure, whatever their background, skills and experience. This brought a freshness of enthusiasms, attitudes and perspectives which is sorely missed in today's profession by many of us who were given such open-ended opportunities to have a dabble into the unknown.

Howe gave many of the staff and volunteers that extraordinary opportunity to work, not only with some exceptional archaeology, but also with a huge number of well-preserved artefacts of a wide range of materials and types. The on-site expectations and experiences were often more than matched by those undertaking post-excavation work. Some of the staff and later the specialists were provided with some of the best material they have ever had in their careers. Several people were employed at Howe through the Manpower Services Commission (MSC) which provided schemes of job training with a wage. We were not only able to provide training and experience but also the opportunity for these people to develop skills in artefact processing and recording, which in one or two people developed

Figure 10.10. Excavating the mound of rubble that encased the Middle Iron Age structures took a lot of hard work. The size of some blocks can be seen in the foreground of the picture. There was no lifting gear, and the stones were moved by brute force into a wheelbarrow to be taken off the site.

into specialist work, while another transferred his skills into the local museums. Without MSC schemes Howe and other excavations of the time would have struggled to find suitably qualified personnel. The scheme was open to abuse, as was advertising for young unqualified people to come and work on the excavation, but I hope social and moral responsibilities prevailed at Howe and people left us with more skills than they came with, and with a true experience of what it was to be an archaeologist.

For the wider public, all the artefacts from the dig stayed on Orkney. Some of the most important and informative finds are on display in the island's main museum with the remainder located in the museum stores. Historic Scotland funded a small project a few years ago to bring some of the documentation up to date by letting this author put the contextual and finds information into a database. This has allowed easier access for researchers. The 1994 publication is now out of print but it has been scanned and is currently available on line via the Archaeological Data Service web site (Ballin Smith 1994). All the documentary archives are preserved and held by the Royal Commission on the Ancient and Historical Monuments of Scotland, Edinburgh.

The publication, the archives and finds are still used by researchers and students. At one time at least two students a year were basing parts of their dissertations or theses on the results of the work at Howe. The publication has also often been cited in the results of more recent excavations and research into the Iron Age. After almost three decades, this is a great compliment to the commitment of all who dug at Howe and helped bring its results to the public domain.

The test of time

It has been interesting talking to my friends and colleagues who took part in the work at Howe and being able to tap into their recollections of that time. What struck me most were their vivid memories: the good things, the bad things, the silly things: what they did next and how it influenced them in their lives and the paths they followed. How many of today's excavations give ordinary people the experiences that Howe provided?

The fact that the excavation of Howe, its finds, its publication and archive are still of use, and are still being used for research, confirms that Howe was an important excavation and that its results are still valued. Other researchers are able to explore the records, to look into aspects of archaeological studies that were beyond our remit as excavators at the time. These include the economy of metalworking, the use of space, ownership and occupancy, politics, *etc.* (see various authors in Turner 2005). Indeed, it is possible to argue that there is much still to be researched to gain further insights, such as the pottery, the buildings and the Neolithic structures.

Howe was a remarkable and challenging site, and in many ways it still is. It remains a standard and a marker, not for any modern archaeological practices, but for the exposure and careful removal of building after building to the bottom of the sequence, and for the detail of the complexities of the archaeological record. The exercise that took place at Howe has not been repeated on similar sites that have been more recently excavated. We are in the position of not knowing whether Howe is a unique site or one that reflected common practices in areas of suitable landscape and resources. Much recording and investigation could be done in areas of coastal erosion in the north of Scotland where brochs are on the verge of literally slipping away.

Howe also remains a warning for those eager to excavate complex sites. Time and expense are factors that are hard to predict accurately and are not to be taken lightly in any similar undertaking. Today, where economic returns are so important, excavations such as Old Scatness on Shetland have had to consider hard commercial enterprise and visitor numbers to be an integral part of the archaeological project and the wider local community. At Howe there was none of that, as archaeological discovery and understanding were the paramount foci of the undertaking, not its responsibilities to society and the local community at large.

Like the brochs at Gurness, Old Scatness and elsewhere, Howe will always be with us. There is however, no longer a stone village and tower to walk through and enjoy. There is no maintenance and preservation of structures, but there is a record, there are stratified artefacts, and a story. The results of Howe have fed into the display and the retelling of the monument at Gurness and in part (whether consciously or unconsciously) set some of the research objectives for Old Scatness, more recently re-dug sites in Caithness (Heald *et al.* 2002, 2006 and Barber *et al.* 2005), and others. Howe has given a wealth of information to the public and for fellow archaeologists: the facts exist and the interpretations can be upheld or still debated.

It is just over 30 years since the beginning of one of the largest and possibly one of the greatest excavations on Orkney in recent times. I call it a great excavation because of its detailed stratigraphy, the preservation and quantity of buildings and the artefacts that survived. It was also a great excavation on academic grounds and remains so today because it has contributed enormously to debates in Iron Age and Neolithic studies and because it widened the debates and pushed them further back in time. It has also helped shape modern approaches to the excavation of complex sites in the Atlantic region of Scotland, and had an enormous influence on the lives of the people who worked there.

Howe was a three-dimensional excavation that gave its excavators an unparalleled, rare, exciting and inspirational experience. The site was excavated without risk assessments and without modern support and administrative networks, but it is a site that remains in the memories of its excavators. Through this chapter I have attempted to explore its results, its achievements, its significance, its contribution to archaeology, to the lives of people that worked there, and its social context. The story is not ended as new research will gradually alter it over time but I hope you will agree with me that Howe was a Great Excavation.

Acknowledgements

Some of the themes of this paper had their origins in a lecture given in 2005. Many of the implications of the work that we did at Howe were discussed in detail with David Lynn and I would like to thank him for that and subsequent discussions, and for reading through this chapter and suggesting things I had forgotten. Dr Colleen Batey and my husband Dr Torben Ballin commented on an earlier draft of this chapter. It is a better contribution for their input and they are gratefully thanked for their help. Dr Charles Tait has also been kind enough to allow me to publish (again) one of his aerial photographs of the site.

References

Ballin Smith, B. (ed.) 1994. *Howe: four millennia of Orkney prehistory*. Edinburgh: Society of Antiquaries of Scotland Monograph Series Number 9. http://ads.ahds.ac.uk/catalogue/library/psas/monograph09.cfm.
Barber, J., Heald, A. and Henderson, J. 2005. Nybster in *Discovery and Excavation in Scotland*, Volume 6, 91.
Calder, C. S. T. 1948. Report on the excavation of a broch at Skitten, in the Kilmster district of Caithness. *Proceedings of the Society of Antiquaries of Scotland*, 82 (1947–48), 122–45.

Callander, J. G. and Grant, W. G. 1934. The broch of Midhowe, Rousay. *Proceedings of the Society of Antiquaries of Scotland*, 68 (1933–34), 444–516.

Cowley, D. C. 2003 Changing places – building lifespans and settlement continuity in northern Scotland, in Downes, J. and Ritchie, A. (eds), *Sea Change: Orkney and Northern Europe in the later Iron Age AD 300–800*, 75–81. Balgavies, Angus: The Pinkfoot Press.

Fairhurst, H. 1984. *Excavations at Crosskirk Broch, Caithness*. Edinburgh: Society of Antiquaries of Scotland Monograph Series Number 3.

Hamilton, J. C. R. 1956. *Excavations at Jarlshof, Shetland*. Edinburgh: HMSO.

Hamilton, J. C. R. 1968. *Excavations at Clickhimin, Shetland*. Edinburgh: HMSO.

Heald, A. and Jacobs, A. 2002. Everley, Tofts, near Freswick, Cathness in *Discovery and Excavation in Scotland*, Volume 3, 64–65.

Heald, A.; Barber, J. and Henderson, J. 2006. Whitegate in *Discovery and Excavation in Scotland*, Volume 7, 104.

Hedges, J. W. 1987a. *Bu, Gurness and the brochs of Orkney. Pt 1: Bu*. Oxford: British Archaeological Reports, British Series 163.

Hedges, J. W. 1987b. *Bu, Gurness and the brochs of Orkney. Pt 2: Gurness*. Oxford: British Archaeological Reports, British Series 164.

Hedges, J. W. 1987c. *Bu, Gurness and the brochs of Orkney. Pt 3: The brochs of Orkney*. Oxford: British Archaeological Reports, British Series 165.

MacKie, E. W. 1974. *Dun Mor Vaul: an Iron Age broch on Tiree*. Glasgow: Glasgow University Press.

MacKie, E. W. 1998. Continuity over three thousand years of northern prehistory: the 'tel' at Howe, Orkney. *The Antiquaries Journal* 78, 1–42.

Turner, V., Nicholson, R. A., Dockrill, S. J. and Bond, J. M. (eds) *Tall Stories: Two Millennia of Brochs*. Lerwick: Shetland Heritage Publications.

Writing Into Land – Haddenham and the Lower Ouse environs

Christopher Evans

First, base-line considerations: the project's where and when (with its 'whys and hows' left to later). Running from 1981–87, the Haddenham investigations were a University of Cambridge research excavation and landscape survey project. Their main focus was the Upper Delphs terrace, a buried gravel peninsula jutting into the southern peat fens north of The Old West River, just west of where the River Great Ouse entered these former marshlands, and where the great 8.75ha causewayed enclosure of its namesake was sited (Figure 11.1). As further related below, it was, however, a project without (strict) borders. Eventually, its remit covered over 5km² and extended south of The Old West, where allied Workers Education Association trial-investigations of Iron Age and Roman sites occurred along the Willingham fen-edge. It also included the buried terraces that flanked the southern side of the main palaeochannel of the Ouse (on which the Haddenham barrow cemeteries lie). In fact, with the imprint of its ancient course snaking across these lowlands, *the River* (together with the idea of 'life in woods' and clearances therein; see also Evans *et al.* 1999) was among the principal metaphors structuring the project's volumes (Evans and Hodder 2006 a and b) and this is a theme that will be returned to in the final section of this chapter.

With the fieldwork now thoroughly published there is no need to dwell in detail upon its many site-specific results. Instead, relieved by only occasional 'memory lane' reminiscence, this contribution will largely be concerned with issues of the project's context and methodologies, as arguably it is in the latter, more than anything else, that Haddenham can lay claim to innovation and, perhaps, some measure of 'greatness'. Nonetheless, we were also incredibly lucky in our sites, and nothing since has been found in the region to rival either the Foulmire Fen long barrow (with its timber chamber miraculously intact), the superb stratigraphic preservation of the HAD V Iron Age compound or the Snow's Farm (HAD III) Roman shrine sited upon a Bronze Age barrow, each of which involved major 'set-piece' excavations.

In hindsight, what we did was ridiculous and for the most part the project was grossly under-funded for what was attempted. Generally operating at an annual level of £5,000–10,000 from English Heritage, it was only with the excavation of the long barrow, and with a Manpower Services Commission (MSC) scheme-input for the digging of the HAD V compound, that anything like adequate funding was approached. With the latter still lacking commensurate post-excavation resources, the project's final publication was similarly done on a shoestring. It nevertheless benefited by having much of its analyses undertaken on *gratis* academic basis, including both student dissertation projects and more major research studies by established colleagues. Equally, in excavation, we enjoyed high labour levels both from summer season Cambridge student-participation of 20–40 *per annum* and, later, the year-round MSC-funded staff (8–10). Perhaps more than any other factor, it was their availability that marks the project (and others of the era) from most of today's developer-funded ventures. Yes, the

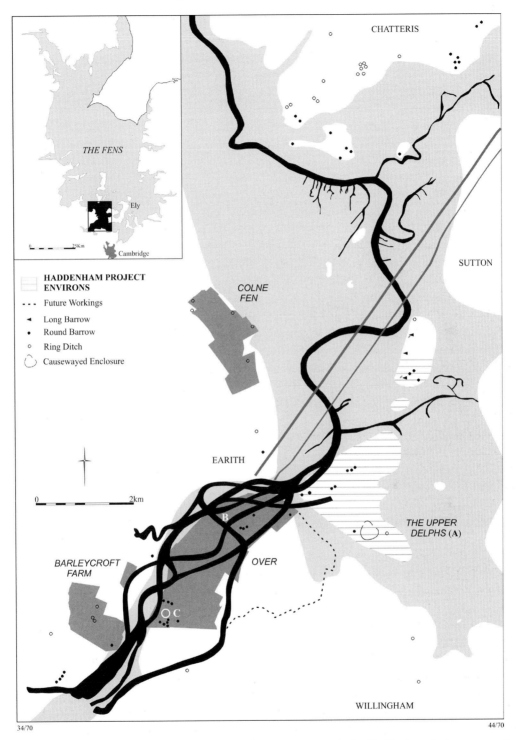

Figure 11.1 A Fenland Delta. The Lower Great River Ouse environs, with the Haddenham Project area indicated. Aside from appreciating what is now known to be the myriad of the river's palaeochannel system, note also the location of the subsequent Ouse Quarries.

basis of archaeology has since certainly become far more professional, with recording generally done to a far higher standard. However, more 'same-type' sites are being dug using the now commonplace (minimal) 10–20% excavation methods, with the consequence that the resultant finds assemblages are just too low to make much impact; few sites, for example, generate the 20,000+ animal bones retrieved from the near-100% excavation of the surface deposits at HAD III or V.

Situation/Context

Ours was always something of a 'salt-and-pepper' partnership: Hodder, then emerging as Britain's leading theoretician – with both *Symbolic and Structural Archaeology* and *Symbols in Action* (1982a and b) appearing in the project's second year – but who had previously directed the work at Wendens Ambo (1982c) and had dug on many sites (including Arbury Villa and Fishbourne), and I, the 'fieldman'. Having earlier worked at Winchester, Bergen and other sites, I had settled in Britain after two seasons at Pryor's Fengate (being part of the same Royal Ontario Museum nexus as Charly French) and was then directing sites for the Museum of London. I met Ian at a party in Cambridge, where my partner was then taking her doctorate. Hitting it off with Hodder (sharing tastes in humour and whisky), I took leave from the Museum to co-direct the second season on the causewayed enclosure and my involvement continued on this basis until 1984, when the project's MSC funding commenced. The Museum was then a vibrant workplace, with debates flourishing about fieldwork methods and sampling (and with Perring, Roskams, Williams and Milne then still in post), and this Cambridge/London axis proved stimulating (if somewhat contrastive).

It is crucial that Haddenham's fieldwork be situated within the research context of its day. If Clark's investigations at Peacock's/Plantation Farm and Hurst Fen are ranked as 'first generation' Fenland sites, then the main second-phase excavations – Pryor's Fengate and Potter's Stonea – had just concluded. Haddenham would, therefore, have to as seen as a third generation project, along with Pryor's early/mid '80s work at Maxey and Etton (and later Flag Fen). With these sites on-going, along with the Coles' Somerset work (Coles and Coles 1986) and the Dutch Assendelver Polder Project (Brandt *et al.* 1987), and as celebrated in Coles and Lawson's 1987 edited volume, *European Wetlands in Prehistory*, the 1980s were indeed heady and ever-promising days of wetland archaeology.

The choice of Haddenham can be seen as complementing a tradition of Cambridge's Fenland fieldwork, the University effectively having the region's marshlands as its 'research backyard'. Starting with Grahame Clark and Harry Godwin's groundbreaking collaborations (see Smith 1997), this would later include David Clarke and John Alexander's work at Great Wilbraham (see Evans *et al.* 2006) and, in the 1970s through the impact of 'Rescue', various Cambridge Archaeological Committee investigations at Earith (summarised in Evans *et al.* forthcoming).

Haddenham's survey context must also be taken into account. Though it was only in the later 1970s that David Wilson first identified the causewayed enclosure on aerial photographs, and it was then that the main Ouse-side barrow cemeteries were also discovered by David Hall during the Fenland Survey Project (1996; see also Hall *et al.* 1987, 175–7, fig. 114), the Snow's Farm barrow/shrine had earlier connections. As part of *The Fenland in Roman Times* initiative, during the 1950s and '60s John Bromwich undertook survey work along the adjacent Cottenham/Willingham fen-edge, which included the discovery of the Snow's Farm barrow/shrine complex (HAD III; his Site 4973 in Phillips 1970). An intriguing character who considered himself working in the mode of Cyril Fox and the tradition of his *The Archaeology of the Cambridge Region* of 1923, Bromwich actually recorded this site during its first ploughing in the 1950s. Along with Charles Bester of Haddenham, who in the 1980s still maintained a personal museum in the village (upon his death his material went to Ely Museum), Bromwich actually cut a small sondage across the site (we retrieved a milk bottle of the day within their backfill; fig. 6). They recovered Roman pottery and metalwork from the complex, and the latter strongly influencing our later interpretation of the shrine's potential imperial connections (through its linkage with the renowned Willingham fen hoard; Evans 1984).

From the outset Haddenham aspired to be 'different': its fieldwork involved a considerable experimental component, and not only saw early applications of phosphate, magnetic susceptibility and soil micromorphology techniques, but also ground penetrating radar (unsuccessfully in the case of the latter). In hindsight, the project had something of a transitional status, with its post-processual interpretative framework supported by relatively strict sampling procedures. Initially, feedback featured in the excavation strategy, and during the first seasons all finds and environmental data was daily inputted into Cambridge's then mainframe computers with the aim of maximising information retrieval to impact upon on-going excavation strategies. Of course, like many excavations of the time (Great Wilbraham providing the most ready example; see Evans *et al.* 2006), these 'totalising' aspirations ultimately proved over-ambitious given the project's limited infrastructure, and after 1982 were largely abandoned.

Complementing this was the implementation of formal, area-wide *landscape sampling* (Figure 11.2). This primarily involved the hand-excavation of many hundreds of metre-square test pits, generally on a 50m grid, across the Delphs and the more deeply buried (palaeo-) Ouse-side terraces. The buried soil from these was 100% sieved, which permitted the plotting of densities of all categories of artefacts in an effort to identify period-based swathes of more intense utilisation and possible settlement. This programme also allowed for a degree of palaeo-topographic prospection/reconstruction and, thereby, dovetailed with the area's palaeo-environmental researches. Not only did the latter include the main Fenland Project investigations (with local environmental cores analysed by Martin Waller, Sylvia Peglar and Anne Alderton), but also project-specific researches across the Delphs by Professor Alan Smith and Ed Cloutman of Cardiff (see Waller 1994).

Site-specific sampling methodologies were also explored. Typical of the era, vast amounts of labour was expended dry-sieving proportional samples of deposits (usually a quarter by volume; 5mm mesh) to control small-fraction artefact recovery. More innovative, however, were the project's attempts to come to terms with the buried soil horizons that effectively masked pre-Iron Age features. The challenge of such strata was something new; for example, the buried soil was only really recognised as such partway through the final season at Fengate, whereas it has now been found on almost all subsequent excavations there (Evans *et al.* 2009). These ubiquitous soil horizons hold a wealth of distributional data – both artefactual and 'chemical' (*i.e.* magnetic susceptibility and phosphates traces) – the trick being to strike upon a reasonable means to sample-investigate their densities.

Although spatial control-samples were taken across this soil level during the first season on the causewayed enclosure, much effort then went into the hand-excavation of this horizon (locally spit-dug, *etc.*), with the result that it was only on the last day that a frustrated Hodder took the machine and widely exposed the terrace gravels, revealing the enclosure's actual circuit. Having learnt this lesson, in the following year two levels of site stripping were implemented. Firstly, down to the buried soil, which was thoroughly sampled (see Figure 11.3), allowing features associated with the Romano-British HAD II enclosure which cut this strata to be excavated; then, secondly, the site was stripped again, this time down to the gravels themselves.

While in terms of methodology there can be little doubt that 1982 was our most satisfying season, from a logistical perspective such approaches could not be sustained. If we were to tackle the causewayed enclosure on a scale in any way appropriate to its size, this double-machining was

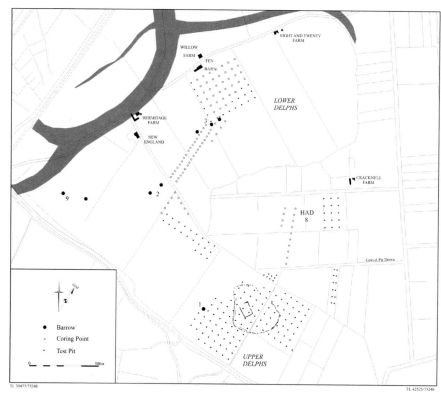

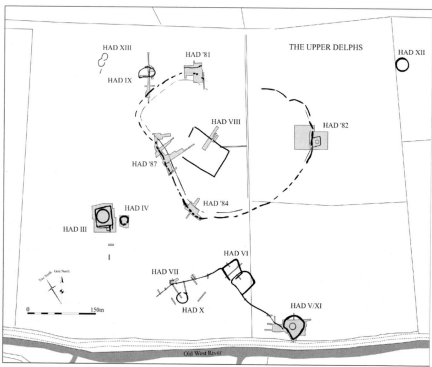

Figure 11.2 Haddenham Project landscape-sampling grid (top) and, below, main areas of excavation on the Upper Delphs terrace.

Figure 11.3 Haddenham '82. Above, a youthful Hodder and Evans stride the '82 site (with metre-test pits being dug into the buried soil). Haddenham always involved a fairly diverse and eclectic staff. Amid the Cambridge trainee students were many of the up-and-coming graduates of the day and 'significant others' (e.g. Pete Rowley-Conwy, Jon Ette, Paul Lane, Roger Matthews, Nick Merriman and Todd Whitelaw), and there was always an interesting dynamic with the MSC staff (three of whose members thereafter went on to forge major archaeological careers). Even in 1983, before having our own scheme, Hodder managed to get hold of a 'travelling' MSC staff from Belfast: tough kids from the Crumlin Road district who went far to distress the well-meant intentions of the earnest Cambridge students. Below, machine-stripping down to the buried soil, with a Roman enclosure emerging (the causewayed enclosure-features being sealed by this horizon; photographs, Gwill Owen).

unfeasible and was consuming too much of our budgets. Thereafter, very much as a compromise, the buried soil investigations were largely restricted to metre-wide transect sampling, with long baulks left running across the causewayed enclosure's ditch and palisade circuits to this purpose (similar total-sieve transects were also excavated across major features on the terrace's Iron Age sites).

Another consequence of the exorbitant share that machining took of our meagre resources, was that we simply could not afford to reopen the same successive-summer season areas. The fields had to be annually returned to the farmers for cropping and, get the balance wrong and open too much, this could lead to undue time-pressure (I can remember having to work all night by Tilley lantern to complete the causewayed enclosure in 1984). Equally, we were probably far too ambitious thinking in 1983 that we could dig both the Snow's Farm shrine and underlying barrow in the same season and, arguably, full justice was not done to the latter.

Working low in the fen, site conditions could, at times, also prove fairly horrific due to depth and/or seasonal flooding (though this, at least, had the unintended bonus of generating photographs suggesting the drainage potential of major prehistoric ditch boundaries and provided first-hand insights concerning their hydraulic logic; Evans 1997a). The worst instance occurred in October during the last season on the causewayed enclosure: the weekend of the notorious 1987 gales. Returning to the site on Monday morning, not only had the University's wooden sheds been blown to smithereens (the same sheds famed for revealing David Clarke's handyman roofing skills at Great Wilbraham; Clark 1989, fig. 34), but water lay over a foot deep across the site's stripped surface, well over the top of the grid posts, and the entire fen was in flood. With the project as a whole poised for completion (the staff soon about to disperse) and with still over a week's digging left of the enclosure's ditch segments, some solution had to be found, as clearly the waters were not about to recede in the near-future. All we could do was to erect sand-bag walls across portions of the site, hire the biggest pump possible (it took six people to manoeuvre this monster) and literally blast the water out. Proving a soggy end to the project, this worked, but we could never pretend that the conditions didn't occasionally effect the excavation standards.

A Wetland Chronicle

Although it was always intended to be concerned with questions of long-term change and the complex interaction between monuments and settlement, initially the project had something of a 'time-sliced' emphasis and was largely directed towards the causewayed enclosure on the Upper Delphs terrace. Indeed, the first two seasons exclusively focussed on that monument. Thereafter, however, the project branched out, both spatially, to include the barrows on the westward terraces flanking the main Ouse palaeochannel, and temporally, to involve later period sites on the Upper Delphs (in the end, its publication was comprehensive and spanned the Palaeolithic to post-Medieval period). While the official justification for this redirection was the necessary provision of context, pragmatism also contributed. Put simply, having what can only be counted as very low finds densities, the results from the causewayed enclosure were not such that it was ever going to attract any significant funding (English Heritage funding always required a degree of competitive spirit and 'active promotion'). Therefore, though that monument saw two further summer seasons (in 1984 and '87), after 1982 other sites were also investigated. Yet it was the return repeat-excavation of the causewayed enclosure that structured the project as a whole and provided its abiding metaphor: Hodder's hermeneutic circle/spiral of study (1992). However, our four-season clockwise progression around its circuit (with, nonetheless, only *c.* 20% of it investigated) was never knowingly conducted. When, in the last act of the project's machining in the autumn of 1987, I returned to the 1981 area and cut a long trench to double-check whether the palisade was present behind the enclosure's ditch-line (it not being identified during the first season), there was certainly no intention of enacting a metaphor – returning (almost 'Elliot-esque') to the project's origins.

Up to the end of the 1970s, causewayed enclosures had essentially been interpreted, *de facto*, as settlements and/or economic exchange centres, with Orsett and Abingdon being obvious exemplars (Hedges and Buckley 1978; Case and Whittle 1982). Yet, with the results from Hambledon Hill becoming available, especially its much-evident dead (Mercer 1980), more ritually based interpretations began to hold sway and came, for example, to dominate Etton's interpretation (Pryor 1998). In the end, the Delphs' enclosure's interpretation reflected something of a compromise between these *either/or* stances. Given its great size, it could never have just been 'domestic' and must have related to mass gatherings, and unassailably ritual deposits were indeed recovered (especially along what was argued to be its straight western façade-like 'front'). Equally, as demonstrated by the causewayed enclosure 'league table' later compiled for its publication (Evans and Hodder 2006a, table 5.5), the Delphs' enclosure actually had the lowest finds densities of any such site. Certainly there seemed insufficient refuse of any kind to advocate substantial occupation and, in fact, its low levels could probably simply be accounted for through 'stays' incurred during its episodes of construction, rather than use *per se*. Nevertheless, recourse to either ritual-and/or construction-only-type explanations seemed inadequate, especially now, as development-related fieldwork over the last decade and a half attests to just how rare and slight is the evidence of substantive Early Neolithic settlement within the region (*e.g.* Garrow *et al.* 2005). Although possible swathes of accompanying settlement activity (*i.e.* 'extended stay'), based on test pit densities, were identified, our sampling at the time was simply too limited to 'side' on this issue with any certainty.

Despite the best of theoretical intentions, our post-1982 extra-causewayed enclosure/other site 'excursions' chronicle an extraordinary run of luck. In 1983 it was decided to investigate the one round barrow known on the Delphs terrace and, also, a small adjacent enclosure. With the latter shown to be of Middle Iron Age date (HAD IV), the Snow's Farm Barrow (HAD III) proved extraordinary, as it had a Romano-Celtic shrine sited upon it; this being the site first tested by Bromwich in the 1950s. Although it only had relatively modest 'architectural' remains, a remarkable series of head-and-hooves votive animal deposits had been set into the floor of its octagonal cella (some of the sheep also having coins placed within their mouths). The building itself was surrounded by middens, which extended throughout much of the shrine's ditched precinct. In total, the site's Roman phases yielded a staggering *c.* 40,000 animal bones – in contrast to only some 2600 pottery sherds and 24 metalwork finds (excluding nails). Mark Beech's analysis of this material (together with Gavin Lucas's study of the pottery and metalwork distributions) provide major insights into the sacrifice and feast dynamics of a small rural shrine. Among the most crucial facets of the site's faunal assemblage was its quantity of bird bone. Amounting to almost 2600 pieces and with 14 different species represented (aside from domestic fowl and Goose), including Duck, Heron, Coot, Cormorant and White-tailed Eagle, this obviously attests to fowling in the terrace's surrounding marshes.

The last decades' spate of both development-led and research-funded excavations (English Heritage's Fenland Management Project; FMP, see Hall and Coles 1994) within the region has clearly demonstrated just how rare are such sites with substantive wetland-specific faunal remains (I only know of three since). This makes the project's excavation of the HAD V Iron Age compound in the following year (1984) all the more remarkable, as it produced comparable 'wet'/'wild' evidence. Located on the lower south margins of the Delphs terrace, the site's alluvial cover accounted for the near-complete preservation of its horizontal stratigraphy (Figure 11.4). Not only were the upcast banks

Figure 11.4 The HAD V Iron Age Compound. Top, aerial shot with the degree of plant-colonisation on the spoil heaps attesting to the length of the site's excavation; below, detail of roundhouse constructed hard on the flanks of the enclosure's upcast bank (note the quality of building's floors; photograph, the author).

and floor surface of its three-phase (seven-roundhouse) sequence intact, but its deep surrounding ditch was completely waterlogged and yielded much worked wood and superb environmental data. The almost two-year long excavation of this site generated vast quantities of finds: over 15,000 sherds and 24,000 animal bones. Respectively studied by J. D. Hill and Dale Serjeantson, wetland species again

Figure 11.5 The Foulmire Fen Long Barrow. Right, showing the undercover excavation of its timber chamber (photograph, Gwill Owen); lower left, the manner of its digging and conservation (with Jon Price in reclining pose and Paul Shand standing centre-stage); upper left, the protective tunnel with the timber structure's excavated façade trench flanking its sides (photograph, Paul Shand).

Heritage's Fenland Management Project; FMP, see Hall and Coles 1994) within the region has clearly demonstrated just how rare are such sites with substantive wetland-specific faunal remains (I only know of three since). This makes the project's excavation of the HAD V Iron Age compound in the following year (1984) all the more remarkable, as it produced comparable 'wet'/'wild' evidence. Located on the lower south margins of the Delphs terrace, the site's alluvial cover accounted for the near-complete preservation of its horizontal stratigraphy (Figure 11.4). Not only were the upcast banks and floor surface of its three-phase (seven-roundhouse) sequence intact, but its deep surrounding ditch was completely waterlogged and yielded much worked wood and superb environmental data. The almost two-year long excavation of this site generated vast quantities of finds: over 15,000 sherds and 24,000 animal bones. Respectively studied by J. D. Hill and Dale Serjeantson, wetland species again featured amongst the latter, including also Crane and Heron, and even Dalmatian Pelican (caches of 'big bird' eggshell were also recovered). In addition, there were also hundreds of beaver bones, many with skinning cuts, which had obviously been taken for their furs. Testing of nearby fen-fast round barrows showed that, during the later 1st millennium BC they had been utilised as procurements stations: places of camping (and tasking) from where marsh resources were obtained. At HAD V what we had therefore found was evidence of a remarkably 'niched' *permanent settlement*. The emphasis here relates to the fact that in the early 1980s, economically determined transhumant-based explanations were still very much in vogue and year-round settlement in this environment was never presumed featured amongst the latter, including also Crane and Heron, and even Dalmatian Pelican (caches of 'big bird' eggshell were also recovered). In addition, there were also hundreds of beaver bones, many with skinning cuts, which had obviously been taken for their furs. Testing of nearby fen-fast round barrows showed that, during the later 1st millennium BC they had been utilised as procurements stations: places of camping (and tasking) from where marsh resources were obtained. At HAD V what we had therefore found was evidence of a remarkably 'niched' *permanent settlement*. The emphasis here relates to the fact that in the early 1980s, economically determined transhumant-based explanations were still very much in vogue and year-round settlement in this environment was never presumed (Evans 1987 offered a critical overview of such approaches).

In the case of Haddenham's later Iron Age compounds, their plant remains, pollen and, even more tellingly, associated ardmarks, all demonstrated that arable production had undoubtedly occurred across the top of the terrace (*i.e.* they weren't pastoralists, but mixed farmers) and, moreover, by the accompanying wild resources it was possible to 'clock' the full year's occupation, beyond just the autumn harvest and spring sowing. This showed that these were unquestionably permanent settlements, with the HAD V community arguably also practising a specialist trade in furs and possibly 'big bird' feathers. Indeed, the wealth of the sites' economic data and unparalleled stratigraphic preservation – augmented by Chris Stevens' and Francis Pryor's observations on the terrace's potential human/animal carrying capacity (and Ezra Zubrow's population modelling) – permitted us to advance a nuanced picture of both the area's initial landscape colonisation and its diverse land-use.

We were only able to undertake such a painstaking excavation at HAD V because of then having had the MSC scheme running. Its participants quickly became adept excavators, and it was only through the availability of such labour that the sheer quantity of 2- and 3-D plotting that the compound's excavation entailed could ever have been faced. Having the scheme also allowed us the freedom to variously survey and test a number of other sites in the area. This included limited dyke survey; following Pryor's lead, this involved the ready use of farmers' machined-cleaned sides of drainage ditches to trace buried islands and search for sites. This led, in 1984, to the discovery of a dense Late Mesolithic/Neolithic flint scatter exposed within the dyke-side along the edge of the Foulmire Fen terrace, located well out in the fen proper and *c.* 3km north of the Upper Delphs terrace. Just northwest of it lay the putative HAD VI long barrow, first found by David Hall in the Fenland Survey. We then took the opportunity to check that it was, indeed, a Neolithic long barrow (and not two conjoining round barrows) by cutting cross-trenches through the topsoil peats and stopping at the mound's upcast, thereby establishing its 'profile-type' and attribution.

Although I was worried about over-stretching the project's resources, Hodder was determined (given the monument's obvious resonance with the causewayed enclosure) to continue with more in-depth testing and – through sheer audacity and good fortune – soon struck the great timbers, and with them the recognition that its wooden chamber was, in fact, wonderfully preserved (Figure 11.5). Thereafter followed a major re-organisation of the project, with 'serious' public resources being directed towards the barrow's careful full-time excavation by Paul Shand and his team over the next year. This equally involved incredible efforts by Jon Price, Ruth Morgan and Richard Darrah to variously cast, lift, temporarily conserve and later study each of its main timbers. As always, the quality of Gwill Owen's photographs of the excavated chamber well conveyed what must have been the reeking (oozing) charnel-house atmosphere when its five interments had been laid into what was the massive bulk of a *c.* 1.50m diameter oak trunk. Split into a box-like construction with its heartwood inward, burial therein would surely have evoked being embedded within a great tree. What was to prove a real sticking-point of the barrow's interpretation was just how the chamber was accessed: from its subsequently closed timber façade-front or by the lifting of its roof? Given its weight, the latter possibility could only be entertained because of what seemed to be a filled hollow within the mound directly above it. It was only afterwards realised that this was, in effect, a collapse crater following the eventual downward slumping of the chamber, demonstrating that no matter what affinities it might have had towards a megalithic architecture and however robust it was, wood – unlike stone – does not stand forever.

Some quantities of later Mesolithic/Early Neolithic flint (and also pottery) were found redeposited within the barrow's mound. Evidently relating to the occupation first distinguished within the field's dyke-side, this must generally correspond with the evidence of clearance from a deep core taken from the Ouse's main palaeo-channel nearby. Dating to 4470–4000 cal. BC (5420±100BP; Q-2814), this remains one of the earliest 'transition horizons' in Eastern England and, clearly, this terrace someday deserves further research (especially as its pre-barrow occupation levels plunge below the marine Fen Clay beds).

While other, more minor, sites were test-excavated on the Delphs over the last years of the project, it really was the trio of extraordinarily well-preserved sites – the Snow's Farm barrow/shrine, the HAD V Iron Age compound and the Foulmire Fen long barrow – that came to shape the project, with the causewayed enclosure remaining like a repeat-theme coda in the background. Almost 'white elephant-like' (or, perhaps better, as 'the 'blind men describing the elephant'), it can be argued that we never fully came to terms with its monumental scale. Due essentially to the inadequacy of sampling of the enclosure's interior, more than any other component of the project, it escaped us.

The Rider Escapes – Historiography and 'Outward Context'

It was essentially in order to emphasise a sense of there always being wider, extra-research area context – and complement a theme that sites are not totalities, and that something will always 'escape' and lead outwards from them – that highlighted inset-sections were employed as a device throughout the two Haddenham volumes. These ranged from historical and ethnographic parallels (*e.g.* Edmonds *viz.* the dynamics of the Appleby Horse Fair, Humphrey on Mongolian Oboo monuments; Lane, Dogon roundhouse abandonment; Mawson, Dinka shrine-building rituals; and Parker Pearson, Madagascan tombs) to the exploration of crucial archaeological concepts (*e.g.* 'tree stories' and Sørensen on gender). However, for reasons discussed below, given its resonance to future regional research, perhaps the most important was Pam Smith's outline of the local antiquarian/archaeologist, John Bromwich (Figure 11.6), with the volumes also including extract contributions from two contemporary local amateur 'village antiquarians'.

One of the pleasures of a project with such a *durée* as Haddenham was the chance to variously explore issues arising from the fieldwork and, also, broader underlying themes (the flow of various modes of interim statements also being encouraged by the 'competitive funding' ethos of the day). This we tended to embark upon separately according to the main thrust of our respective research interests at the time: Hodder largely concerned with matters of methodology – the nature of long-term continuities, the hermeneutic of study and the archaeological process generally (1992; 1999a and b) – whereas I tended to be more concerned with the historical – variously the construction of the regional past (Evans 1997b) and the historiographic roots or 'archaeology' of the subject's conceptual building blocks (*e.g.* causewayed enclosures and roundhouses; Evans 1988 and 1989a). This divide between our general *vs.* specific interests was, though, by no means absolute (see Hodder 1989; Evans 1985 and 1989b), and we each held that these approaches gave the project, both during its fieldwork and writing, much wider resonance.

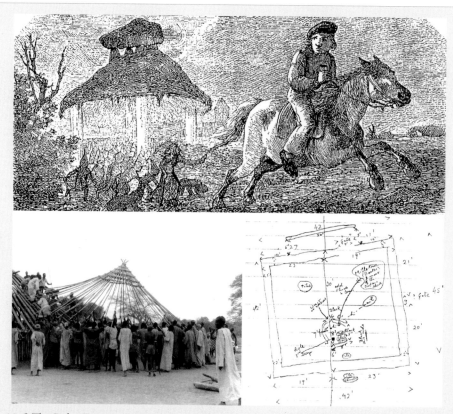

Figure 11.6 The Rider Escapes. Top, nineteenth-century Danish engraving showing a wayward rider fleeing from the temptation of trolls gather beneath an elevated barrow/megalith (Holbeck and Pio 1967, 37); highlighting the notion that something will always escape (while obviously resonating with the Snow's Farm barrow/shrine complex), this image came to serve as one of the project's abiding metaphors (Evans and Hodder 2006b, fig. 10.4). Lower left, volume-inset photograph of Dinka shrine-building ceremony (ibid., fig. 7.30; photograph, Andrew Mawson); lower right, one of Bromwich's 1950s sketch plans of the Snow's Farm/HAD III site as exposed through its initial ploughing (ibid., fig. 7.3).

In terms of the Cambridge Archaeological Unit's subsequent fieldwork projects in the region, it is the latter, historiographic dimension that has proven to have the greatest impact. In the Unit's forthcoming Colne Fen, Earith volume, the work of the local antiquarian, Charles Tebbutt, features in much the same way that Bromwich did in Haddenham's. Similarly, our recent Fengate monograph (Evans *et al.* 2009) highlights the local researches by E. T. Leeds and Wyman Abbott, with the publication of Abbott's long-lost notebooks taking up the better part of a chapter. In fact, that volume marks the first in a new series by the Unit, *Historiography and Fieldwork* (with Mucking's Prehistoric and Roman phases being its second and third releases). Its main thrust is that we cannot just treat the efforts of forerunners as picturesque scene-setting, but – and as in a Foucaltian spirit – we invariably write/dig after 'origins and others', with fieldwork observation as much determined by what has been written as by what is in the ground before us.

Same-River-Twice

Haddenham continues to have an active research context and 'casts a long shadow'. Shortly after the founding of the Cambridge Archaeological Unit (CAU) in 1990, we were fortunate enough to secure the fieldwork in Hanson's (then ARC's) Lower Ouse Valleys quarries at both Colne Fen, Earith and Needingworth (see Pollard 1996 for work in their St Ives pit; see Evans 2000 concerning the impact of Haddenham's methodologies on the FMP). As chance would have it, both lay immediately adjacent

Figure 11.7 Over Quarry, 2007. Above, against the background of the Haddenham Project's Upper Delphs fieldwork (A) and the marked great 'diagonal' of the Bedford Level (upper left) is the patterning of evaluation trenches; (B) indicates the location of the earlier excavation at the southern end of the Godwin Ridge, whose test pit-grid is detailed below (see fig. 1.B for location; upper aerial image, Ben Robinson; site photograph, Dave Webb, CAU).

to the Haddenham area and we have always considered them as a direct extension of its fieldwork and as together constituting one massive wetland archaeological project; one now amounting to more than 1000ha. This being said, the research directives of the two quarries, at least originally, differed greatly. The 140 ha Earith quarry straddled the fen-edge just north of the Bedford Level (Figure 11.1) and, based on the quality of its aerial photographic coverage and the morphology of its cropmark enclosures, its focus was upon the Iron Age and Roman periods. It eventually involved the excavation of seven separate later Iron Age compound-settlements and, also, two massive Romano-British complexes; one – *The Camp Ground* – a major inland barge port (accompanied by dense settlement) relating to the operation of the Car Dyke canal system (see Evans and Regan 2005). However, the chronological focus of these investigations had to expand when a major Bronze Age fieldsystem was found extending through the southern third of the area. With associated settlement swathes investigated, the fieldwork has also involved the excavation of three earlier Bronze Age ring-ditch monuments, two with accompanying cremation cemeteries.

Having relatively thin topsoil cover (with no buried soil surviving), Earith's fieldwork programme has been relatively conventional. Although involving gridded surface-collection (after commissioned ploughing of settlement sites) and an extensive palaeo-environmental component, there the recovery of sites is relatively straightforward; the same is not true of Needingworth. Extending over both sides of the river at Barleycroft Farm and Over (just above Earith and where the Ouse debouches into the fen; Figure 11.1), generally having 1–3m peat/alluvium cover, there the problem has been the discovery of sites at depth. A battery of techniques have been applied to this problem, but, augmented by many kilometres of trenching (Figure 11.7), the backbone of its prospection has been the extension of the main Haddenham landscape sampling grid. Now with upwards of a thousand test pits dug, this has resulted in the recovery of a wide array of deeply buried prehistoric sites throughout the lower floodplain reaches and, moreover, allowed for the mapping of artefact densities on an unprecedented landscape-scale (see Evans and Knight 2000 and 2001 for summaries).

The standard application of these sampling techniques was also prompted by the project's prime research directive: *the status of a major river in prehistory* – by period, a communication corridor and/or territorial divide? – to which purpose, methodological consistency across its two banks is an absolute necessity. Yet, of course, things are rarely so simple. An intense palaeo-environmental programme with Steve Boreham of the Department of Geography has demonstrated the entire idea of *the river* to be erroneous. Instead, there was a delta-like web of secondary and major channels with islands left intervening, on which the main barrow cemeteries cluster (this kind of revelation is characteristic of long-term landscape study and evokes the Heraclitus-passage entitlement of this section: 'you can't go down to the same river twice' – both you and it are invariably different).

The Lower Ouse quarries provide a number of 'hindsight lessons' in relationship to Haddenham's fieldwork. Primarily, there is the matter of scale (and funding). Though we always were aware in the 1980s that the restriction of our limited area-investigation curtailed recovery, this came strikingly home when in the winter of 1995/6 we tackled the first main site at Barleycroft, the Barleycroft Paddocks. There we undertook excavation across *c.* 5ha; in other words, a level of exposure we could never have dreamt of at Haddenham. What resulted was not just the finding of a major Mildenhall-attributed, Early Neolithic pit cluster settlement (*ibid.* and Garrow 2006), but also a 2nd millennium BC fieldsystem with associated settlement. This, in fact, was the first fieldsystem of the period found in the region since Pryor's Fengate and, moreover, it also included a post-built longhouse set within a Down Farm-like paddock (Evans and Knight 2000 and 2001; Yates 2007, 95–6, fig. 10.6) – in short, exactly the kind of evidence we suspected to be missing from Haddenham's record.

The Ouse River-side investigations also highlight the benefits of patience and long-term landscape commitment. This manifests itself in two ways. First, is the realisation of just how long it takes when, operating 'blind' in an area, for true patterning to emerge and to achieve a real appreciation of sub-regional archaeological character. The most obvious exemplar is the dotting of the Ouse landscape with Early Bronze Age ring-ditches and its paucity of henge monuments (in contrast to, for example, the Welland Valley; Pryor and French 1985 and Pryor 2002). The second point (in contrast to the Barleycroft Paddocks' 'fast return') is just how long it can take to recover the kind of sites actively anticipated. To wit, the HAD V settlement's wild species-augmented faunal assemblage remained unique for almost 25 years, with no other local sites yielding anything comparable. Indeed, one of the issues raised in terms of that Iron Age compound was just how a community had achieved the specialist fowling and trapping knowledge needed to procure such a range of wild species. It was only after a long series of near-annual campaigns that, in the winter of 2007/08, we came across a site with a comparable wild assemblage (including 'big birds', beaver, pike and other fishes): a later Bronze Age midden settlement (including bronzes) situated on a marked, roddon-like gravel ridge flanked by major palaeochannels of the Ouse at the north end of the Over quarry.

The Ouse Quarry campaigns are still on-going, and the project will continue well after my eventual retirement. On the one hand, they can be seen as a direct continuation – albeit greatly elaborated in their methodology and scale – from Haddenham, and also reflect the CAU's commitment that there need be no intrinsic difference between fieldwork in research and development sectors, as both require academic prioritisation and sound methodological practice. Yet, conversely, the Ouse excavations themselves equally enriched and 'rooted' Haddenham's final publication in the local landscape. If we had been able to, according to the intended schedule, produce the project's volumes in the late '80s (as opposed to appearing nearly twenty years after the end of fieldwork), their scope and flavour would have been markedly different. This is not to make a virtue out of necessity; but, then, having only a bare minimum of any local excavation context, Haddenham would have had to have been only presented in a 'Fen-wide' or national/international perspective. Hopefully, the final product has maintained this sense of 'grand view', but their delay has also given them a more considered, immediately sub-regional resonance: *appropriate local context only being established through time.* Now, a very different regional prehistory is possible than during the 1980s. A knowledge, for example, of what should be expected of the region's Neolithic settlements has been established, just as there also is a much firmer basis upon which to model its prehistoric settlement densities and appreciate the changing fabric of the land, and this even extends to an awareness of a 'bunching-up' of occupation in the fen-edge river valleys through the impact of marine flooding. Where there was *a* Fenland archaeology, there are now beginning to be many and the emergence of such local complexity is encouraging. With the first of the Lower Ouse volumes currently in preparation, after now working for more than 25 years in the same landscape (admittedly interrupted with fieldwork projects in very different climes; *e.g.* Mongolia, the Himalayas and Cape Verde Islands), it still only remains a privilege to, as it were, be able to 'write into land'.

Acknowledgements

It is a nice conceit to think that long-term fieldwork projects are akin to kids: you tend and cherish them, and duly send them out into the world (often with no small measure of angst); therefore, it is only a pleasure when afforded the opportunity to (re-)visit off-spring. Of course, my greatest debt of thanks is to Hodder, and Haddenham throughout was hugely formative and an enriching experience. Both Ian and I were always grateful to the project's main backers: variously John Coles, David Hall,

Francis Pryor, Geoff Wainwright, Philip Walker and Tim Williams. While this chapter has managed to 'plug' the input of many of the project's key specialists, for the sake of its flow the work of the tens of others who participated are here duly acknowledged, as are also the sterling and much-tried efforts of the project's long-term staff. The same is also true of the Unit's subsequent Lower Ouse fieldwork, for which there is here only scope to thank Charly French, Mark Knight, Roddy Regan and Marc vander Linden, and also acknowledge the co-operation throughout of the various Hanson Quarry managers: Ian Briggs, Brian Chapman, Paul Geeves, Hilton Law and Alex Smiles. This chapter's illustrations attest to the well-honed graphic skills of Andrew Hall of the CAU.

References

Brandt, R. W., Groenman-van Waateringe, W. and van der Leeuw, S. E. (eds) 1987. *Assendelver Polder Papers* I, Amsterdam (Cinqulia 10).

Case, H. J. and Whittle A. W. R. 1982. *Settlement Patterns in the Oxford Region: Excavations at the Abingdon Enclosure and Other Sites.* Oxford/London: Council for British Archaeology.

Clark, J. G. D. 1989. *Prehistory at Cambridge and beyond.* Cambridge: Cambridge University Press.

Coles, B. J. and Cole J. M. 1986. *Sweet Track to Glastonbury: The Somerset Levels in Prehistory.* London: Thames and Hudson.

Coles, J. M. and Lawson A. J. (eds) 1987. *European Wetlands in Prehistory*, 169–201. Oxford: Clarendon Press.

Evans, C. 1984. A shrine provenance for the Willingham Fen hoard. *Antiquity* 58, 212–14.

Evans, C. 1985. Tradition and the cultural landscape: an archaeology of place. *Archaeological Review from Cambridge* 4, 80–94.

Evans, C. 1987. 'Nomads in Waterland'? – Prehistoric transhumance and Fenland archaeology. *Proceedings of the Cambridge Antiquarian Society* 76, 27–39.

Evans, C. 1988. Monuments and analogy: The interpretation of Causewayed Enclosures, in Burgess, C., Topping, P., Mordant, C. and Maddison, M. (eds), *Enclosures and Defences in the Neolithic of Western Europe*, 47–73. Oxford: British Archaeological Reports, International Series, 403.

Evans, C. 1989a. Archaeology and modern times: Bersu's Woodbury 1938 and 1939. *Antiquity* 63, 436–60.

Evans, C. 1989b. Perishables and worldly goods: Artefact decoration and classification in the light of recent wetlands research. *Oxford Journal of Archaeology* 8, 179–201.

Evans, C. 1997a. Hydraulic communities: Iron Age enclosure in the East Anglian Fenlands, in Gwilt, A. and Haselgrove, C. (eds), *Reconstructing Iron Age Societies: New Approaches to the British Iron Age*, 216–27. Oxford: Oxbow Books.

Evans, C. 1997b. Sentimental prehistories: The construction of the Fenland past. *Journal of European Archaeology* 5, 105–36.

Evans, C. 2000. Testing the ground – Sampling Strategies, in Crowson, A., Lane, T. and Reeve, J. (eds), *The Fenland Management Project: Summary Volume*, 15–21. Lincolnshire Archaeology and Heritage Reports Series No. 3.

Evans, C. with Beadsmoore, E., Brudenell M. and Lucas, G. 2009. *Fengate Revisited: Further Fen-edge Excavations, Bronze Age Fieldsystems and Settlement and the Wyman Abbott/Leeds Archives* (CAU Landscape Archives Series: Historiography and Fieldwork). Cambridge: Cambridge Archaeological Unit.

Evans, C., Edmonds, M. and Boreham, S. 2006. 'Total Archaeology' and Model Landscapes: Excavation of the Great Wilbraham Causewayed Enclosure, Cambridgeshire, 1975–76. *Proceedings of the Prehistoric Society* 72, 113–162.

Evans, C. and Hodder, I. 2006a. *A Woodland Archaeology* (The Haddenham Project: Volume I). Cambridge: McDonald Institute Monograph.

Evans, C. and Hodder, I. 2006b. *Marshland Communities and Cultural Landscape* (The Haddenham Project: Volume II). Cambridge: McDonald Institute Monograph.

Evans, C. and Knight, M. 2000. A Fenland Delta: Later Prehistoric land-use in the lower Ouse Reaches, in Dawson, M. (ed), *Prehistoric, Roman and Post-Roman Landscapes of the Great Ouse Valley*, 89–106 (Council for British Archaeology Research Report 119). York: CBA.

Evans, C. and Knight, M. 2001. The 'Community of Builders': The Barleycroft Post Alignments, in Brück, J. (ed.), *Bronze Age Landscapes: Tradition and Transformation*, 83–98. Oxford: Oxbow Books.

Evans, C., Pollard, J. and Knight, M. 1999. Life in woods: Tree-throws, 'settlement' and forest cognition. *Oxford Journal of Archaeology* 18, 241–54.

Evans, C. and Regan, R. 2005. The Roman Camp Ground, Colne Fen, Earith. In Malim, T. (ed.), *Stonea and the Roman Fens*, 164–66. Stroud: Tempus Publishers.

Evans, C. with Appleby, G., Lucy S. and Regan, R. forthcoming. *Process and History: Prehistoric and Roman Fen-edge Communities at Colne Fen, Earith* (*The Archaeology of the Lower Ouse Valley*, Volume I). Cambridge: McDonald Institute Monograph.

Garrow, D. 2006. *Pits, settlement and deposition during the Neolithic and Early Bronze Age in East Anglia*. Oxford: British Archaeological Reports, British Series 414.

Garrow, D., Beadsmoore, E. and Knight, M. 2005. Pit Clusters and the Temporality of Occupation: an Earlier Neolithic Site at Kilverstone, Thetford, Norfolk. *Proceedings of Prehistoric Society* 71, 139–57.

Hall, D. N. 1996. *The Fenland Project Number 10: Cambridgeshire Survey, The Isle of Ely and Wisbech* (East Anglian Archaeology 79). Cambridge: Cambridgeshire Archaeological Committee.

Hall, D. N. and Coles, J. M. 1994. *Fenland Survey: An Essay in Landscape and Persistence*. London: English Heritage.

Hall, D. N., Evans, C., Hodder, I. and Pryor, F. 1987. The fenlands of East Anglia, England: Survey and excavation, in Coles, J. M. and Lawson, A. J. (eds), *European Wetlands in Prehistory*, 169–201. Oxford: Clarendon Press.

Hedges, J. and Buckley, D. 1978. Excavations at a Neolithic causewayed enclosure, Orsett, Essex, 1975. *Proceedings of the Prehistoric Society* 44, 219–308.

Hodder, I. (ed.) 1982a. *Symbolic and Structural Archaeology*. Cambridge: Cambridge University Press.

Hodder, I. 1982b. *Symbols in Action*: *Ethnoarchaeological Studies of Material Culture*. Cambridge: Cambridge University Press.

Hodder, I. 1982c. *The Archaeology of the M11: Excavations at Wendens Ambo*. London: Passmore Edwards Museum.

Hodder, I. 1989. Writing Archaeology: The site report in context. *Antiquity* 63, 268–74.

Hodder, I. 1992. The Haddenham causewayed enclosure: a hermeneutic circle, in Hodder, I. (ed), *Theory and Practice in Archaeology*, 213–40. London: Routledge.

Hodder, I. 1999a. *Archaeological Process: An Introduction*. Oxford: Blackwell.

Hodder, I. 1999b. The wet and the dry: Symbolic archaeology in the Wetlands, in Kawanabe, H., Coulter, G. W. and Roosevelt, A. C. (eds), *Ancient Lakes: Their Cultural and Biological Diversity*, 61–73. Ghent: Kenobi Productions.

Holbeck, B. and Pio, I. 1967. *Fabeldyr og Sagnfolk*. Copenhagen: Politkens Forlag.

Mercer, R. 1980. *Hambledon Hill – A Neolithic Landscape*. Edinburgh: Edinburgh University Press.

Phillips, C. W. 1970. *The Fenland in Roman Times* (Royal Geographical Society Research Series 5). London: Royal Geographical Society.

Pollard, J. 1996. Iron Age Riverside Pit Alignments at St. Ives, Cambridgeshire. *Proceedings of the Prehistoric Society* 62, 93–115.

Pryor, F. 1998. *Etton – Excavations of a Neolithic Causewayed Enclosure Near Maxey, Cambridgeshire, 1982–7*. London: English Heritage.

Pryor, F. M. M. and French, C. A. I. 1985. *Archaeology and Environment in the Lower Welland Valley* (East Anglian Archaeology 27). Cambridge: Cambridgeshire Archaeological Committee.

Pryor, F. 2002. The Welland Valley as a Cultural Boundary Zone: An example of long-term history, in Lane T. and Coles, J. (eds), *Through Wet and Dry: Proceedings of a conference in honour of David Hall*, 18–32. (Lincolnshire Archaeology and Heritage Reports Series No. 5 and WARP Occasional Paper 17). Sleaford: Heritage Trust for Lincolnshire.

Smith, P. 1997. Grahame Clark's New Archaeology: the Fenland Research Committee and Cambridge prehistory in the 1930s. *Antiquity* 71, 11–30.

Waller, M. 1994. *Flandrian Environmental Change* (Fenland Project Number 9/East Anglian Archaeology 70). Cambridge: Cambridgeshire Archaeological Committee.

Yates, D. T. 2007. *Land, Power and Prestige: Bronze Age Field Systems in Southern England.* Oxford: Oxbow Books.

Philip Barker's Wroxeter

Paul Everill and Roger White

In a career as illustrious as Philip Barker's, it seems foolish to try to single out one aspect for special attention. However, at the IFA conference session that forms the basis of this volume, it was revealing that Wroxeter was mentioned in a number of papers (for example Everill, this volume) and in much of the following discussion, but no-one had attempted to present a paper specifically on it. It was almost as if Wroxeter as a site, and in particular Philip Barker's work there, was already a by-word for a 'Great Excavation' and needed no further recommendation. It became clear, however, that there was a need for a discussion of the impact it had on British archaeology. This chapter was born out of subsequent discussions between the authors, both of whom consider Wroxeter to be central to their career development, and consider Philip Barker a key role model in their current efforts to train the next generation of archaeologists.

Roger White paid to take part in the training school at Wroxeter in 1976 and has maintained an active involvement ever since. He was one of the supervisors when Paul Everill was a trainee in the summer of 1989 – the penultimate year of Philip's summer training school there. Of course, given the sheer scale of the site, excavation at Wroxeter both pre- and post-dates Philip's involvement. Graham Webster had already established his own University of Birmingham training excavation there in 1955, having previously assisted on the training excavation run by Dame Kathleen Kenyon in 1953 (White 2006, 166). Kenyon had first worked at Wroxeter in 1936, but she was not the first high profile individual to become linked to the site. In fact the list of names associated with Wroxeter is indeed an illustrious roll call and demonstrates the power of the place to inspire all sorts of people (Barker and White 1998, 12–31). Thomas Telford, not renowned for a compassion for historic buildings let alone an interest in them, recorded a Roman bath house at Wroxeter in 1788 (White 2007). Seven decades later, in the 14 May 1859 issue of the journal *All the Year Round*, Charles Dickens published an article entitled 'Rome and Turnips', which had been inspired by the excavations of Thomas Wright at Wroxeter. Later that same year Charles Darwin, himself a native of Shropshire, astounded the world with the publication of his magnum opus *On the Origin of Species*. However, his last piece of research was a lower key affair for which he had studied the depth of soil overlying the archaeology at Wroxeter and other Roman towns. *The Formation of Vegetable Mould Through the Action of Worms* was published in 1881, the year before Darwin's death. Another local man, Wilfred Owen, used to visit Wroxeter regularly with his brother and it provided the inspiration for one of only two odes that he is known to have written. *Uriconium: An ode* is believed to have been written *circa* July 1913 and is often described as his first war poem (Stallworthy 1974, 88–90). There is the very real possibility that Owen was sketching out his stanzas watching the students of J. P. Bushe-Fox, including the young Mortimer Wheeler, being instructed in the art of excavation at Wroxeter.

If thou hast ever longed
To lift the gloomy curtain of Time Past,
And spy the secret things that Hades hath,
Here through this riven ground take such a view.

(*Uriconium: An ode*, First Stanza, Day Lewis 1963)

Against this impressive backdrop, Philip Barker was first asked to assist Graham Webster at Wroxeter in 1966, after he had been appointed to a lectureship in the Extra Mural Department at Birmingham. The two worked together until 1985, with Philip continuing to direct excavations there for a few further seasons. Both Graham and Philip were dedicated to the principle of providing high-quality training for archaeologists. However, Philip brought open area excavation to Wroxeter at a time when the process was still largely scorned by those raised on Mortimer Wheeler's box and baulk approach and, over a number of years, convinced Graham that this new methodology was both appropriate and effective. White (2006) provides a detailed overview of the often complex relationship between Philip and Graham and the difference in their approaches. It is not our intention to repeat that exercise, but simply to examine, sometimes reflexively, the effect of Philip's approach at Wroxeter and to ask: What is the legacy of a great excavator and a great excavation?

Reminiscences of Wroxeter Alumni

During the 1970s and 80s, the twin excavations at Wroxeter by Philip and Graham had a total workforce of around 150 each year. However, by 1990 these numbers were greatly reduced - largely as a result of changes in the way British archaeology was funded, but also because the two directors had reached convenient points at which to move away from the field and concentrate their energy on publishing results. The experience of trainees at Wroxeter also changed over the years, as ideas developed and methods were perfected.

Peter Pickering was a trainee on Webster's excavation in 1959 – several years before Philip became involved. Peter had started a career as a Civil Servant, after a degree in classics at Oxford. He had done no excavation as part of his course, though he had spent a few days at a dig in Lincoln, but when it came time to organise his summer holiday he came across a programme for the Wroxeter training course, and booked. During his time there prisoners from a local prison did the heavy work, while the trainees trowelled and drew sections *etc*. He recently found some letters that he had sent to his parents at the time, and in one of them he had written:

> I cannot say that I am a great archaeologist, but I learnt a lot. I found a coin in my hole, and, although I did not realise it, a most interesting wall which ran in an unexpected direction. I also did a very wicked thing by agreeing to the suggestion of a prisoner that he should remove an oil-drum [*i.e.* amphora] which was clinging to the side of my hole. They were very cross with me. But they forgave me. All last week I stayed up until 2am… I learnt a lot in these conversations about the archaeological world, and how much they all hate each other! And how to control amateurs who don't know nearly as much as they think they do. (Peter Pickering, pers. comm.)

Peter remained involved in archaeological societies, but never had the opportunity to take part in any further training excavations because of work and family commitments. He concluded his account of his time at Wroxeter by saying that there is not much I can remember about the techniques taught by Webster, I fear. All I can say is that ever since 1959 I have subconsciously believed that proper archaeology has trenches, with baulks, sections and layers. All this open area and context stuff seems vaguely wrong to me – though I know it isn't. (Peter Pickering, pers. comm.).

Lyle E. Browning was at Wroxeter in 1974, also on Webster's site. He had dug first for Alan Carter at Norwich and, later, for Donald Mackreth at Peterborough and so he had already been trained in stratigraphic excavation by the time Mackreth – a Wroxeter veteran himself – suggested he take part in the training excavation to further hone his skills. Lyle recalls that there was amazement amongst Webster's team that Barker had taken so many seasons to remove so little 'dirt', but, at the same time, there was real acknowledgment of the results that had been obtained by his methods. Lyle also remembers the effect that Philip's personality had on the way he went about his work.

> We went over to Barker's dig and I remember a story that Barker told about a vicar who'd come to visit and was up on the photographic tower and remarked about the shops all having different coloured stones defining them and Barker laughed and said "Oh, yes, of course" and explained that he'd not seen the wood for the trees until the vicar pointed it out.[1] Deprecating sense of humour at times, but with eyes wide open for any new input that could help, regardless of the source. Open minded evaluation was the hallmark. That has always stayed with me as a way to approach life. (Lyle E. Browning, pers. comm.).

Lyle, who returned to the USA in 1979, was immensely influenced by Philip's approach. He still uses what he calls the 'Carter / Mackreth / Winchester method' of stratigraphic excavation in his work. During much of the 1980s, Lyle ran the Virginia Department of Transportation archaeology program, before moving into 'CRM' (Cultural Resource Management) archaeology. He states that Barker's techniques have 'moved across the pond and are alive and well' (Lyle E. Browning, pers. comm.).

The year that Lyle worked at Wroxeter was also the year that Mike Corbishley, later to become head of English Heritage's Education Department, was appointed supervisor by Philip. Mike, like Lyle, already had archaeological experience when he first worked at Wroxeter as a volunteer in 1973. He was teaching it in secondary school in Colchester to some very receptive students, including Dominic Powlesland, Tim Williams and Paul Barford and also part-time for the Workers' Educational Association, but Philip's reputation attracted a wide variety of people, including experienced unit diggers who spent their holidays working at Wroxeter. Mike soon became the senior site supervisor, and towards the end of the project he effectively ran the training component. He recalls the principles behind the training excavations as follows:

- Students were to be given the opportunity to engage in real archaeology. Both Phil and I were adamant that those training schools where lower standards were applied, simply because it was training, were not acceptable.
- We encouraged applications from people of all ages who wanted to be trained to work on archaeological excavations, whether as professionals or amateurs. We were also taking university students at a time when some universities could not provide their own training excavations.
- [The] schools were, essentially, practical training on site with lectures/seminars as a subsidiary part of the training.
- Students were not treated any differently from the volunteers and, in fact, we were always keen to see that the volunteers received as much training as they needed (Phil and I were both (ex-)teachers). We engaged in long discussions before the schools started about the 'morality' of taking money from some while paying others. Students were also included in all the social aspects of the site itself (cinema evenings, outings to other sites *etc*).

- Students had to do the work on the site themselves. We dismissed any idea that the volunteers would empty buckets and wheelbarrows (for example) for students, simply because they had paid to come to the Wroxeter training schools. (Mike Corbishley, pers. comm.).

These shared principles were very much in evidence throughout the years of the training schools. By 1989, when Howard Williams participated, the quality of the direction and supervision was a significant feature of the Wroxeter experience. He describes it as a 'very well run training excavation that incorporated teaching and practice effectively' (Howard Williams, pers. comm.). He recalls specialists being brought in to train students on survey equipment and to give talks on geophysics, church architecture and other aspects of the site's history, alongside regular evening lectures on aspects of the site and the excavation. The fieldwork itself was generally undertaken at a pace that allowed individuals to learn at a self-determined rate – although there was pressure to complete some tasks – and provision was made for trainees with a range of physical and mental abilities. He also recalls that the wide range of ages and backgrounds of the trainees provided a real sense of inclusiveness and team spirit. It was not a training excavation dominated, as many were, by undergraduate students. Instead 15 and 16 year olds worked alongside students on their university training dig, and tradesmen and professionals spending their summer holiday at Wroxeter. 'Apart from the ubiquitous insane older student and the ubiquitous overbearing ex-military type, this was a real benefit – it wasn't a group of students of the same age' (Howard Williams, pers. comm.).

Importantly, there was also an expectation that trainees at Wroxeter would do some background reading on the project and this reinforced a sense that it was part of ongoing academic research. Equally important were the discussions regarding the presentation of the site and of the excavations. The value Philip and his team placed on the principles of community involvement and education were clear to all of the trainees and made a lasting impression on many, including Howard. Currently a senior lecturer in archaeology at the University of Chester, Howard sums up his memories of Wroxeter by saying that

> Implicitly these are all points that I have tried to integrate, with different levels of success, into my own, more modest attempts to run field projects. Equally importantly, I don't recall the problems I face as a site director today being a problem at Wroxeter – *e.g.* constant complaints about limitations on mobile phone recharging, accusations and obsessions with health and safety, and dealing with students who become problems and gain difficulties only because their medical histories are withheld from the director for confidentiality reasons.
>
> As for Barker himself, my memories are rather less clear. I don't remember him being there most of the time apart from to lead a few visits and take some pics. I remember him calling me a fool, which probably was and is true, so I can afford him a firm judge of character. (Howard Williams, pers. comm.).

After the end of the official Barker era training schools the University of Birmingham continued to send its students to Wroxeter and Philip remained involved, albeit in a more peripheral role. In the summers of 1991 and 1992 Nick Armour, today a site director for the Cambridge Archaeology Unit, took part in the excavation on the northern defences far removed from the centre of the city which had become 'scheduled to within an inch of its life' by English Heritage (Nick Armour, pers. comm.; Esmonde Cleary *et al.* 2006). The quality of the supervision remained a significant factor, and Nick describes Gwilym Hughes, the site supervisor and now Chief Inspector for Cadw, as being 'absolutely fantastic. An excellent teacher' (Nick Armour, pers. comm.). At that time Nick had already spent a year working for the Essex County Council Unit, in a gap year before university, and felt that he did not really need training. He recalls that

In some ways I was right. I could hoe gravel and dig postholes! What I saw at Wroxeter was a completely different order of magnitude. The memory I have that stands out is of a lecture Philip Barker gave on the late/post RB 'squatter' occupation in the basilica. The quality of work was simply astounding. Every floor layer, every repair (even repair of a repair) documented and sequenced. Post holes and beam slots sometimes only a few millimetres in depth yet all revealed, excavated and recorded. And from this huge body of evidence careful interpretation leading to the previously unrealised details of a late RB city in decline and beyond. It fired two main observations that I still hold today. Firstly, as I tell students and anyone else who will listen, there are only three things to remember when practising archaeology – definition, definition, and more definition! If you can't see it properly you won't recognise it, excavate it, record or interpret it properly. Secondly, if you don't apply the highest standards of technical expertise to the smallest of details as well as the largest then the evidence with which you present your interpretations is flawed and ultimately worthless. It's usually the small stuff that illuminates the big stuff rather than the other way around. In the context of a whole Roman City a faint smattering of postholes and beam slots may not seem to count for much but they have powered the entire field of late Roman studies for the last 20 odd years. Nuff said! (Nick Armour, pers. comm.).

Nick was not the only Wroxeter alumnus to also mention specifically the social life on the digs. He recalled parties down by the Severn that caused some consternation for the supervisors, and the 'simmering term-time romances that exploded into flames of passion at Wroxeter'. These included the innocent couple who finally got together after a year of missed opportunities and 'inadvertently advertised the whole thing to the rest of the campsite (her head was up against the tent pole...)' (Nick Armour, pers. comm.). However, it is clear that the real legacy of Wroxeter for Nick was in the painstaking approach to the archaeology pioneered by Philip, and in the importance placed on the quality of supervision and training.

One trainee in particular had a unique insight into the personality and working methods of Philip Barker. In 1968, 14 year old Jeremy Barker joined his father at Wroxeter for the first time, and was a regular fixture each year until the mid 1970s. For him, 'it seemed the most natural thing in the world for the Barker family to become nomadic every summer and to mount the expeditions to Hen Domen in July and Wroxeter in August' (Jeremy Barker, pers. comm.). Jeremy's recollections reveal the extent of Philip's commitment to the principle of 'education for all' and 'willingness to enlighten anybody who wished to listen (and most likely quite a few who didn't)'. It was not unknown for him, on wintry evenings, to dress in an old RAF flying jacket and drive 15 miles in his unheated Austin 10 to deliver a lecture to a local society. Jeremy does recall, however, that 'these evening outings, however, took their toll and my Father once had the dubious distinction of falling asleep in one of his own lectures' (Jeremy Barker, pers. comm.).

It is also clear that Philip's passion for the past came from a desire to create a better future. As he once said, 'we should learn from the past, not live in it'. This may appear a strange thing for an archaeologist to say, but it was this forward thinking which enabled him to develop and refine the excavation techniques for which he has become so well known. (Jeremy Barker, pers. comm.).

Jeremy's first season at Wroxeter, in August 1968, was memorable for a number of reasons. On the international stage it was, of course, the time that the Soviet Union ruthlessly suppressed demonstrations in Prague. One of the volunteers taking part in the excavation was a Czech academic whose wife was still in Prague – though it later transpired that she was thankfully safe and well – and for Philip it brought back moving wartime memories. That season Jeremy shared a tent with old friend Charles Hill and, unbeknown to Philip, they used the 'Old Work' as goal posts for their kickabouts amongst the ruins. It was also the year that the term 'Surgery of the Earth' was coined during a conversation between Philip and John Hill MD (Charles' Father) at Sidoli's Italian restaurant in Shrewsbury. In general terms, however, Jeremy states that his, foremost memories of working with Dad at both Hen Domen and Wroxeter are of his infectious passion, energy and humour (not necessarily in that order). His measured and meticulous method of excavation may not be to everyone's taste but appears to have set a standard or yardstick that others can use for comparison. In other words, if you have the time and the money this is how you would set about all archaeological excavations… As we all acknowledge Dad was, by all accounts, a remarkable man, and, believe you me, a very tough act to follow. (Jeremy Barker, pers. comm.).

A trainee's scrapbook – Paul Everill

In 1989, having found the CBA leaflets on careers in archaeology at my school, I decided that I would be one of the 8% of graduates that managed to get a job. In 2008, in contrast, my experience suggests that only 8% of archaeology undergraduates actually want a career in archaeology, and many training excavations do not succeed in inspiring the remainder (Everill 2007). However, the CBA's advice at the time was clear and simple: get as much experience as you could to make sure you stood out from the crowd. Having been sent the application leaflet for the Wroxeter training school, I was able to convince my school that this would serve as my 'work experience' in the summer following my GCSEs. My parents paid the small fee, I got my old tent out of the loft and by Saturday 19 August 1989 I was listening to an introductory lecture by Philip Barker (Figure 12.1). I am sure I was an unremarkable trainee, but for me the two weeks I spent there was packed full of firsts. I still remember the camaraderie of my fellow trainees. I remember doing the 'Shadow's Walk' on one of the tables in the food tent with a friend - much to everyone else's amusement; I remember the thrill of my first love; I remember being introduced to rum and coke in the 'Horseshoe' on the day I got

Figure 12.1. Excavation Team Photo, 1989. Paul is crouched in the front row wearing a jacket, and Roger is to his right, at the end of the row. Philip stands extreme left.

my GCSE results; I remember the sheer exhausting satisfaction of working outdoors; and I remember, more than anything, that each passing day confirmed in me the desire to be an archaeologist. In fact, when I look back, I simply cannot believe that all my memories would fit into two weeks, but there you have it.

I kept a scrapbook and diary during the training school and, looking at it now, it is plain to see the impact that the tutoring of Philip, Mike and Roger had on me. I copied out drawings illustrating stratigraphic principles and typed up my notes on context recording, the history of the site, and dating techniques on my parents' prehistoric Amstrad word processor when I got home. My diary records that I spent the first Sunday and Monday revealing the remains of a wall, and had my first ever significant find of a small bronze coin on only my second day on site. Tuesday was spent in the finds hut and on Wednesday I was back on site 'cleaning a really boring pebble floor' – finding it hard to concentrate as I was nervous about my impending GCSE results. By the following Sunday I volunteered for surveying to 'get out of trowelling', but it is clear that I was fascinated in all the aspects of the archaeological process. Interestingly, from my current perspective of someone who now trains students, my comprehension of stratigraphic principles was surprisingly good for someone new to archaeology. This, I assume, must be due to the way it was taught on site and in the evening classes, and is a good reflection of the quality of the staff that Philip gathered around him.

The staff perspective – Roger White

In more than 30 years of work at Wroxeter I have been fortunate to have seen the progress of discovery on this site from all possible angles. I first began as a paying student on Graham Webster's training school in the scorching heat of 1976. In 1978 I came back as a paid volunteer on Philip Barker's site, returning every year for full seasons from 1979 until 1985 when I had the sad duty of supervising the backfilling of the basilica site. These years included being made assistant supervisor in 1980 and full supervisor from 1981. From 1986–90 I taught on the same Birmingham Training School that I had been a student on a decade before, working on the extremities of the site and combining this from 1987 onwards with employment as the post-excavation researcher writing up Philip's site. I had peripheral involvement in the University of Birmingham excavations from 1991–3 (Department rather than Extra-Mural) but then in 1994–1999 was field archaeologist with the Wroxeter Hinterland Project, employed by the Birmingham University Field Archaeology Unit (now Birmingham Archaeology) as a Leverhulme Research Fellow. What was it about excavating at Wroxeter that clearly had such a profound effect on my life and chosen profession?

My initial involvement was the perceived requirement to get training. I had always wanted to be an archaeologist and felt that if I wanted to get anywhere I had to participate in a training excavation so as to learn the basics. That done, I felt free to volunteer when in 1978 my Canadian cousin asked if I could find us both a dig to take part in. By then I had experienced prehistoric excavations and reasoned that he would prefer to find artefacts in abundance: Wroxeter was an obvious choice from the CBA Calendar of Excavations, not least because I knew the set up. My initial experience was not positive: I was put down a large archaeological trench, excavated by Graham Webster in the early 1960s, and told to empty it. I learnt later this was Mike Corbishley's idea of a fitting task for a Webster-trainee! If that had been my only experience then perhaps the story would have stopped there but one day, deep down in the trench, Phil's head appeared alongside Mike's and, looking at the results of my work and listening to my responses to their questions about what I thought was going on in the visible sections and how I had defined the edges, I was redeemed and put to other, more Barker-like tasks of cleaning and defining on the surface. By the end of my third week (the fourth of that season) I was hooked by both the quality of the archaeology and the camaraderie of the team excavating it and could hardly wait to get back to the site in 1979.

What were the hallmarks of Phil's approach? As someone just starting out, his most important characteristic was that he was always prepared to listen to anyone's opinion about the site. Instead of only seeking the supervisor's view, he would ask the diggers directly: what was the surface like to excavate? What did *you* think was going on? This was no tokenism: he had no time for those who used people as 'trowel-fodder'. To him, there was no such thing as 'mindless trowelling'. Your attention must be focused on the task and surfaces in front of you: you had a responsibility to the archaeology and that meant that you didn't have time for too much chatting and certainly not to listen to music on site, which would be too much of a distraction. In consequence radios were banned (as would have been Walkmans or iPods were they around at that time).

In practical terms his approach was that the excavators worked together as a team: in a trowelling line if you were a quicker, cleaner troweller than your neighbour, you were expected to take more of the archaeology so that the line advanced together. The overall effect required was precise and accurate: if you were asked to *clean* a surface, he (and the supervisors) would look in your bucket to make sure you were only taking the very crust off the surface to freshen it. No stones must be removed. When digging you were instructed never to take off more than one bucketful at a time: too much loose meant you couldn't see what you were doing to the archaeology. If you couldn't determine how layers inter-related, clean, and clean again until you could. If there was still no answer, take off a spit of 5cms and then try again. Once you found an edge, always dig from the known to the unknown until you had resolved which was earlier. That way, if things went wrong you would not have damaged the archaeology too much. Such rigour may sound rather anal but in reality it emphasises that Phil's defining approach was that the archaeology should *emerge* rather than you as excavator guessing what was there and digging the site according to your preconceptions. This can be contrasted to Graham's approach which was very much about deciding what the Romans had been trying to do and then digging accordingly. When they did not do what he had expected them to do, he was confounded:

> On the very last day of [the] 1953 [season at Great Casterton], an unexpected wall was uncovered. But a new wall in that particular place spelt trouble for my carefully nurtured hypothesis. I was not prepared to contemplate such an inconvenient find … Eventually the students virtually had to drag me to their find and I was forced to gaze on this horror … In no way could it conform to my carefully constructed logical building sequence … such was the shock that I walked off the site in a state of mental turmoil (Webster 1991, 121).

It was Phil's meticulous, precise and sensitive approach to the archaeology that sticks in your mind. If you worked for Phil, you never looked at an archaeological surface in the same way again. You would forever be seeking out the nuances and subtleties of the archaeology that he so keenly observed. Why was that stone worn and not those round it? How long did such wear take to generate? Why was that surface different from its surroundings? I have in my Wroxeter archive a very characteristic Phil document. Entitled '*WP84: 22 hard questions, not in order of difficulty*', it poses as questions 22 of his observations of the archaeology of the baths basilica that season which had puzzled him and which he sent to all his supervisors asking for a response to see if they knew what the answers might be. The questions range from (3) *Where did the charcoal and the ash at the west end [of the nave] come from? And why?* to (13) *What was the function of the basilica at this time? What function could it have had which generated no rubbish?* concluding with (22) *What the hell does it all mean ???* Such approaches could help deal with that most difficult of archaeological problems: the fixed interpretation. Any site will gradually accrue interpretations of the archaeology that become more and more fixed through being explained first on site and then in public lectures so that they become very difficult to retract. At Wroxeter, the gravel street was one such account, as was the discovery of the frontages on *insula* 2 and their relationship to the discovery, always puntilliously acknowledged to A. H. A. Hogg, of Building 10. The problem with these stories is that they can become difficult to prove to others – 'you had to be there to see it' – but worse they can lead to an uncritical approach. The first point will be picked up later in the narrative but the second point is one that comes back to the questions asked by Philip. In asking these he not only wanted an answer – he wanted evidence too. If you were going to demolish his pet theory, he wanted to see an equally plausible explanation put in its place, backed with the evidence of the archaeology. Where possible this would involve going out on site and looking at the archaeology. If not, then a search of the archive was called for. Once convinced, he would happily ditch an interpretation, or place yours alongside it as a viable alternative.

This is certainly how I remember Phil as a Director. His role was not to be on site 'Directing' but to roam as an interested, and extremely well-informed bystander, whose task it was to ask the awkward question of the supervisor, to notice the details that you, as someone trying to cope with the multitude of tasks and personnel, did not have time to ask. This could, of course, be infuriating. I remember on one occasion racing up to the drawing office in a fit of righteous anger to rail at the site draftsman about Phil's 'interference' in what I was doing on site. She tried to calm me, mouthing that he was next door but it was too late: I had had my very voluable say. He calmly emerged when I'd finished as though nothing had happened, and walked away, leaving me initially seething but then feeling very foolish. Such episodes were very rare as he was a genuinely easy person to get on with, though demanding. One of his more demanding, but also rewarding, tasks, was to ask you to get up early in the morning, at sunrise, to capture particular effects that the low sunlight had on the surfaces of the site, often highlighted by a light dew. Here, his artist's eye was all too evident and it is telling that although we had Sidney Renow, a site photographer of brilliant technical ability, it is Phil's photographs that mostly appear in the basilica report because he knew how to take a photograph that captured the archaeological nuances. The helper's role was to pose scale, arrow and labels so he could frame the picture quickly while the light was with him.

There is no doubt that this ability to capture such detail came from his artistic training and is echoed in his very visual approach to his excavations. Go to the Wroxeter archive today and what strikes you is the huge quantity of drawings and photographs. As has been noted (Cool 2006, 231–2), this is a feature of the report too: nearly 200 loose-leaf drawings, enough to paper a wall, speak volumes about the core of Phil's approach. It led to the greatest weakness of his style, as well as its greatest strength. The weakness was in the written record. I cannot recall him writing context cards, despite his interest in and awareness of the importance of the record. Initially, records had been in books tied to each grid recording Layers or Features (F. nos.) and supplemented by huge single squares of permatrace drawing film for each 5m grid but these records too had been written by the site supervisors. These books were replaced in 1974 by cards and a single sequence for each of the five areas of site, lettered A–E. By the 1980s these had been replaced by printed pro-forma context cards that are in most respects the same as those in use today. It was the supervisor's task to fill these in and keep an accurate record of what was being done, including drawing up the Harris matrix. This was never monitored by Phil so that it was apparent to me, as the person who actually carried out the writing up, that the record could be quite variable or even poor in places. I do not wish, however, to give the impression that Phil was in some way shirking his responsibilities. Running a huge workforce, actually making the dig happen in the first place and ensuring that it ran without hiccup, was a full-time job. He had no choice but to rely on his supervisors. What redeemed the record was the unique and huge archive resource that was the quadrupod photograph collection (Renow 1985) and the equally voluminous drawn archive.

Drawings, of course, were his forte. As he had taught art in his first career after his war-time service in Coastal Command this was hardly surprising. Planning was done on sheets of drawing film – permatrace – in the late 1960s still brand new and favoured for its stability and ability to be drawn upon in the wet. Drawings were made when an archaeological horizon had been reached – a 'phase' or 'sub-phase'. This was, of course subjective and caused some disagreement at a later stage as will be seen. Drawings were to be as realistic as possible, and coloured using crayons. Not surprisingly the defining image of the site was of draftsmen and women standing hunched over the lightweight aluminium drawing frames that Phil had designed and had made in the University's engineering department (Figure 12.2). For those of us who were artistically challenged, this task could be a nightmare: peering down through the grid, striving to compensate for the shift of the surface beneath the grid according to the angle of vision and the height of the frame above the ground. I remember once despairing of being able to reproduce on drawing film what looked remarkably like a pile of cornflakes but which was, in fact, a heap of frost-shattered tiles that had once been a hearth. 'But Phil', I said, 'it's impossible to draw this!' when he remonstrated with me for lapsing into a conventionalised representation of the tile. Quietly he took the pencil, rubbed my efforts out and impeccably drew it for me. Infuriating, but the perfect response too: not only was it possible but it was also important to get it right.

Phil was correctly worried, of course, that one could not capture in two-dimensions the subtleties of the surfaces and so he also employed as a back-up the vertical stereo photographs, taken in Vericolour by a quadrupod tower and printed at 1:20 scale. It took nigh on a decade of dedicated drawing by three draftswomen to draw these up but the record they have made of the site is second to none and helped immeasurably in writing it up. It was the drawn record that came to the fore on the one occasion when I can recall real dissent between Phil and some of his supervisors. The occasion was a time when some of the younger supervisors had begun their careers with the Department of Urban Archaeology, now MoLAS, which was then developing its famous digging manual. They had returned to Wroxeter in the early 1980s full of the new mode of single-context recording used in London and which they then proceeded to use on those areas of the site that they were digging in preference to 'phase-planning'. While Phil was open to new ideas, the imposition of a new recording system without his agreement or discussion was a step too far but although upset he did not stop them, seeking always to avoid confrontation. My experience in writing up this part of the site, however, was a difficult one. In terms of the matrix it was very clear what the sequence of layers was. However, all I had in terms of drawn record was a single outline of each context with no adequate photographic or drawn corroboration of what they looked like and how they related to each other except in the strict stratigraphical sense. It is to this day very difficult to visualise what these layers were and how to interpret them. In the heat of the moment, the same group had challenged Phil to demonstrate to them the existence of Building 10 from the records he had kept of the site. It was the ultimate challenge and at first it proved very difficult to achieve because of its sheer size but on re-assembling all the relevant plans Building 10 once again emerged from the sea of drawn rubble, identifying itself by the plaster-packing between the rubble, coloured pink on the drawings, and, once identified, demonstrably forming a rectangular shape symmetrical about the two padstones that had initially identified the Building to A. H. A. Hogg and

Figure 12.2. A familiar Wroxeter sight: hoards of planners on the baths basilica, 1984.

Figure 12.3. Excavation Team Photo 1985, with the catering staff and the English Heritage directly employed labour who maintained and consolidated the site throughout the year.

Phil. Of the two recording systems, there is no doubt in my mind that Phil's was the better one, and the one that was more capable of reinterpretation. The problem with single context recording was, and is, that one has to take for granted the interpretation offered at the time. Reinterpretation is virtually impossible. It might also be added that this episode underlined another key Barker tenet: that it is impossible to understand a site purely from the record. You have to understand it on site first, record it and then work out the detail. It is no good hoping that it will 'all come out in the wash' later on: if you don't understand it on site, you stand no chance of making sense of it during the writing up.

I wish to conclude with one element of the excavation process that is rarely considered but which shows Phil as nothing short of a genius. As with the army, an excavation marches on its stomach. Without abundant food to fuel it, an excavation will completely grind to a halt. Phil's approach was masterful and streets ahead of his time. On many excavations, cooking and domestic work was one of the chores that was shared out on a rota basis. Wroxeter was no exception other than that the actual cooking was done by Cynthia and Ian, a husband and wife team who ran catering courses in Worcester. Wroxeter was their way of providing placement training for their students. Thus Wroxeter was doubly a training excavation in both excavation and catering. They learnt how to keep hungry diggers fed to a budget: we were grateful for the fantastic meals whose scents wafted so enticingly across the site. Phil was clever too about breaking up the long day: on site at 8.30 with no more than a cup of tea, one would be ready at 10 for a full English breakfast and the 45 minutes that one had to enjoy it. Then lunch at 1 with another 45 minutes before tea at 3.30 with freshly baked cakes or buns ending at 6 with a welcome collapse, for the supervisorial staff at least, into the delights of a drink while waiting for the evening meal at 6.30 (these drinks not, alas, provided by Phil but from our own pockets). It was little wonder that we all wanted to come back year after year.

Conclusion

So what was it about Wroxeter that made it a great excavation? It was not primarily the site although that played its part in providing the most astonishing quality of archaeological preservation and detail, as well as copious amounts of finds. Graham's excavation too had its loyal followers who came back year after year to experience their own brand of camaraderie and Graham's approach to excavation. Yet it is clear that when people talk of Wroxeter as a great excavation they mean Phil's rather than Graham's or anybody else's. This rather suggests that what makes a Great Excavation is a Great Excavator and there is little doubt that Philip Barker has a claim to have been one of the greatest excavators that British Archaeology has produced. If this is the case, then perhaps the real question is: What makes a great excavator? From what has been demonstrated here we would highlight two traits. First was Phil's unsurpassed ability to interpret the archaeology, to notice the detail and to be open to what the archaeology was saying to him rather than bring his own preconceptions to the site and have them confirmed by the archaeology. Second was his ability to treat the opinion of all equally on site, from the lowliest digger, including the prison labourers he initially worked with, to the most senior of visitors. All were able to express their opinion to him and be taken seriously. All felt that they could have an input. Diana Murray, now Chief Executive of the Royal Commission in Scotland, was a planner on the baths basilica site in the 1970s when the revolutionary discovery of the post-Roman levels was first being realised (Barker 1975) and what she recalled in conversation were the debates among the whole team in the evenings after work. Interpretation was debated collectively[2] but refined by Philip, Kate Pretty and others in the supervisory team. Phil's willingness to engage in archaeological thought and debate, his openness to new ideas and interpretations, and his huge energy and commitment to archaeology – it should never be forgotten that he was an instrumental player in the foundation of both Rescue and the IFA – mark him out as a truly great man in an exceptional generation of archaeologists.

References

Barker, P. A. 1975. Excavations at the Baths Basilica at Wroxeter 1966–74: interim report *Britannnia* 5, 106–117.

Barker, P. A. 1977. *Techniques of Archaeological Excavation* (1st edn.) Batsford, London.

Barker, P. A. and White, R. H. 1998. *Wroxeter: life and death of a Roman City*. Tempus: Stroud.

Barker, P. A., White, R. H., Pretty, K. B., Bird, H. and Corbishley, M. J. 1997. *Wroxeter, Shropshire. Excavations on the Baths Basilica 1966–1990*. London: English Heritage Archaeological Reports 8.

Cool, H. E. M. 2006. *Eating and Drinking in Roman Britain*. Cambridge: Cambridge University Press.

Darwin, C. 1881. *The Formation of Vegetable Mould Through the Action of Worms*.

Day Lewis, C. (ed.) 1963. *The Collected Poems of Wilfred Owen*. London.

Dickens, C. (ed.) 1859. Rome and Turnips. *All The Year Round* Issue 3 (14 May), 53–8.

Esmonde Cleary, S., Ellis, P., Mecksepper, C. and White, R. 2006. Excavations on the Northern Defences, 1991/2, in Ellis, P. J. and White, R. H. (eds), *Wroxeter Archaeology. Excavation and Research on the Defences and in the Town, 1968–1992*, 5–12. *Transactions of the Shropshire Archaeological and Historical Society* 78 (2003).

Everill, P. 2007. A day in the life of a training excavation: teaching archaeological fieldwork in the UK. *World Archaeology* 39(4), 483–498.

Renow, S. 1985. *Vertical Archaeological Photography*. Birmingham: The Institute of Field Archaeologists Technical Paper No. 2.

Stallworthy, J. 1974. *Wilfred Owen*. Oxford: Oxford University Press.

Webster, G. 1991. *Archaeologist at Large*. London: Batsford.

White, R. H. 2006. Excavating Wroxeter at the End of the Twentieth Century, in Ellis, P. J. and White, R. H. (eds), *Wroxeter Archaeology. Excavation and Research on the Defences and in the Town, 1968–1992*, 165–9. *Transactions of the Shropshire Archaeological and Historical Society* 78 (2003).

White, R. H. 2007. Thomas Telford: Rome, roads and bath houses. *Proceedings of the Thomas Telford Day School, Madeley, 8th September 2007*, 8–14. Telford: Wrekin Local Studies Transactions.

Notes

1   It is quite likely here that what was being pointed out was the different coloured platforms of buildings on the south aisle in phase Z: see Barker *et al.* 1997, fig. 204, a photo taken by Philip.

2   In the acknowledgements to Philip's 1975 article he thanks 'my colleagues on and off the excavation whose criticisms and suggestions have formed the basis for much of the interpretation offered here'.

'Erik Bloodaxe Rules OK': 'The Viking Dig' at Coppergate, York

Richard Hall

Pre-Norman York, before Coppergate

With its cathedral, twin castles, five guild halls, nineteen surviving medieval parish churches, a wealth of timber-framed buildings, and the remains of a major Benedictine abbey and medieval hospital, as well as 2½ miles of city walls, York still retains a vivid impression of the imposing late medieval city that it once was. As for its earlier history, an origin in the Roman period is betrayed by visible traces of various buildings, and remains of the legionary fortress defences which stand up to 5.8m (19 feet) tall in places. Nothing, however, survives above ground from the centuries between the Roman army's withdrawal from Britain in *c*. AD 410 and the Normans' arrival in York some six and a half centuries later. Yet even before the archaeological discoveries described below, some clues, both written and tangible, did survive to testify to York's historic importance and archaeological significance during that early medieval period.

Eighth-century Anglo-Saxon writers referred to events at York, the epicentre of the independent Anglo-Saxon kingdom of Northumbria. They mentioned kings, a cathedral, a monastery and overseas merchants (Rollason 1998). The *Anglo-Saxon Chronicle*, a brief year-by-year summary of key events, becomes the main source of knowledge about what happened after a Viking army captured York in 866. For nearly a century Viking kings either controlled, or plotted to control, the city and its region. Even after Erik Bloodaxe, the last Viking king of York, was expelled in 954, there was a strong Scandinavian element in the population. Traces of this Scandinavian influence are most obviously preserved in many of the city's street names, such as Ousegate, which end in the element *-gate*. This derives from the Old Norse word *gata*, meaning a street, and became part of the local dialect. Also, some of the city's churches, most notably St Olave's [St Olaf's], are dedicated to saints originating or popular in Scandinavia.

This Scandinavian influence remained strong right up to and beyond the Normans' arrival. By that time, as William the Conqueror's *Domesday Book* makes clear, the city, called *Jorvik*, was one of England's largest. Yet in the early 1970s *Jorvik* was essentially a lost city, not impenetrably enmeshed in dense jungle vines or cut off on a precipitous mountain peak, but mundanely buried below the picturesque remains of its later medieval successor.

In contrast to coins, pottery and massively constructed stone buildings, which had been easy to identify as Roman when they were found by chance in the eighteenth and nineteenth centuries, very few Viking-Age objects apart from coins were recognised until the later nineteenth century. No Viking-Age structures were identified until the early twentieth century; and even then they were thought to be merely wood-lined tanpits, rather than the basement structures that they really were (Hall 1991). They were found in Ousegate, and it was on building sites in this vicinity that nineteenth- and early twentieth-century workmen found many of the objects of metal, bone and other materials which were eventually identified as dating to the Viking Age (Radley 1971). The Yorkshire Philosophical Society's Museum, now The Yorkshire Museum, acquired probably the finest collection of everyday Viking-Age objects in England to be seen outside London. Yet despite the best efforts of various excavators, particularly in the 1950s and 1960s, Viking-Age York still remained elusive, and impossible to characterize, for the investigations in which Viking-Age deposits or structures were identified had either been small in scale or located in parts of the modern city where conditions did not preserve buried remains in good condition.

So, when York Archaeological Trust for Excavation and Research (YAT) was established as an educational charity in 1972, one of its objectives was to discover remains that would plug this chronological gap. The newly established Trust realised straight away that plans put forward by Lloyds Bank to extend their branch in Pavement, a continuation of Ousegate, could offer an opportunity to investigate Viking-Age York. The bank's proposals involved the creation of new subterranean vaults; so YAT, conscious of the archaeological riches that might lie undetected here, approached Lloyds and asked if it could do the digging. Lloyds agreed and, what's more, generously donated £1000 towards the cost of the excavation, at that time an unusual and very welcome gesture. Georgian cellars had already removed the uppermost archaeological layers and, on lifting their floors, YAT's archaeologists immediately started to uncover Viking-Age layers. By the end of their work three important and novel facts had been established (Addyman 1991).

Firstly, they found that about 9.5m (30 feet) of archaeological layers lay between the modern street level and the underlying natural geological deposits. Such a deep build-up is very unusual; it resulted from the rapid accumulation of layer upon layer of domestic rubbish and discarded building materials such as thatch, wattlework and wood. Together these ingredients had given these layers an organic-rich, 'peaty' appearance.

Secondly, and closely related, was the exceptionally good organic preservation throughout most of these deposits. This was because they had been kept moist by groundwater seeping down the natural valley slope towards the River Foss. These layers never dried out but had compacted, excluding the free circulation of oxygen and thus denying life to the bacteria which normally destroy buried objects. In particular, objects made from organic materials which normally rot to dust quickly after they are buried – wooden bowls, leather shoes, textiles from clothing – were preserved in remarkable condition. Objects made from other materials such as iron, bone and antler also survived well; the only casualties were items made of horn or linen. Overall, this presented the archaeologists with a much more complete picture of daily life than they could normally hope to recover.

The third discovery at the Lloyds Bank site was that these 'peaty' soils also preserve the small, often microscopic, remains of seeds, plants and beetles which, in their lifetimes, favour very specific habitats. Experts could identify these remains, and deduce what conditions had been like in their immediate vicinity. They could then provide remarkable insights into both urban living conditions and the natural, semi-natural and man-made landscape in the surrounding countryside, as well as into topics such as past climate, diet and health which often remain elusive to the researcher.

All of this was a revelation, exposing aspects of the Viking-Age urban past that had been undreamt of in the archaeological world. The only problem was that the Lloyds Bank trenches, because of their restricted size, had given just a tantalizing, key-hole view into this Viking-Age city. But they had demonstrated the gains to knowledge that might be won if an archaeological vista could be opened up in larger scale excavations.

Opening Coppergate

Fortuitously, a proposal by York City Council to redevelop a vast, partly derelict area in Coppergate, just 75m from the Lloyds Bank site, soon gave a glimmer of hope (Figure 13.1). Importantly, the site was right in the heart of that part of York where builders and other workmen in the nineteenth and earlier twentieth centuries had found most of the Viking-Age objects which had ended up in The Yorkshire Museum. The proposals were at an early stage in 1975 when Peter Addyman, York Archaeological Trust's founding Director, set about lobbying the Council for permission to excavate before the redevelopment got underway. Eventually agreement came that YAT could have two years to excavate while the development was tendered and planned, and funding came from the Department of the Environment (DoE, the predecessors of English Heritage). So, in May 1976, we started the excavation by hammering out the concrete floor of a suite of cellars near the street frontage on four properties at 16–22 Coppergate. Within a few days traces of wooden walls, wattle fences and other organic materials revealed that preservation here was as good as that seen at Lloyds Bank; and pottery and other datable objects proved that the modern cellars had provided a short-cut into the Viking Age.

This was the start of what was to become known as 'The Viking Dig' (Figure 13.2). But having rapidly confirmed that the site was prolific in new information about urban development in the Viking Age, we turned our attention to later centuries, as we extended the area under excavation. Firstly we investigated down slope, nearer to the River Foss, where Viking-Age features were still covered by the remains of a sequence of later medieval and post-medieval buildings extending up to the eighteenth century (Hall and Hunter-Mann 2002). They were excavated in the same detail as the Viking-Age levels, giving us the most comprehensive and extensive picture of town life in secular medieval York that has yet been uncovered. The impact of the better building methods of these later centuries on the archaeological remains was clearly visible. From the thirteenth century onwards, as tiles were increasingly used for roofing instead of thatch, and as the bases of major structural timbers were no longer placed in the ground but were supported on stone sill walls, so the organic content of the soil was diminished. Archaeological preservation became less good because the later medieval builders were able to construct longer-lasting houses. Nevertheless, we could trace how the plots of land were more densely and extensively built over as the medieval period progressed. We also found remarkable objects, ranging from a medieval toilet seat (Figure 13.3) to a gold ring with a pearl and garnet setting (Figure 13.4), a testimony to the affluence of the medieval landowners hereabouts in what, at one time, was one of the most fashionable neighbourhoods in medieval York (Ottaway and Rogers 2002).

Meanwhile excavation continued on the Viking-Age layers below the modern cellars. As the weeks passed, the wooden walls initially seen there were gradually exposed. They had been fabricated from horizontal oak planks laid edge upon edge, one on top of another, and defined rectangular wooden buildings measuring about 7.5 × 4m (24'6" × 13'). These were cellars or semi-basements, with their floors as much as 1.8m (6 feet) below the contemporary ground surface. Archaeologists in other cities such as London and Chester had excavated such buildings before, but only as ghosts, with all their timberwork long since rotted away. Here, details of the woodwork were preserved up to ground level,

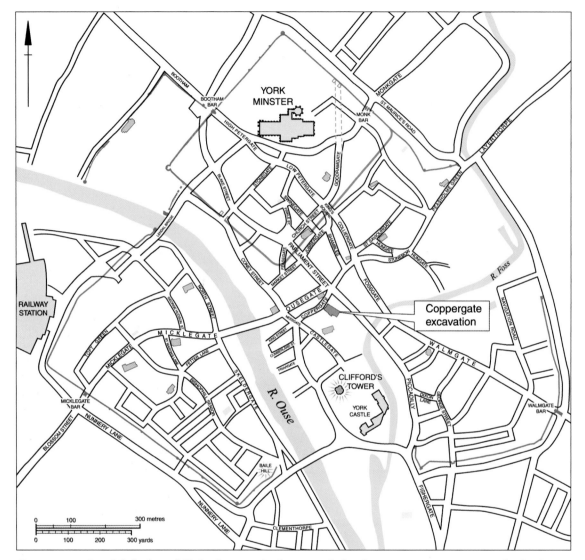

Figure 13.1. Simplified plan of York, showing the location of the Coppergate excavations outside the Roman fortifications. © York Archaeological Trust.

and we could see the massive foundation beams, and the upright posts which rested upon those beams and held the horizontal planks in place. These are the best-preserved buildings in the Viking world in terms both of the condition of the timber and the height to which they remained standing (Figure 13.5). We could even see the tool marks left when the timbers were originally felled and shaped, and could work out how the Viking-Age craftsmen went about their task (Hall 1994; in prep.).

Tree-ring dating experts from the University of Sheffield were able to tell us that many of the timbers had been felled in AD 974/5 and this was, presumably, when the buildings were erected. This is a precision which archaeologists always want but seldom get. So whereas previous discussions of Viking-Age York and beyond had often been conducted in terms of centuries, we had pin-point accuracy, and could use this to extrapolate to other layers and features which did not themselves contain precisely dated timbers. Archaeological dating doesn't get much better than this.

It was already clear that if we were to dig deeper into the Viking-Age layers and to expose any Anglo-Saxon and Roman remains that might lie below, we would have to be very wary of destabilising surrounding buildings. And if we wanted to excavate right up to the modern street frontage where, it might be anticipated, the most important Viking-Age buildings stood, then we would have to

Figure 13.2. The Viking Dig in full swing. © York Archaeological Trust.

Figure 13.3. Thirteenth-century toilet seat discarded in a pit. © York Archaeological Trust.

Figure 13.4. Thirteenth-century gold, pearl and garnet ring. © York Archaeological Trust.

Figure 13.5. Semi-basement building of oak planks, posts and beams erected c. 974/5 © York Archaeological Trust.

shore up the site's perimeter. From a timing point of view it seemed feasible to go to this trouble and expense, for York City Council had indicated to YAT that their various negotiations about the site's redevelopment were taking longer than originally predicted, and so we could have an extension to our original, two-year, timescale. Technically, however, such shoring would not be easy, for hammering piles into the ground might itself damage potentially vulnerable surrounding buildings such as the landmark medieval lantern tower of All Saints church, directly opposite our site. Advice indicated that hydraulic piling would be needed, at a cost of £76,500; a huge sum of money in 1978 which neither YAT nor DoE could find. At this point The Scandinavian Bank came to the rescue, offering to underwrite the costs on the basis that YAT would, eventually, repay the money (which we did). And so, in the summer of 1978, the piling was installed.

The significance of Coppergate

The dig was the first (and is still the only) excavation to reveal a large swathe of Viking-Age York. The substantial scale of the investigation was one reason for its importance, for instead of small-scale 'key-hole' archaeology in which it is often impossible to grasp the big picture, here we were dealing with 1000 square metres, extending over what, from the Viking to the Victorian era, had been four adjacent property plots or tenements (Figure 13.2). Urban archaeology on this scale is the exception rather than the rule, and opens up a townscape vista, in which the typical can be differentiated from the unusual, and patterns of occupation and behaviour can be recognised.

Although many of the dark brown 'peaty' layers which characterized the Viking Age looked remarkably similar to the inexperienced eye, they could be picked apart by the archaeologists, and by the end of the excavation we had identified, recorded and excavated nearly 40,000 'contexts', each a piece in an enormous three-dimensional jig-saw puzzle. Although the stratigraphic relationships between individual layers were often complex, the sheer depth and marvellous preservation of the deposits meant that it was possible to distinguish successive phases of activity within the Viking-Age in considerable clarity. This is in stark contrast to what might be expected in most parts of York, and in other English towns, where these conditions are generally not present. In these other parts of York the whole two centuries of the Viking Age might be represented by a total depth of deposit only 10–20 cm (4–8 inches) thick, in which the archaeologist would be hard pressed to identify more than one or two major episodes of activity. Seeing how the Coppergate site developed *within* the Viking Age was enormously important.

Having sufficient time to work our way methodically through this deep and complex stratification was yet another crucial factor. We were fortunate that a variety of reasons, ranging from the nation's economic condition via York City Council's procedural requirements to the developer's own timetable for design and construction, meant that we did not vacate the site until September 1981, having had a total of five years and four months of virtually continuous excavation. The series of extensions to our occupancy allowed a measured approach to the archaeology rather than any panic response to the successive deadlines; we were attempting to square the circle, finding a middle path between making the most of understanding the detail of each moment in historic time while pushing on to ensure that we got the overall chronological picture of how the area had developed over the centuries. Even so, we did not quite manage to reach the bottom of the archaeological layers over the entire area; although the entire street frontage was excavated, approximately half of the backyard areas behind were not investigated beyond the early tenth-century layers. Nonetheless, the earliest Viking-Age, Anglo-Saxon and Roman deposits were seen in an area measuring about 500 metres square, enough to give us a representative sample of this vicinity.

The archaeological discoveries from each of these other periods made significant contributions to knowledge and, although they are not what made 'The Viking Dig' famous, they should not be forgotten, for they both put the Viking-Age remains in context and indicated the lasting importance of that key period. At the base of the excavation, as much as 6.75m (22 feet) below the modern surface, we found a succession of Roman buildings, first of timber and then of stone, set out at an angle to the later street (Ottaway 2004, 88, 138; Ottaway in prep). A small later Roman cemetery, with bodies buried in wooden coffins, was also found. Unsurprisingly, Roman artefacts and pottery were found throughout these and later layers (Figure 13.6).

After the end of the Romano-British period, *circa* AD 400, the Roman buildings and cemetery fell out of use and the site was, apparently, abandoned; we identified no signs of any occupation or major activity here during the Anglo-Saxon period from the fifth to the mid-ninth centuries. However, one extraordinary object made during this era was unearthed during the archaeological watching brief that we kept after the excavation had finished, during the construction of the Coppergate Centre. An iron helmet, decorated with bronze plates, and with a neck guard comprising two thousand links of mail, was recovered by YAT's archaeologists only a few metres beyond the edge of the former excavation. An object of high prestige and value, it is the best preserved of only a handful of Anglo-Saxon helmets which are known today (Figure 13.7). Why it was buried here in a wood-lined pit remains a mystery (Tweddle 1992).

However, the most revelatory discoveries, which led to the most revolutionary reappraisals of received archaeological and historical wisdom related, as we had hoped, to the Viking Age. For example, they revealed exactly the size of the semi-basement urban houses and workshops in the tenth and eleventh century; tiny by our standards, they had a floor area of only 30 square metres (320 square feet). They were positioned with their narrow, gable end at the street frontage, thus allowing the maximum number of properties to be squeezed into the available space. This is a sure sign that their builders believed that this was a good place to live and to do business; certainly they stood on one of Jorvik's busiest streets, leading towards the only point where the River Ouse was crossed by a ford or bridge, on the site of the later medieval and modern Ouse Bridge.

Findings

The structures with semi-basements represented the rapid adoption of a new building form in Coppergate; they were cut down into the remains of earlier Viking-Age buildings constructed in a wholly different technique, with screen walls made by weaving wattles (flexible rods of wood) around upright stakes planted in the ground (Figure 13.8). These earlier buildings were roofed in thatch, the weight of which was supported on upright timber posts or staves (vertical planks) set immediately outside the wattlework screen walls. They were single storey buildings, which were slightly shorter but slightly wider than their two-storey, semi-basemented successors, and each had a large, centrally positioned hearth designed to contain the fire risk. Intense charring of the woodwork, and layers of charcoal and ash, proved that fires did destroy some of these buildings, and their fabrication was clearly not so robust as that of the semi-basement buildings, made from oak planks, posts and beams, which eventually superseded them. Although they were remarkably well preserved, given the materials employed, their small posts and wattlework did not offer opportunities for tree-ring dating. Instead,

Figure 13.6. Roman cornelian intaglio of a charioteer © York Archaeological Trust.

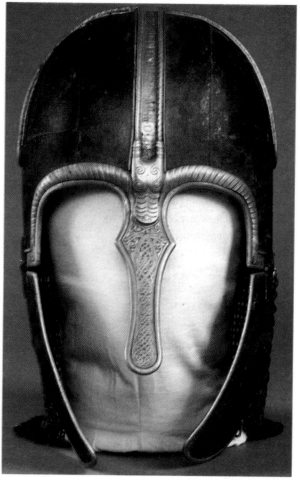

we had to rely mainly on the artefacts, such as coins and pottery, found in and around them. These indicated that buildings were first erected here sometime within the period *c.* 900–25.

This is an important date, for it was at this time that the street of Coppergate must have been laid out, and the fence lines which separated one property from another were first established. This act of Viking-Age redevelopment had a formative influence, for all subsequent rebuildings on this site down the centuries to the Victorian era more or less respected the boundaries that were instituted in the early tenth century. The idea that a period of Viking control might have encouraged such enterprises was entirely novel, and caused a major revision of perceptions of what the

Figure 13.7. Iron and brass helmet, c. 750–75. © York Archaeological Trust.

Vikings did for towns; urban growth rather than destruction was suddenly the watchword. Equally importantly for York, the fact that this redevelopment was discovered on a site at the heart of the Viking-Age city suggested that it was in these decades, in the early tenth century, that Jorvik 'took off' as a boom town. The evidence excavated at Coppergate suggested that the period *c.* 850–900, within which the Vikings first captured York, was one where some activity and occupation took place, and that this in itself marked a change, as the site had been deserted for four hundred years and more. However, the early Viking-Age occupation was not as intensive as it became in the 10th century.

Just as the evidence for buildings and their layout re-wrote our understanding of these aspects of Viking-Age York, so too did the artefacts associated with them. As one commentator has recently remarked 'The material culture of Viking York in the tenth century is difficult to match in any other excavated town in Western Europe' (Schofield 2007, 122). Some items were accidentally lost in the earth floors within the buildings; more came from the backyards behind them, for the Viking-

Age inhabitants of Coppergate had disposed of much of their rubbish, broken objects and other garbage either by throwing it into rubbish pits there or simply by discarding it behind their houses and workshops. There was no shortage of material; in total, we recovered about 50,000 individually interesting objects ('small finds' in archaeological jargon), as well as about 250,000 sherds of pottery and five tons of animal bones.

Bones of domesticated farm animals, fowl and fish, combined with other domestic food debris such as oyster and cockle shells, and traces of fruit and vegetables, allowed Viking-Age diet (and farming practices) to be reconstructed in great detail (O'Connor 1989; Kenward and Hall 1995). A good diet it was, too, drawing on the agricultural produce of the region and supplementing it through hunting and wild-fowling. Clearly the occupants of 10th-century Coppergate were adequately, if repetitively fed. How, then, did they pay for this food?

The answer again came from the rubbish, which included traces of the raw materials, manufacturing waste and by-products, failed products and sometimes, by accidental loss, the finished products of their craftsmanship. These items gave wholly new insights into the technologies available to satisfy the growing consumer markets of the 10th and 11th centuries. Essentially, the raw materials of the countryside were brought into Jorvik to be fashioned into necessary and desirable goods, which were bought in part by villagers from the city's hinterland. Each of the excavated properties was occupied by a craftsman who specialised in the mass production of particular items. In the earlier tenth century

Figure 13.8. Excavating two post and wattle structures of early-mid tenth-century date; a large, stone-lined hearth is at the centre of each. © York Archaeological Trust.

it was metalworkers who predominated here (Ottaway 1992). They seemed at home with any high temperature job, working with iron, copper, lead, silver and gold (Bayley 1992); a small quantity of high-lead glass beads and rings was also made (Bayley and Doonan 2000). Everyday requirements such as iron knives were one staple; cheap base-metal copies of higher quality jewellery, particularly disc brooches, were another. The evidence for the techniques they used was often unusually full, and sometimes unique; the skills and methods of the craftworkers could be reconstructed in great detail. Perhaps the rarest artefact found in the excavation was an early 10th-century coin die (Figure 13.9), a technical masterpiece with a shank resilient and malleable enough to withstand thousands of heavy blows, yet sufficiently hard-headed to maintain a crisp impression on each of the thousands of silver pennies that were struck from it (Pirie 1986, 33f).

Later the properties were home to woodturners who took blocks of alder, maple and other woods, and turned them on a rotary lathe, gouging out the bowls and cups which were standard table ware in the Viking Age (Morris 2000). Indeed, it was this craft that gave the street its name, Coppergate, the *gata* or street of the cupmakers. Other crafts practised on an industrial scale included leatherworking to make shoes, belts, harnesses, scabbards and sheaths (Mould, Carlisle and Cameron 2003). Both amber and, on a smaller scale, jet, were shaped, drilled and polished to make beads, pendants or rings (Mainman and Rogers 2000, 2498–2518), and bone or antler were utilised by specialists to make combs and other household items (MacGregor, Mainman and Rogers 1999). Textile making was carried out on a domestic scale, and there was evidence too for dyestuffs and dyeing; this was a colourful era (Walton 1989; Rogers 1997).

Imported artefacts testified to Jorvik's contacts throughout England, Scotland and Ireland. Additionally, there were items from Scandinavia, and from north-west Europe, as one might expect. Wine, for example, was imported from the Rhineland, along with lava quernstones which were top of the range for grinding grain (Mainman and Rogers 2000, passim). More surprising were silks that probably originated in Byzantium (Istanbul) (Walton 1989, 360–81), a cowrie sea-shell of a species which lives only in the Red Sea (Kenward and Hall1995, 781), and a coin purporting to be a silver dirham minted in Samarkand (Pirie 1986, 55). It was, in fact, a genuine contemporary forgery; but it and the other exotica illustrate the far-flung geographical spread of the networks of overseas contacts into which Jorvik was plugged.

Public archaeology

These exciting discoveries – and there were many, many more which can't be mentioned here – were both the product and the rationale for another remarkable facet to 'The Viking Dig': its success in engaging an enormous public interest. From its earliest days YAT had, whenever possible, opened up excavation sites to the public and welcomed the media, in order to bring our work to the widest audience. The Coppergate excavations were no different; from an early stage people were paying 10p to come, pick up an information leaflet and have a look at men and women digging a hole.

Another extraordinary innovation came with the realisation that YAT needed to enlist the interest and support of people who might not normally think that an archaeological excavation could be worthwhile. By issuing press releases to the media the excavation soon began to command column inches and air time not just locally and regionally, but nationally and internationally. Underpinning all was the fact that this was not just media hype; we were shedding totally new light on what some people called 'the dark ages'.

A major leap forward came when, after the dig had featured on a popular BBC early evening televison programme, a wealthy businessman, Ian Skipper, who had been enthused by what he had seen, came to inspect us at first hand. After a rapid tour of the site he professed himself incapable of having the patience to excavate, but very willing to help YAT raise enough money to finance the excavation by encouraging yet more paying visitors. He briskly volunteered to meet the cost; and thus the visitor experience was substantially upgraded and made to appear much more inviting and attractive. The name 'The Viking Dig' was emblazoned tastefully on the perimeter hoarding, and the visitors rolled up in droves. There are no overall figures, but I estimate that over the entire five year and four month duration of the excavation, in the heart of this tourist town, somewhere between 500,000 and one million people visited the site. They clearly enjoyed it; some people stayed for hours, watching as some rare or delicate item was lovingly disinterred.

Many other people helped to raise the profile of the excavation. HRH Prince Charles, HM Queen Margrethe of Denmark, Crown Prince Harald of Norway, King Carl Gustav of Sweden and Vigdis Finnbogadottir, President of Iceland, became Patrons of the excavation; an Anglo-Scandinavian royal flush which was an unbeatable combination. All save the Swedish king managed to fit a visit to the dig into their busy schedules. On the academic front Dr David Wilson, then Director of The British Museum and the country's leading Viking-Age archaeologist, agreed to become our Academic Adviser; and Magnus Magnusson, instantly recognisable television presenter of archaeology programmes and respected translator of Icelandic sagas, agreed to act as Chairman to a Committee of Stewards, which added both lustre and lucre to the campaign. Commercial businesses and associations and groups of various kinds in Scandinavia and the USA contributed to the fundraising which, nevertheless, was still underpinned by English Heritage and its predecessors, assisted latterly by The British Academy.

The project didn't end when the last layer was exposed, identified and recorded. Ian Skipper had prompted the development of a concept that eventually, in 1984, opened to the public as the Jorvik Viking Centre. This is a permanent display both of what we had excavated and how we think this part of the Viking-Age city may have looked, sounded and smelt in the year 975. Completely innovative in its approach to displaying excavated remains, it has welcomed over 16 million visitors, giving them an introduction to the Vikings, to Viking-Age York and to archaeology. It has won numerous educational and tourism awards, both regionally and nationally, and spawned another award-winning York Archaeological Trust attraction, a hands-on introduction to archaeological techniques called DIG! And as research into the data excavated at 'The Viking Dig' continues, the displays have been updated to keep abreast of the latest thinking.

The experience of the Viking Dig also affected the approximately 600 people who were part of the excavation or research teams. Some went on to jobs in academic archaeology, into archaeological posts in central or local government, or into professional archaeological units, while others became stalwarts of local archaeological societies and community archaeology groups. Researchers who investigated specific components of the data found that they became national or international experts because this vast and well-preserved body of material opened up hitherto hidden aspects of the past. Just as the display at the Jorvik Viking Centre conjured up new means of presenting the past, so the care and preservation of the organic material prompted advances in archaeological conservation which left York Archaeological Trust's Conservation Laboratory and Archaeological Wood Centre at the forefront of their profession.

Of course, there is still much to find out about the Viking-Age city; key sites and topics – the Viking-Age cathedral, the possible royal and aristocratic residences, the waterfronts, the defences, to

Figure 13.9. Iron coin-die, c. 925, inscribed 'St Peter's Money' but with a Viking sword at centre and a Thor's hammer below. © York Archaeological Trust.

name but a few of the most obvious – remain in obscurity. 'The Viking Dig' is not an archaeological panacea; but it has been an exciting, ground-breaking, project which has re-written urban history, discovered the lost city of Jorvik and provided a benchmark for future studies of Viking-Age towns in Britain (Hall *et al.* 2004). There was never a dull day at the office on 'The Viking Dig'.

For information on archaeology in York, visit the website www.yorkarchaeology.co.uk.

Acknowledgements

Thanks to all who participated in the excavation and in the analyses and dissemination of the discoveries, whose work and expertise I have drawn freely upon in the account above; and to those whose efforts and support behind the scenes made it possible.

References

Abbreviations
AY: *The Archaeology of York*, ed. P. V. Addyman (London or York: Council for British Archaeology).

Addyman, P. V. 1991. Lloyds Bank, Pavement, in Addyman and Hall 1991, 180–237.
Addyman, P. V. and Hall, R. A. 1991. *Urban Structures and Defences* (AY 8/3).
Bayley, J. 1992. *Non-Ferrous Metalworking from Coppergate* (AY 17/7).

Bayley, J. and Doonan, R. 2000. Glass Manufacturing Evidence, in Mainman and Rogers 2000, 2519–2528.

Hall, R. A. 1991. Structures at 5–7 Coppergate, with a re-assessment of Benson's observations of 1902, in Addyman and Hall 1991, 238–50.

Hall, R. A. 1994 *Viking-Age York*. London: B. T. Batsford and English Heritage.

Hall, R. A. in prep. *Medieval Urbanism in Coppergate: Defining a Townscape* (AY 8/5).

Hall, R. A. *et al.* 2004. *Aspects of Anglo-Scandinavian York* (AY8/4).

Hall, R. A. and Hunter-Mann, K. 2002 *Medieval Urbanism in Coppergate: Refining a Townscape* (AY 10/6).

Kenward, H. K. and Hall, A. R. 1995. *Biological Evidence from 16–22 Coppergate* (AY 14/7).

MacGregor, A., Mainman A. J. and Rogers, N. S. H. 1999. *Bone, Antler, Ivory and Horn from Anglo-Scandinavian and Medieval York* (AY17/12).

Mainman, A. J. and Rogers, N. S. H. 2000. *Finds from Anglo-Scandinavian York* (AY17/14).

Morris, C. A. 2000. *Wood and Woodworking in Anglo-Scandinavian and Medieval York* (AY17/13).

Mould, Q., Carlisle, I. and Cameron, E. 2003. *Leather and Leatherworking in Anglo-Scandinavian and Medieval York* (AY17/16).

O'Connor, T. P. 1989. Bones from Anglo-Scndinavian Levels at 16–22 Coppergate (AY15/3).

Ottaway, P. 1992. *Anglo-Scandinavian Ironwork from Coppergate* (AY17/6).

Ottaway, P. 2004. *Roman York (2nd edition)*. Stroud: Sutton.

Ottaway, P. J. in prep. *Extra-Mural Roman York* (AY).

Ottaway, P. and Rogers, N. 2002. *Finds from Medieval York* (AY 17/15).

Pirie, E. J. E. 1986. *Post-Roman Coins from York Excavations 1971–81* (AY18/1).

Radley, J. 1971. Economic Aspects of Anglo-Danish York. *Medieval Archaeology* 15, 37–57.

Rogers, P. W. 1997. *Textile Production at 16–22 Coppergate* (AY 17/11).

Rollason D. W. 1998. *Sources for York History to AD 1100* (AY1).

Schofield, J. 2007. Urban Settlement, Part 1, Western Europe, in J. Graham-Campbell and M. Valor (eds), *The Archaeology of Medieval Europe. Volume 1. Eighth to Twelfth Centuries AD*, 111–28. Arhus: Arhus University Press.

Tweddle, D. 1992. *The Anglian Helmet from Coppergate* (AY 17/8).

Walton, P. 1989. *Textiles, Cordage and Raw Fibre from 16–22 Coppergate* (AY 17/5).

The Manpower Services Commission and La Grava

Evelyn Baker

Introduction

The site of 'La Grava' or Grove Priory, together with its associated system of field closes covering some 19 acres (7.8 hectares), lies on the Bedfordshire border south of Leighton Buzzard (Figure 14.1). It was the core of a royal manor granted by Henry I to the Order of Fontevrault in 1164 and converted into a monastic grange and administrative centre for the Order's five English houses. Continuing royal interest ensured its use as a residence on progresses and contributed to a chequered pattern of ownership during the wars with France. Fontevrault finally lost its possession in the fifteenth century and it declined into a farmstead that itself had disappeared by the early part of the last century.

The La Grava project was described by an English Heritage Inspector of Ancient Monuments advising on the preparation of the final report as, 'one of the most important and certainly the most extensive excavations of a medieval manorial and monastic site to have been undertaken in the 20th century'. The whole site was almost completely excavated between 1973 and 1985. During virtually continuous work from 1976, 18,500m² of sometimes dense stratification were excavated by hand. Intermittent periods of post-excavation analysis followed during the next 23 years, and the publication of the final report is expected 35 years after work first began.

The project came out of the creation of county archaeological planning advice and underpinned development of the Bedfordshire County Archaeology Service (BCAS), now Albion Archaeology, thus contributing to and benefitting from the transformation of archaeological work over the last four decades. It is highly unlikely that the project would have taken place at any time after 1990, when PPG16 confirmed management of the archaeological resource as part of environmental planning; it probably could not have been afforded at any time before 1975 and after 1988, the period when employment schemes funded by the Manpower Services Commission (MSC) provided resources beyond what was available from the developer and the public purse. The length of the project and its regular review in response to site discoveries, methodological advances and new academic contexts made it a monument to flexible rather than formulaic management.

This is a personal account of archaeological Manpower Services Commission schemes on the site of 'La Grava', run through Bedfordshire County Council. Using archaeological work to deliver wider social benefits required an often difficult balancing act between giving valuable work-experience to the long-term unemployed and running a viable fieldwork project. Archaeologists benefitted also, as through developing appropriate fieldwork techniques and training opportunities; several are now senior professionals (Figure 14.2). With today's technical advances, recording is more systematic (if sometimes

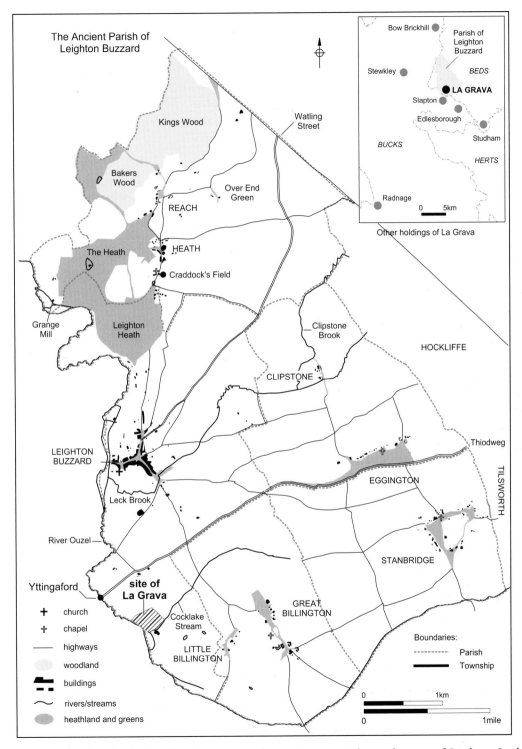

Fig 14.1. Location plan for the La Grava excavation; the area in tone is the royal manor of Leighton. It almost certainly extended well into Buckinghamshire in the 10th century (Albion Archaeology).

over-rigid) and with far less scope for omissions. Nevertheless, raw graduates learnt in depth the practicalities of their profession in what were essentially the apprenticeship schemes encouraged by the (then) Institute of Field Archaeologists and English Heritage, but supervising unemployed people of all ages and abilities. Thanks are due to the hundreds of MSC scheme staff who worked at La Grava and other Bedfordshire sites; the more mature profession of the twenty-first century owes a huge debt to these unemployment measures.

Fig 14.2. Photograph of MSC staff in the snow at La Grava on Good Friday (Baker and Albion Archaeology).

Context: The early 1970s

In 2008 you have to be well over 50 years of age to have been involved in the public recognition of the archaeological crisis caused by 1960s development and the creation of RESCUE. By the time MSC schemes emerged in 1975, the vision of a few publicly funded Regional Archaeological Units was giving way to an untidier and incomplete pattern of Units based on some counties and cities. Emphasis was shifting towards the appointment of County Archaeological Officers, hoping to tackle the problem at source by ensuring development proposals took account of archaeological considerations, either by diverting impacts or ensuring proper recording before destruction.

In 1972 Bedfordshire County Planning Department acquired England's third County Archaeologist; this was David Baker who initiated the La Grava excavation and commented helpfully on this paper. The job title of 'Archaeological Liaison Officer' marked an intention not to excavate but to facilitate. Fortunately a small fieldwork budget was provided because the initial task of assembling a basic Sites and Monuments Record immediately revealed major threats from existing planning permissions to a Bronze Age barrow cemetery, a late Iron Age farmstead, a Roman villa and a medieval priory.

This dire situation threw into sharp relief the contrast between what had been done in the 1960s and what was required in the new post-RESCUE world. My own experience derived from training in fine art (painting) and a steady drift sideways into archaeology during the 1960s through digging and drawing at Fishbourne Roman Palace and Porchester Castle, and supervising at Elstow Abbey in Bedfordshire. The rescue work I supervised in Bedford and at Bedford Castle from 1970–72 was done on the old pattern, with short, intensive, volunteer-staffed excavations in the spring and summer holidays.

This approach was carried through into the early years of County Council involvement with archaeology largely on a seasonal basis with volunteers and a few paid staff. This was the approach to my work at Warden Abbey in 1974, and to the first two years at La Grava. An Archaeological Field Team of four young professionals was formalised at local government reorganisation in 1974. When the impossibility of spreading them around the major rescue projects became all too apparent, it was decided to follow up rumours on the grapevine about the potential usefulness of the new MSC Job Creation Programme schemes.

The economic difficulties of the early 1970s led government to introduce a series of short-term temporary employment schemes. Harold Wilson in the 1974 Labour Party Manifesto described 'what was universally acknowledged to be the gravest economic crisis Britain had faced since the war'. The situation was grim, with prices rising between 15% and 20% every year, the cost of foodstuffs nearly doubling and oil four times the cost a year earlier. There was misery and poverty, with people without jobs for several years, giving up all hope and becoming unemployable. UK industry was hit as new technologies, global competition, recession and company closures led to staffing cuts and structural unemployment. The outlook for that and future generations was bleak. Political parties focused on the issue, but it was Labour that declared:

> We shall transform the existing Manpower Services Commission into a powerful body, responsible for the development and execution of a comprehensive manpower policy. Redundant workers must have an automatic right to retraining, with redundancy leading not to unemployment, but to retraining and job changing.

Between 1975 and 1983 MSC schemes benefitted La Grava, other Bedfordshire excavation projects, and initially the parish survey programme. It began with JCP (Job Creation Programme), creating temporary jobs for young people. This was followed by STEP (Special Temporary Employment Programme), YOP (Youth Opportunities Programme) in 1978, CEP (Community Employment Programme) and CP (Community Programme). Later schemes became increasingly unsuitable for archaeological fieldwork, and it all ended in the late 1980s.

Some remarkable excavations were undertaken of sites that would otherwise have been destroyed without trace, despite the obvious drawbacks of workforce limitations and an extremely restricted facility to plan forward. One problem was that, while it was sometimes possible to acquire sufficient resources for fieldwork, it was quite impossible to persuade developers to pay for post excavation analysis, let alone provide considerable sums for adequate publication. It must be remembered also that even the most prestigious excavations then were generally staffed by undergraduates or recent graduates, only sometimes supervised by experienced excavators. Many of the present older generation of lecturers and senior professionals, training today's archaeologists, pass on knowledge not gained in the lecture room but in the field.

The opportunity

Though the local parish council knew the site as 'our priory', it had been tentatively classified as a village by the Deserted Medieval Villages Research Group from aerial photographs taken in the early 1950s by Dr J. K. S. St Joseph. Planning permission for quarrying had been granted in 1969 for extracting a 20m depth of sand of such quality that it was exported to Saudi Arabia; revocation of the consent even on an obviously schedulable site was out of the question. The only option was excavation.

Project designs at the time were in their infancy, or even embryonic, and the justification for work was largely in terms of investigating what variants of plan might be found in the process of 'collecting' a rare kind of monastic house. Consequently, excavation strategy evolved during the thirteen years of nearly continuous fieldwork. It responded to changing appreciation of the scale of archaeological opportunities offered by the project, innovative archaeological techniques, a developing organisational capability, the decelerating advance of the destructive quarry face and the availability of resources, quantitatively and qualitatively.

It was predicted at the outset that the entire site would be destroyed by about 1977. It was hoped that the surviving evidence for a relatively small alien cell of Fontevrault of less than three centuries' duration would be relatively simple, and that an overall plan could be secured through extensive stripping once trial trenches had located the main areas of buildings. An initial survey of the earthworks identified three possible locations, and trial trenches were mechanically excavated across two of them.

They showed relatively shallow stratigraphy coming down on to mixed natural boulder clay. Two adjacent areas were excavated in seasonal work with volunteers during 1973 and 1974: one comprised much robbed multi-period wall foundations but discrete structures could not be identified; the other found stone structures overlying timber features that were difficult to detect in the mixed boulder clay. By the end of 1974 it was clear that work on this scale was not recovering information quickly enough. The site was technically challenging; the problems of understanding apparently well-preserved and complex evidence were exacerbated by difficult soil conditions.

Larger scale work in 1975 and early 1976, with DoE grants increasing from three- to four- figure sums, allowed the employment of two experienced supervisors, Humphrey Woods and Dominic Powlesland, in order to speed up exploration of the site as the quarry deadline approached. Both found footings for large masonry structures but were unable to resolve definitely whether there had been a standard claustral plan.

By 1976 it was clear that the quarry's slower progress into Chapel Field would give an opportunity for several more years' work, that complex evidence had survived relatively well, and that complementary historical documentation I was assembling in parallel was raising further questions. These pointed towards a changing identity from manorial site to alien priory and back again, including royal use of the site. They required definitive clarification of sometimes alternating place-name evidence that this indeed was the documented site; they raised the question of how these changing uses might be reflected in the archaeological record (see below). The only way forward was the excavation of large areas, but the resources were not available. Abandonment of the site was deferred only by the series of MSC schemes, which continued with one small break from September 1976 until 1984, albeit with constant uncertainty whether further schemes would be approved. Throughout, we were fortunate in having a helpful tenant farmer, since we were occupying some of his best pasture. Without his agreement the owners, the Church Commissioners, would never have continually renewed our licence to excavate. The agent, with whom I mostly dealt, while militarily punctilious, was unfailingly supportive and understanding.

Between 1976 and 1981 work continued on the total excavation of the main platform, and showed its buildings did not conform to a monastic claustral plan, but were a manorial type whose status seemed consistent with the recorded royal visits. At least five main phases were identified. At the turn of the decade, as the quarry face began its delayed entry into the north end of the field, an examination of the outer closes began in sequence of vulnerability, continuing in 1982 and 1983. Extensions of the area excavation on the north-west and south-east of the main platform led work into a much larger part to the east and south, containing the main medieval agricultural buildings (Figure 14.3). Ground conditions had frustrated their location by geophysical survey, so their discovery during precautionary mechanical trial trenching raised a major problem, exacerbated by the increasing incompatibility of the later MSC schemes with this kind of archaeological work. A special grant from the newly created English Heritage funded employment of a fully professional team (the first) in the last eighteen months of the project, and allowed completion of fieldwork in August 1985, just in front of quarry overburden stripping.

Reconciling work experience and archaeological research at La Grava

A new kind of labour force was provided by MSC schemes, different from the usual groups of senior school and university students and local society members, nearly all volunteers. Bedfordshire had a relatively low unemployment rate, so most of the people available in the local job market were long-term unemployed, lacking motivation, with few skills and poor education. There was no local university able to supply unemployed archaeological graduates eager for work-experience, though a few redundant graduates were recruited.

MSC policy for the turn-over for workers and supervisors was intentionally rapid in order to get as many unemployed as possible into any sort of work. It was considered fair that if employees had benefited for 12 months, other, needier, candidates should be given an opportunity. The name of the game was figures, even if they then went back to Job Centres immediately afterwards. A suitable ratio of supervisors had to be strongly fought for; retaining them, their knowledge of the site and their relationship with staff, became increasingly difficult. Supervisors needed to be unemployed for many months yet strict time limits were imposed on their employment on schemes. Continuity on complex area excavations with initially untrained staff was essential but not always achievable; sometimes it was possible to persuade sympathetic MSC managers of the benefit to both archaeology and staff, and exceptions were made. Many MSC staff returned to La Grava several times after statutory gaps of unemployment, so we could build on their experience of the site. A large proportion regained confidence and got 'proper jobs'. The percentage leaving the scheme for full-time 'proper' employment in Bedfordshire was high. Even Andrew Selkirk has admitted that 'The "graduates" from archaeological MSC projects were exceptionally successful in getting jobs afterwards.'

Motivation was a problem and a challenge. Although everybody had considerable training both on and off site there were those who found digging demeaning, even though we all undertook our share of physical work. Site conditions were rugged. All records, survey equipment, cameras and water supply had to be carried three-quarters of a mile across fields and across a rickety bridge over the Ouzel twice a day for the 13 years. Only the last two years saw relatively decent accommodation. On occasions the first task was to clear the excavation of snow and hope that the sun would deal with the permafrost. Figure 14.2 shows diggers coming onto the site in the snow on Good Friday one year.

The least favourite task was finds processing, as always, and staff would prefer to be in the field in the worst of weather. Some enlightening graffiti were found in the finds cellar of the excavation base then in use at Bedford when it was finally cleared out. The most difficult people to manage were, however, not the general run of unemployed people, but disgruntled graduates, usually non-archaeological, discovering the hard reality that the world was not in fact their oyster. A few became world experts on medieval monastic/manorial archaeology after a month or two and demonstrated how creatively disruptive intelligent people can choose to be. Yet serious disciplinary problems on an isolated site were comparatively few. Accusations of rape and racial prejudice, alcohol, misuse of substances and violence were rare (and generally unfounded). Competent supervisors soon learnt how to cope as illustrated by that vital site document, the Day Book (Figure 14.4).

Some found the work, pay, long hours and poor site conditions not to their liking. A percentage 'played the system' and only took jobs because of sanctions if they did not; some preferred leisure and 'moonlighting'. This minority rapidly found excuses to leave, shirked work or had mysterious illnesses that coincided with weekends or festivals.

The Youth Opportunities Programme was one of the easiest schemes to manage. Most sixteen-year-olds thought digging was romantic and enjoyed adverse conditions that others would find impossible, revelling in mud, snow and ice. They responded well to personal attention; the highlight of their year was a Christmas feast cooked on site. This group benefited more than others in training for basic skills:

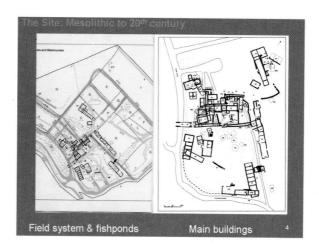

Fig 14.3. Plan of the principal buildings at La Grava; 108 were excavated, ranging in date from the 6th to 17th centuries (Baker and Albion Archaeology).

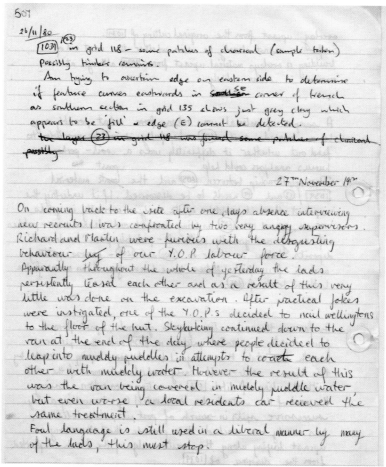

Fig 14.4. An extract from site Day Book No 8, p. 507; as well as an invaluable day-to-day record of ideas about the archaeology, these books are a social document. That day the YOP staff were clearly not in a mood to work (Baker and Albion Archaeology).

they learnt tea could only be made after the water had bubbled. The novelties of getting up in time for the van to leave Bedford and organising a packed lunch were a great strain for some. They learnt about rotas for routine tasks; they quickly acquired surprisingly good digging and drawing skills.

They had their moments: Campden Tablets in the tea; mud flinging fights; graffiti; nailing wellies to the hut floor; burying antler 'picks'; peeing out of the van window while moving. One youngster came to us at the Job Centre's request because he was being mercilessly bullied in his job as a chicken strangler – and became hugely loyal and a real charmer. He was not over-bright and it was with some relief that we saw him blowing up condoms at a Christmas party – at least someone had seen to that part of his education. One man was fascinated by what we were able to tell him about a silver coin he had discovered; perhaps he was one of our failures since he became a notorious local criminal, but at least he did not steal from us. One senior field officer had an unrivalled empathy with the disadvantaged young and moved out of archaeology into the social services; largely through him young people learnt to build satisfactory relationships with other trainees and members of staff, with personal growth and self realization.

Several hundred people passed through the various MSC schemes at La Grava, many acquiring the highly valuable transferrable skills that archaeology provides. One man with no formal qualifications was inspired to go to college in the evenings; he gained two 'A' Levels, then a first class degree in archaeology at Durham followed by a doctorate; he is now a respected academic who has worked with BCAS/Albion Archaeology on several occasions. Others who began as supervisors at La Grava have become higher-ranking professionals in many branches of archaeology.

MSC schemes and the development of local services

The Bedfordshire County Planning Department, where the archaeological capability was planted in 1972, had a tradition of countryside conservation, but at that time the idea of historical conservation was only just beginning to take root. Many of its staff could not understand why archaeologists were there at all, let alone why an invasion of the long-term unemployed complete with muddy boots should be unleashed upon them.

Fieldwork was viewed with some suspicion, especially for its entrepreneurial tendencies in securing the first MSC scheme and later the first personal computer obtained by the County Council, let alone its enviable popularity with the public (Figure 14.5).

There were advantages and disadvantages to running archaeological MSC schemes from a local authority base. On the positive side, initially the County Council provided some cash and essential in-house assistance through first rate legal, photographic, administrative and graphics services, personnel, payroll and financial advice, surveyors, land agents, the County Records Office, Heath and Safety experts and colleagues dealing with the Sites and Monuments Record (now HER) and Historic Buildings. The latter enabled a more thorough documentary analysis covering the whole Royal Manor to place it in its historical context. In a large parent organisation, support for archaeology varied hugely; political antennae were all-important in cultivating useful acquaintances, knowing where to get assistance and to persuade others that they wanted to give it. The interface between Council red tape and MSC accountability was often difficult, but for much of the time the situation was blessed with key people on both sides who saw administration as a means to an end rather than an end in itself.

On the negative side, MSC workers were very much regarded as transitory staff, and were at the bottom of a heap beneath permanent established specialists, themselves under the highest form of life, the generalist planner. Even archaeological professionals taken on as supervisors were largely invisible when job grades and salaries were assessed: no acknowledgement of degree status or number of staff supervised; no fast track promotion; no pension scheme. Yet these were some of the most difficult and sometimes stressful staff and projects to manage – out in the field all year round and travelling considerable distances every day. Designated drivers were paid a little extra, but were expected to put in a full day's site work every day; the two hours travelling were not otherwise paid. Most excavation was considered common labouring by the 'suits' since digging occupied a large percentage of work time, always with the jibe 'this is your hobby, isn't it?' Abnormally low pay was a problem that dogged schemes for many years and echoed through field units long afterwards; their influence on pay scales has also been far-reaching.

Methods and MSC

The special circumstances of the La Grava project created methodological opportunities and challenges. From 1973 to 1975–76 when the site was dug seasonally with students and volunteers, the site record mostly consisted of traditional notebooks, plans, sections and

Fig 14.5. The cover of a catalogue created for an MSC exhibition which was hugely popular, especially with schools; cartoon by Andrew Pinder, MSC Supervisor (Albion Archaeology).

photographs. The complexity of evidence on the site became clear from early trenches on the main core of buildings, first seen through multiple destruction spreads and robbing as a palimpsest of walls going out into trench edges in all directions. Features cut into a mixed boulder clay subsoil tended to disappear back into the body of the clay without trace, appearing only after weeks of weathering by the elements, and then often fleetingly as subtle differences in colour or texture confirmed in section or by their content.

These conditions, which effectively ruled out strict working within easily defined phases or areas, stimulated the development of other recording methods. The timescale of the quarry and the MSC schemes on a site that would be totally destroyed allowed stratified sequences to be fully excavated on a greatly extended timescale, unusual in 'rescue' situations. Very large open-area working was applied to the main concentrations of buildings on the central platform, the outer court to the south-east, the barn area to the north, and some of the outlying investigations. It uncovered wide areas and took them down systematically across the site, with the control of upstanding sections, recording in a way that allowed the evidence to be manipulated and reinterpreted subsequently. Excavation on this scale was essential in order to make sense of the complex interconnecting and overlapping building sequences, many of which had little intervening open space to demarcate them.

Site excavation and recording methods had to be capable of combining MSC requirements of general employment training for a transient labour force of greatly variable abilities, with the need to get a reliable archaeological result capable of systematic and detailed review during the period of analysis, after the quarry had destroyed the site. The low proportion of skilled supervisors forced a conscious decision not to undertake full matrix compilation and comprehensive preliminary phasing on-site. On the other hand, archaeologists were used to dealing with inexperienced teams, spotting those with talent, providing necessary training and generally making the best of things. Photographs show an almost military discipline that is rarely seen now. The cry of 'clear up your loose' heralded a break and woe betide anyone who left piles of soil on the ground, and who did not clean their tools and leave them under an up-turned barrow. This enabled good overall site photographs unmarred by heaps of loose soil. The system produced an acceptable level of consistency in observation and recording thanks to the control provided by a succession of capable senior supervisors. Modern methodologies were born under these adverse conditions and those excavation techniques are still the basis of those used today, albeit with the almost total absence of scientific equipment so customary now. Geophysics was in its infancy, so a vital tool was unavailable for reconnaissance. There were no computers to facilitate recording and data analysis, electronic survey equipment or GIS; everything had to be done manually with recording and analytical systems devised to suit.

The system comprised four independent but interrelated elements: individual pro formae sheets for collecting contextual information; detailed coloured drawings as sets of overlays, and supplementary drawings for specific details and general overviews; the photographic record; and a series of day books or site diaries giving an evolving interpretation. The aim was to construct a series of interconnecting statements about the site during lengthy excavation, yet provide the possibility of modification according to subsequent detailed analysis and assessment. At the start of the post-excavation programme this system enabled independent analyses of the stratigraphic evidence from the context sheet records, and of finds with their dating, before the data was then assembled into an integrated whole. Whilst it was hoped that the final conclusions would not vary too greatly from the evolving on-site interpretation based upon the day-books, the system was designed to allow for (and in the event was able to support) changes of view and refined reinterpretation derived from systematic analysis.

More than 5,400 context sheets were completed. 1,500–2,000m^2 of complex multi-period stratified deposits were exposed at one time, and with even larger areas in the outer court excavations of the early 1980s. Much of the site was urban in character in a rural setting. Context recording had to be organised flexibly in order to control large amounts of data which a simple unique numbering system would have scattered widely numerically. Guidelines were issued for describing soil make-up and content in order to impose consistency and accuracy, together with a thesaurus of key words. Munsell colour charts were initially used, but later discarded in the face of serious difficulties over allocating relatively coarsely differentiated soil/colour numbers to the more subtle distinctions recognisable in the ground with the tricky subsoils. Substituted verbal descriptions were also usually inadequate, varying according to the individual making the record. In these circumstances the on-going dialogue of site diary interpretation was crucial.

More than 1,100 multi-context coloured site drawings at 1:20 scale were made, designed to 'reconstruct' the whole site in the same sequence that it was excavated (Figure 14.6). Each type of material was colour-coded consistently for all drawings. A detailed stone-for-stone technique was used requiring the minimum of archaeological value-judgements from the ordinary members of the team, though some showed considerable talent for this work, and produced particularly useful records. This response to staff skills stronger in literal graphics than in verbal expression chimed well with the need to produce drawings capable of subsequent interrogation and interpretation. Drawings tried to produce what was seen instead of the simplified line drawings suitable for digitising (then not yet available anyway). In parallel with these multi-context detailed drawings, overall outline plans were made of features and contexts at scales of either 1:50 or 1:100, similar to all-feature plans. With complex areas or features, supplementary drawings were made, which could also be overlaid in sequence. All recording is inevitably subjective and selective, yet these drawings were no less 'objective' than context sheets whose compilation had already inevitably taken the record through a level of interpretation. These coloured drawings proved to be of immense worth in both the fieldwork phase when the patterns they revealed informed continuing excavation, and later when structures were being dissected and analysed in post-excavation.

The photographic record comprised 212 films taken by site staff, supplemented by high level shots by the County Photographic Unit. There is some video material of the excavations in 1984 and 1985. In addition, the archive contains a series of vertical views taken as a substitute (in times of greater pressure from the mineral extractor) for detailed drawing over comparatively blank areas such as courtyards. These took the form of single metre squares shot through a drawing frame; they could be rectified and traced off to complete the coverage.

Eight day books and site diaries containing extensive notes, observations and sketch drawings recorded on-site interpretation as it developed and changed. These are an essential part of the site archive. Their purposes were to:

(a) complement the 'objective' record;
(b) provide a record of changing hypotheses and excavation strategies;
(c) recall the assumptions behind the excavation strategies when returning to exposed contexts after weeks or months;
(d) assist the recording of data too subtle or indeterminate to be fully comprehended within standard pro formae;
(e) present the various arguments about areas where the evidence seemed ambiguous or conflicting;
(f) act as insurance against the further deterioration in resources which always seemed possible;
(g) assist post-excavation analysis by people who had not seen the site; and
(h) act as a social document, recalling the management of staff, as well as other circumstances colouring the decisions of the day such as weather and site morale, all of which had an effect on the site.

Post-field, post-MSC

It has taken over three decades since the first trial trench to get this report ready for publication, largely due to stop-start funding although, like several substantial Bedfordshire projects of the late 1980s and early 90s, there was always the risk that it would simply be 'archived' rather than formally published. Fortunately, Geoffrey Wainwright, then English Heritage's Chief Archaeologist, had the foresight to recognise the significance of the La Grava project, and its imminent publication is due to his personal intervention. These particular circumstances have worked to the project's advantage. The large amount of data and the recording method have enabled analyses not possible on smaller or partially excavated sites, and full advantage has been taken of methodological changes and new research insights to produce a more considered and useful publication than would have been possible in, say, the 1990s.

Fieldwork finished in August 1985, at a time when the need for a methodical and critical approach to post-excavation work was generally understood, but the procedures now familiar as MAP2 (English Heritage 1991) had not yet been devised. During the next two years the field record was consolidated and a post-excavation research design prepared as a retrospective document stating research aims and

Fig 14.6. A detailed, coloured site drawing by MSC staff; the 'layers' of drawings were colour coded to ensure complete coverage of any one stage of excavation. They made a crucial contribution to post excavation interpretation (Baker and Albion Archaeology).

priorities, together with a full methodological statement. The five-year programme of work funded by English Heritage proved insufficient to complete a report on 13 years excavation by 1992. In the ensuing seven-year hiatus, work continued, only partly supported by local funding. This allowed the research design to be substantially reviewed, to produce an improved publication format, and, crucially, to incorporate a new dimension of analytical research into the spatial geometry of individual buildings and the whole settlement through its various phases.

The system devised for structural analysis and for interrogating the record about all aspects of the site was structure-led in order to facilitate handling the large quantities of data. However, the importance of all other evidence was recognised by fully integrating as many other aspects as possible at earliest stages of analysis. Procedures were devised for an overview of evidence dealing with the basic structure, the fixtures and structural elements, functional (subsidiary) structures within them, the way they were used, the objects used in association with them and contemporary features relating to them. The aim was to determine which structures, or parts of structures, functioned together at any one time, what those functions were, and how they worked as part of the settlement at different periods. A series of *pro formae* was devised for examining each structure or group of structures throughout its life. They helped impose a minimum standard on all building evidence, and form the core of a consistent archive for structural aspects of the site. They are complemented by artefact correlation charts which denote all the material aspects of each structure, internally and externally, throughout its existence.

Analysis of construction types has produced the basis for a regional type series of building and repair techniques. There were many ancillary features such as hearths, ovens, kilns, watercourses, drains, ditches, roads, cisterns and pits (Figure 14.7). An extensive illustrated body of finds has been organised and described by function and divided into those used for building and those that denote activities. The largest pottery assemblage in Bedfordshire supports discussion of trade patterns, function and cooking techniques. Plant and seed evidence was sparse, but confirmed how demesne land was distributed and changed. Animal and human bone studies have described life-styles of permanent and temporary residents, adding complementary information to building, artefactual and documentary evidence. Some early examples of archaeomagnetic work on hearths and ovens independently confirmed part of the dating framework. Detailed documentary and topographical work was undertaken.

Developing the spatial analysis of landscape and structures in the hiatus between the last two tranches of funding was a large task because all work had to be undertaken by hand using geometry instruments and light box to take measurements from field drawings. The analysis covers a hierarchy of planning within the site:

1) the layout of the buildings' area within a measured, planned landscape comprising boundary ditches parallel and perpendicular to each other;
2) the design of the principal courts of buildings as a framework for regular disposition of buildings and spaces; and
3) the metrology of individual buildings through time and their spatial relationships to each other.

This approach enabled some innovative analyses that could not otherwise be attempted. Ratios of domestic/service, agricultural and ecclesiastic accommodation and associated yards have been tracked through time, together with structural expansion, contraction and function, and changes in hearth/oven types, roofs, floors and wall types.

This most recent analysis countered the initial view that the settlement had developed organically, with little obvious organisation except for the physical separation of functions into broad zones by ditches, roads or walls. It identified remarkable discipline in the development of the core site and its adjacent farmland, from post Romano-British times. Campaigns of work could be identified, and insights gained into how medieval masons and carpenters set about major remodelling.

The archaeology and history of La Grava

So what did all this produce? By any standards La Grava has been a project with remarkable characteristics, the like of which we may not see again, not least because, unless the financial climate continues to drastically deteriorate and MSC in another guise provides the resources (including sufficient properly paid professionals and scientific support), it would be prohibitively expensive. It had a wider landscape context, site planning within which strict design provided continuity over several centuries, over a hundred structures including a chronological framework of stratified sequences of buildings, a wide spectrum of ancillary structures and industrial processes, a variety of building techniques, a large pottery assemblage, a wide range of associated artefacts, good environmental evidence including a small, short-lived cemetery, early independent dating and royal connections. Moreover, excellent documentation placed La Grava onto the national and international stage, providing a rare human element and suggesting the historical reasons for changes detected archaeologically on site.

The chronological sequence and the extent of settlement continuity is also impressive. Though there is evidence of all periods from the Mesolithic onwards, the main report will deal with the story from the 6th century onwards. The publication starts with a planned settlement measured in *perticae*, stemming from a Romano-British beginning. It continues with a 10th-century Saxon Royal Manor, which for some time had been in Danish hands; there was a crucial treaty with the Danes at Yttingaford in 906. The 11th century manor was carefully planned in poles, and seems to have been based on the earlier pattern. The Domesday royal manor may have had two centres, with the possible minster and administration in the town of Leighton and the royal hall at La Grava. In 1155–56, a post-Anarchy survey of the manor by the Constable of England described a run-down complex and proposed replacements for grain, stock, and eight measured agricultural buildings; large sums were spent in the following year. In 1164 the manor was given to the double Order of Fontevrault in Anjou in place of a cash grant by Henry I in 1129. Fontevrault immediately invested in the manor which already had a substantial settlement at La Grava. Documentary evidence suggests a large estate resolutely exploited to provide income for the great but impoverished mother-house.

Detailed changes in the form and function of the settlement mirrored the complex history of the site, its royal and enhanced ecclesiastical status and its role at the hub of a major agricultural enterprise (Figure 14.8). Royal and ecclesiastical interest in the site is reflected in extensive documentary evidence; structures indicate a monastic grange planted on the pre-existing royal site in the 1160s, converting an extant high status, masonry chamber block into the priory chapel. Queen Joanna of Sicily, sister to Richard I, may be a posthumous royal patron, enabling considerable rebuilding and enhancement soon after 1200, when Fontevrault was in financial difficulties. It was then the residence of the Procurator of the Order in England with buildings to match his status. Permission to have a chapel and right of burial was granted to Fontevrault in 1220, probably regularising an existing situation (Figure 14.9).

After the start of the Hundred Years War, La Grava reverted to a Royal Manor with resident chaplain, in the hands of high-ranking royal women. Princess Mary of Woodstock, daughter of Edward I, was a nun at Amesbury and custodian from at least 1305 to 1332. Maud (Plantagenet) de Burgh, Countess of Ulster, was custodian from 1338 followed by Edward III's daughter Isabel in 1357. Alice de la Pole, Duchess of Suffolk (and Chaucer's granddaughter) was granted custody from 1413, and she was probably responsible for building the late medieval complex. Major rebuilding in the mid 15th century entailed most medieval buildings being demolished, but some good quality stone ones were incorporated into a substantial timber-framed manor house layout. At about the same time the

Fig 14.7. Photograph of one of the many service buildings under excavation by MSC staff; the bake house (S23) with smoking bay to the left, huge ovens and scullery in the foreground (Beds CC Photographic Unit, Baker and Albion Archaeology).

Fig 14.8. Photograph of some of the wide variety of agricultural buildings under excavation by MSC staff; almost the whole outer court was cleared by hand to ensure that structures were not missed (Beds CC Photographic Unit, Baker and Albion Archaeology).

Fig 14.9. Photograph of the core of the site, the chapel (S16) left, prior's cross-wing (S54) centre and hall (S7)n (right) marked by MSC staff (Beds CC Photographic Unit, Baker and Albion Archaeology).

lower court was virtually abandoned, the demesne separated from the rest of the manor, and the land put down to sheep, thus preserving the majority of the buildings.

Later ownership was complicated, with many changes of hands. In 1446 the Suffolks were required by Edward IV to give it to Eton College, and in 1479 it went to the Dean and Canons of St George's Chapel, Windsor. The mother of Edward IV, Princess Cecylle, was custodian from 1480; she was granted the demesne block detached from the rest of the manor.

The 16th century saw gradual decline; the property was leased into private hands. In 1581 wealthy gentleman farmer Clement Duncombe was licensed to build a new dwelling house (Grovebury), only metres away on the other side of the boundary stream; the old manorial buildings were dismantled and the materials probably re-used. A number of important gentry then farmed the land. The last surviving building was the first masonry structure, the chapel, finally robbed so thoroughly that it could still be seen in 1973 as a rectangular depression in the meadow called Chapel Field.

Conclusion

Little of this complex and intricate story could have been obtained without the Manpower Services Commission schemes. At best, a local Field Unit watching the top-stripping would have noted extensive medieval structures and wondered at lost potential. The project that actually happened was formed by, and helped inform, several crucial methodological and scientific developments in modern British archaeology, exemplifying difficult issues, some of which remain unresolved.

At the strategic level is the choice between preserving and digging. Today, the site would have been scheduled and consequently preserved, not least for the documentary indications of its rarity and the physical indications of good below-ground survival. When the final report is published others must judge in hindsight whether the already quoted view of its significance would justify excavating it now, always assuming, rather optimistically, the availability of equivalent or greatly improved resources. In the last few years there has been some shift in the terms of the debate between preservation for the benefit of future generations and excavation to achieve greater understanding now. What can the story and results of the La Grava project contribute to this discussion?

Also strategic is the issue of project management which has informed archaeological activity progressively throughout work on La Grava, in the field and out of it. In many ways the project was shaped by these developments, though not always directly. Initially, realising the need to plan post-excavation work ran ahead of the means of doing it. Later, advances in digital presentation and a more relaxed approach to academic publishing credits allowed the production of a more effectively usable report structure, with a synthesis supported by specialist technical evidence and overviews, and a very large archive. Serendipitously, gaps in resourcing and the competing demands of managing other projects and programmes allowed or enforced time for fruitful reflection and research which has enabled much more to be obtained from the site archive than would have been possible on a shorter and more rigid timescale.

On a more technical level, the structural recording systems, tailored to the capabilities and training needs of field staff, did not go so far down the road towards single-context planning as to make the record difficult to interrogate in much delayed post-excavation analysis, even with the difficult-to-predict arrival of computers. The disciplined insistence on keeping archaeological and documentary analyses separate until a final stage of synthesis helped show up what neither record could demonstrate and helped identify more clearly which conclusions were a matter of informed speculation. What was produced by a large-scale near-complete excavation is a useful comment on the efficacy of sampling strategies – how to adequately sample complex stratigraphy, and at what stage does a carefully devised academic tool become compromised by shortage of resources for field work?

Turning to contemporary preoccupations, thirty years ago this and similarly resourced projects demonstrated what would now be called the 'public value' of archaeology in terms of helping the unemployed, Today, other kinds of 'public value' are sought, with the emphasis on communication and different kinds of involvement. It would be anathema today to use a publicly-funded unemployment scheme for work that eighteen-year-old planning guidance defines as a responsibility of the developer. Yet the transition from MSC schemes to Field Units largely reliant upon developer-funded projects did bring with it still unresolved issues about professional standards and levels of pay and conditions.

Viewed as part of the history of archaeology, much about the La Grava project would today be seen as distinctly politically incorrect, but it is no less memorable for that, certainly for its participants and hopefully also for readers of the soon-to-be-published report. What was done and how it was done were definitely of the later 1970s and earlier 80s, but it did rely upon the wider social provision represented by MSC schemes, and their outcomes were as important for their participants as the research outcomes are for wider historical and archaeological understanding. MSC excavations were superb training grounds and were the origins of many of the methodologies in use today: context sheets, planning grids, type series, budgeting and project designs, remote sensing and independent dating, the value of environmental and documentary evidence, and exploring computerised aids. They established the need for planning archaeologists and Historic Environment Records, and paved the way for PPG16 and PPS5. Historically, MSC schemes were vital building blocks for many of today's archaeological organisations, and the roots of today's more mature profession.

References

Anon, 1974. *The work of the Manpower Services Commission in the Journal of Industrial and Commercial Training*. MCB UP Ltd.

Baker, D., Baker, E., Hassall, J. and Simco, A. 1979. Excavations in Bedford 1967–1977, *Bedfordshire Archaeological Journal* 13.

Baker, E. M. 1981. The medieval travelling candlestick from Grove Priory, Bedfordshire. *Proceedings of the Society of Antiquaries London* 61(2), 336–345.

Baker, E. M. 1983. Grove Priory and the Royal Manor of Leighton; interim report on excavations from 1973–1981. *CBA Group 9, South Midlands Archaeology* 4, 5–9.

Baker, E. M. 1983. Grove Priory and the Royal Manor of Leighton. *Bedfordshire Magazine* 18, 321–327.

Baker, E. M. 1988. Grove Priory alias the Royal Manor of Leighton, Bedfordshire. County Planning Department.

Baker, E. M. 1997. Grove: Royal Manor, Alien Priory cum Grange or Lost Minor Palace, in De Boe, G. and Verhaeghe, F. (eds), Military Studies in Medieval Europe: Papers of the Medieval Europe Brugge 1997 Conference, Volume 11, 227–36. Zellik.

Baker, E. M. *et al.* 1999. Grove Priory, unpublished Updated Project Design. Bedfordshire County Council.

Baker, E. M. 2001. Grove Priory, in Crabtree, P. J. (ed.), *Medieval Archaeology: an Encyclopedia*, 147–8. New York and London: Garland Publishing Inc.

Baker, E. M. in prep. *La Grava: The archaeology and history of a royal manor and alien priory of Fontevrault*, English Heritage and CBA.

Blunden, J. and Curry, N. 1985. *The Changing Countryside*. Open University/Croom Helm.

Davies, B. 1979. *In Whose Interests? From Social Education to Social and Life Skills Training*. Leicester: National Youth Bureau.

Gladstone, D. 1995. *British Social Welfare past, present and future*. London: Routledge.

Manpower Services Commission, 1982. *Manpower Services Review*. London: Manpower Services Commission.

The Job Release Scheme, 1978. *Department of Employment Gazette. Volume 86. No. 8*. London: HMSO.

Manpower Services Commission, 1984. *Annual Reports' 1976–1984*. London: Manpower Services Commission.

Mucking: Real heritage heroism
or heroic failure?

Paul Barford

The open-area rescue excavation in advance of gravel quarrying at Mucking in southeast Essex under the direction of Margaret U. Jones (1916–2001) was one of the largest projects of this type in Europe. It covered a massive area and went on continuously for 13 years between 1965 and 1978, producing an incredibly rich and diverse data set making it relevant to specialists in various periods on an international scale. It therefore occupies a special place in the history of British archaeology. Affected by several significant changes that took place in British archaeology in the past four decades, it arguably also had an influence on archaeological policy in more ways than one.

The area excavated was a portion of the edge of a rural gravel terrace (centred on NGR TQ 673803) in one of the most depressing industrially exploited parts of southern England. Here the infertile dusty soils formed on Boyne Hill Thames terrace gravels abut the loamier soils of the slopes to the west leading down to the marshlands along the estuary coast. The hilltop is rather exposed to winds and bad weather blowing in from the North Sea but has extensive views of the Thames Estuary at the point where it widens. The road which bounded the quarry on the east seems an ancient route leading to a natural crossing point at the head of the estuary at nearby East Tilbury. The 1965–1978 excavations showed that this exposed marginal landscape had been particularly desirable in the past for settlement. This multi-period site with a continuous series of episodes of settlement for some 3000 years or more provided a detailed and extremely informative cross section of the history of the region.

The excavation developed in a phase of British archaeology when archaeology and public opinion were awakening to the destruction of Britain's buried archaeological heritage, and when quarrying was seen as particularly high on the list of threats. In the 1950s and 1960s in Britain the use of aerial photography of cropmarks had been revealing a previously unsuspected density of archaeological features and sites across the sand and gravel areas of the British countryside leading to an altered perception of ancient landscapes, areas of which many hectares annually were being irrevocably destroyed by development and quarrying. A number of publications (*e.g.* RCHME 1960) were drawing attention to the potential scale of the destruction, and the response was increased efforts to document the cropmark sites by aerial photography before they disappeared without record. Resources were however insufficient to mitigate more than a relatively small proportion of the destruction by meaningful excavation. On the few sites that were investigated, rescue archaeology took the form of the investigation of only sample areas, followed up at most with a watching brief of the rest of the destruction. A typical example was the excavation carried out for the Ministry of Public Building and Works (MPBW) in 1958–65 at Roughground, near Lechlade (Gloucestershire), where some 10 ha of an extensive complex of Roman ditched enclosures and a stone-built villa was partially investigated during topsoil stripping and gravel extraction (Allen *et al.* 1993). The excavation was directed by Margaret Jones, a freelance field archaeologist who had previously worked for the MPBW on a number of sites in Buckinghamshire and Yorkshire and also at Old Sleaford, Lincolnshire (Elsdon 2001, Pitts 2001, Webb 2001).

The area that was excavated and recorded in detail at Mucking before its destruction by gravel quarrying covers an amazing 18.2 hectares (45 acres), making it one of the flagship sites of the rescue archaeology movement. The numbers of finds and records generated run into hundreds of thousands. Yet, it was in this very success that the roots of the ultimate tragedy of Mucking lay. While well known through a constant stream of interim reports issued during the project (a bound volume of which is 45mm thick), the full publication of the results of this massive piece of research seems a prospect very distant, if no longer visible. A site atlas was published over a decade ago (Clark 1993), and at the time of writing, only a few other selected aspects of the results of the excavation have reached print despite three decades having passed since the excavation finished.

What was found?

The Mucking excavation established itself as a forerunner in the study of total landscape archaeology; the excavator was fond of referring to it as a 'multi-period palimpsest', a document written on by many generations for whom the Mucking landscape was home. Earlier sporadic activity is evidenced by a few redeposited Mesolithic flints scattered across the site, mostly associated with the silted hollows left by long-fallen trees. There are several areas where Neolithic pottery and lithic assemblages are associated with pits, some of them forming discrete concentrations. There were also burials, including a Beaker inhumation with 11 arrowheads. A number of Early Bronze Age ring-ditches (barrows) and burials formed a row along the valley crest and in several areas between them were contemporary pottery and lithic assemblages. A large part of the excavated area was divided up by a later field system delimited by narrow and shallow ditches dividing it up into large rectangular units, possibly Middle Bronze Age, though few settlement features could be associated with them.

Then in the Late Bronze Age the terrace was dominated by two small circular enclosures. The bivallate South Ring was 76m in overall diameter, and its main entrance faced the river. The second one some 800m to the north was the univallate North Ring at the north-eastern end of the gravel terrace, overlooking Mucking Creek. These were associated with an abundance of artefactual material, pottery and objects of fired clay including briquetage for on-site salt-drying.

The Early Iron Age was represented by enclosures, round houses, pits and postholes and an unenclosed cremation cemetery largely at the south end of the site; more than 100 round-house sites lying within penannular eaves-drip gullies were also found. Two complexes of round houses had attached compounds (the largest of which was re-used as a Romano-British cemetery). The same type of features continue into the Middle Iron Age which is followed by a Later-Iron-Age phase apparently without much of a break, making this a potentially important site for following cultural transition in this period. A complex of frequently renewed curved and rectangular ditches in the centre of the site (the so-called 'Banjo' complex), perhaps providing banks for sheepfolds, belongs to the final pre-Roman occupation.

The Early Roman phase sees a continuation of the same material culture (pottery and fired clay) for a few decades. About the time of the Roman conquest, a precisely rectangular 1.5 acre partly double ditched enclosure with a single north-facing entrance and a military profile ditch was erected on the site of the southern Late Bronze Age circular enclosure. Together with a sub-rectangular 'native' enclosure of similar size at the north end of the site, this earthwork was incorporated into a Roman field system which ran along the crest of the slope. A double ditched enclosure in the middle of the east side of the site seems to have been part of a farmstead. These fields apparently belonged however to farms on the more fertile and heavier soils downslope. A villa somewhere in the region is hinted at by building materials (roof and flue tile fragments, patterned wall daub and window glass), found redeposited as rubbish in ditches and wells. Pottery kilns were established on the edges of this field system, in several cases dug into the fills of partially silted ditches. A number of corndrier flues (made of flint, tile and chalk) and timber lined wells were also found in the excavated area. There were also several small cemeteries. One was sited within the earlier Iron Age ditched enclosure mentioned above and contained 80 graves, the majority being inhumations with grave goods, with body 'silhouettes' and some in coffins with nailed joints. Two further Romano-British cemeteries containing 30 and 20 burials (cremations as well as inhumations, including one in a stone coffin) were also found, one within the double ditched enclosure, the other outside the main outfield boundary ditch.

The Anglo-Saxon settlements dating from the early 5th century to the 7th century spread along half a mile of terrace, both inside and outside the area of the Roman field system. They were represented primarily by the dug-out floors of so-called sunken huts. Over 200 have been excavated, and traces of several dozen ground level post-buildings ('halls') have also been found, making this one of the largest excavated early medieval settlements in Europe. The huts and halls seem to lie in two groups, separated by two Saxon cemeteries which are a notable feature of the excavations. What was left of Cemetery 1 contained only 60 inhumations. Cemetery 2 was the first sizeable Saxon cemetery in England known to have been completely excavated; it contained nearly 800 cremation and inhumation burials. The amount of early 5th century domestic pottery is notable, while from both huts and graves came late Roman military belt fittings which attracted much attention at the time of the excavation. Three sceatta coins were found in the lower fill of one sunken-floored hut and are among the latest Saxon finds from the site.

In the Middle Saxon period, settlement moved away (presumably to the vicinity of Mucking village) and the terrace edge was abandoned becoming marginal waste. Part of the area however contains Medieval field boundaries and the cross-shaped beam-slots of a mid-fifteenth-century windmill were found here. There was an extensive post-medieval ditched field-system extending across almost the entire area. These were all excavated by the Mucking project as part of the investigation of the total landscape history (as well as to recover the redeposited artefactual material in their fills, the distribution patterns of which, over the huge area investigated would give evidence of earlier areas of activity). The sequence ends with a series of modern sheep burials and Second World War bomb craters.

How did it happen?

The excavation was not initially intended to go on for so long; in one sense it 'just happened'. The area of Thurrock had long been known among antiquaries and amateur archaeologists as rich in chance finds made during extensive brick-earth, gravel and sand digging from the nineteenth century onwards, though few finds were known from Mucking and East Linford. Gravel-working after 1938 (Barton 1962, 57) destroyed what were probably Roman kilns just across the road from the Mucking excavation site. When in the early 1950s two boys found some sherds on a quarry spoil-heap and took them to their local museum, a small-scale rescue excavation funded by the MPBW took place in October and December 1955. Typically for the period, only a small area was imperfectly sampled mostly by small-scale trenching as resources allowed. The examined area contained Iron Age and

Roman ditches and pits and Saxon features and was clearly a part of an extensive multi-period site. The results were fairly promptly and fully published (Barton 1962), and it is worth noting that the report of even this small investigation extended to fifty pages. Despite the clear cognitive importance of the site, by the time the Mucking excavation started, the whole area around Barton's excavations had been totally quarried away with no other record made.

As the gravel to the west of the road was exhausted, it was natural for the quarry companies to look for new sources along the terrace to the east where the poor soils were relatively unprofitable to farm. The tenant farmer (Thomas Lindsay of Walton Hall Farm, Mucking) in an effort to improve profitability had grubbed out the hedges to turn some 50 acres into a prairie-like landscape for extensive barley, but in fact in the dry summers only certain areas of the field supported much of a crop. The limited areas where the crops grew better were over the rich tangle of loam-filled ditches and other features left under the ploughsoil by past users of the land. Lindsay jokingly used to say that he wasn't really growing barley on the thin soil, he was growing crop marks! During one hot summer in the mid 1970s, the only corn worth harvesting was along the silted ditches, cropmarks that had been recorded by the Cambridge aerial photographer Professor J. K. St Joseph in June 1959. He saw a tangle of features including a circular cropmark which he interpreted as a double-ditched henge and an enclosure which looked suspiciously like a Roman fort overlying it. Revisiting the site annually for the next few years he gradually revealed the existence of an 800m long zone about 300m wide extending along the terrace edge containing a complex of contiguous cropmarks of enclosures and ditches clearly of several different periods of land-use (see Riley 1993, fig. 2). From the air it was especially obvious that much of the area around had already been destroyed by quarrying and development; the pattern was already truncated at the southeast end where they had been quarried away unrecorded over the road (where Barton's site had been). The rest would clearly soon be totally destroyed by further expansion of the quarrying. St Joseph published a note in *Antiquity* (1964) drawing attention to the importance of and threat to the site: 'so many buried monuments lie in areas liable to be worked for gravel that all cannot be investigated. Here a chance is to hand, either to save a remarkable site from destruction, or to ensure careful excavation before it is too late. Excavations […] might be unusually rewarding'. The local response was immediate; a local museum curator (from Southend Museum) and the district's chief librarian attempted to get some 40 acres of the area covered by the Mucking cropmarks scheduled under the Ancient Monuments Acts. Had this happened, the need for the rescue excavation might have been obviated, but (despite some of the interim accounts suggesting that this had been done), the process of protecting the site was not in fact initiated.

As a result, the Ancient Monuments Branch of the MPBW decided to carry out a small scale excavation of a portion of the complex, and engaged the itinerant excavator Margaret Jones to carry out the task. This she was to do with a small team of hired manual labourers and local volunteers from the Thurrock Local History Society which, together with local notables, she had contacted as soon as she arrived in the area. The general tendency in those days, even for state-supported rescue archaeology, was to operate by something akin to partisan tactics; a small task force would descend on an area for a few weeks, do some digging and then move away to deal with other sites, accumulating in the process a backlog of information from excavated sites they were unable to devote time to processing and publishing (they were only paid to do the digging).

The initial investigation began on 5 September 1965 after the barley harvest and was expected to last eight weeks.[1] In the end, the initial funding was extended and Jones stayed there eight months digging through the winter. Iron Age and Roman features (including burials) were found and recorded in a desperate race against the quarrymen's dragline (Anon. 1966). The atmosphere of the project is well summed up in a recollection of Jonathan Catton:

> My first visit to Mucking (December 1965) was when my father, a local doctor, was asked by Margaret Jones to look at the Roman cemetery body stains and some bone survival. I remember well arriving on the bleak stark hill top overlooking the marsh and estuary. There was snow on the ground. Margaret (dressed in three layers of clothing, a woolly hat and gloves) and an assistant were huddled around a paraffin burner trying to break a chocolate bar for their break. She sparked into life when a new young volunteer appeared, soon a trowel was thrust into my 10 year old hand and I was directed to a dark stain of earth, under the dragline (the driver of which was having a break). It was a small unurned cremation, charcoal and a few flecks of cremated bone. For me it was the start of an odyssey into the world of archaeology' (J. Catton pers comm. August 2008).[2]

It was clear to Margaret Jones that relying only on what can be garnered from cropmarks, surface evidence and extemporary small scale excavation of random parts or cursory 'watching briefs' of the complex of sites threatened by destruction was not an adequate basis for reliable knowledge. Information of the quality that Mucking could clearly provide was precious and finite and if destruction could not be stopped, Jones held that it is incumbent on the archaeologist to make every effort to create as full a record of it as possible, on the principle of: 'the logical aim of 100 per cent examination before 100 per cent destruction' (Anon. 1966). She set about using her somewhat forceful manner to convince others to accept such a vision.[3] In effect she was trying to bridge the gap between the under-resourced rather amateur approach to archaeology of the period and the firmer footing of modern institutional archaeology as a discipline fully conscious of its role in conserving the historic environment as a fragile, finite and valuable resource.

Just after her fiftieth birthday, Margaret Jones came back with her husband Tom[4] to the site after a break of a month in June 1966. In order to place the next phase of the excavation on a more formal operational footing, a committee was set up with the support of the local history society to establish a semi-permanent excavators' camp, which was followed by an excavation committee which was to function throughout the dig to monitor the work and seek and administer various grants. Over the next few years MPBW funds were made available to carry out the excavation of several areas.

Recording the palimpsest

In 1966 parts of the 'fort' and 'henge' to the north-east of the area recorded in 1965 were investigated. The first century AD rectangular enclosure was investigated and the 'henge' turned out to be something quite different, a Late Bronze Age enclosure of a type then poorly known in Britain. While the perception of the site had up until then been mainly as a prehistoric and Roman one, the discovery, dug into the late fills of Roman ditches, of the first sunken huts with Early Saxon pottery in them was to give the site a new significance as one of only a few settlements of this period known to any extent. Then in the winter of 1967 the first of the site's two Anglo-Saxon cemeteries was discovered during quarrying of an area to the northeast devoid of any cropmarks and which had thus reluctantly been sacrificed to the quarry without more than a cursory examination. Paradoxically this area was being quarried because the quarry management had been persuaded to adjust their plans to exploit an area with few cropmarks in order to give the excavation more time in the areas where such remains were known. In the end part of the cemetery was destroyed before finds were noticed on the gravel conveyor-belt. The cemetery had to be excavated on the quarry edge in the shadow of the dragline, as is shown in a dramatic photo captioned 'brinkmanship in archaeology' published in *Current Archaeology* (Anon 1973). There are many questions about that complex of features and its relationship with the rest of the Anglo-Saxon landscape which cannot now be answered, even though they were found as part of one of the largest landscape excavation projects this country has seen, because the excavated part of the cemetery is isolated from the rest of the site by a large uninvestigated area. From 1968, the funding allowed excavation to carry on all the year round, a British first. The Joneses moved (from the rented accommodation on a Tilbury council estate) to caravans on the site, which were to be their permanent home for the next decade and a half.

The underground traces surviving from a long sequence of consecutive changes in the superimposed ancient landscapes were manifested as a palimpsest of negative features (such as ditched enclosures, gullies, pits, postholes, graves and house sites) with more or less loamy fills dug into the loose sandy gravel. These were revealed in plan (as soilmarks) when the plough soil and the subsoil had been stripped off. Mucking was one of the first sites where regimes of topsoil stripping by machine (box scrapers and front bladed diggers) integrated with the work of the quarry company were developed. The excavation was from the beginning totally open area, and it was from the beginning apparent that horizontal patterns were more revealing than the vertical stratigraphy which was still the main focus of other excavation strategies of the mid 1960s. The distribution of features and finds in their fills was indicative of zones of activities, but the pattern needed recovery over as large and continuous an area as possible in order to be correctly read.

The excavation methods adopted in the early years (described briefly by Jones 1968, 228–230: cf Clark 1993, 11) were developed with several considerations in mind. The first was the need for them to be consistent with the nature of the deposits being examined, loose extremely pebbly sandy loams differing often by very subtle variations in colour and consistency (better seen in winter digging than in dry summer conditions). The second was an obvious need to maintain complete consistency of method from one end of the site to the other over a number of years and despite changes of excavation teams. Thirdly, the human factor: it had to be understandable to the people from varied backgrounds employed as excavators (see below). The features were excavated by a horizontal 'spit' technique (usually three inches, or six inches in deep ditches). This allowed the drawing of 'horizontal sections' of the feature fills which were then supplemented by vertical sections in the baulks (the plans and sections of the many thousands of postholes however were measured and sketched in the notebooks). Documentation of the stratigraphy was done in a dig-diary form in the supervisors' notebooks (supplemented by the directors' own field notes). Most of the major features are documented in some superb photographs taken by Tom Jones (after careful critical scrutiny of the degree to which the area had been prepared).

In considering the excavation methods adopted in the mid 1960s it should be remembered that the stratigraphic methods of excavation and recording, which were in more general use all over Britain by the time the Mucking excavation finished, were in their infancy and were developed on other sites largely after Mucking was well underway. Those who came to the site from other excavations by the end of the 1970s surprised by and sometimes critical of the less fashionable excavation techniques they found at Mucking and indeed this was fuel for rumour and folklore. Some of this has spilled over into the literature (Dixon 1993; see Barford 1995). This 'Black legend' has served latterly to justify the failure of a proper report to appear. Actually, as an excavation methodology, when properly applied, the Mucking system worked perfectly adequately for the purposes for which it was devised, and the paper records and other parts of the archive probably have no more problems hectare for hectare than any similar excavation carried out under such conditions at the same period.

For reasons of consistency, the use of a site measurement system based on feet and inches was maintained throughout, and again by the end of the excavation this seemed incongruously old-fashioned to those brought up thinking in the less intellectually-demanding metric. In the circumstances, it was logical, even though by the end of the dig it was getting increasingly more difficult to obtain equipment (steel tapes and graph paper especially) in imperial measurements. Features were not consecutively numbered, but each intervention (feature, ditch segment, trench etc) was given a co-ordinate (northings by eastings) in feet and inches. Some classes of features however were sequentially numbered for ease of reference (the most enduring were the numbers of Anglo-Saxon SFBs and all the graves).

The increased government allocations for rescue archaeology in the early 1970s were to ease a little the accessing of continued funds for the Mucking excavation (Margaret Jones was one of the founder members of RESCUE). Mucking was a showpiece site demonstrating the new government committal to the recording of the country's archaeological heritage threatened by development under an (initially) booming economy. Mucking remained however unique in the scale of the response. Jones bemoaned the fact that:

> … in spite of an official report published in 1960 on the growing loss of sites through gravel quarrying, Mucking is still the only gravel pit rescue where a deliberate attempt is being made to record the entire palimpsest of ancient landscapes, rather than specific features. Its significance therefore derives not only from its discovery of new material. It is also a type site for method, based on the positive attitude that quarrying provides unique opportunities (Jones in Bruce Mitford 1975, 133).

She was hoping that the publication of the results she was obtaining would confirm the validity of the holistic approach and lead the government to adopt it more widely. The intimate integration of her archaeological research with the quarry programme was a forerunner of the developer funding approaches of the following decade. The integration was not however always seamless:

> Rescue archaeology in a gravel pit was in the 1960s a question of opportunism […] successful archaeological operations […] had to depend on constant adjustments to fit the way the quarry worked and the demands of its personnel, which were in turn affected by such imponderables as required outputs, the thickness of the gravel, and the weather […] it was a constant battle to keep ahead – a battle not always successful… (Jones 1993, 6–7).

Despite the full co-operation of the quarry company (Hoveringham Gravels Ltd), some areas were inevitably only available for excavation for a short time between topsoil stripping and quarrying, thus could only be the subject of salvage work and watching briefs. This explains the blank areas visible at the south end of the site plan in the Site Atlas and the strip of uninvestigated areas over most of the northwest side of the quarried area.

Slowly the excavation moved piece by piece in a north-easterly direction across the peaceful rural landscape with its splendid views in front, and always very closely followed by the noisy machines marking the inexorable spread of the quarry. By the early 1970s, one complex of Roman field enclosures over 300m across was behind them. On the west edge of the excavated area was encountered a confusing tangle of Latest Iron Age ditches (labelled the 'banjo' enclosures) which continued in use into the early Roman period apparently without a break. This was followed by the discovery of another Anglo-Saxon cemetery. This one, unlike the first, was excavated almost in its totality (one of the few in Britain where this has been achieved). The following years were spent investigating a second complex of Roman enclosures on the east side of the site (including a rectangular enclosure with a double ditch) and then a sub-rectangular enclosure which had Late Iron Age beginnings. By

Figure 15.1. Mucking, Essex: Excavation in progress in the late 1970s. Hand clearing of freshly-machined area behind the conveyor belt. Dragline in the distance, recently quarried area in foreground. Excavation huts and toolshed in background (excavation archives, photographer unknown).

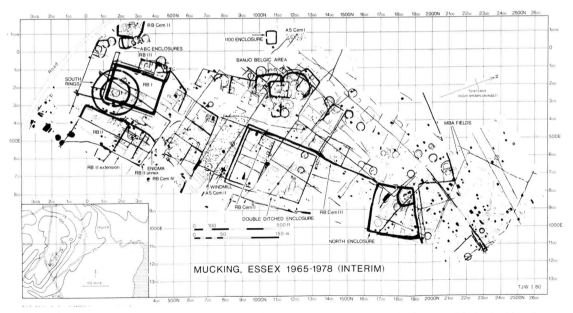

Figure. 15.2. Mucking, Essex: Plan of the investigated part of the site, the soilmarks shown in black. At this reduction the huge number of smaller features is barely visible and the scale of the excavation difficult to appreciate (Clark 1993 after John Webb and others).

1975 the excavations moved away from the area of Roman activity, and much of the evidence was of prehistoric activity, though the Anglo-Saxon settlements extended in this direction too.

Throughout the whole period, the excavators kept their project in the public eye both at national and local level, through a series of interim reports (full bibliography Clark 1993, appendix A, 37–8). Many of them were written for a local history society publication (*Panorama – Journal of the Thurrock Local History Society*). These pieces of popular writing show the importance the excavators attached to maintaining links with the local community and keeping them involved in the development of this major project which had developed on their doorstep. Indeed, it has been argued (Randall Bingley pers. comm.) that the Mucking excavations had a crucial role in developing interest in the local heritage in the region among the public and local government administration. The excavators gave many talks and conference papers on a variety of topics, and interested many senior academics both at home and abroad in their findings (in particular the Anglo-Saxon ones) and the progress of the investigations, for example making a point of regularly showing their finds at the Exhibits at Ballots of the Society of Antiquaries. There was a readable and informative account of the first part of the excavations written in 1973 (Jones 1975) and also two important interim reports in the Antiquaries Journal, though no third Interim report for the Antiquaries Journal at the end of the excavations was prepared; presumably Jones was counting on the appearance of the final report in the next few years, given adequate resources. There is little doubt that a lot of this publication activity should be seen as a kind of propaganda, keeping the project in the public eye in the light of the still somewhat precarious situation of state financing with the increasing economic crisis of the mid and late 1970s. Fortunately the Ministry and from 1970 the DoE, was able to continue to fund the project to a very satisfactory degree. It has been estimated (not all expenses are now determinable) that the Directorate of Ancient Monuments and Historical Buildings (DAMHB) of the DoE had funded the excavations to the tune of at least £85,000 (Clark 1993, 13).[5] The local council, assured that the finds from this prestigious project would form the centrepiece of the collections of the new museum being planned, also made substantial financial grants to the project and supplied help in kind, including working and storage space in the new Central Library and Museum Complex.

The excavations proper came to an end in 1977, though in 1978 more work (directed by Jonathan Catton) was done around the quarry margins as they were dug away as the gravel on the rest of the site had run out. On the other side of the quarry was another circular enclosure cropmark, and trial excavations (by the present writer) of part of it damaged by previous quarrying had revealed it as a Late Bronze Age enclosure analogous to the one excavated in the 1960s. The quarry concession now included the field containing this cropmark, but instead of making this part of the brief of the Mucking excavation team (perhaps understandably) the mitigating excavation was entrusted to the DoE's Central Excavation Unit directed by Dermot Bond. Sadly, only the immediate area of the cropmark was excavated in 1978 and the ditch fill itself was only sampled. After topsoil stripping of the rest of the area to be quarried away, Margaret Jones (who still lived in her caravan on the site – now moved down nearer the farm) continued salvage work with weekend volunteers for a few months in 1978–9 as best she could on what was left, revealing much evidence of Late Bronze Age activity associated with the enclosure and other features. Thus it was that the long series of excavations themselves came to an end.

The first part of the project had achieved its primary aim: a considerable portion of the archaeological evidence in the ground had been turned into paper records supplemented by the collected artefacts, ecofacts and soil samples. These were to provide the raw material for the final report presenting the results of the work. The archive produced however was vast: an estimated 44,000 features had been excavated. Ann Clark (1993, 14) estimates the total number of finds from the site as 1.7 million.[6] There were some six tonnes of ceramic sherds alone to be processed, 5000 plans, several thousand photographs and 363 site notebooks to be studied. In the field, the finds had of course been separated into categories and given a preliminary examination in the excavation finds hut. They were boxed according to category, feature and hundred-foot grid square. Special finds which seemed to need showing to specialists or used for exhibition were separated out (they were called '55's because initially field notebook 55 was used to list them). Grave assemblages were however kept together and separate from that of the settlements (the post-excavation of the cemetery assemblages was directed by Tom Jones). The Mucking finds were initially stored in a Thurrock District Council facility in Tilbury (where some were involved in a freak flood in September 1968) with some also in a government store in Acton near London where the Joneses were able to work on them on the rare occasions when they left the site for any length of time. One result of this was a journal article concerning several Roman kiln groups (Jones and Rodwell 1973). This in the end was to be the only part of the site to have been published in full by the excavator and showed some of the problems that this involved. From about 1972, all the material from the excavations was taken to the store in the newly-built Thurrock Central Library and Museum complex.

The digging team

The Mucking investigation could not have taken place without the many thousand people from many walks of life who took up tools to rescue the archaeological evidence of this unique site before it was destroyed by the dragline. Over 5,000 people from Britain and abroad took part in the excavations. They were called 'volunteers', though they received a small sum of money called 'subsistence' for immediate needs. Most of them were students: 'mega-excavations like Mucking were products [...] of a definite ethos of students of the 1960s and 1970s' (Jones 1993, 10). The team was truly international; as well as from Britain, young people from the Netherlands, the USA and Australia came to take part in the work. Jones realized that young eastern Europeans from Communist countries were eager to visit 'the west' and could be persuaded to come simply by providing an official 'invitation' which was needed to get a visa; they also proved usefully resilient to the rigours of excavation life. Thus it was that for several summers the excavation was staffed with young people first from Czechoslovakia and then from the mid 1970s from Poland. In the 1977 season, like many other excavations of the period, the usual student labour force was supplemented by a Job Creation Project (Manpower Services Commission) for the long term unemployed. Jones was unimpressed by their attitudes to hard work in the field (though MSC employees were later to make an important contribution in the post-excavation office work).

Being an all-year dig, Mucking was also a fixture on the digging circuit; on the team (especially in the autumn and winter) one usually could find talented individuals who had spent the last decade or so moving from excavation to excavation. Other long term residents were using the project as a refuge from everyday life in a counter-culture search for themselves, all adding colour to the specific community which an excavation always creates. In the months in the depths of winter there might be just over a dozen excavators, while in the summer university vacation period there may have been a hundred or more. This obviously affected the pace of the work.

Having an excavation of this stature as a permanent fixture in the neighbourhood stimulated local awareness of archaeological matters and there was active outreach to the local community. This was to pay dividends in offers of help. The site welcomed local amateur archaeology enthusiasts who each weekend and on public holidays rain or shine would spend a day or two, week after week digging for the fun of it on the quarry edge on the bleak hilltop with Margaret Jones (who took very few days off while there was archaeology still to be rescued). Some of these 'Mucking weekenders' became very competent diggers.

The peculiar place that was the excavation camp, isolated from the outside world in the middle of the lunar landscape of the quarry floor and with its sparse vegetation, was the epitome of what the dig was about. This collection of make-do shacks and primitive utilities was a focus for a loose scatter of diggers' own tents and home to the constantly shifting populace of excavators. Yet it engendered a specific team spirit and folklore among them. Those who had been on the site longer graduated to living in one of the several wood and tar-paper shacks; another permanent structure was converted from a large lorry donated by a local firm as a dormitory. The key structure was a large pensioned-off contractor's hut which served as cook house, mess hut and shelter for various activities. To one side were chemical toilets in corrugated iron privies with next to them out in the open, sawn-off plastic container washbasins with their strong carbolic soap and a tendency to freeze in winter. Here too was what passed for an open-air 'shower'. Water was from a huge black tank (theoretically it was to be 'heated by the warmth of the sun') filled by a plastic hose that snaked up from the distant farm, when it did not freeze. The Joneses endured similar rigours in their three caravans (one each and one for guests) situated nearer the quarry working face and guarding the site at night.

The excavation camp was a model of economy; it could not have functioned without the help of local firms who gave items such as food and detergents from their charity allocations or any surplus equipment that may be useful. The diggers were fed on the cheapest brand from the local cash and carry prepared by a succession of creative cooks (Jones 1993, 9) and often eked out with vegetables which the farmer allowed to be gathered from the crops in the fields (most of which was otherwise destined for cattle feed). Jones was delighted when a Polish camp cook demonstrated that an appetizing soup can be prepared from the leaves of beetroot. The tasty wholemeal bread, baked on site from a proprietary ('scofa') mix remains a permanent memory.

Even in those days, these 'refugee camp' living conditions would raise eyebrows, but luckily for the Excavation Committee, 'official bodies who might have invoked stringent regulations and frowned on so Bohemian a settlement instead took a helpful line' (Jones 1993, 9). 'Mucking is no holiday camp' wrote the journalist Tina Brown of Punch (30 June 1976) after she visited the site:

> Mrs Jones has devised a stunningly repulsive application form to weed out the loafers [...] It is an outdoor camp with minimum equipment. There is piped cold water serving outdoor wash places and chemical sanitation [...] the turnover unsurprisingly is rapid. Mrs Jones's nightly task is casing the new application forms sent in by vacationing students, actors between jobs, dole collectors on holiday from unemployment and archaeology students desperate or dedicated enough to work for £12 a week.

Elsdon wrote in Jones' obituary (2001), 'a generation of respectable middle-aged archaeologists still boasts of being dosed with patent medicine, learning to bake their own bread and other rigours among the Thames gravels. To have dug with Margaret Jones at Mucking remains a badge of honour'. It would be interesting to collect their reminiscences (see Carney 2002).

Total landscape rescue: Utopian idea?

The excavation team worked hard in all weathers to give Margaret Jones' credo '100% destruction means 100% rescue' substance in action. For those that knew the site and watched the subtleties of the evidence emerge and relate to what previous recording had revealed, this was entirely logical. Mucking was a site which it would have been very tempting to sample. It had a very clear record of excellent cropmarks, which revealed a pattern of interconnecting ditches and a scatter of large features like sunken-floored huts which it might have seemed easy to interpret merely by sampling a few limited areas. Full excavation of the area concerned, field by field showed how erroneous this notion would have been. Jones was dismissive of 'armchair exercises with air photographs and maps' and pointed out that her work at Mucking was 'helping to dispel the illusion of easily-won data. Cropmarks do not provide more than a partial glimpse of ancient settlements: they rarely reflect minor features, nor […] are they capable of reliable interpretation without excavation'. (1975, 8). 'Cropmarks are to be regarded as site indicators, never as site plans' (Jones 1974, 31). The fact that some features do not appear in the cropmarks should not need any emphasis, but it was precisely the destruction of Anglo-Saxon Cemetery 1 in an area that had been written off as having limited archaeological significance on the basis of pre-quarrying evaluation, which brings this point home. Similarly, while the cropmark 'blobs' representing Anglo-Saxon sunken featured huts were usually obvious and easily plottable on a map as cropmarks, the extent of Anglo-Saxon posthole buildings, pits, post-hole fence lines and other elements of the same landscape were not.[7]

Various strategies were used by Jones to attempt to predict (for grant application and general logistics purposes) what lay ahead. Early on in the excavation it became clear that, with or without the cropmark evidence, neither fieldwalking surveys nor trial trenches gave any indication of the complexities to be found under the ploughsoil, and indeed their interpretation often gave false information. Tony Wilkinson (1988, 6) had similar experience nearby in his work on the A13 and M26 investigations.

The evidence from Mucking showed that the small scale sampling by excavation after evaluation was simply unreliable. By the time the total landscape excavation at Mucking was well underway however, this was what was being routinely advocated in the British archaeological establishment as a mitigation strategy. Mucking provided a clear example of a case where it was impossible to predict what information about the past large areas of a site like this will contain. Not only would selecting areas to investigate by more or less arbitrary means, while leaving others to be destroyed without record, have produced woefully incomplete data, but also a dataset warped by certain inbuilt assumptions imposed by the excavation method. On the other hand, subsequent events were to show that total excavation of even a shallowly-stratified rural site of this type can – without the application of suitable resources and strategies – produce an overwhelming amount of data to be processed in order to disseminate the results (and the lessons one can learn from a project of this nature). The message of Mucking is perhaps that current rescue archaeology mitigation strategies on sites of this type give us the alternative of incomplete or even bad data, and too many data.

Organizing and disseminating the results

After the digging was over, Margaret and Tom Jones (together with assistant director Jonathan Catton) moved to the sixth floor of the Central Library and Museum complex in Grays, Thurrock, in effect occupying almost the entire Grays Museum store where most of the material from the excavation was now archived. The Mucking Excavation became MPX, Mucking Post-Excavation (Jones 1979a; Clark 1993, 12–14). Although conditions were somewhat cramped, between 1978 and 1985 a small group of dedicated people (six DoE funded staff and ten part time MSC staff) worked away in these storerooms trying to make sense of the enormous body of archaeological information concentrated there. Problems were bound to be caused by the processing of the information on an unprecedented scale produced by the work of thousands of people over 13 years non-stop excavation and always pressed for time under rescue conditions. The task ahead of Jones was vast, and as Sheila Elsdon (2001) noted, 'The challenge to write up that huge corpus of recorded detail came when she was ageing and tired after long years of continuous digging. It overwhelmed her.' (Margaret was 62 when MPX began.)

The form of the publication was also a question. Mucking spanned several generations of change in this respect. When the excavation began, the model to be striven for in the case of excavations which were too large to fit into a local archaeological journal were as hefty volumes in the Reports of the Research Committee of the Society of Antiquaries series. Presenting a site of this size and nature in that form would require several dozen volumes. Then the first site publications in fasicule form began to appear as part of the *CBA Research Report* series in the mid and late 1970s. The publication of the 'Frere Report' (1975), with its various levels of data, laid down new principles for the publication of major sites and Mucking Post Excavation was to put them into practice. In November 1976 Margaret Jones produced a conspectus for a level II archive (presenting the totality of the excavated data as urged by the Frere Report) and a series of volumes of definitive reports on 'successive human landscapes'.

Computerisation was seen as the answer to the problem of handling the vast amount of data. Although computers were finding increasing uses in archaeology in the 1970s, Mucking was one of the pioneers of the use of computer databases on a large scale (Clark 1993, 12–13, Catton *et al.* 1982). The computerised record would comprise the 'level III' database which would then form the basis for creating the published 'synthetic description'. A database would be manually compiled which would link together records of the various types of evidence in a way which seemed very time consuming manually. Unlike a major urban or similar site with deep vertical stratigraphy which can be divided into vertical phases, the material of which can be processed within discrete chronological blocks, the main key to the chronological development of the Mucking site was in terms of spatial arrangements over massive areas, and this was dated by the contained artefactual material. A lot of this was difficult to 'spot date' at the time, since Mucking itself was to become one of the type sites for pottery sequences of the region in several periods. One of the main aims of this system was to be able to document where in this vast spread of features certain types of material had been found and to examine their spread across the site (Catton *et al.* 1982, 36).

The software and hardware available at the time seemed to give the possibilities of achieving the aim. For several reasons however this promise was ultimately not to be fully fulfilled (see Clark 1993, 12–14) which was very frustrating to those who had put the effort into inputting these records. Part of the problem was perhaps an over-optimism on the part of the post-excavation team concerning the capabilities of the computer technology of the period.[8] Jonathan Moffett (1989) who compiled the original software to the archaeological specifications was later critical of the approach which he saw as to some degree based on the attitude that the computer database 'will make the data self-explanatory', a model where the computer is 'fed masses and masses of data in the great hope that when the button is pressed a report will appear out of thin air'. This however is not a totally fair assessment of what MPX was attempting. By the time the 1983 Cunliffe Report (with its emphasis on the 'new technology' of microfiche) appeared marking a new stage in the development of the debate on the form of publication of major projects, problems were emerging in both the progress and results of the initial computer processing of data in MPX.

By 1983 the 'golden age' of rescue archaeology was beginning to come to an end and questions were being asked about when (or rather, whether) the Mucking project would reach its conclusion. This coincided with, and indeed may even have been part of the catalyst for, a growing awareness in the early 1980s that in general, post excavation archiving and publication of the results of an excavation can be a more time-consuming and costly process than the excavation itself. Current project management systems derive from such an awareness. At the time though while such an awareness was still rudimentary, it perhaps was less clear than it is now that the resources assigned to this project, though not by any means inconsiderable were wholly inadequate to the task before it.

The setting up of the Excavation Backlog Working party in 1984 (Butcher and Garwood 1994) allowed some of the work on specific portions of the excavated material to be contracted out (including to the present writer). Parts of the Mucking project were funded from this project so that it would not make significant inroads on the 'current projects' budget. Tensions however began to develop between MPX in Thurrock and the DoE Management Team (Clark 1993, 13–14). Despite this MPX struggled on with MSC staff until time came for Margaret and Tom Jones to retire, and this phase of the project came to an end in the last months of 1985. According to DoE records between 1978 and Dec 1985, the AMHB had provided £254,000 to the post excavation (not counting technical services over the decades such as conservation, illustration and analyses provided by HBMC staff); Thurrock Borough Council, in addition to its earlier (not insubstantial) grants also bore many of the day to day running costs of the MPX unit.

The British Museum steps in

By this time, the decision had been taken to make a fresh break with previous work, and that the most fitting location for this enormous nationally important excavation archive was not in a local museum, but the British Museum. This caused mixed feelings locally, Thurrock was losing a well-renowned resource which they thought had been promised to them as the core to their new museum collection[9] but would no longer have to bear the mounting costs of maintaining the rest of the archive. Thus it was that in 1985–6 the newly-created Mucking Management Committee (MMC) (Clark 1993, 14–7) supervised the wholesale transfer of the excavation archive to the British Museum's (BM) Blythe Road store in Hammersmith. Here under joint BM/English Heritage (EH) control the material was to be reorganized in a form suitable for the BM accession system, but also the processing and publication of the material was to be brought to fruition. To carry out this programme, the MMC engaged a small team of post-excavation staff (some of whom had not seen the site itself and had no experience with its rich archives and the work already done on it) and outside specialists under the direction of Ann Clark (who for a number of years previously had been working on part of the Mucking Publication Programme for EH). This new project was to last from February 1986 to March 1989, but was later extended in a reduced form until 1992. The task once again however proved beyond the financial and personnel resources made available. The post-excavation project was terminated in 1993, due to financial overspend, apparently just as many of its initial analyses were about to be completed. This part of the project is reported to have cost English Heritage a further £372,515.

Part of the problem was that for a number of reasons, which have never been properly justified in a comprehensible form, except calling on the 'black legend' of some vague 'problems inherent in the record' (Clark 1993, 2), the MMC decided that they were unable to work with the system of co-ordinates which was fundamental to the excavation recording system and that before work could begin in earnest it first had to completely reorganize the archive and assign feature numbers to all the major features and cuts (Clark 1993, 14–17). As a result, 'the logistics of working through the paper archive [...] were sufficient to absorb the BM/EH team for the majority of its three year programme. Hence the integration of the finds and records was hardly begun, let alone any but the most basic phasing of the site'. As a result and unbelievably, 'In practice, the vast secondary archive produced by MPX was not investigated systematically' (Clark 1993, 2 and 14). One of the few achievements of this MMC programme was however the publication of the Site Atlas (Clark 1993). This was published as a series of loose plans at consistent scale (1:180) of all the excavated areas in an oversized folder accompanied by a slim booklet containing some background information (setting, geology, excavation methods and other material), and a short four-page text (pp. 6–10) contributed by a now thoroughly disheartened Margaret Jones. It is ironic that after all her effort, this was all that she was able to contribute to the final report of her own project. The 'Site Atlas' is better than nothing, but is however a very scrappy and unsatisfying volume lacking in balance and with a long list of errata seen as the publication was being prepared (pp. vii–I). It is however notable that in the course of the Blythe Road project, Dermot Bond's (1988) report on the excavation of North Ring and a limited area around it appeared. Despite having the full resources of the English Heritage Central Excavation Unit behind it, and covering only a minute fraction (about one fiftieth or less) of the area of the main Mucking site, its publication only appeared ten years after the main dig had finished. In other words, the report had taken almost as long to produce as the duration allowed the comparatively small teams of MPX and the Blythe Road MMC team for their work. Another work that appeared in 1993 was Helena Hamerow's report on the Anglo-Saxon settlements which was written for a post-graduate degree and drew heavily on data already organized by the team in MPX, though with some annoying omissions (most of the Anglo-Saxon pits, other features and deposits between the obvious houses) and minor errors in use of existing specialist reports. The projected volumes concerning the site's prehistoric and Roman phases were not completed. The volume on the Anglo-Saxon cemeteries (by Sue Hirst and Dido Clark) has been announced as 'imminent' since 1993, the year when their main excavator Tom Jones died of a stroke.

Mucking was probably the most significant of the few of the 'Backlog' sites that failed in the end to be published. As the original Blythe Road project began to draw to an end, MAP1 and then MAP2 appeared, and it is tempting to believe that Mucking was one of the most notorious failures of the existing system which were the catalyst for their writing. Margaret Jones died in March 2001 without any assurance that the work to which she devoted much of the latter part of her working life, and on which others had worked so hard would ever be completed.

Back to Cambridge

After the publications of 1993, there then followed a break of thirteen years in which very little seems to have happened, and funding for the Mucking projects which were still ongoing seems to have been minimal. In 2006, however, the British Museum commissioned yet another new team, this time from the Cambridge Archaeological Unit (CAU) based in the University of Cambridge, to attempt to complete the site's publication programme. It is perhaps ironic that the results of an excavation which started with St Joseph's aerial photos should end up being brought to final publication in Cambridge. The new team received two years' money (part of it from the Aggregates Levy Sustainability Fund) to

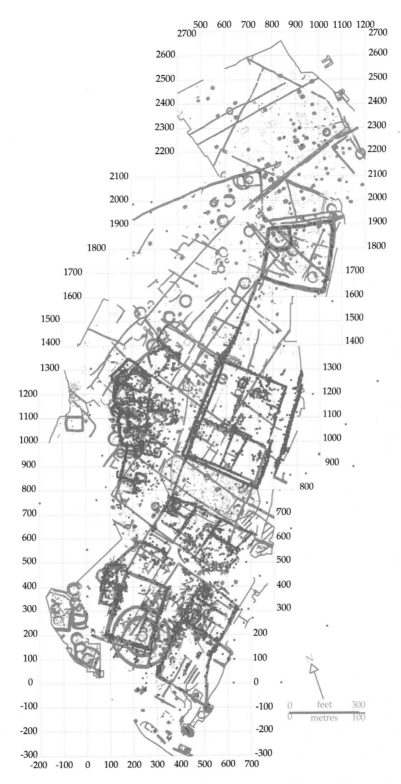

Figure 15.3. Mucking, Essex: Fruits of the revival of the MPX database: distribution plot of all Roman pottery fragments against the background of the excavated features, defining areas of depositional activity of varying intensity across the landscape. At the north end of the site the material mainly occurs in the late fills of earlier features (Plot courtesy of C. J. Evans CAU).

consolidate the existing data and post-excavation research from the excavations of the prehistoric and Roman phases of the site and 'conduct a limited amount of further archival work on the prehistoric pottery assemblages'. The aim of this was to make 'phased site plans, feature gazetteers, prehistoric pottery reports and period-based assessments of the archives' available digitally via the Archaeology Data Service website so that it would be presented to a sufficient standard to allow it to be usable by others as the basis for further synthesis.[10] After two decades, in 2007, it proved possible to get the old computer files of the MPX database up and running and finally produce the three dimensional plots of artefact distributions across the site which were to have been the vindication of the '100% rescue' ethos (Figure 15.3). It is projected that work on the archive will result in the production of two further paper volumes (Evans and Lucy, forthcoming; Lucy, Jefferies and Taylor forthcoming).

The end?

The tale of Mucking prompts a few reflections. Above all it is clear that British archaeology of the 1960s and 1970s was not ready for the Mucking project and its indomitable director Margaret Jones. Neither were the Joneses prepared for the consequences of their decision to rescue this piece of threatened archaeological heritage from unmitigated destruction. In one way the story of this project may be characterized as one of heroic failures and compromises, but only as the epitome of the general situation of the discipline as a whole as it grew and developed with archaeological experience and expertise in the last half century. In this, Mucking played no small part, which is part of its legacy.

The saga of Mucking is a typically British one, a tale of an idealistic struggle against the odds, of brave and sometimes rash decisions and compromises, and of (in the excavator's own words) 'make-do and mend, and ad hoc-ery', a sequence of events which owes much to 'fluke and fashion' (Jones 1979b). Much was achieved, but a number of circumstances, easier to see with hindsight perhaps than they were at the time, have conspired to make this a story without a final victorious end, a sobering tale some might say of missed opportunities and to a large degree unrewarded effort. Mucking suffered precisely because of its uniqueness and scale and the nature of the available resources. As Ann Clark (1993, 1) noted, the period over which this massive project stretched 'has seen considerable changes in excavation methods and post-excavation strategies, of many of which Mucking has been both a pioneer and victim'. The history of British archaeology is strewn with tales of more or less heroic failures; Mucking may well count as a most heroic achievement in some ways as well as one of the most bitter of failures in others. An extraordinary record however has been made and permanently curated for posterity of some extraordinary archaeological evidence, which but for the dedicated work and extreme efforts of many people over several decades, would have been totally lost. It sadly still remains to be seen how this can be used to full benefit to enhance knowledge of the past.

Acknowledgements

Any attempt to briefly summarize this massive project is fraught with risk, not only due to its enormous scale, but also because it is many things to different people, perhaps more than many other excavations. This chapter presents one of a number of possible accounts, inevitably personal anecdotal, and condensed by hindsight. The writer dug at Mucking 1975–77, worked through the documentation and finds in the first MPX 1978–1991, and then on some of the material as a consultant 1983–5. I would like to thank Jonathan Catton, Randall Bingley, Chris Evans and Pamela Irving for their comments and help. I am grateful also to John Schofield for information on the scheduling history of the site.

References

A Correspondent [M. U. Jones] 1966. Race to win secrets of ancient sites, *The Times* (29 May 1966).

Anon [A. Selkirk?] 1973. Mucking: the Saxon Cemeteries, *Current Archaeology* 50, (3) (May 1973), 73–80.

Allen T. G., Darvill, T. C., Green, L. S., and Jones, M. U. 1993. *Excavations at Roughground Farm, Lechlade, Gloucestershire: A Prehistoric and Roman Landscape.* Oxford: Oxford University School of Archaeology.

Barford, P. M. 1995. Re-interpreting Mucking: countering the black legend, *Anglo-Saxon Studies in Archaeology and History* 8, 103–10.

Barton, K. J. 1962. Settlements of the Iron Age and pagan Saxon periods at Linford, Essex, *Transactions of the Essex Archaeological Society* (iii ser) 1. 2, 57–104.

Bond, D. 1988. *Excavations at the North Ring, Mucking, Essex.* East Anglian Archaeology Reports 43.

Brown, T. 1976. [column in] *Punch* (30 June 1976).

Butcher, S. and Garwood, P. 1994. *Rescue Excavation, 1938 to 1972: A Report for the Backlog Working Party of the Ancient Monuments Advisory Committee of English Heritage.* London: English Heritage.

Carney, T. 2002. *Memories of Mucking* [in:] *Thurrock Gold*, Thurrock Local History Society.

Catton, J. P. J., Jones, M. U. and Moffett, J. C. 1981. The 1965–78 Mucking excavation computer database, in I. Graham and E. Webb (eds), *Computer applications in archaeology*, 36–43. London: University of London Institute of Archaeology.

Clark, A. 1993. *Excavations at Mucking, Volume 1: The Site Atlas.* English Heritage Archaeological Report 20. London: English Heritage.

Cunliffe, B. W. 1983. *The Publication of Archaeological Excavations. Report* of the Joint Working Party of the Council for British Archaeology and the Department of the Environment. London: Department of the Environment.

Dixon, P. 1993. The Anglo-Saxon settlement at Mucking: an interpretation, *Anglo-Saxon Studies in Archaeology and History* 6, 125–47.

Elsdon S. 2001. Margaret Jones [obituary], *The Independent, Saturday, 31 March 2001* [http://www.independent.co.uk/news/obituaries/margaret-jones-728978.html].

Evans, C. J. and Lucy, S. with contributors, forthcoming. *Mucking, Essex – Excavations by Margaret and Tom Jones* (1965–78): The Prehistoric and Roman Landscape CAU Landscape Archives Series: Historiography and Fieldwork No. 2.

Frere, S. 1975. *Principles of Publication in Rescue Archaeology.* Ancient Monuments Board (England). London: DoE.

Hamerow, H. 1993. *Excavations at Mucking, Volume 2: The Anglo-Saxon Settlement,* English Heritage Archaeological Report 21. London: English Heritage.

Hirst, S. and Clarke, D. forthcoming. *Excavations at Mucking 3: the Anglo-Saxon Cemeteries.*

Jones, M. U. 1975. An ancient Landscape palimpsest at Mucking. *Essex Archaeology and History* 5, 6–12.

Jones, M. U. 1979a. Mucking Post Excavation 1979, *Panorama* 23, 47–57.

Jones, M. U. 1979b. Operation Mucking. *Essex Archaeological Society Newsletter* 68, 8–9.

Jones, M. U. 1993. Background, in Clark, A. (ed.) Excavations at Mucking, Volume 1: The Site Atlas, 6–10. English Heritage Archaeological Reports, 20. London: English Heritage.

Jones, M. U. and Jones, W. T. 1968. The cropmark sites at Mucking, Essex, *Antiquaries Journal* XLVIII(ii), 210–230.

Jones, M. U. and Jones, W. T. 1974. The Mucking Excavations, the interim plan 1965–1973, *Panorama* 17, 31–39.

Jones, M. U. and Jones, W. T. 1975. The crop-mark sites at Mucking, Essex, England, in Bruce-Mitford, R. (ed.), *Recent archaeological excavations in Europe, 133–87.* London and Boston: Routledge and Kegan Paul.

Jones, M. U. and Rodwell, W. J. 1973. Romano-British pottery kilns at Mucking: Interim Report on Two Kiln Groups, *Essex Archaeology and History* 5, 13–47.

Lucy, S., Jefferies, R. and Taylor, N. forthcoming. *Mucking, Essex – Excavations by Margaret and Tom Jones (1965–78): The Roman Cemeteries.* CAU Landscape Archives Series: Historiography and Fieldwork No. 3.

MAP 1 = English Heritage, 1989. *The Management of Archaeology Projects*. London: Historic Buildings and Monuments Commission.

MAP 2 = English Heritage, 1991. *The Management of Archaeological Projects* (2nd edn). London: Historic Buildings and Monuments Commission.

Moffett, J., 1989. Computer perceptions in archaeology 1: the deep thought syndrome, *Archaeological Computing Newsletter* 20, 11–16.

Pitts, M.,2001. Margaret Jones Archaeologist at the sharp end of history [obituary], *The Guardian*, Wednesday 2 May 2001. [http://www.guardian.co.uk/news/2001/may/02/guardianobituaries.education].

RCHME, 1960. *A Matter of Time: An Archaeological Survey of the River Gravels of England*, Royal Commission on Historical Monuments (England). London: HMSO.

Riley, D. N., 1993. The Mucking Cropmarks, in Clark, A. *Excavations at Mucking, Volume 1: The Site Atlas*, 23–25 and fig. 2. English Heritage Archaeological Reports 20. London: English Heritage.

St Joseph, J. K. 1964. Air reconnaissance: recent results, *Antiquity* 51, 217–18, Pl. XXXVIl(b).

Webb, J. 2001. Margaret Ursula Jones [obituary], *Panorama* 43 [http://www.thurrock-community.org.uk/historysoc/mujones.htm].

Wilkinson, T. J. 1988. *Archaeology and Environment in South Essex: rescue archaeology along the Grays Bypass 1979–80*. East Anglian Archaeology 42.

Notes

1 These investigations were initiated by S. A. Butcher and J. G. Hurst then assistant inspectors of the Inspectorate of Ancient Monuments in the MPBW and they remained concerned with the excavations throughout its further development.

2 Jonathan Catton became one of Mucking's weekend-diggers for a few years and then an excavator during successive summer school holidays, then 'special excavator' and supervisor. In 1973, after he had left school and excavated in Saxon Southampton for 6 months, he returned to Mucking as Senior Supervisor and then an extremely competent Assistant to the Director until the end of digging (he directed the Margins excavations in 1978). He then became Data Manager in post excavation in Thurrock Museum until 1985.

3 It is undeniable that Margaret Jones' personal character and undoubted intellectual abilities had a great influence on all phases of the development of the Mucking project. Pitts (2001) records that her nickname in MPBW was 'Boadicea' and notes 'while her actions could be frustratingly obstructive, her personality could command respect, and even warmth'. By her closer circle, she was more often referred to as 'Mudge' from her initials which she habitually appended to annotations in field notes and other texts.

4 Tom became deputy Director of excavations, responsible for site photography and the recording of the evidence from the cemeteries. His overall influence on the project itself however was relatively slight in comparison to that of his rather more dominant wife (though the frequent sharp exchanges of opinion between them on site are an inseparable part of the site folklore). Nevertheless they functioned relatively well as an archaeological team, despite their apparent shortcomings as life-partners.

5 The pound though of course changed its value quite considerably between 1965 and 1977. It would be interesting to see this sum calculated at today's values to compare with the sums later assigned to post-excavation work.

6 C. J. Evans (pers. comm. July 2008) tells me that the current estimate differs from that published by Clark; his team's work suggests there were 500 000 finds and records of 18 000 features.

7 It is a matter for extreme regret that Hamerow's report almost entirely fails to make this information available for use.

8 A machine which (though one of the most advanced at the time) had pitiful capabilities compared with the home computer on which this text was written.

9 Though in fact council minutes show that as late as 1983 the problem of the ownership of the finds had still not been properly regulated (R. Bingley pers. comm.).

10 Information from English Heritage Aggregates Levy Sustainability Fund summaries. 2007/2008 http://www.english-heritage.org.uk/server/show/ConWebDoc.12455

Growing up with Wharram Percy

Bob Croft

Archaeological research at Wharram Percy has influenced two generations of professional archaeologists and researchers. It has been the focus for academic research, developed methodologies of on-site interpretation, and produced an amazing insight into the development of medieval rural settlement on the Yorkshire Wolds. Wharram is a significant symbol of archaeological research, and was and still is a crucible for the development of medieval archaeology. This chapter also illustrates aspects of the social interactions that occurred at Wharram and includes some observations on what was, in my opinion, one of the great excavations of the twentieth century.

Wharram Percy – people and place

It was 60 years ago in 1948 that Maurice Beresford – then a newly appointed lecturer in Economic History at Leeds University – first visited the earthwork remains of Wharram Percy in North Yorkshire. His interest in deserted or 'lost' villages was to lead to what was to become a major research project, and the foundation of a whole area of academic research into the history and archaeology of medieval rural settlements across Britain and Europe. Wharram Percy – the place – was the catalyst that brought together the economic historian Maurice Beresford (the 'prolix professor') with the archaeologist John Hurst (the 'man from the Ministry') and it was the influence of these two very individual characters that brought about one of the greatest archaeological projects of the twentieth century (*The Times* 2006) (Figure 16.1). Together they ran the excavations at Wharram Percy and were largely responsible for setting up the Deserted Medieval Village Research Group (DMVRG) in 1951. They developed a working relationship that continued without a break from 1953 until John Hurst's untimely death in 2003. For over fifty years generations of archaeologists, scientists and other scholars have worked on the information excavated from this rather remote chalk valley in the East Riding of Yorkshire and a new generation of archaeologists continues with this detailed research today. During the main excavation seasons many leading archaeologists would visit the site to catch up on recent discoveries, to meet up and be part of the Wharram experience if only for a day or so.

Wharram and the study of medieval rural settlement

As work gathered pace at Wharram itself, there was a wider debate about how best to recognise and (as we would say today) designate the increasing number of deserted village sites that were being mapped.

Very few medieval village sites were scheduled monuments before the work of the DMVRG. During

Figure 16.1. John Hurst and Maurice Beresford outside Wharram Percy Cottages in 1974. Note the old sign for the Deserted Medieval Research Group above the door and a cast of the so-called 'Wharram lady'. (Photograph Paul Stamper).

the 1960s Beresford and Hurst were involved in coordinating research on all the deserted medieval villages across England. They invented the term DMV – still in wide use today to describe medieval earthworks in local historic environment records. They produced a report that was then passed to the Ministry of Public Buildings and Works (MPBW) with a list of the fifty best-preserved DMVs in the country and the suggestion that the best six should be taken into the care of the state, or 'Guardianship'. Wharram Percy was at the centre of these proposals and in 1967 the Ancient Monuments Board, under the chairmanship of Sir Mortimer Wheeler, visited Wharram and following their visit commended the DMVRG list to the ministry. Wharram Percy was set to be a direct beneficiary of this new interest in DMVs. Negotiations were set in motion with the landowners, Lord Middleton who owned the village site and the Church Commissioners who owned the church, and all agreed to place the site in the care of the MPBW with the church taken into care in 1972 and the village two years later. 1974 was a pivotal year for Wharram Percy as it entered a new phase of research, consolidation and interpretation brought about with the financial support from government funds.

Alongside the research on protecting medieval settlements through Guardianship John Hurst carried out a review of archaeological research in England and it is clear from this survey that Wharram was one of the key sites. The report was published in 1971 in a milestone book called *Deserted Medieval Villages* covering England, Wales and Scotland (Beresford and Hurst 1971). The history of the foundation of the DMVRG is intimately bound up with the origins of the discipline that was to become medieval archaeology in Britain. A partial history of this particular area of research is documented in Beresford and Hurst (1990) and Chris Gerrard has compiled an excellent general guide to the development of Medieval Archaeology in the UK (Gerrard 2003). However, a more definitive account of the development of the archaeology of the medieval village remains to be written and whoever takes on this task will need to research and weigh up the role that Wharram Percy has had, and continues to have in the subject.

Open-area archaeological excavation techniques on medieval rural settlements were developed at Wharram from 1953, and the project grew into one of the first and most extensive multidisciplinary projects anywhere in Britain (Wharram I, 1979). The site was a training excavation for university students and the impact of university support can be traced back to the 1950s and 1960s when Professor H. C. Darby recruited and financed an annual field party of students from the Department of Geography, University College London. It was this support that enabled the summer digging season to run for three weeks and set the pattern for summer excavations that was to continue until 1990 (Beresford and Hurst 1990, 32). A number of other university departments have been actively involved with supplying students to work at Wharram and these include Lancaster, Sheffield, Leeds Polytechnic and University and most notably the archaeology department at the University of York.

Excavation in the 1960s and '70s concentrated on the parish church of St Martin and part of the churchyard (excavated 1962–1974). This excavation was the first complete excavation and analysis of a parish church in England (Bell and Beresford *et al.* 1987). The subsequent analysis of the site and skeletal remains has turned out to be one of the most significant archaeological excavations of a medieval church and churchyard in England. Recent scientific analysis of almost 700 skeletons has provided evidence of medieval diet, diseases and cranial surgery (Mays 2007). I worked on the excavations at Wharram Church over three seasons and anyone who was there when they discovered the carved Saxon grave slabs, now identified as re-used Roman sarcophagi, will remember the precarious nature of the final recovery and excavation of these slabs on the last evening of the dig using torches and car headlights to provide sufficient illumination. It was largely due to the heroic efforts of a few dedicated archaeologists and others that this work was completed. Looking back it is easy to see how things should have been done differently: there was limited equipment, limited Health and Safety provision, and limited budgets. But equally the excavation involved considerable energy, enthusiasm and perhaps most importantly of all an intelligent and ever-developing research agenda with a sprinkling of luck. No one involved with the earlier work at Wharram would have imagined that the project would still be running over fifty years later. Many archaeologists, historians, geographers and landscape researchers and other scholars have given years of their lives to the excavation and research at Wharram, each person contributing in some way to making it a great excavation to work on.

The South Manor

Some background to the history of the archaeological work is needed to understand how the research questions developed and were addressed. I am very familiar with a small area of the Wharram hillside known as the South Manor area and use this to illustrate the point. The early work on Area 10, including the excavations of the undercroft of the South Manor house (excavated in 1956 and 1957), was extensive and complex, revealing the well-preserved stone foundations of a twelfth-century manor house which is still one of the type-sites for Britain. Later excavations around the South Manor area (excavated by David Andrews 1977–78 and by Paul Stamper and Bob Croft 1980–1990) (Stamper

Figure 16.2. Paul Stamper giving a guided tour of the excavations at the South Manor site 1982. The timber fence posts mark the positions of Saxon postholes. (Photograph: Paul Stamper archive).

and Croft 2000) examined the question of settlement continuity on this site from Roman through to Saxon and medieval times (Figure 16.2). After twelve seasons of excavations a complex story emerged for the South Manor area, and Julian Richards has suggested that this area was already a high status settlement in the 8th century but was not at that stage part of a nucleated or planned settlement (Richards 2000). Excavations at the South Manor site addressed the question of continuity, a topic that was very popular in the late 1980s. After ten seasons of work we discovered some evidence for this: a huge amount of Saxon pottery, some well-stratified features and important evidence of occupation and land use dating from Roman times through to the sixteenth century, but direct proof of continuity on the site remains elusive. The value of such detailed investigations enables others to check and re-examine the archaeological evidence as other research questions are posed for the area. The analysis of well-preserved Saxon-building remains and occupation material has enabled Richards to review the evidence and to go on to suggest that Wharram was one of the estates granted to a Scandinavian settler who set about establishing a planned settlement (Richards 2000). Few could have thought that such an observation could have been made when the South Manor phase of the Wharram Percy project started. The evidence from this relatively small investigation has provided information that is of national significance – it has looked at the very origins of the apparent medieval settlement pattern in this valley and shown that it is likely to be of Scandinavian influence. Such observations as this pose some significant questions that need to be addressed across a larger geographic area.

But what has the research work at Wharram brought to the study of medieval settlement studies – and indeed archaeology more widely – in the UK and beyond? One of John Hurst's famous expressions was 'another first for Wharram', and the list of its achievements, many of them indeed 'firsts', is impressive. It includes:

- The development of excavation techniques and research strategies suitable for the study of thinly stratified medieval sites.
- The first methodical, full-scale excavation of medieval peasant houses.
- The first comprehensive excavation and analysis of a parish church and a large part of its graveyard.
- The systematic investigation of other components of the medieval village including a mill, vicarage complex and the village boundaries.
- Promoting the idea of deep and long-term landscape change, and its multi-disciplinary investigation including a detailed landscape survey of the parish.
- Developing understanding and debate via publications including a soon-to-be completed series of thirteen research reports
- Being among the first earthwork sites where management and interpretation techniques were developed to facilitate long-term protection alongside the site's enjoyment by the public.
- Largely through the involvement of John Hurst, being at the heart of the emergence of medieval archaeology in the 1950s and the bodies that promoted this such as the Deserted Medieval Village Research Group (founded 1952, from 1986 the Medieval Settlement Research Group) and the Society for Medieval Archaeology (founded 1957).
- One of the largest, and longest-running, examples of a multi-disciplinary archaeological research project devised and carried out using largely voluntary labour.

Wharram post-excavation work

The analysis and publication of archaeological excavation reports is notoriously slow and in this regard Wharram is no exception. Wharram had a legacy of unfinished reports but, thanks to a substantive grant from English Heritage, the West Yorkshire Joint Archaeological Service directed by Dr Stuart Wrathmell is nearing the end of coordinating the analysis and report writing of the post-excavation programme. Stuart worked as a supervisor at Wharram for many years and was ideally placed to take on the mammoth editorial and coordinating task of completing the Wharram post-excavation programme. The Wharram post-excavation programme has benefited by the involvement of many specialist contributors, and Ann Clark and Peggy Pullen have coordinated much of this work. The post-excavation programme has been running for eighteen years and the end is at last in sight. Everyone who has worked at Wharram is indebted to Stuart for his determination, professionalism and the academic rigour that he has brought to the Wharram publication programme. I have not attempted to look in any great depth at the more recent academic and research questions posed and answered at Wharram; that is not what this chapter is about. There is no doubt that the achievements from the research work at Wharram have greatly influenced the whole discipline of medieval archaeology and rural settlement studies. The bibliography gives a list of the most recent archaeological reports and that list alone shows just how important Wharram is for the study of medieval rural settlement, not just in the UK but also as a site of international importance.

Paul Stamper and I finished the excavations on the South Manor area in 1990 and then had the task of preparing the excavation report and interpretation of the site. Most of this post-excavation analysis took place at Vessey Pasture Farm, the new headquarters of the successor project that inherited the Wharram equipment and administrative structure including the support of Maurice Beresford and John Hurst. Vessey became the focus for further research work in the wider environs of Wharram, and University students from Sheffield and York have used this farm since 1991. However the long-term viability of this successor project to Wharram is somewhat in doubt. We completed our analytical and descriptive work and the information was passed over to Stuart Wrathmell and the WYJAS to await the specialist reports and detailed analysis of the finds. The report was edited by Stuart and published as a York University Archaeological Monograph No 10 in 2000. The publication of the report represented a major achievement – the completion of the South Manor excavation that had started twenty years earlier.

Wharram – the social significance

But what of the more social elements of the excavation project? This was one of the key questions set by John Schofield in his brief for the IFA conference session from which this book derives, so I have attempted to document some of this to add to the more holistic picture of Wharram Percy, providing some details of the social and domestic side that ran parallel to the archaeological excavation. Many of these details will not be recorded in any of the published literature on Wharram so this is an attempt to record a brief snapshot of the social side of Wharram. Looking back, perhaps through some rose-tinted spectacles, it is the symbiotic relationships between people and the place that helped to form the genius loci that characterised the 'Wharram experience'.

For three weeks of each year from 1950–1990 Wharram was not a Deserted Medieval Village. Rather, it was a self-sufficient community providing opportunities to learn about archaeology and to live and work with other people. It was in many ways a social experiment and one that influenced the lives of everyone who worked at the site. It is estimated that over 5000 volunteers and supervisors have worked at Wharram since the project began. The excavations at Wharram Percy did, in effect, bring a community and a population back to the valley, a population probably higher than it was for much of the history of the village.

To live and work in the Wharram landscape is incredibly addictive. Most people who visited Wharram as part of the excavation projects have come back at some point, and many archaeologists returned to dig at the site for many years, often taking leave from other professionally-paid jobs for the opportunity or privilege of working there.

Feeding the 5000

'In the beginning Maurice created the Wharram dig and cooking was non-existent and all was sandwiches and Thermos tea. And Maurice said let there be a kitchen and cooking and there was a kitchen and cooking and he saw to it that it was good' (Watt 1990). This quote is taken from an excellent resume of the history of Wharram catering prepared by Johnny Watt, a report that is already an important record of the social history of the excavation.

Wharram mealtimes were an important part of the Wharram experience (Figures 16.3–16.5). All food was prepared for communal consumption. The food queues to get into the kitchen were an institution in themselves and an important part of the social interaction of the day. They enabled archaeologists from different parts of the site to meet and discuss current discoveries or to sort out social arrangements for the evening or for a day off. In the early years at Wharram everyone worked

Figure 16.3. For many seasons a large marquee was set up as a finds tent in the cottage gardens. This photograph taken in July 1986 shows a typical grouping of diggers at a tea break. (Photo: Paul Stamper archive).

Figure 16.4. One of the key activities of Wharram – 'Fourses' and the search for tea and biscuits followed by bread and jam. (Photograph shows Paul Herbert, Chrissie Milne, Bob Croft, John Hurst, Andy Gray, Colin Treen, Ann Clark and Jonathan Watt) (Photo: Paul Stamper archive).

a seven-day week but in the later years diggers were allowed to have one day off a week. The role of chef to the excavation was an important job. For over twenty years Maurice Beresford was in charge of ordering food and catering. From the 1970s a specialist cook was put in charge of the kitchen and a variety of meals were prepared for the diggers. In my experience at Wharram there were two key characters who worked as cooks, they were Glen Battesby (in the mid 1970s) and Johnny Watt who was responsible for the last ten years of cooking at Wharram – the busiest years of the excavation often with over 100 people at each mealtime. Some of the most amazing meals were cooked on simple calor gas cookers and rings. By the late 1970s two electric cookers were installed. The kitchen was one of the hubs of the excavation headquarters in the cottages. The ringing of an old ARP hand-bell at 0800 hrs announced that breakfast was ready. The bell was rung at all meal times. The working day followed this pattern:

Breakfast	0800–0850
Elevenses	1100–1130
Lunch	1300–1400
Fourses	1630–1700
Dinner	1900
Coffoco	2100 onwards (the term Coffoco was allegedly invented at Wharram to describe the coffee or cocoa options available as an evening drink)

Many diggers will remember the sound of the bell echoing up the stairs of the dormitory or drifting across the field as one of the early risers was deputed to go into the tent field and wake up the diggers. From the 1970s onwards the archaeological supervisors traditionally cooked breakfast. One of the staple foods of Wharram was the 'Wharram porridge', cooked in a large aluminium saucepan and stirred with a purpose made 'porridge paddle'. The challenge of porridge production followed by the cooking of over 100 fried eggs was always a good start for the day! One of the lasting rules that I learnt from working at Wharram was the need to ensure that breaks, food and regular meals were fixed and served on time if an archaeological excavation project is to run smoothly.

The tradition of communal cooking at Wharram can be traced back to the involvement of East Moor Approved School in Leeds under the supervision of the late Bill Callow who in the 1960s set up the kitchen in the farm workers cottage (Wharram 1 vii). In the first years that I visited and worked at Wharram in 1972 and 1973 I had to pay for food, but by 1974 funding was available to provide free food to the diggers.

Food preparation rotas along with washing-up duties were all part of the daily routines of working at Wharram Percy. The duty rotas continued right up to the final season in 1990 and the task of coordinating the daily list was the responsibility of Francesca Croft (nee Hurst) from 1980 –1990. Today this task would be carried out on an elaborate computerised spreadsheet, but in the 1980s it was carefully drawn up on a large piece of graph paper and constantly changed and added to as the excavation progressed. In later years it was always the duty of the supervisors to wash-up after the evening meal and this could often be a time-consuming task washing-up for over one hundred people. Speed and efficiency improved as the need to finish washing-up in time to catch a lift to the local pub at North Grimston or Thixendale, both about an hours walk away from the site if you missed the often limited lifts. The kitchen still survives in the cottages at Wharram Percy complete with its sink and some of the original shelving. The templates and guide graffiti for the different pan sizes can be clearly seen drawn in black marker pens onto the kitchen walls, all part of the care and organisation brought to the cooking and catering under the supervision of Johnny Watt (Figure 16.5).

The arrival of electricity to the cottages transformed the evening activities at Wharram. One of the key events celebrated with great pomp and ceremony including a pageant with Latin script was the opening of the first shower cubicle in 1975. Use of the shower was carefully monitored with time slots for males and females and an honesty box was set up to collect the extra 20p for the electricity. A second shower cubicle was commissioned in 1983, which meant that the men's dormitory had its own shower unit (Figure 16.6).

York University arrives

In the 1980s the project entered a further phase of development and expansion with the arrival of York University Archaeology Department under the direction of Professor Philip Rahtz (Figure 16.7). Philip brought with him a number of professional staff that all helped to supervise the excavations in the area of the North Manor. A number of the undergraduate students from York went on to obtain professional archaeological jobs. The impact of York University Archaeology Department on Wharram Percy was considerable and wide ranging. It gave a significant boost to the academic research objectives that were emerging in medieval settlement studies and it provided an injection of new blood into the whole project. It put the research at Wharram into the vanguard of multi-disciplinary projects around the UK and it was one of the first projects to work on such a scale across a wide landscape.

Wharram Percy was an important social and cultural experience for me. It taught me how to live and work with a wide range of people 24 hours a day; how to work outdoors in all weathers and live without a flushing toilet for three weeks. It also taught me how to dig a cesspit and empty an incredibly full elsan bucket – a technique requiring an unusual gait and arm action. The main item of clothing needed for such an activity is a pair of Wellington boots and not the ubiquitous leather sandals loved by so many 1970s archaeologists, myself included. The subject of sandals did in fact become the subject of artefact studies themselves. As ever, Wharram was at the cutting edge of best archaeological practice investigating the archaeology of archaeologists. In *c.*1978 Paul Stamper and Glenn Foard supervised the digging of a large cesspit on the edge of the cottage garden. At a depth of 1 m it was clear that they were excavating an earlier rubbish pit containing good dating evidence of tins of corned beef and other domestic refuse. They also discovered a layer that contained two well-preserved leather sandals dating from the 1960s. Much excitement ensued and the finds tent was alerted to receive a rather special small find. These were identified as being an early pair of John Hurst's sandals and as such were duly photographed and recorded in the appropriate manner.

Wharram – a social experiment

The project provided a great opportunity to get involved with a long running social experiment. Today we are familiar with reality television shows that bring together a range of different people who are then given a range of meaningless tasks to complete under the watchful eye of a television camera and several million viewers. Wharram provided a similar opportunity and the whole project was carried out under the watchful eye not of a 'Big Brother' figure but Maurice Beresford, Emeritus Professor in Economic History at Leeds University.

Throughout its life Wharram provided the opportunity for social interaction alongside a well-organised archaeological research excavation. In the 1950s and 1960s the interaction of borstal boys with students provided its own challenges to the organisers and the individuals. In the 1970s and

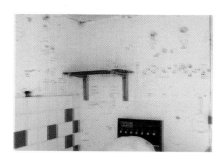

Figure 16.5. Detail of the kitchen wall in the Wharram Percy cottages showing the graffiti marks for the kitchen appliances. (Photo: Bob Smith).

Figure 16.6. Ceremony and procession to mark the grand opening of the men's shower at Wharram in 1983. (Photograph WP archive).

Figure 16.7. Group photograph taken by Sebastian Rahtz on 23 July 1981

1980s archaeology students and volunteers working with professional supervisors did most of the work during the main three-week summer excavation season – usually the last three weeks of July. It was the development of the training excavations involving UK and foreign students that made Wharram a melting pot of social and cultural interaction. Students and volunteers came from many parts of the world with a large number coming from Europe notably Holland, France, Sweden and Italy and others from the USA and Canada. The link with archaeology students from Holland was particularly productive and many students returned for several years, some going on to work as supervisors.

Maurice was one of the last great polymaths who worked tirelessly in each area of his research. He is well known for his academic work on medieval settlement studies, deserted villages and urban history but he was also an influential figure in the administration of Leeds University and working with prison reforms in West Yorkshire (*The Times* 2006). Maurice will be best remembered by a whole generation of archaeologists for the morning meetings held at 0900 hrs when both Beresford and Hurst provided the diggers with a wide range of information ranging from the duty rota, the names of important visitors expected that day, national news items if relevant and a report on the weather (always from John Hurst). The mass meeting usually concluded with an impromptu lecture on an important social issue of the day that usually involved Maurice Beresford showing off his skill in remembering every new digger's name and making them feel part of their new happy family. It made the new arrivals at this archaeological village community feel at home on their first day on site. On one occasion the site was to be visited by Lord William Whitelaw and Lord Middleton at a time when Lord Whitelaw was a senior figure in the Thatcher government. Prior to the arrival of the noble Lords, Maurice was at his acerbic best at the morning meeting touching upon the political issues of the day. Each mass meeting was brought to a close with the unique and distinctive voice of John Hurst with the instruction, 'Everyone on site please'. Once heard never forgotten.

John Hurst and Wharram

It was in 2003, however, that all things Wharram came back to the top of my list. In April of that year John Hurst was attacked in the street and died of his injuries. I was appointed John's academic and literary executor meaning that all the Hurst archives had to be sorted and passed on to the appropriate repositories. John was a great horder of papers, reports and information. He had a whole barn full of archives that related to the history of the development of medieval archaeology in Britain. At various times in his life he was on the committees as an officer and later President of the Society for Medieval Archaeology, Society for Post Medieval Archaeology, the DMVRG and later the Medieval Settlement Research Group along with one of his other great passions in life the Medieval Pottery Research Group.

Wharram formed an important foundation stone in John's life and it influenced a lot of what he did for the Ministry of Public Buildings and Works although he was always very clear to define boundaries and to identify any potential conflicts of interest. He started his career with the government in 1954 as an Assistant Inspector of Ancient Monuments and progressed through the ranks of the civil service until his retirement from English Heritage in 1987 where he had reached the title of Assistant Chief Inspector of Ancient Monuments. In 1987 he was made a Fellow of the British Academy. I had the challenge of sorting out John's copious notes and papers and ensuring that this important archive was not discarded. This was a somewhat daunting task and it was eventually tackled with the help of the indefatigable Paul Stamper who helped to sort and move the archives first into the care of English Heritage and then on to their final resting places. The Wharram archives were passed to the Wharram project in the West Yorkshire Joint Archaeology Service; the Medieval Pottery archives were passed to the British Museum; the Society of Antiquaries of London generously accepted John's general archaeological papers; and a wide range of local history material was donated to the Centre for English Local History at the University of Leicester. For a fuller appreciation of John Hurst's contributions to medieval archaeology see the most informative obituary prepared by Dr Lawrence Butler for the British Academy (Butler 2006).

The Wharram re-union

Wharram Percy was an important part of John Hurst's life. For many years in the 1960s and 70s there was the annual Wharram reunion, usually the first Saturday in December, held at 67 Gloucester Crescent in the heart of Camden Town. It was common practice for John Hurst to start his annual lecture with the phrase: 'Well it is rather incredible but the story has changed again'. We would then be entertained with a report and slide show on the latest conclusions from the previous season's excavations followed by a short (or long) discourse from Maurice on some aspect of his Wharram linked research or some erudite observations on the social value of the 'Wharram experiment'. The visits to Gloucester Crescent and the Betty Ewins buns and biscuits will be fondly remembered by many of the staff and volunteers that made up the Wharram Percy team. Another first for Wharram was the use of the 'Wharram Weekend' to further research. This was usually a three day working weekend that required a certain degree of youthful enthusiasm, or madness, to stay in the cold, damp Wharram cottages in March or October and working during the day to hand dig evaluation trenches. This 'Time Team' style model was introduced by John Hurst in the late 1960s and continued for about twenty years. (Figure 16.8)

A number of Wharram picnic events have been held in recent years and it was in 2003 that John Hurst and Maurice Beresford last visited Wharram together. Maurice Beresford's last visit to Wharram was on 24 July 2005.

Wharram Percy in the twenty-first century

To many people today Wharram Percy is a name on a brown tourist sign pointing towards a rather inaccessible dry valley, twenty minutes walk from the nearest car park. For the determined visitor who makes the pilgrimage from the inadequate English Heritage car park down to the valley they will find a locked up nineteenth-century cottage, a roofless medieval church, a rather silted up pond and some faded, cattle licked information panels. The visitor experience today to one of English Heritage's premier guardianship sites is very different from the whole 'Wharram experience' that was available when the project was running as an archaeological research and training excavation. Archaeological excavation and research is sadly missing at many of the nationally important sites around the country and public understanding and enjoyment of the heritage is diminished as a result.

I consider myself one of the fortunate ones who happened to be in the right place at the right time. Wharram provided me with a range of contacts and opportunities that are so often lacking in British archaeology today. In my view it is time to consider the next research questions that previous work at Wharram have posed. Has the time come to unlock the sleeping giant that is Wharram Percy? There are still many questions to be asked of the Wharram landscape and I hope that further research and excavation will one day continue to look at this very special but perhaps not so unusual DMV.

Figure 16.8. Cartoon by Chris Mahany depicting a typical Wharram Weekend. For many years Wharram had two working weekends one in October and one in March where additional recording work was carried out. This cartoon depicts Maurice Beresford, John Hurst with souwester hat; Jim Thorn seated drawing and Betty Ewins digging.

Figure 16.9. Philip Rahtz, Edwina and Bruce Proudfoot and Betty Ewins at Wharram Percy cottages in July 1982

Wharram Percy – was it a great excavation?

I have had some time to reflect on the subject of what constitutes a great excavation and my personal view is that it was the scale, longevity and enthusiasm of the excavations and excavators at Wharram that gave it the essential characteristics that constitute a 'great excavation'. I do however conclude that it was a product of its own time. It was a series of circumstances and opportunities that coincided with the immense energy and intellectual endeavour of two very singular individuals who made Wharram happen. To the thousands of students and volunteers who visited or worked at Wharram it was and still is a very special place. Research at Wharram Percy has contributed to the development of medieval settlement studies and in many ways was one of the key building blocks for the whole discipline. It led the way in the idea of using archaeological research to study a whole landscape through time – it started out as a medieval village project but in the end told the story of a changing landscape with its fantastic time depth. Much of this pioneering work must be down to the far-sighted vision of John Hurst – in the early years few archaeologists thought that digging up an old vicarage garden

The Sleeping Lord of Wharram

Figure 16.10. R. T. 'Dicky' Porter completed the early earthwork survey of Wharram Percy. This version of the earthwork survey shows the hidden image of a sleeping giant – as modified by Bob Croft onto a Christmas card.

or a nineteenth-century farmhouse would be particularly worthwhile or revealing. It is amazing how attitudes change. Wharram can claim another first for much of this work.

In preparation for this chapter I have discussed the social side of Wharram with a wide range of archaeologists and it is clear that each decade of the excavation reflected the wider social, economic and sexual mores of the time. I am particularly indebted to Paul Stamper for his help and advice and it is he who has identified three main social phases. Firstly there was the *Austerity Years* of the 1950s into the 60s, typified with a diet of blancmange all round and the excitement of tiddlywinks played in the railway tunnel; this was followed by the *hairy 1970s* and the final decade was typified by the *second generation Wharram families* supplemented by the *student of the 1980s*.

On the last day of the excavations in 1990 at an emotional final party Professor Maurice Beresford quoted the following lines from Samuel Butler: 'Yet meet we shall, and part, and meet again, where dead men meet, on lips of living men'. Wharram is indeed a site that will be spoken about for many years to come and I hope that by the time you have finished reading this collection of essays you will agree with me that Wharram Percy deserves to be on anyone's list of Great Excavations.

References

Beresford, M. W. 1954. *The Lost Villages of England*. London: Lutterworth Press.

Beresford, M. W. 1989. A review of historical research (to 1968), in Beresford, M. W. and Hurst, J. G. (eds) *Deserted Medieval Villages*: 3–75. Gloucester: Alan Sutton.

Beresford, M. W. and Hurst, J. G. 1971. *Deserted Medieval Villages*. Woking: Lutterworth Press.

Beresford, M. W. and Hurst J. G. 1990. *Wharram Percy Deserted Medieval Village*. London: Batsford.

Butler, L. A. S. 2006. John Hurst – in British Academy obituaries.

Gerrard, C. 2003. *Medieval Archaeology – Understanding Traditions and Contemporary Approaches*. Abingdon: Routledge.

Gilchrist, R. and Reynolds, A. 2009. *Reflections: 50 years of Medieval Archaeology 1957–2007*. Society for Medieval Archaeology Monograph Series, Number 30. Leeds: Maney.

Hurst, J. G. 1971. A review of archaeological research (to 1968), in Beresford, M. W. and Hurst, J. G. (eds), *Deserted Medieval Villages*; 76–144. Woking: Lutterworth Press.

Hurst, J. G., 1984. The Wharram Research Project: Results to 1983. *Medieval Archaeology* 28, 77–111.

Hurst, J. G. and Rahtz, P. A. (eds) 1987. *Wharram Percy Church of St Martin*. Society for Medieval Archaeology Monograph Series, Number 11 Leeds: Maney.

Richards, J. 2000. *The Anglo-Scandinavian evidence*, in Stamper, P. and Croft, R. A., 195–200.

Stamper, P. and Croft, R. A. 2000. *Wharram: A study of Settlement on the Yorkshire Wolds, vol. 8 – The South Manor Area*. York University Archaeological Publications 10. York: University of York.

The Times 2006. Obituary for Maurice Beresford. *The Times* 2 January 2006.

Watt, J. G. 1990. Wharram Recipes, Including a Short History of Wharram Catering (private publication).

Wharram I (Andrews, D. D. and Milne, G. 1979). *Wharram. A Study of Settlement on the Yorkshire Wolds, I. Domestic Settlement, I: Areas 10 and 6*. Society for Medieval Archaeology Monograph 8.

Wharram III (Bell, R. D., Beresford, M. W. and others 1987). *Wharram. A Study of Settlement on the Yorkshire Wolds, III. Wharram Percy: The Church of St. Martin*. Society for Medieval Archaeology Monograph 11.

Wharram IV (Rahtz, P., Hayfied, C. and Bateman, J. 1986). *Wharram. A Study of Settlement on the Yorkshire Wolds, IV. Two Roman Villas at Wharram le Street*. York University Archaeological Publications 2B.

Wharram V (Hayfield, C. 1987). *An Archaeological Survey of the Parish of Wharram Percy East Yorkshire. 1. The Evolution of the Roman Landscape*. Oxford: British Archaeological Reports, British Series 172.

Wharram VI (Wrathmell, S. 1989). *Wharram. A Study of Settlement on the Yorkshire Wolds. VI. Domestic Settlement 2: Medieval Peasant Farmsteads*. York University Archaeological Publications 6.

Wharram VII (Milne, G and Richard, J. D. 1992). *Wharram. A Study of Settlement on the Yorkshire Wolds. VII.*

Two Anglo Saxon Buildings and Associated Finds. York University Archaeological Publications 8.

Wharram IX (Rahtz, P. and Watts, L. 2004). *Wharram. A Study of Settlement on the Yorkshire Wolds. IX. The North Manor and the North-West Enclosure.* York University Archaeological Publications 9.

Wharram X (Treen, C. and Atkin, M. 2005). *Wharram: A Study of Settlement on the Yorkshire Wolds. Water Resources and Their Management.* York University Archaeological Publications10.

Wharram XI (Mays, S., Harding, C. and Heighway, C. 2007). *Wharram: A Study of Settlement on the Yorkshire Wolds. The Churchyard.* York University Archaeological Publications 11.

West Heslerton:
Past, present and future

Dominic Powlesland

Context

It is a privilege to be offered the opportunity to write reflexively about West Heslerton within the context of 'Great Excavations'. When we began a six week rescue excavation at Cook's Quarry, West Heslerton in 1978 no one could have predicted that research work focussed upon West Heslerton and the Vale of Pickering would still be in progress in 2008 (Powlesland et al 1986). The Landscape Research Centre (LRC) was established as a charitable trust in 1980 to oversee the work of the Heslerton Parish Project. Our work has comprised multiple unique or stand-alone but interlinked projects with a primary focus upon a single landscape; at heart demonstrating that archaeological research is an iterative process. The Heslerton landscape has through continuous re-investigation given an insight into a density and continuity of occupation that, whilst unparalleled, is likely to reflect levels of activity which prevailed in appropriate settings in river valleys throughout lowland Britain (Powlesland 1980; 2008).

It should be stated at the outset that the importance of Heslerton is based upon the sum of the many projects undertaken over a large area rather than on any single component, and that these include both excavation and survey in its broadest sense. Equally important is the need to reflect upon the benefits of long-term support from English Heritage in its various incarnations since the early years when the Rescue archaeology fund was managed by the Department of the Environment. It would be wrong to imply that funding has been continuous or without severe limitations at numerous points during the life of the project as a whole; however, regardless of those difficulties, research has continued generating results that challenge established views regarding much of the archaeology of Eastern Yorkshire from the Neolithic to Medieval periods. More importantly, Heslerton has contributed towards nationally important issues regarding excavation and recording methodologies, landscape survey and remote sensing, the role of aggregate landscapes in the archaeology of lowland Britain, training in field archaeology, and the very concepts that underlie 'Landscape Archaeology' as a discipline.

Although this chapter and the instigation and direction of the various Heslerton-based projects are largely the product of one individual, 'Great Excavations' and archaeological fieldwork are the products of many. The components that combine to form great projects are the archaeological resource, the people who do the work – which in the case of Heslerton amount to more than a thousand people over the thirty year time span (the vast majority of whom were volunteers), the research frameworks and directives that drive the research, and the funding bodies who support the work despite the perceived 'risk' inherent within it. Viewed from a chronological viewpoint work in Heslerton has reflected and responded to fundamental changes affecting the practice of archaeology in Britain which have taken place over the last three decades, a period during which government funding has declined at a rate that inversely matches the massive increase in public interest in the subject. In the same way as the various excavations have been a barometer of student fashion, providing a degree of entertainment to the local population, they have directly reflected not only changes in the nature and direction of field archaeology but also other issues such as the changes in legislation regarding volunteers and subsistence payments, or health and safety regulations which have effectively made it impossible or at least uneconomic to contemplate carrying out excavations on the same basis now as we were able to during the late 1970s. Whilst one would not wish (in our increasingly litigious society) to initiate projects today with the same lack of on-site facilities or financial limitations that characterised the excavation campsites in the late 1970s and early 1980s, they did provide a social environment where archaeology was the pre-eminent focus of all-night discussions in the site hut, particularly once the subsistence allowance which amounted only to beer money had run out before the end of the week. The scale of the endeavour that is generally encompassed in reference to Heslerton could not be summarised in the space available here; this chapter is concerned with illustrating aspects of the various projects undertaken over more than 30 years, projects that have combined the most important two facets of archaeology – that it should generate new and challenging results and that it should be fun.

The headings 'Past', 'Present' and 'Future' used below reflect major phases in the research undertaken by the LRC, 'Past' being concerned with the main phase of large excavations which were the primary focus from 1977 to 1999, 'Present' primarily concerned with large scale landscape evaluation and remote sensing projects, and 'Future' concerned with the challenge and potentials of the Heslerton landscape and its identified resource in terms of long term management and development.

The chapter is dedicated to the memory of four individuals, all of whom contributed to the work and the experience of the Heslerton research programme – John Hanson (scholar and phenomenally able assistant who could 'tut-tut' like no other), Barry Prestwood (East Yorkshire linguist and esteemed excavator of burials), Andrew Jagger (in his first week in a full-time post) and Robert Gourlay (whose busman's holidays brought an annual laughter fest – Figure 17.1) – and all of whom we lost far too soon; and to the future of the unknown but considerable number of progeny arising from Heslerton-related pairings.

Past

Cooks Sand Quarry

Archaeological research at West Heslerton was initiated, following a salvage excavation undertaken by John Dent of the Humberside Archaeological Unit in 1977, after an employee of Cook's Sand Quarry reported the discovery of Anglian burials exposed in a newly stripped part of the quarry. That the site was reported at all is a testament to the contribution of the late TCM Brewster, the excavator of nearby Staple Howe, who had been head teacher at West Heslerton primary school where he taught the three 'R's' – archaeology Reading, archaeology wRiting and archaeology aRithmetic – during the 1950s and 1960s (Brewster 1963, 1981). In the spring of 1978 an application was made through North Yorkshire County Council to the Department of Environment (DoE) for funding for a rescue excavation. John Hurst, assistant chief inspector of ancient monuments at the time, later admitted, fortunately without regret, that he had misread the site name and granted funding thinking it was for another known Early Anglo-Saxon cemetery in the south of England; had it not been for this simple twist of fate it is likely that the Vale of Pickering would have remained substantially an archaeological blank with the exception of the few burials examined by John Dent, the Vatchers' excavation of the East Heslerton Long Barrow, the excavations at Star Carr, Tim Schadla-Hall's teams' work around Lake Flixton and Brewster's excavations at Staple Howe and Devils Hill, West Heslerton (Vatcher 1965, Moore 1950, Clark 1954, Schadla-Hall 1977a; 1977b; 1988, Brewster 1963; 1981). There were additionally a number of records pertaining to Heslerton in the County Council Site Index (the forerunner of the Sites and Monuments Record (SMR)), including material recorded by Brewster from field-walking undertaken by the primary school children. Synchronous with the start of the first season of rescue excavation at Cook's Quarry, archaeological attention was focussed on the area with the start of a regular programme of air-photography which still continues. A number of other air-photographers also started to fly over the Vale on a regular basis, contributing both to the County Council SMR and ultimately the National Monuments Record.

It was quickly realised during the first six week excavation in the late summer of 1978 that not only was the Anglian cemetery more extensive than had formerly been considered, with areas surviving beyond the limits covered in the previous winter's salvage work, but also that there was a considerable body of important prehistoric evidence situated to the north of the active quarry in areas for which planning permission for extraction had already been granted. It was also realised that the potential importance of the site was greatly amplified on account of the presence of extensive areas of blown sand. This had buried much of the site, protecting the archaeological deposits from plough damage and, at the same time, reducing the visibility of the archaeology in conventional field survey, surface collection or air photography. We were not to know then that the sandy soils on the southern margins of the Vale of Pickering which, at that time, were considered almost valueless as agricultural land, had been the setting for some of the densest and most comprehensive sequences of human settlement so far identified in rural England. Changes in agricultural practices and cropping regimes and in particular extensive irrigation have changed the status of these formerly unproductive sandy fields; increasingly they have been used for growing root crops with invasive ploughing regimes which have led to truncation of the blown sands and increasing damage to the buried archaeological resource.

It was argued from the outset that the chance discovery of archaeological evidence at Cook's Quarry should be set against broader research objectives, and that the basis of excavation should not simply be a response to the fact that something was there; the very severe limitations of the rescue archaeology budget for England were such that if funds were spent in Heslerton it was likely that funds might be harder to raise for other sites elsewhere in the region. Whilst the first rescue excavations and initial programme of air photography were taking place a research design was developed which attempted to place the rescue excavations in a landscape context and to identify aspects of the Cook's Quarry site which addressed the issues and research questions which were increasingly being promoted by the national period societies or reflected gaps in the regional archaeological record. It was argued, for instance, that in the case of the Early Anglo-Saxon or Anglian cemetery, rescue excavation could be justified on the basis that the site offered the potential for the recovery of rare types of data, particularly mineral-replaced organic materials, and that, unusually, there was a good chance that the limits of the cemetery could be defined. All too often chance discovery had revealed small numbers of burials adding to the dataset of burials rather than contributing to the understanding of cemeteries. In this context West Heslerton remains one of very few cemeteries in the North of England where the full extent and burial capacity have been defined.

By 1980 a research design, 'The Heslerton Parish Project' (HPP), had been prepared and distributed widely in the academic community for comment (Powlesland 1981). This project design established

Figure 17.1. Robert Gourlay demonstrating dumper driving technique in 1980.

a research framework within which to place the Cook's Quarry excavations; it was not constrained by a focus upon any particular archaeological period or activity; rather it emphasized a multi-period and multi-faceted landscape-based approach reflecting different environmental zones within the landscape. The approach was articulated through a theoretical landscape transect extending from the River Derwent in the centre of the Vale of Pickering to the Great Wold Valley to the south of the north-facing scarp slope of the Yorkshire Wolds. The landscape along the southern side of the Vale of Pickering (and also that along the northern side) could be broken into a number of distinct eco-zones based upon the combination of soils, elevation, land form and environmental conditions; these eco-zones extended both to the east and west of the research area centred in Heslerton. Although environmental determinism may be unfashionable within some spheres of archaeological research, it would be impossible to explain the human settlement and other activities in the Vale of Pickering from the Prehistoric to Medieval periods outside this context. It was argued then, and it has now been confirmed, that in broad terms the archaeology of one Vale-edge parish – Heslerton – which combines the villages of East and West Heslerton, reflects activity over a much larger landscape extending both to the east and west of the main research area. Rather than being exceptional, this situation is likely to be the norm in most of the broad valley environments of lowland England and is particularly the case in those valleys where the valley floors and edges are the locations of extensive sand and gravel deposits. The sands and gravels with their associated light, well drained soils provided an ideal setting for early settlement enhanced by the close proximity of different environmental and economic resources, as in the case of Heslerton, between the wetlands at the centre of the Vale of Pickering and the low chalk uplands of the Yorkshire Wolds.

Whilst the presence of extensive areas of blown sands on the southern side of the Vale of Pickering is not a unique situation in British valley landscapes, it is exceptional. The blown sands have, in some places, secured the preservation of stratigraphic components that would normally not have survived in the plough-truncated landscapes that dominate rural archaeology both in Britain and Europe. Moreover, the gradual accumulation of blown sand over time has had a most unusual effect on the physical nature of the archaeological deposits in Heslerton, particularly at Cook's Quarry, where the gradual introduction of the iron-enriched red-ochre coloured blown sands have changed the colour of the soils over time; this has been confirmed by an analysis of the Munsell colours of the dated features, reflecting a transition from Neolithic features filled with almost black soils to Iron Age features with reddish fills. This simple observation regarding the relationship between soil colour and chronology reflects the continuous programme of work in Heslerton over a long time; it is most unlikely that this characteristic would have been noticed if excavations in Heslerton had been a one-off event.

The first seasons of rescue excavation at Cook's Quarry reflected levels of funding and expectations which, whilst the norm thirty years ago, would be unacceptable to many engaging in field archaeology today. The staff and workforce were all effectively volunteers receiving a small subsistence allowance and free food in return for long days of fieldwork in difficult conditions, six days a week. People brought their own tents and camped next to the excavation where a single cold tap provided water for cooking and washing. A single small Portakabin acted as kitchen and dining room, a small garden shed acted as site office; a chemical toilet in a rickety DoE hut, which failed to survive the intense gales of the Vale of Pickering in autumn, provided the rest of the facilities. It is remarkable how one is able to look back with elements of fondness to a time when the 'Men from the Ministry' would deliver the site hut from a store a few miles away one day, the bolts to put it together the next day and the windows on the third.

The adverse climate of the Vale of Pickering and the hard days spent on site encouraged the entire team to eke out their subsistence payments. The Dawnay Arms pub in West Heslerton was the indirect recipient of a large percentage of the excavation grant over many years. The pub provided warmth and generosity from a village population in an area which at the time was far more isolated than now, in which the latest student fashion (or lack of it) was a cause for amusement and enquiry rather than horror. The advice from the local policeman that travelling to and from the pub along the A64 Trunk Road by dumper truck, with multiple people in the bucket holding two torches for headlights and another two coloured with a covering of red underwear for rear lights, was not the best approach, even if the driver did not drink – reflecting a time when there was much less traffic than today and in which advice was given personally rather than the more draconian response we might expect now. The use of a tractor and trailer with real lights on a later occasion, to visit the pub in Yedingham 3 miles away, would not have caused so much excitement had the driver not passed the owner; that too was a once in a lifetime experience.

The 'Brewster effect' on the village meant that the villagers knew both what archaeology was and that it was 'worthwhile', and encouraged a generosity that might have been less extensive had he not had such an influence through the school. The levels of support over the years included everything from villagers coming digging to providing fruit and vegetables, carpentry and other skills free of charge, or providing photographic materials at cost. The concept of a stand-alone 'community archaeology project', had not of course been invented at that point, but in real terms the excavations at West Heslerton and the team that undertook them became very much a 'possession' of the village population, leaving the occasional critic in the pub in no uncertainty as to who thought it was important – the 'locals'.

It would be easy to fill an entire and very entertaining volume with tales of the remarkable individuals who made the West Heslerton excavations fun or frustrating, and in real terms it is the eclectic collection of individuals who made them 'Great Excavations' for those that spent time working on them. Reports that the Thursday night parties were amongst the best in British archaeology or that the projects were amongst the hardest work are not entirely unfounded; however, the wider impact of the excavations is best observed by the fact that large numbers of people who volunteered at West Heslerton are to be found working in archaeological units and academic institutions throughout Britain and abroad; in many cases individuals have, after the event, argued that the experience and training that they received at West Heslerton made a fundamental and positive contribution to their career development.

Although almost all the excavations undertaken by the LRC in the Heslerton research area have been rescue excavations undertaken ahead of mineral extraction, or to recover evidence under threat from plough damage, they have also been conducted as research excavations. The nature of the research questions raised and the approaches adopted to target them has changed continuously in response both to results returned from fieldwork and also to new challenges arising from factors such as global warming and changes in agricultural practice. If one of the purposes of archaeological research is to challenge what we know and secure data that allows us to change our understanding of the past and its people then the various projects operated by the LRC have succeeded well. The combination of exceptional deposit survival, multi-activity and multi-period evidence examined over large areas, initially through excavation and air photographic survey and more recently through large area geophysical survey, has generated results that seriously challenge established views of the past.

The multi-hectare, multi-period and multi-activity nature of the excavations carried out over a thirty year time-span covered areas with very different ground conditions, varying from vast areas of soft sands to large areas of hard, ice-fractured chalk bedrock. Each year one had to learn how to work different soils and identify the most suitable approaches to excavation; as with almost all aspects of the research process this involved a degree of trial and error. We were annually faced with large open area excavations in frequently challenging conditions, not helped perhaps by the often unrealistic ambitions regarding what could be done in a seasonal excavation based on what seemed like realistic ideas of what was anticipated.

The learning and re-learning process associated with very long-term field projects, even in a single location like Heslerton, ensures that interest or excitement is not diminished. During the first season a 'colleague' questioned why the excavation was not being run by a 'Prehistorian'; rather it was being run by an archaeologist with no particular chronological bias. Whilst it was true that the excavation of the first Fengate/Peterborough pit group encountered represented a new experience, one is aware of potentially hundreds of declared Prehistorians who have yet to have the pleasure of excavating such a feature group. This question reflected the time in the late 1970's when major differences emerged in the intellectual paths followed by field archaeologists, more concerned with excavation, recording and stratigraphic analysis, than institutional archaeologists often pre-occupied with theory rather than practice. Almost everything encountered in the early excavations represented a new experience from which we hope we learned; the excavation of prehistoric settlement and other evidence at Cook's Quarry prepared us well for the excavation of the Early to Middle Saxon settlement at West Heslerton, the character of which has so much more in common with prehistoric archaeology than with the Roman or later Medieval periods (Powlesland 2003a; 2003c).

As the excavations at Cook's Quarry expanded, the need to establish the landscape context became increasingly important. As early as 1980 we attempted to use geophysical survey to identify features at Cook's Quarry ahead of stripping the area; the results showed nothing; sadly with no useful result at all the first surveys were not extended over areas where we now know results should have been forthcoming. Without sufficient evidence to show the potential a large area at the northern end of Cook's Quarry, with important archaeology, was later lost without observation during quarrying as our case for funding was not accepted. A by-product of the decision not to excavate this area meant that when a new planning application was later submitted for the adjacent area the lack of evidence meant that no archaeological condition was attached to the approval and a considerable area, which we now believe to have contained extensive activity, was lost without observation. More irritatingly, following the resumption of work at Cook's Quarry under arrangements related to a more recent planning application in accordance with PPG16, we have discovered that in the intervening years erosion of the western quarry face had removed up to four metres of ground along the whole of the quarry edge. Given the scale of the areas examined this might be considered a minimal loss; however, it appears to have included the centre of an important round barrow and most of a Neolithic timber mortuary structure which, when identified in 1982, extended back into the section, but was completely lost by the time the western half of the barrow was investigated 20 years later. Elsewhere, a failure to understand or at least interpret the evidence when first encountered led to some spectacularly exciting reversals of opinion as, for instance, in the case of an area of narrow v-shaped features considered at first to be Late Bronze Age ard marks but later shown to be wheel ruts in a Late Bronze Age trackway.

During the five seasons of excavation investigating more than four hectares at Cook's Quarry, it became clear that the established interpretation of the archaeological landscape, in which the Vale of Pickering was an area of very limited activity in contrast to the Yorkshire Wolds to the south or North York Moors to the north, was fundamentally flawed. Not only were the excavations revealing unexpected areas of Late Bronze Age/Early Iron Age open settlement, but these were set within an area delimited to the north and south by extensive earlier monument complexes including Neolithic Hengiform enclosures and Late Neolithic/Early Bronze Age Barrows. Massive post pits interpreted as parts of a Neolithic Avenue have since been shown to form part of a much more extensive and probably long- lived arrangement of massive posts situated between the northerly of the two barrow cemeteries and the edge of the former wetlands *c.* 400m to the north.

Not only were the excavations revealing an unanticipated density and range of activity indicating that Prehistoric and later activity along the southern edge of the Vale of Pickering was as dense as or denser than that found on the Wolds. The exceptional position of the Wolds in the established picture of the prehistory of the North of England owes most to the fact that the earthen monuments incorporated a lot of stone and thus survived as visible targets for examination by antiquarians and early archaeologists like Greenwell and, more importantly, Mortimer whose contribution to the archaeology of Eastern Yorkshire is as great as that of Pitt-Rivers to the archaeology of Wessex (Greenwell and Rolleston 1877, Mortimer 1905). The blown sands which had completely buried one of the barrows allowed us to examine the construction sequence in a way that would otherwise not have been possible revealing that, in this case and, it seems most likely, in the other examples excavated at Cook's Quarry, the barrows had started life as flat cemeteries bounded by a slight ditch (Figure 17.2). Only when the enclosed area had absorbed a number of burials was a mound put over the top and a much larger ditch dug, presumably in part to provide material for the mound, after which secondary burials were inserted through the mound and into the partially filled ditch. The key factor here is that the mound represents a late addition sealing multiple graves rather than being raised over a single primary grave. Had the mound been truncated by ploughing (as is so often the case), the evidence of sequence would have simply been lost.

Whilst the excavations revealed dense multi-period and multi-activity evidence, air photography began to show that the evidence from Cook's Quarry did not exist in isolation. The excavated area reflected a lower density of activity than areas to the north of the quarry, where patchy crop marks revealed an Iron Age and Roman 'ladder settlement' following the margins of the ancient wetlands that had formerly dominated the valley floor. Those areas that most closely matched the environment at the quarry appeared to have a poor crop-mark response, probably a consequence of the covering deposit of blown sand.

The initial phase of excavation at Cook's Quarry was concluded by the end of December 1982. Whilst it was clear that the Prehistoric evidence could be fully published at that time, sampling trenches had revealed that the Anglian cemetery extended to the south of the A64 trunk road that bounded the site to the south. Other trenches 500m further south had revealed Anglian structures and finds demonstrating that the settlement was broadly contemporary with the cemetery; a wrist clasp found in the settlement proved to be from the same mould as one from the cemetery. Excavation resumed whilst the report on the Quarry site, incorporating a summary of the Anglian evidence, was put together, the report being updated later to reflect discoveries made in 1985. The initial excavation report was completed within 18 months and published shortly afterwards in the Archaeological Journal; the completion of the report in such a short time (much of which was not funded) was a considerable achievement (Powlesland *et al.* 1986).

The discovery of multiple Anglian burials to the south of the excavated area, and the recovery of a small bronze-bound wooden bucket cut in half by the plough, provided a strong case for extending the excavation. In 1985 excavation resumed (Figure 17.3). The western limit of the Anglian cemetery was identified in an area that will shortly be quarried whilst to the south the full extent of the cemetery and its relationship to a Late Neolithic/Early Bronze Age monument complex became evident. Excavation of the Anglian cemetery was completed during the winter of 1987/8. The excavation team was small, the ground conditions were difficult and excavation of the graves complex, not helped by the variable survival of the skeletal material and snow-bound conditions that prevailed for what seemed like an eternity during the previous winter. The location of part of the roof of the site hut, which had blown off during a particularly aggressive gale, remained a mystery for some months until it was finally found several fields away; it has to be admitted that the presence or absence of the roof made no real difference to the temperature in the old wooden shed that served as the site office.

The Anglian cemetery

The West Heslerton Anglian cemetery remains the most extensively excavated example of its type in the north of England, totally excavated with the exception of a strip though the centre which lies beneath a main road. Not only were we able to identify the full extent of the cemetery and recover an exceptional resource of mineral-replaced organic and costume evidence, we were also able to pose questions regarding the cemetery as a whole and its relation to the prehistoric monument complex within which it was set. It was clear that the prehistoric monument complex comprising a post-circle, a hengiform monument and a number of small barrows, must have been maintained or managed, most likely through controlled grazing, to have survived as a visible feature of the Early Anglo-Saxon landscape in an environment where blown sand activity would otherwise have buried and hidden the monuments. One is tempted to wonder if the practise of grazing sheep in churchyards reflects a method of managing sacred sites developed in the prehistoric past. The realisation that the Anglian cemetery had been deliberately associated with the prehistoric monument complex, and that in Eastern Yorkshire this would appear to have been the norm rather than an exception, was to inspire research investigating this relationship both locally and elsewhere in England (Lucy and Reynolds 2002, Williams 1997).

During the late 1970's and early 1980's Sites and Monuments Records were being developed in a

Figure 17.2. Excavation concludes on a buried Barrow 1M, at Cook's Quarry 1981.

Figure 17.3. Barry Prestwood attempts to unfreeze a burial during excavation in the winter of 1986/7.

number of counties and North Yorkshire, under the driving force of the then County Archaeologist, Mike Griffiths, was amongst the first to establish a comprehensive computer-based SMR. It was also a time when the first computer-based excavation records were being developed. In the case of Heslerton, which was initially established as a County Council project, the excavation record was developed in tandem with the SMR as a component of the SMR. The two-year design process which went into the definition and creation of the excavation record is reflected in the fact that the overall structure of the computer-based record has hardly changed over the last 28 years despite the tremendous changes that have taken place in computing; many new components have of course been added as changes in technology have allowed, but the core structure has remained the same. The role and nature of computing applied to the archaeology of Heslerton has been discussed elsewhere (Powlesland 1984; 1986; 1987; 1991; 1997 and Powlesland and May forthcoming); however it must be noted that it has been fundamental to the development of the excavation record over nearly three decades, a period in which a single individual, Christine Haughton, has recorded almost all the finds, within the discontinuous and challenging employment environment that has characterised the Heslerton projects as a whole.

The excavation of the cemetery was amongst the earliest excavations to be documented digitally in the field, with 3D recording of all finds positions and all recording undertaken using hand-held computers (Figure 17.4). To ensure the best recovery of mineral-replaced organics and textile materials, novel excavation techniques were developed to recover increasingly large soil-blocks; this work culminated in the recovery of almost an entire burial in one case (Grave 86 [2BA31]). Although this maximised the recovery of particularly rare and important data it contributed to significant delays in the conservation programme and thus the report production phase. The publication of the excavation report concerning the Anglian Cemetery was finally completed in 1999; it also employed innovative techniques (Haughton and Powlesland 1999). The grave catalogue, laid out on the basis of assemblage rather than the traditional materials-driven layout, employed extensive use of object scans made using a flatbed scanner, drawings of both ceramics and objects published from pencil originals, and the use of unedited scanned field-drawings. The grave plans themselves, produced directly from the excavation in a Geographic Information System, were for the most part digitised from large-scale 1:5 prints from vertical photographs.

The Anglian settlement

Once compilation of the cemetery report had begun and whilst we awaited the completion of various specialist reports, the soil-block excavation and conservation programme, fieldwork was resumed. Our attention was directed towards the excavation of the settlement that had been discovered in 1982 (Figure 17.5). In contrast with the cemetery, discovered by chance during aggregate extraction, the settlement was discovered through a pro-active sample trenching campaign directed towards finding the settlement, conducted with undergraduates from York University as part of their fieldwork training. The sampling approach adopted was based upon the 'here seems a good place for a building' principle rather than any elaborate random or statistically based sampling programme; our approach worked and structures were identified in multiple locations. Subsequent experiments using the excavated data-set and various different sampling approaches and densities have shown that with both random and grid based sampling very much lager areas would have had to have been exposed to characterise the nature and extent of the settlement. Field-walking and surface collection survey failed to reveal the presence of the Anglian settlement, a reflection perhaps of the poor survival of Early-Middle Saxon ceramics in the soil, the fact that it appears that most domestic refuse was incorporated in temporary middens which were spread on the fields and that, with the exception of those areas used for the middens, much of the settlement was kept remarkably clean. The discovery of the location of the settlement was an important breakthrough given the exceptional rarity of known settlements with associated cemeteries; however, it was ultimately realised that the area that was covered in the sampling trenches was insufficient to identify the total extent of the settlement. The number of sample trenches was constrained by what could be achieved without dedicated funding, through purely voluntary arrangements. In addition to identifying the location of the settlement the sample trenches were intended to identify the levels of preservation of any deposits encountered; it was quickly realised that the settlement archaeology was being actively eroded by ploughing.

It is difficult to reflect on the origins of the excavation of the settlement without hindsight. The prevailing intellectual position at the time defined the limitations within which the potential settlement was perceived; the suggestion that it might be as large as ten acres was considered by some as too ambitious. In fact, the extent of the settlement was to turn out to be nearer to 30 acres. Had the settlement turned out to be as small as originally suggested the excavation would still have been large, complex and very time consuming; even working with an almost entirely volunteer team the excavation would still seem to some expensive. The exceptionally low comparative database of known and excavated Early-Middle Saxon settlement evidence, and the prevailing model of settlement development based on a very limited number of excavated features from a single site (Mucking in Essex) (Barford, this volume), had an indefensible influence on the way settlement of this period was conceptualised. An inherent desire to see Early Anglo-Saxon 'history' as articulated through very much later documents such as the Anglo-Saxon Chronicle, the concept of the Dark Ages and a whole range of attitudes derived from nineteenth- and early twentieth-century imperial sensibilities, contributed towards a view of the immediate Post-Roman past in terms that are now totally unsupportable. The extant Anglo-Saxon evidence base, at the time almost entirely based on the partial excavation of cemeteries and the odd very rich grave, encouraged attempts towards social reconstruction on the basis of grave assemblages, and the development of increasingly complex typologies of objects employed to date the dead in total isolation from the living contexts articulated through settlement.

Having discovered the settlement, we had to accept a degree of responsibility for its future. With a team in place but without any project income whilst we awaited the completion of a number of external components of the cemetery excavation report, a detailed research design was developed which examined various options with regard to the settlement. The cheapest option was of course simply to allow the 'site', whatever its nature, to be lost to the plough; it was argued in the light of this being the first identified instance of a cemetery and an associated settlement in the North of England, particularly one where the majority of the cemetery and its limits had already been defined, the deliberate sacrifice of the settlement would be unacceptable. We could have campaigned to have the site removed from agriculture; this would have required either the purchase of the land for the State or annual compensation payments for the foreseeable future. Whilst in simple terms this approach might have secured 'preservation', what, precisely, would we be preserving, and what would be the purpose of preserving something which at that stage comprised an ill-defined area of settlement evidence of unknown nature and unknown date range. It is difficult to argue for the preservation of something of which we have virtually no understanding, especially since this would have been an exceptional approach which might have diminished interest in any similar sites in the region on the basis that there was already a preserved example. The costs of preservation through land purchase were not

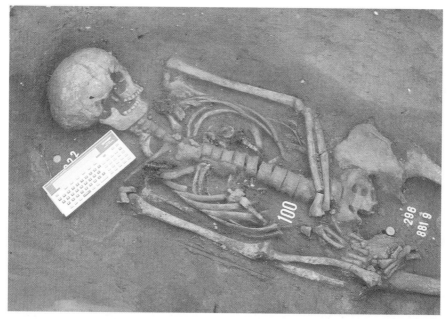

Figure 17.4. At Heslerton hand-held computers have been used for capturing the primary record in the field since 1984.

Figure 17.5. The first post-hole building identified in the Anglian settlement in 1982 is re-exposed in context in 1986.

Figure 17.6. Air photograph showing the first of the vast trenches opened over the Anglian settlement.

significantly lower than the anticipated costs of excavation and would have still required investment in excavation to identify the limits of the settlement; had this been done the full scale of the occupation area might have emerged earlier than it did, with a consequent increase in the costs for preservation through purchase. With very large parts of rural England subject to ever more invasive damage from modern intensive agriculture it is easy to see why plough damage was not considered in the same light as, for instance, mineral extraction as the basis for securing rescue funding. Plough damage is an irreconcilable problem in the archaeology of Britain and most of Europe; moreover, the extent is not predictable and the degree of damage and rate of archaeological truncation is changing as farmers adapt both to technological changes in agricultural practice with ever larger machines and also to changes arising from global warming and changes in the crop types being grown. In the case of Heslerton it was argued that the intellectual premium returned through excavation and the potential to address fundamental issues regarding Early Anglo-Saxon settlement, landscape and population, would justify the expenditure. The trial excavations had revealed that whilst some areas had already been truncated by long term ploughing, in others plough damage was actively taking place but had not yet totally compromised the buried evidence. After lengthy discussion, a budget considerably less than had been requested was agreed and plans for what was to become one of the largest excavations in Europe began. The scale of the excavations at Cook's Quarry had been large, with multiple hectares examined in the final year; the Anglian settlement excavation made those early excavations seem small. Not only did the excavation progress with huge open areas, but the excavation teams and infra-structure were also larger than had been the case in the previous decade.

The excavation of the northern third of the settlement between 1987 and 1990 took longer and was more challenging than had been expected; the overall scale of the excavation and subsequent workload earned Heslerton a reputation for hard work and tremendous archaeological returns (Figure 17.6). At that time, whilst developer funding was being introduced and finally formalised through PPG16, there was considerable criticism from some of the emerging archaeological units concerning the role of volunteers on excavations. In the case of West Heslerton, the majority of the workforce were volunteers, including most of the site assistants and supervisors, who had effectively undertaken an apprenticeship in previous seasons before being given supervisory responsibility. This approach to developing a skills base made a huge contribution towards the uniformity of the record and methodology used in the field; inexperienced excavators would learn how to excavate and record within the context of our methods and recording systems which, in the early 1990's, were unique, employing handheld computers for recording in the field and the global recovery of individually lifted and located finds.

The costs of the excavation would have multiplied many times, and effectively been uneconomic, had we worked only with well-paid professional staff; besides, West Heslerton provided extensive and in-depth training to literally thousands of volunteers who were subsequently able to secure full-time employment with the expanding commercial units during the early 1990's. Since the first season of work in West Heslerton, payment and subsistence scales had been very low; the seasonal nature of the excavations was determined both by the scale of resources available and by the availability of the sizeable volunteer workforce needed to effectively investigate the very large areas being examined. Despite project funding arrangements intended to see the project operate over a number of years, the inevitable variations arising from the increased scale of the project meant that the battle to secure funding continued to operate on the basis of annual applications, with the associated periods of worry and depression as we waited to see if funding would be secured for the next stage. Although the project was directed and operated by the LRC, the Department of the Environment and later English Heritage grants were managed by North Yorkshire County Council (NYCC) until 1995, at which point NYCC opted to transfer any responsibilities for the project to the LRC. With project funding available solely on the basis of annual grants, the local authority would not risk engaging any staff as employees and thus the project staff were all either self-employed or volunteers receiving a daily subsistence allowance and free food. Despite limitations in funding, very large numbers of volunteers and ultimately staff returned on an annual basis; they returned because the project was a challenge and it was fun; much of the reputation about how hard the work was, was amplified by the team who were justifiably proud of the tremendous achievements. It was easy to be a workaholic within the context of the settlement excavation; however, it was a matter of policy that the key staff – most of whom worked very long days and frequently seven days a week rather than the six days worked by the volunteers – whilst expecting people to work hard, would ask no-one to do anything that they would not do themselves, nor expect them to work as hard as they did. The organisation of the excavation, with small groups of volunteers managed by experienced site assistants who were in turn looked after by site supervisors who did most of the recording, and managed progress on an area by area basis, was considered by some critics, who had not worked in Heslerton, to be too hierarchical, old-fashioned and in some ways non-democratic; others suggested that 'a single proper employee would achieve four times as much as a volunteer in the same time'. Those that criticised from the outside generally did so from well-paid positions in large excavation units who, for some reason, felt threatened by the presence of volunteer run excavations; they did not consider the extensive training that was provided. The singular fact exists that even if the desire had been there, English Heritage did not have the resources to provide a four-times larger budget and thus the excavation would not have taken place and the site and training benefits would have been lost. Any suggestion that, by leaving the control of the recording with the site assistants and supervisors, the excavation was not engaging the volunteers in the process is absurd and defies the logic of apprenticeship; the supervisors acted as experienced mentors compiling the record with the volunteers, for many of whom this was their first direct experience of practical archaeology.

By 1990 it became clear that the Mucking model of shifting settlement did not fit the evidence coming out of the ground at West Heslerton; clear evidence of different activity zones seemed to indicate a much more static and long-lived arrangement, with some fluctuation in scale and focus over time but within a settlement that seems to have been established over a large area which contracted over time. The presence of different zones devoted to housing or craft and industry is more representative of an integrated village or settlement with proto-urban ambitions rather than a group of loosely clustered farmsteads.

Further evidence of specialised activity zones were discovered in the central third of the settlement during the early 1990's. By the time the final huge area covering the southern part of the settlement was stripped in 1995, it was realised that there were severe flaws in our own interpretation of the settlement sequence, in particular the suggestion that the settlement had developed in a de-novo location. During the final season it became clear that, far from being laid out on new ground, the settlement had developed to incorporate a Roman sacred complex which appears to have been active from the late Iron Age at least (Figure 17.7). The excavation of the settlement extended over a much larger area than had originally been anticipated; further funds were provided to cover the excavation of the Anglo-Saxon deposits in the southern part of the site, where a considerable depth of earlier deposits survived in the base of a dry valley, but there was neither time nor the resources, both economic or human, to include the excavation of these deposits; these were re-buried at a depth which should secure their survival from plough damage at least for the immediate future. The final season had been by far the most exhausting for all involved; with up to 110 people on site at any one time, the pressure on the core team was relentless. The size of the team, which was determined by the scale and complexity of the excavation, was not ideal. The presence of a very large number of people on site made the physical process of excavation possible, but put extraordinary pressure on other aspects of the work such as the lifting, cleaning and recording of the finds.

Landscape surveys

Whilst the excavations took place on the Anglian settlement, air-photographic survey continued on an ad-hoc and annual basis; this included the identification of other possible Anglian settlement sites in the immediate area. In addition to conventional oblique air photography, a NERC multi-spectral survey which also included high resolution vertical air photography was carried out in 1992. Since the flights undertaken in 1978 to photograph the first season of excavation in progress, a compelling body of air-photographic evidence has revealed a picture of a landscape with very dense activity over huge areas from the late Prehistoric period onwards (Figure 17.8).

Gradiometer survey was tested (again) by the English Heritage geophysical survey team as part of the pre-excavation planning in 1990, and produced remarkable results; this triggered a series of experiments designed to test the viability of geophysical survey as part of the excavation process, with areas being surveyed after the removal of the plough-soil (Lyall and Powlesland 1996). The results were exceptional and, by 1995, the use of high resolution survey after removal of the plough-soil over

Figure 17.7. Excavation in progress during the final season on the Anglian settlement in 1995.

the southern third of the settlement provided a plan showing areas where stratigraphic relationships appeared to be visible in the survey alone; without this resource it is debateable whether the excavation of more than 3 ha of dense archaeology could have been achieved at all. The realisation that the area was very well suited to geophysical survey by gradiometer was to have far-reaching implications for the interpretation of the excavated areas and the understanding of the landscape as a whole.

Present

Once the detailed assessment of the Anglian Settlement Excavation was complete, energies were focussed upon the analysis of the evidence and the production of the various specialist reports contributing to the completed excavation report (Powlesland 1998, Tipper 2004). New projects, initiated during gaps in the work programme associated with the Anglian Settlement Analysis

Figure 17.8. Crop marks showing multiple flat burials around a group of ditched barrows seen first in 1984 and not again until 2006.

programme and a return to Cook's Quarry, where excavation resumed in 1998 under arrangements covered by PPG16, have continued to generate new and challenging data. The singular focus of the LRC upon the archaeology of a single landscape, in which all projects are effectively linked to each other or overlap, poses conceptual problems for grant giving bodies better used to projects which are less dependent upon each other. The work has generated results which challenge fundamental concepts of landscape population and development from the prehistoric to medieval periods. The ad-hoc but extensive programme of air photography initiated in 1978 and still continuing had, when combined with the results of the NERC multi-spectral flight in 1994, revealed a landscape which had been transformed from an area considered in the mid 1970's as an archaeological blank to a fragmented but densely settled area, particularly in the sandy area between the edge of the former wetlands that dominated the centre of the Vale of Pickering to the foot of the Yorkshire Wolds to the south (Donoghue, Powlesland and Pryor 1992, Powlesland, Lyall and Donoghue 1997, Powlesland 2001). By 2000, the returns from airborne survey were diminishing, with known sites appearing on a regular basis but few 'new' sites being identified.

Geophysics and particularly gradiometry had been shown to be very effective, giving more detailed or, more importantly, complementary evidence in relation to the air photographic record. In 2000 an

English Heritage project was initiated to gather large area geophysics in the area between Sherburn and East Heslerton as a method of interpreting the gaps in the air-photographic record, and assembling evidence that would allow us to address the development of the landscape as a whole rather than on a site-by-site basis. The results from the large area survey were extraordinary and, with the introduction of the Aggregates Levy Sustainability Fund (ALSF) in 2002, it was realised that the survey could be extended to encompass the landscape around the Cook's Quarry site. A second NERC multi-spectral survey project in 2005 together with further ALSF funding to cover the examination and integration of all the NERC data and some targeted additional geophysics, have generated a multi-project dataset covering most of an 11 by 3 km area on the southern side of the Vale of Pickering; this forms the largest contiguous geophysical survey of its type in the world (Powlesland *et al.* 2006). The combined core of geophysical data forms a single contiguous survey covering a little short of 1200ha, within which are more than 20,000 discrete features (Figure 17.9).

The impact of the ALSF funding has been tremendous; it has facilitated work which would probably never have been possible within the constraints of English Heritage Commissions projects. By combining ALSF and English Heritage Commissions projects we have been able to assess both the methods used to evaluate large landscapes and also generate results which show that we have fundamentally misunderstood the scale, density, complexity and continuity of human settlement in the Vale of Pickering from the Prehistoric to Medieval periods, and would argue that this is probably the case for most similar valley landscapes in lowland Britain. We can argue that the Vale of Pickering does have exceptional qualities,

Figure 17.9. A small part of the massive geophysical survey around Heslerton showing part of an Iron Age and Roman ladder settlement and cemetery.

particularly the fact that the River Derwent drains through the valley inland rather than into the North Sea about a kilometre from its source; this may have encouraged settlement in what we may see as a sacred space; we should, however, be careful in placing too much emphasis on this.

If any aspect of the work in Heslerton is unique and critical it is the continuity and scale of effort applied to a single landscape that makes it unlike any other project in Britain (Powlesland 2003b). Within the context of this chapter one could perhaps question the relevance of the vast geophysical survey projects; however, these are completely relevant as they provide the context for the excavated 'sites' within the landscape, and evidence which both changes and enhances the interpretation of the excavated evidence. The combined remote sensing data undermines fundamental archaeological concepts such as the very existence of 'sites' and the way that we have viewed them either as excavated trenches or isolated crop-marks in a vast emptiness, the unstudied or unknown. The term 'site' is of course fundamental to the LRC recording strategy but, as used, it refers not to any particular archaeological entity; rather, it references an individual field as mapped at the start of fieldwork; the first phase of excavation at Cook's Quarry was concerned with Site 1.

If the results of the excavation of the Anglian settlement and cemetery are viewed in isolation against the tiny comparative dataset for England, then they seem exceptional. However, the remote sensing work and particularly the geophysical survey projects, whilst poor at revealing further cemeteries, show a wholly unanticipated density and scale of Early-Middle Saxon settlement on account of the very distinctive geophysical signal of the Grubenhäuser. Any temptation to see Early Anglo-Saxon settlement in terms of small clusters of gradually shifting farmsteads in isolated pockets in the landscape is compromised by the realisation that within ten kilometres of West Heslerton there are two much larger Early-Middle Saxon settlements and at least ten smaller examples. The detailed chronologies of these settlement features can of course only be established through excavation, but the comprehensive picture which has emerged provides nothing to indicate a break in continuity of field-systems and population from the Iron Age through to the Medieval periods. The shift in settlement location, for instance, from the ladder settlement that followed the edge of the wetlands to the settlement site at West Heslerton, appears to emphasise continuity of the open space and fields between them rather than any discontinuity. Even in the Neolithic and Bronze Age the excavations both past and ongoing at Cook's Quarry, combined with the remote sensing in which we know that the prehistoric evidence is grossly under-represented, show a densely utilised and open landscape with arguably a much higher population than we find for instance on the Yorkshire Wolds (Powlesland 2008). To the casual onlooker, looking down on the landscape in the Vale from the top of the Wolds, there is effectively no trace of the Medieval Rig and Furrow which remains visible, despite the truncation by modern ploughing, in the geophysical survey results. It is the imposition of the Rig and Furrow, established prior to the Norman Conquest that represents the biggest change to the landscape at any time prior to enclosure, effectively erasing everything that went before with the exception of the parish boundaries, and thus invalidating any attempt to articulate the Prehistoric or Post-Roman landscape through visible remains.

Future

If the hidden landscape of the Vale of Pickering is to be more than an interesting footnote in the archaeology of Europe then we, as a community, have some responsibility for it. We have seen that it includes areas that are or have been exceptionally well preserved, and that these are actively being truncated by industrial agriculture. The wetlands that dominate the centre of the Vale of Pickering, from Star Carr on the edge of Lake Flixton to the relict lakes and channels identified through auger survey

Figure 17.10. Excavation at Cook's Quarry in 2007 covering areas of Early Bronze Age settlement and a cemetery and associated enclosure of Late Bronze Age date.

in the centre of the Vale of Pickering, are rapidly desiccating as a consequence of global warming and increasingly determined drainage schemes, with the inevitable loss of the entire environmental record from the Palaeolithic to Medieval periods. Current estimates indicate that the environmental record will be effectively totally compromised within a decade; it is depressing to realise that had our initial work incorporated proactive sampling in the wetlands 30 years ago, we would have probably secured a detailed environmental record with greater resolution and chronological depth than is possible even now.

At a time when terms such as 'heritage management' or 'protection through designation' seem to be given ever more space in government policies, the management challenge to secure the future of the fragile resources identified through the LRC research programme is very significant, not least since we have spent in the region of two million pounds identifying and quantifying the resource. If the resource identified in Heslerton is to make a real impact on our understanding of the past, then part of any long term management strategy must include investigation. It needs to be studied and interpreted rather than simply mapped; moreover, it does need some sort of protection both from the ravages of industrial farming and from systematic treasure hunting, with the associated and chronic loss of dating evidence.

The demise of the large volunteer excavations such as West Heslerton or Crickley Hill, and the realisation that the two-week 'training' digs mounted by universities are hopelessly inadequate as platforms for training professional field archaeologists, leaves us desperately short of training platforms, whether it be for the excavators that will transform archaeology in the future, or the materials specialists upon whom we rely to identify and interpret the material culture evidence that provides the human context for the excavated contexts. The training problem is amplified by the disproportionate number of undergraduate places to archaeological employment opportunities. We are encouraged at every turn to include 'community engagement' within our research designs even in areas with minimal populations and thus an exceptionally limited community resource in terms which suggest political correctness. The excavation and other research at West Heslerton demonstrate how long-term projects become embedded within a community. Amongst the distinctive features of the large excavations in Heslerton were the open days attended by thousands of people, visits from schools as far afield as Kent and Lancashire, and the constant interest shown not only by the Heslerton 'locals' but by those form nearby towns (Figure 17.11). The excavations, and the diggers without whom they could not have taken place, were part of the community.

We are faced with a challenge which requires an innovative solution; whilst there are clearly many important individual components in the mapped archaeology of Heslerton, it is the contiguous nature of the geophysical and air-photographic evidence, showing a landscape rather than a number of important 'sites', that is the unique and valuable characteristic. Securing preservation through subsidised management agreements, which effectively would need to run forever, would be uneconomic, and simply scheduling large areas without restricting agricultural activity would be pointless. Logically the only way to preserve the resource would be to take a large section out of conventional agriculture altogether. This could be achieved through a purchasing programme directed towards establishing a perpetual land trust

Figure 17.11. Potential archaeologists of the future from West Heslerton School assess a Roman Building in 1995.

for an archaeological and environmental research park; non-invasive agricultural use could continue and the park could then become the setting for a permanent research and training base. Through the development of research and training excavations the intellectual benefit of securing the resource would be realised; moreover, by creating a permanent visitor centre and educational resource public engagement can be assured. Such a park would form a living laboratory using the investigation of the buried resource both to train archaeologists and members of the general public and develop archaeological field techniques. Without investigation, preserving the resource becomes purposeless and, even with a continuous programme of excavation, only sample areas could be studied; it would take over a thousand years to excavate even a half of the area covered by the geophysical survey. By combining excavation with reconstruction, the link between buried archaeology and the physical past can be established in terms which can be understood by all, from school-children to the retired.

The importance of the archaeology of the Heslerton landscape is predicated upon a uniqueness that is a reflection of work undertaken rather than an archaeological reality; if the undoubted importance of this work is to be fully realised then we need to establish other comparable long term projects elsewhere in Britain and beyond. Finding locations in which to develop comparable projects should not be a problem; securing the long-term funding to facilitate such projects, which requires a long-term and proactive approach from funding bodies, might be difficult. Finding the individuals prepared to devote 30 years of their lives to such a project, especially if it has to built upon a sequence of annual applications for funding without any guarantees of even short-term continuity and employment, may be the biggest challenge of all.

References

Brewster, T. C. M. 1963. *The Excavation of Staple Howe*. East Riding Archaeology Research Committee.
Brewster, T. C. M. 1981. The Devil's Hill. *Current Archaeology* 76, 140–41.
Clark, J. G. D. 1954. *Excavations at Star Carr*. Cambridge: Cambridge University Press.
Donoghue, D. N. M., Powlesland, D. J. and Pryor, C. 1992. Integration of Remotely Sensed and Ground Based Geophysical Data for Archaeological Prospecting using a Geographical Information System, in Cracknell, A. P. and Vaughan, R. A. (eds), *Proceedings of the 18th. Annual Conference of the Remote Sensing Society, 197–207*. Dundee: University of Dundee.
Greenwell, W. and Rolleston, G. 1877. *British Barrows*. Oxford: Oxford University Press.
Haughton, C. A. and Powlesland, D. J. 1999. *West Heslerton – The Anglian Cemetery*. Yedingham: Landscape Research Centre Monograph 1, 2 vols.
Lyall, J. and Powlesland, D. J. 1996. The application of high resolution fluxgate gradiometery as an aid to excavation planning and strategy formulation. *Internet Archaeology* 1 (http://intarch.ac.uk/journal/issue1/index.html).
Moore, J. W. 1950. Mesolithic sites in the neighbourhood of Flixton, north-east Yorkshire. *Proceedings of the Prehistoric Society* 16, 101–08.
Mortimer, J. R. 1905 *Forty Years Researches in British and Saxon Burial Mounds in East Yorkshire*. London: A. Brown and Sons.
Powlesland, D. 1980. West Heslerton – the focus for a landscape project. *Rescue News* 21, 12.
Powlesland, D. J. 1984. Pots, Pits and Portables. *Practical Computing*, 6 (6), 144–6.
Powlesland, D. J. 1985. Random access and data compression with reference to remote data collection: 1 and 1 = 1, in Cooper, M. A. and Richards, J. D. (eds), *Current Issues in Archaeological Computing*, 17–22. Oxford: BAR (271).
Powlesland, D. J. 1986. On-site computing: in the field with the silicon chip, in Richards, J. D. (ed), *Computer usage in British Archaeology*, 39–43. Birmingham: Institute of Field Archaeologists.

Powlesland, D. J. 1998. West Heslerton – The Anglian Settlement: Assessment of Potential for Analysis and Updated Project Design, *Internet Archaeology* 5. (http://intarch.ac.uk/journal/issue5/pld/index.html).

Powlesland, D. 2001. The Heslerton Parish Project: An integrated multi-sensor approach to the archaeological study of Eastern Yorkshire, England, in Forte, M. X. and Campagna, S. X. (eds), *Remote Sensing in Archaeology*, 233–235. XI Ciclio di Lezioni sulla, Firenze.

Powlesland, D. 2003a. The Heslerton Parish Project: 20 years of archaeological research in the Vale of Pickering, in Manby, T. G., Moorhouse, S. and Ottoway, P. (eds), *The Archaeology of Yorkshire An assessment at the beginning of the 21st century*, 275–292. Leeds: Yorkshire Archaeological Society.

Powlesland, D. 2003b. *25 years research on the sands and gravels of the Vale of Pickering*. Yedingham: The Landscape Research Centre.

Powlesland, D. 2003c. The Early-Middle Anglo-Saxon Period, in Butlin, R. (ed.), *Historical Atlas of North Yorkshire*, 62–65. Leeds: Smith Settle.

Powlesland, D. 2008. Why Bother? Large scale geomagnetic survey and the quest for 'Real Archaeology', in Campana, S. and Piro, S. (eds), *Seeing the Unseen, Geophysics and Landscape Archaeology, papers presented at the XVth. International Summer School for Archaeology, University of Sienna, Grosseto July 2006*, 167–182. London: Taylor & Francis.

Powlesland, D. and Haughton, C. 1985. *Archaeology and Computers*. London: Council for British Archaeology.

Powlesland, D. J., Haughton, C. A. and Hanson, J. H. 1986. Excavations at Heslerton, North Yorkshire 1978–82. *Archaeological Journal* 143, 53–173.

Powlesland, D., Lyall, J. and Donoghue, D. 1997. Enhancing the record through remote sensing: the application and integration of multi-sensor, non-invasive remote sensing techniques for the enhancement of the Sites and Monuments Record. Heslerton Parish Project, N. Yorkshire, England. *Internet Archaeology* 2. (http://intarch.ac.uk/journal/issue2/pld/index.html).

Powlesland, D., Lyall, J., Hopkinson, G., Donoghue, D., Beck, M., Harte, A. and Stott, D. 2006. Beneath the sand: Remote Sensing, Archaeology, Aggregates and Sustainability. A case study from Heslerton, the Vale of Pickering, North Yorkshire, England, *Archaeological Prospection* 13(4), 291–299.

Powlesland, D. and May, K. Forthcoming. Excavations in Heslerton – DigIT: experiments in digital recording. *Internet Archaeology*.

Reynolds, A. and Lucy, S. J. (eds) 2002. *Burial in Early Medieval England and Wales*. Society for Medieval Archaeology Monograph 17.

Schadla-Hall, T. 1987a. Early man in the eastern Vale of Pickering, in Ellis, S. (ed.), *East Yorkshire Field Guide*, 22–30. Cambridge: Quaternary Research Association.

Schadla-Hall, T. 1987b. Recent investigations of the Mesolithic landscape and settlement in the Vale of Pickering, CBA Forum 1987. *CBA Group 4 Newsletter*, 22–3.

Schadla-Hall, T. 1988. The early post-glacial in Eastern Yorkshire, in Manby, T. G. (ed.), *Archaeology in Eastern Yorkshire*, 23–25. Sheffield: University of Sheffield.

Tipper, J. 2004. *The Grubenhaus in Anglo-Saxon England. An Analysis and Interpretation of the Evidence from a most distinctive building type*. Yedingham: Landscape Research Centre.

Vatcher, F. and L. de, 1965. East Heslerton Long Barrow, Yorkshire: Eastern Half. *Antiquity* 39, 49–52.

Williams, H. 1997. Ancient Landscapes and the Dead: the reuse of prehistoric and Roman monuments as early Anglo-Saxon burial sites. *Medieval Archaeology* 41, 1–31.

Great Expectations, great excavations: The view from the trenches

Paul Everill

In *Great Expectations*, Pip, Dickens' central character, has the opportunity to enjoy a simple life of hard physical work and straightforward, honest friendships. Instead he is seduced by the opportunity to live as a wealthy gentleman, pursuing the love of a woman who has been raised to be cold and heartless. Had Dickens been writing 120 years later, perhaps Pip would have been serving his apprenticeship not to a Blacksmith, but on a Manpower Services Commission archaeological placement. His decision to take the chance offered to him to become a gentleman might instead be a conversion course to start a career as a lawyer. Biddy, the warm, loving and honest girl of Pip's childhood might be a metaphor for life as an archaeologist; wealthy yet emotionally truncated Estella, life as an accountant. Had Pip been offered a Great Excavation, rather than a Great Expectation, perhaps his life would have been rather happier.

So what makes an excavation great, from the perspective of those who occupy the less glamorous positions on a project? Clearly it is not the facilities or the accommodation. In fact, perversely, it often seems to be the case that the worse, or more peculiar, the facilities the more likely an excavation is to achieve mythic status. My first year undergraduate excavation in 1992 is memorable largely for the rats and the mad, dreadlocked sheepdog locked in the hayloft. In the old orchard where we camped there was also a chemical toilet, concealed in a cubicle made from corrugated iron and sheets, which we took in turns to empty into a large pit. Most evenings were spent sitting round a bonfire drinking, and the morning alarm call was provided by someone walking amongst the tents with a stereo. I got up early one morning just to do that job and chose to play *Ride the Lightening* by Metallica. It was a memorable experience, but I would not describe it as a 'Great Excavation'. For two weeks I dug test-pits that produced a lot of 'negative' evidence and not much else. I did, however, have a good time doing it.

In contrast, my very first excavation in 1989 encapsulates what I think a Great Excavation should be. I had just turned 16. Instead of doing my work experience in a shop I had arranged to do it on a training excavation in the Midlands. I was only beginning to learn about archaeology and so the fact that the site was Wroxeter and one of the directors was Philip Barker meant very little to me at the time. This project is described more fully elsewhere in this volume, but the standing remains at Wroxeter and the sense of the city's enormity and importance were incredible. To be a part of that, and to take part in the tours that we gave to the public only emphasised to me that an archaeologist holds a privileged position. An archaeologist seemed somehow to be almost a shaman or a priest, negotiating the public's relationship with the past; an intermediary through whom the relationship was conducted, and yet someone who was also allowed access to that dangerous interface where irreparable damage to the remains might be caused. It was seductive and I was hooked.

I found when conducting qualitative interviews with commercial archaeologists (Everill 2009) that many of them told very similar stories. My own interest in archaeology seems to go back to a childhood memory of finding a cow mandible while digging a vegetable patch with my Dad when I was eight or nine years old. I cleaned it up and displayed it in a temporary exhibition on my bedroom floor, alongside pretty pebbles and old coins, for which I charged a penny entrance fee. Then I took it to school to show my class, only for one of the older boys to pull all the teeth out. I was convinced it was a dinosaur jaw and was outraged by this vandalism. The 'Invisible Diggers' interviews give a definite sense that the participants fell into one of two camps. By this I mean those that had a very early interest in archaeology, perhaps even before they really understood what archaeology was, and those that became archaeologists through their degree, or later in life. A common story amongst 'born' archaeologists was of early forays into excavation and experiencing the thrill of discovery at an early age. Equally, a number cite frequent family trips to famous archaeological sites as early factors in their interest. Here are three examples:

> I excavated my dead Guinea Pigs when I was about 10, so *[pause]* I did the typical 'I want to do archaeology' because my parents took me round Roman villas when I was a kid and I was absolutely fascinated by it all.

> I found a lovely little arrowhead when I was about 7 or 8 years old. From then on I thought 'Wow, this is incredible' and I was digging holes *[pause]* I found a dead *[pause]* pig cemetery in the village *[pause]* probably wasn't very old at all *[pause]* and I dug all that up and took it into school...

> I went back to France when I was 15 as well and realised that I really was an archaeologist ... I don't know if there's such a thing as a natural archaeologist, but I just knew I was [one]. ...

Whether a 'born' or 'converted' archaeologist, a great excavation seems to consist of a number of similar themes. My research and my own experience have highlighted the importance of camaraderie and the social side of archaeology. These aspects, among others, were underlined in the brief accounts that were sent to me by archaeologists who felt they had worked on a great excavation.

Fishbourne

Jude Jones started digging with Barry Cunliffe at Fishbourne in 1964 and worked there until excavations finished at the end of the 1960s. He later offered Jude a place at Southampton University, but she says that she was frightened of the science that seemed to be central to the discipline at the time and she opted instead to pursue a singing career. Summarising her time at Fishbourne she commented that she dug at other sites, for other people, right through her early 20s and nothing really bettered it. It was 'a magical time and place' (Jude Jones, pers. comm.). Jude recently decided to return to archaeology and she completed her BA at Southampton in 2007. Describing her time at Fishbourne she told me that

> A group of us used to spend most of the summer digging for Barry at Fish, Porchester, Bath and later Danebury and many of them were doing archaeology degrees – some with Barry at Soton, some at the Institute and some elsewhere. Quite a few have since made a name and I'm told Hodder dug at Fish – can't say I remember him – but then he'd probably say the same about me – it was a big site. (Jude Jones, pers. comm.).

Fishbourne was an ideal site for a trainee, with logical Roman archaeology which was very easy to see on the ground. Jude comments that

Figure 18.1. Jude drawing at Fishbourne. Trench in north corner of West Wing. c. 1966 © Jude Jones.

the site supervisors trained us quite strictly and there was the usual ethos of proving oneself – in terms of physical ability (no mechanical diggers) and understanding what was going on. Barry was very good at explaining the archaeology to us and used to take us round the site about twice a week on walkabout explaining what was happening in the other trenches. (Jude Jones, pers. comm.).

The diggers were accommodated in a school in Chichester, or later in tents or potting sheds next door to the scout hut which also served as their canteen. At night they became, in Jude's own words, 'the terror of Chichester' and she learnt a great deal about how to drink, what to drink and how to cope with hangovers first thing in the morning. She also noted that same feeling I had at Wroxeter, that archaeologists seemed somehow separate from normal society.

It was also the first experience I had of being a combatant rather than a civilian. Archaeology seemed to me at the time to be something which set its practitioners apart – it was hard, dirty and *dangerous* – the rest of the population were mere civilians. (Jude Jones, pers. comm.).

Sutton Hoo

John Wood worked at Sutton Hoo during the 1985 season. The project was well funded, via the British Museum and the BBC, which enabled the archaeologists to be more inventive and experimental than might have been possible on a smaller budget. It also meant that the project featured a number of times on the BBC programme 'Chronicle' and became fixed in the public consciousness as an example of good archaeology. John describes the remains as remarkable and clearly enjoyed the social aspect, but he seems certain that it was the direction of Martin Carver that made the project such a success. Carver introduced the project to the team by saying, 'We are all students of archaeology here' (John Wood, pers. comm.) and this approach certainly seems to have created a real sense of camaraderie. John went on to describe how

> the excavation was run by BUFAU under the 'command' of Martin Carver whose military background could be seen oozing from every pore of the project. If there was anything that made the whole thing such a success it was the organisational abilities of Martin Carver. (John Wood, pers. comm.).

During the 1985 season John witnessed some weird, wonderful and inspired experimentation. Aerial photography was tried using kites, hot air ballooons and a 'borrowed' Chinook from the local USAF base. Another innovation was the use of different methods for preserving and analysing the 'sandmorphs' – the 3D cast of the inhumations in the otherwise friable sand. In the case of the 'ploughman' (see Figure 18.2) the body was sprayed with a consolident, vinamul, to preserve it. The experimentation does not seem to have been limited to the site, however, and John recalled with great affection Carver's experiments to produce the perfect 'digger's lunch'. These experiments seem to have been successful.

> I have to say they were sandwiches to die for, as what was finally decided on was a delicious honey-like wheat germ, rustic bread from one of the local bakeries… Tasty, nutritious and filling! But that just showed you the detail that Carver went into, not to mention so much else that made the project the Greatest of Excavations. (John Wood, pers. comm.).

Mont Beuvray

Kenny Aitchison, the IfA's 'Head of Professional Development', began his digging career at the stunning location of Mont Beuvray in Burgundy. It was here that Bibracte once stood – the capital of a powerful Gaulish tribe and centre of resistance to the Roman invasion. It was at Bibracte that Vercingetorix was proclaimed leader of the Gaulish coalition in 52BC, and where Caesar finished writing his *Gallic Wars*. In 1984, President Mitterand's government launched a pan-European research project at Mont Beuvray. In 1990, Kenny, who had started doing a geography degree, but later switched to archaeology, found himself on an Edinburgh University excavation of part of the huge rampart of this important site. Of course, as is often the case, it was not just the archaeological remains that inspired his interest. The social side of the project was also hugely important and ensured that it was a positive first experience of archaeology. Despite that, only two of the nine students featured on this postcard (see Figure 18.3) from the early 1990s are still involved in archaeology (Kenny Aitchison, pers. comm.).

The real significance of this site, as far as Kenny is concerned, goes beyond being the site of his first taste of archaeology. In 1996 he returned to Mont Beuvray as the Site Director. Several years later, after starting work at the IfA, he found himself managing aspects of the Mont Beuvray project's European funding in 2003. It seems Kenny is destined to have a life-long relationship with this site and it is hard to quantify what that really means. His interest in French, Iron Age archaeology, and enjoyment of the pan-European nature of the project, clearly means that he will never move completely out of that sphere. In Kenny's words, 'the site doesn't come back to haunt me but it is a big part of my life' (Kenny Aitchison, pers. comm.).

Figure 18.3. Postcard from Mont Beuvray from the early 1990s featuring excavations.

The Invisible Diggers survey

Figure 18.2. Wendy Locker excavating the 'ploughman' burial 1985 © John Wood.

Clearly it is difficult to be specific as to what makes an excavation 'great'. It seems to mean different things to different people – even on the basis of the three brief case studies just presented. Is it the magic of a place, the organisation or a long-term connection that determines an excavation's greatness? However, there are a number of common themes, such as the quality of the work being undertaken, camaraderie, social life etc. The data gathering for the Invisible Diggers project (Everill 2009) included an online survey of commercial archaeologists to obtain demographic, employment and other relevant information. This proved to be a great success, and the survey received 329 responses – a reliable 15.67% of commercial archaeologists in the UK. It was interesting to assess the figures for what one might consider the major 'push' and 'pull' factors in commercial archaeology (Tables 18.1 and 18.2). These show that aspects such as the archaeology itself (i.e. the actual remains and the process of excavation); simply being able to work outdoors; the camaraderie; and the social life score very highly, with 44.68% of respondents answering that they love 'all of the above' about their jobs. However, where single aspects were highlighted the archaeology itself was far and away the most important element. When asked what they hated most, around a quarter answered 'all of the above' to a choice of the pay; the quality of people employed in the profession (both digging staff and unit management); incestuous relationships (meaning the sexual as well as professional relationships that can become complicated in a small profession); and bad weather. Pay was the standout single issue with 35.87% of respondents choosing to highlight that alone, but the quality of staff/management also featured prominently. Table 18.3 compares the responses in the Love/Hate questions with the responses to the question regarding how long the individual intends to remain within the profession. This database query was performed to see if there were any particular issues that were retaining staff, or driving them away. At first glance it seems that there is little to be gained from this data, as there are no striking push or pull factors apparent. However, those who chose to highlight 'the archaeology' as the single element they loved

Table 18.1. Aspects of the profession viewed most positively.

What do you love about commercial archaeology?		
Archaeology	133	40.43%
Being outdoors	19	5.78%
Camaraderie	11	3.34%
The social life	2	0.61%
All of the above	147	44.68%
None of the above	15	4.56%

Table 18.2. Aspects of the profession viewed most negatively.

What do you hate about commercial archaeology?		
Pay	118	35.87%
Quality of staff/ management	60	18.24%
Incestuous Relationships	21	6.38%
Bad weather	13	3.95%
All of the above	87	26.44%
None of the above	27	8.21%

Table 18.3. Aspects of the profession viewed most negatively.

Question	Answer	% of group who answered the following when asked how long they intend to stay in the job	
What do you love about commercial archaeology?	All of the above	As long as I can	50.34%
		Trying to get out now!	18.37%
	The Archaeology	As long as I can	63.27%
		Trying to get out now!	10.53%
	Being outdoors	As long as I can	31.58%
		Trying to get out now!	47.37%
	Camaraderie	As long as I can	54.55%
		Trying to get out now!	27.27%
	Social Life	As long as I can	50%
		Trying to get out now!	50%
	None of the above	As long as I can	53.33%
		Trying to get out now!	33.33%
What do you hate about commercial archaeology?	All of the above	As long as I can	41.38%
		Trying to get out now!	27.59%
	Pay	As long as I can	59.32%
		Trying to get out now!	13.56%
	Quality of staff or management	As long as I can	55%
		Trying to get out now!	28.33%
	Incestuous relationships	As long as I can	76.19%
		Trying to get out now!	4.76%
	Bad weather	As long as I can	69.23%
		Trying to get out now!	0%
	None of the above	As long as I can	81.48%
		Trying to get out now!	7.41%

about their jobs were also those most keen to remain in the profession, with only 10.53% trying to find alternative employment. The other interesting figures to come out of this suggest that, apart from those who indicated that they 'hated' all of the options, none of the single issues of this small selection were really responsible for driving people away. In fact even the issue of pay still scored a high percentage of respondents who intend to stay in the profession as long as they can. This apparent paradox merely indicates that single issues are not enough to drive people away from the profession when the strength of feeling towards it remains high. Instead, the highest percentages of people trying to leave the profession were those whose answer, when asked what they loved most about it, did *not* include 'The Archaeology'. This was one of the most revealing statistics to come out of the survey and highlights the vocational nature of employment within commercial archaeology. All of which causes many people to ask 'if this is true, why are there no "great excavations" in the commercial sector?' The answer is simple. There are, and this chapter would not be complete without reference to two recent examples.

Bradley Fen

Fraser Sturt, now a lecturer at the University of Southampton, spent a number of years at the Cambridge Archaeological Unit from 2002. During this time he worked on the Bradley Fen project, which is widely regarded as one of the most innovative commercial projects of recent years. Directed by Mark Knight, the Bradley Fen project sought at all times to combine reflexive approaches with rigorous standard recording methodology. They were also fortunate in that the archaeological remains were of a spectacular nature. Fraser comments that there is a gulf between a great archaeological site and a 'great excavation', noting that the two are not necessarily the same.

> The archaeology of Bradley Fen was definitely great, with Bronze Age hoards, intact wicker work and burnt mounds all found close together and this certainly contributes to its fond place in my memory. However, what really made the excavation was the process of engagement engendered by the site supervisor Mark Knight. (Fraser Sturt, pers. comm.).

Fraser describes how he and a friend had been transferred from elsewhere and had arrived at Bradley Fen expecting it to be just another site. Instead, Knight introduced the site in such a way that the newcomers were instantly considering some of the unique issues of the location, and ultimately felt a real connection with the work that was being undertaken.

> What stands out in my memory is how the complexities of the site were introduced, how we were thinking about what it would have been like to live on this wet edge, where differences of centimetres in elevation led to very different archaeologies. This process of discussion and involvement continued throughout the dig culminating in the group excavation of a Bronze Age hoard on a late Friday afternoon and early evening. (Fraser Sturt, pers. comm.).

As Fraser himself says, 'rather than doing a job, we were investigating the past'. I believe that this connection with a site does not differ between academic, rescue and commercial projects. Each has the ability to inspire, provided that there is the right combination of archaeological significance, camaraderie, expertise and leadership.

Heathrow Terminal 5

Gareth Chaffey had only been working in commercial archaeology for 15 months before he was first sent by Wessex Archaeology to join the Framework team at the Terminal 5 extension of Heathrow Airport. It had first started as a MoLAS project in 1996, before being expanded to a full excavation under the auspices of Framework from 1998 to 2006. For him, and many within the profession, Framework was a real eye-opener.

> The nature of sites run by Framework Archaeology allows for a completely different approach to archaeology in Britain. Framework is a joint venture between Wessex Archaeology and the Oxford Archaeological Unit, joined in partnership to cope with the high staffing demands of working for BAA on large airport projects. The joint venture allows Framework to draw upon the resources of both Wessex and Oxford, including site staff, specialist managers, administrative support, and technical facilities. (Gareth Chaffey, pers. comm.).

Framework, however, was more than the sum of its parts. Instead it was seen as an opportunity to revalue the process of excavation and interpretation, so that those staff who worked on site, excavating individual features, were given an integral role in the analysis of the site. As far as staff like Gareth were concerned it wasn't simply the geographical size of the project that made it a 'great excavation'. More significant was the fact that over 90 archaeologists were employed on T5, and an opportunity was taken to reposition site-based archaeologists within the process of knowledge production. The site did, however, incorporate an enormous area (Figure 18.4) and, as Gareth states, 'it was largely the size of this project that allowed the methodologies of Framework Archaeology to come to the fore and to be developed'. This is, of course, true. A large budget and a well-defined research agenda do inevitably provide opportunities to lay out one's intentions early on. In the case of Framework there was a clearly established intent to redefine the role of site-based staff – including the direct inputting of data into a computer database – in an attempt to counter the more widespread practice of 'deferred interpretation' (Andrews *et al.* 2000). As far as Gareth was concerned, Framework 'genuinely appreciated the digger, who was actively encouraged to fully interpret the features, to always think about the archaeology'. Gareth continues that

> Nowhere in the country have we been able [through excavation] to view such a large and comprehensive multi-period landscape; to have all information to hand at the touch of a button via an enormous database from which we can query just about anything relating to the historical landscape. The date range of the material extends from the Mesolithic to the recent past; although the major elements comprise a Neolithic Cursus and associated monuments, an extensive system of Bronze Age field enclosures and trackways and a sequence of Iron Age and Roman settlement remains and enclosures. (Gareth Chaffey, pers. comm.).

Their experiences, however, were also social in nature and included archaeological field trips to Avebury or Butser; parties in the accommodation that had been provided; and the often symbiotic relationship between an archaeologist and their local pub, all of which were remembered fondly by Gareth.

Conclusion

Clearly the definition of a 'Great Excavation' is a very personal thing. One archaeologist's 'Great Excavation' might be another's 'miserable month in a tent'. However, one can determine a number of recurring factors that contribute to the perceived success of a project in this sense, and this seems to be true of both academic and commercial projects.

Figure 18.4. A view across part of the excavation at T5 © Wessex Archaeology.

- The quality of the archaeology
- The quality of project management/ supervision
- The success of the training (where applicable)
- The quality of the camaraderie/ team spirit
- The quality of the recreational/ social component

And finally, to ensure that a project with all of those elements receives the recognition it deserves, its legacy is also crucial. Sufficient numbers of people need to have worked on it and remained in archaeology long enough to tell other people about it. For this reason the truly great excavations are those that have become semi-mythologised and part of the folklore, or even popular culture, of archaeology. In some cases it is because individual site directors, with a gift for self-aggrandisement, have spent their entire careers trying to convince others that their site falls into that category. However, the genuine article is the site where the diggers themselves acclaim it as a truly 'Great Excavation'.

References

Andrews, G., Barrett, J. C., Lewis, J. S. C. 2000. Interpretation not record: the practice of archaeology. *Antiquity* 74: 525–30

Dickens, C. 1994. *Great Expectations*. Penguin Popular Classics (New Edition)

Everill, P. 2009. *The Invisible Diggers: A study of British Commercial Archaeology*. Heritage Research Series 1. Oxford: Oxbow Books.

Great excavations, developer funding and the future

David Jennings
(with contributions by Søren Churchyard and Hank Covethon)

Foreward

by David Jennings

As all students of the latest incomprehensible ramblings of theoretical physics will permit, it is possible that an object from the future could materialise in our time. Miraculous as it might seem, I am able to report such an occurrence and present it for your consideration. More remarkably the object, a manuscript that appeared upon my study desk, is relevant to the very subject of this book.

This scientific marvel presented me with a dilemma: whether to continue with my own poorly muddled thoughts with respect to 'Great Excavations' and the world of 'developer funding'. But I have concluded that the opportunity to present a 'retrospective' and arguably therefore more 'objective' view of our times seemed too good to miss. As a consequence, I will shortly pass the narrative to Mr Søren Churchyard. Naturally, as he has not yet been born I am unable to provide you with any details of his life, other than the sparse details contained in this paper. I am also aware that through the publication of this article, I might in fact be creating the possibility for the events that have led to the 'singularity' (a suitable science-fiction term) of the appearance of his text upon my desk – that cannot be helped and I leave these complexities for the likes of Kyle Reese, John Connor or other interested 'terminatorologists' for resolution.

Mr Churchyard's own text presents a fragment of a play (entitled *Archaeological Life*) by another hand, and I shall leave it up to him to explain the unusual events that led to (or will lead to?) its discovery.

A Fragment of 'Archaeological Life'

by Søren Churchyard

Discovery

My interest in antiquated technology has led me to make a number of interesting discoveries and sent me on obscure peregrinations along the backwaters of intellectual endeavour – none more so than recently when I encountered a fascinating fragment of an impassioned dramatic work – *Archaeological Life*. Set in the twenty-first century it encapsulates the tensions that gripped the transition in the forms of organisation of the archaeological discipline. But before I get ahead of myself, it might be useful to explain how I came by this intriguing work.

My antiquarian sensibilities being what they are, I do not routinely deploy avatars to 'multi-task' all aspects of my life. Clearly, I am not totally primitive and my avatar selves are used for the 'professional domains' of existence, but for leisure activities, I restrict myself to a single physical presence. Friends and family complain that such atavism severely restricts my social life, and indeed the practicalities of travel are tiresome. But I still prefer the physicality of organic life-forms and the embarrassment and absurdity of 'life-synching' with multiple, differently intoxicated, versions of one-self after their nights of excess, only confirms what some might call a prejudice. Still I digress.

However, the simplicity of my existence can cause problems, and on this occasion it was only through extreme good fortune that I was able to retrieve the situation. It went like this: reviewing the Christies Classic Computing Sale, my interest was captured by an early twenty-first century Samsung X1 laptop – Lot no. 583. A relatively standard machine with quaint technologies now long forgotten, like Bluetooth and Microsoft Windows Vista, it had nevertheless been a singular gap in my collection of the Korean electronics company's products from the first half of the twenty-first century. I had resolved to bid for it (naturally in person not, as I have explained above, using a virtual self) but a combination of transport problems and the filial duties owed to my mother (or at least her avatar no. 14) conspired to ensure that I arrived late at the auction and missed the bid!

Distraught, but ultimately philosophical, I accepted my fate and resigned myself to a series of 'told-you-so' conversations with relations and acquaintances – 'it wouldn't have happened if you'd used an avatar!'

You can imagine my surprise, therefore when I went to the retro-zone to indulge in the arcane activity of 'shopping,' to see the very same item in the window of one of the stores. Despite a hefty price, I simply had to possess that computer. Stealing myself for a lengthy negotiation, I emerged an hour later the proud owner of my antique laptop.

Of course, one of the pleasures of owning these ancient machines is the forensic examination of their hard-drives, and it was during one of the final sweeps of the fragmentary data dumps that I came across part of the text for a play – *Archaeological Life*. While I am still engaged in trying to reconstruct a biography for its author, Hank Covethon, the text is sufficiently interesting to merit wider circulation. I will present it for you here – verbatim – and then offer some comment upon it.

An Archaeological Life: A Play in Three Acts

by Hank Covethon

Characters

AMBROSE: The local doctor and amateur archaeologist
AVANT: Eminent archaeologist
DE COOPER: A recently retired professor. Formerly teacher of NINA and EARNEST
CYPHER: Amateur archaeologist and EARNEST's uncle
EARNEST: Contract archaeologist
NINA: Contract archaeologist

ACT ONE

A pub in an isolated part of the country. An archaic ale-house that the frenzy for theme and gastro-pubs has by-passed. In the centre a series of wooden benches are arranged around an oblong table upon which there are numerous empty pint glasses. AVANT, DE COOPER, CYPHER *and* AMBROSE *are seated at the table.*

AVANT: It might be I'm becoming a curmudgeonly old devil, but the other day this young man came to see me about some ditches he'd found. He's working down the road for TC Archaeology, some bunch of cowboys I've never heard of – probably Trash and Cash Archaeology! And do you know what he wants? Advice! That's right, no bloody idea what he's looking at! I've been working on this landscape for twenty years and it was obvious that his ditches clearly related to Charlton Heath, but he had absolutely no idea! I thought why the hell are these people being let loose on our heritage!

DE COOPER: Quite right! It's the same in Budcaster, people blundering around on sites about which they know next to nothing. Recently, I heard about a site going on close to one of my excavations in the 60s. So I went down there and I practically had to sweep some wet-nosed buffoon out of the way to actually get on the site and look at the archaeology. He blithered something about health and safety and permission from the client – but I would have none of it! The archaeology seems to be forgotten about – it's a bureaucracy gone mad!

AMBROSE: Listen to you two! Really, you should know better, two eminent archaeologists, I would have expected some charity. Didn't you ever have to learn? Or look for assistance from others?

DE COOPER: Well I guess so, but that's not the point.

AVANT: Dear Doctor, it's rather the system that's at fault and I think that after all my years of dedication I've a right to express my dissatisfaction with the archaeological world.

DE COOPER: Yes, I have to agree with Avant, Ambrose my old friend, there's much that's wrong with the world of archaeology today. In a system driven by the market, where is the space for research? It would be like you being asked to undertake open heart surgery – no disrespect old soul – but as a GP you don't expect to nor do you have the training to do it. But in archaeology, some people think that you can turn up anywhere, start hacking away at the archaeological body, and then we seem to be surprised when we soon have a cadaver on our hands!

AMBROSE: Oh please leave my day-job out of this discussion! I came here to indulge my private passions, but one piece of advice, you might want to ease up on the sauce, don't you think?

DE COOPER: Nonsense, we're just getting started! Three more of the same gentlemen?

AMBROSE: Well, it would be churlish to deny such hospitality

AVANT: Of course, just to keep you company. [CYPHER *nods his agreement.* DE COOPER *goes to the bar.*] Time to visit the gentleman's chamber, I think. [*Exits stage.* EARNEST *and* NINA *enter and move over towards the table.*]

CYPHER: I knew a man who once tamed a, now what was it? A crow? No! That's it I remember now – a seagull! The damnedest thing, flew around this lake all day, screeching and keening, it drove him quite demented in the end. [*Gesturing to the empty seats of* AVANT *and* DE COOPER.] A bit like our two old birds. Now is that a simile or a metaphor or....[*Drifts into silence.*]

[*A pause.*]

EARNEST: Good evening Uncle, it looks like it's already been a long night.

CYPHER: Earnest, pull up a pew!

EARNEST: [*Ironically.*] I see our really brilliant people are here! [*Angrily.*] I'm more talented than the lot of them put together, if it comes to it. [*Tears the hard hat off his head.*] Those hacks have a stranglehold on archaeology. They don't recognise or put up with anything except what they do themselves, everything else they sit on and crush. But I don't accept it!

AMBROSE: Another angry soul! What a pleasant evening this is turning into. I do hope that you, Nina, will be able to calm some of these tormented spirits!

NINA: Not much chance with Earnest, he's in a foul mood. I'll go and help De Cooper with the drinks. [*Goes to the bar*]

AMBROSE: Really Earnest this black mood is rather tiresome, and not at all attractive to the ladies, take it from one that has known the pleasures of the affairs of the heart – as you understand, I am speaking only as a friend.

EARNEST: It's Nina and me – is it obvious that I love her? But I suspect that she only has eyes for De Cooper. I first saw them at the TAG disco together, in December. He was strutting around like a constipated chicken. So undignified. How I am sick of myself and this situation! I'll go crazy if I have to carry on like this!

AMBROSE: Yes I'm afraid that's a malady that no physician can help you with, but perhaps you can help to cure the two malcontents of their opinion of the dismal state of modern archaeology. Come use that mind of yours and lift yourself above these personal storms.

EARNEST: The affected way that they promote their tired ideas about how archaeology is heading for disaster – how utterly I loathe it all. Oh, I've made such a fool of myself. I used to idolize that miserable, gout-ridden professor – worked my fingers to the bone for him. In the past, Nina and I've squeezed every drop we could out of grant funding and we've haggled over our tins of baked beans and cheese like a couple of miserly peasants. We've gone short ourselves so we could scrape odd funds together to keep a couple of hundred pounds in the dig budget. I was proud of him and his great learning, if that doesn't sound strange? He was the very breath of life to me. Everything he wrote or uttered seemed inspired. But by God, what does it look like now? Not a page of his work will survive him. He's totally obscure, a nonentity. A soap bubble! And I've made a fool of myself, I see it now, a complete fool. But Nina doesn't see it.

[*Their conversation continues but our attention moves to the bar.*]

NINA:	[*At the bar.*] Need any help?
DE COOPER:	Nina, can I get one for you?
NINA:	Oh, yes please, that would be nice. A half of lager please
DE COOPER:	How's the site going?
NINA:	A difficult day with the main contractors, but we're making progress with the main area of the settlement.
DE COOPER:	Looked at the phosphates in the occupation areas yet?
NINA:	Not part of the brief I'm afraid.
DE COOPER:	That's the problem. When I dug at Budcaster, I didn't have a brief and I didn't have my hand held by a curator. It was up to me – the unrepeatable experiment! I made damned sure that I got everything I could off that site and it made my career. Rewrote the history of the development of medieval towns in Britain.
NINA:	[*Taking a sip from her drink.*] Yes, main volume out this year?
DE COOPER:	[*A flash of anger, then concealed by embarrassment.*] Rome wasn't built in a day! But seriously, don't you deplore this modern state of affairs. [*Picking up drinks and heading back to the table.*] So much work but of so little value. Just how many more times do we need to look at a 10% sample of the Iron Age settlements of Borsetshire? [*Sitting.*] If I had even 5% of the funds poured into these developer-funded projects at my disposal, I could lead a new revolution in our understanding of the medieval world.
EARNEST:	Oh not again! Must we repeat this mantra? [*Mimicking DE COOPER.*] 'Archaeology today is terrible! Standards have been driven down by competition; there is no coherency or co-ordination in the work that is undertaken and research is ignored for commerce!'
DE COOPER:	Well, I'm glad to see that the years in my lectures have taught you something other than mimicry. I could not have put it better myself.

[AVANT *returns to the table*]

EARNEST:	Yes but the problem is that this description denies reality! In reality, standards have been driven up over the past twenty years. I remember those archives from the 60s and 70s – notebooks and scraps of paper. Trying to write up those sites was like trying to knit with custard! In reality, there never was a golden age of archaeological research; rather it was an evolutionary stage in the development of the discipline. It is not that the discipline is eroding, it is simply changing.
AVANT:	What did you put in his Chum? This pup seems to be rather snappy tonight!
AMBROSE:	I believe that Anteros has been shooting his leaden arrows! [*Responding to bemused looks.*] The demise of a classical education is to be regretted greatly!
AVANT:	You are purposefully Delphic!
AMBROSE:	Bravo! Indeed.
DE COOPER:	But if your claim for evolution rather than degradation is to be accepted Earnest,

explain what has happened to all of the great excavations. Remember that session at the IFA conference in Reading? Speakers were lined-up and gave accounts of their excavations, chosen as great by popular vote, and not a single one derived from the world of modern developer-funding. Indeed, I remember someone asking the question ' Where are the great excavations of today?' The room was packed with people from your world of developer funding No one could name a single one! You could practically see the tumble-weed blowing through the the hall. So if this more advanced condition of the discipline doesn't generate a single candidate for *greatness*, but by the popular opinion of the practitioners in the discipline, a whole session can be filled with accounts of great excavations from more *primitive* times, perhaps you could enlighten some of us dinosaurs as to the error of our ways.

EARNEST: If you insist. First, let's look at this claim to greatness. Aren't you rather ashamed? Doesn't it seem hyperbolic or rather overblown to claim greatness for these endeavours? Admittedly, there have been significant and deeply informative excavations and those that you might call socially interesting, but great? Finding a cure for cancer, stopping armed conflict, gaining the independence of India like Gandhi – these things I can see might give rise to a claim for greatness, but digging holes in Britain and fulminating on the finer points of the Neolithic. That's not great, it's using a heroic language to mythologise the discipline's past.

AVANT: I think he's wriggling. It still doesn't explain the absence of any great developer-funded excavations. Why is no-one romanticizing the present?

AMBROSE: La Rochefoucauld states that 'Philosophy triumphs easily over past and future ills; but present ills triumph over it.'

NINA: So dear doctor, you think we are merely deceiving ourselves? It's a function of history and imagining the future, that can't be sustained in the chaotic and unresolved nature of the present?

AMBROSE: Isn't it our dissatisfaction that drives us towards a better future? Perhaps, without recognising it we certainly would be condemned to atrophy.

EARNEST: The social and economic context has also changed. Many of these great excavations took place over many seasons and relied heavily upon volunteers, amateurs and academics. They were to an extent a removal from the everyday flow of life – an escape. God, on one project I seem to remember that radios were banned on the camp-site, because 'people came to get away from the everyday world.' Now, it's my full-time job. It's been professionalised. I don't know of many professions that talk about themselves in terms of greatness. We're simply maturing.

CYPHER: So you're saying we're not comparing like with like – or apples with apples as they say? Do you know I once knew a chap that often compared fruit and vegetables. What do you prefer, he would say, banana or carrot? Orange or cabbage? Cherry or chard? Different things, but you can have a preference, which might even be good for the body and soul.

AVANT: Cypher, you are too deep. Now how about getting in another one for you and me?

CYPHER: [*Speech becoming slurred.*]Excellent idea! [*Goes to the bar.*]

DE COOPER: But perhaps that social context, I mean of those earlier excavations, was important. It's not solely about the academic results of the work, but also about the experience of archaeology and the access that our excavations gave to the public – they could be directly involved in discovery. Nowadays, they're lucky if they can see the site on an open day, and don't talk about actually taking part in it. Ambrose will like this – I remember a phrase coined by Kierkegaard from the Ancient Greek – symparanekromenoi – goodness knows if I've pronounced that correctly.

AMBROSE: Passable! Hidden depths, hidden depths!

DE COOPER: Thank you! It means 'the fellowship of buried lives'. And it struck me that it is that experience that strikes at the core of what people value when they take part in a dig – it's their fellowship with buried lives. Their connection with people that have gone before. Perhaps that's one reason why our work has been considered great!

EARNEST: If you want an answer, let's not get distracted by discussions of value.

NINA: But clearly, that which is deemed great is also considered valuable, so you can't totally ignore reflections on value.

EARNEST: But please let's avoid the definition debate. Look at it another way. Coming back to my proposal that we're seeing an evolution, a burgeoning maturity of the discipline – let's look at the role of single excavations. It's clear that the scale and range of research now being undertaken as a result of developer-funding far outstrips anything we have seen before in the history of archaeology. As such, the capacity of a single excavation to substantively change our understanding is diminished. I mean that the focus of our research needs to change. The Victorian paradigm of the type site, lavishly published and used as a platform for a series of sweeping generalisations about the past looks increasingly tenuous as a methodology.

AVANT: I'm not sure that I'd quite agree with your characterisation.

EARNEST: Well let's try a thought experiment. Let's imagine that in one thousand years we dug a hole of any conceivable archaeological scale in the middle of London. Do we consider that we could accurately reconstruct a comprehensive understanding of life in the 21st century? No! But we've archaeologically played a similar game for the past one hundred years.

AVANT: Your argument is a parody! I'm not aware of too many *comprehensive* reconstructions on the basis of a single excavation. Rather each excavator tries to examine their site against the background of other knowledge and contributes to the debate where the site seems to have some additional or complementary information.

EARNEST: But we need to recognise that we have to move beyond the site and we need new forms of working and analysis. Our problem has changed. It is not that we have a paucity of data. For large parts of British archaeology we have an engorged mass of under-utilised data. We have neither the tools nor the research structures to transform the discipline from a site focus to a truly integrated landscape focus. We need to work across organisational boundaries in larger cross-functional teams. In other words it's less about the *great man* view of the history of archaeology – the Mortimer Wheeler or General Pitt Rivers. It's about combined efforts. Its also about using Information Systems technology to permit major synthetic programmes.

DE COOPER: So you're contending that there are no more great excavations because the scale of analysis is moving to a wider level? But surely as your colleagues' day-to-day activities are still focussed at site level, they still predominantly experience archaeology as a site-based activity? So how come none of those sites made it into the Reading conference session? [CYPHER *returns and sits down rather heavily.*]

EARNEST: I'll respond another way if I may. If you're trying to argue that the endeavours and abilities of the four thousand people now employed in UK archaeology amount to less than the efforts of the several hundreds undertaking the same work in the 60s, 70s and early 80s, then I think that highly improbable. The aggregate results of human endeavours tends to be the same.

DE COOPER: I don't think that's what is being said. Avant and I were saying just before you came in that it's the system that compromises the results. I wouldn't dare to insult the abilities of the current generation. Let's accept that there have been the good and the bad, the incompetent and the stunning expert in every phase of history.

CYPHER: [*Increasingly slurred*] Like that King and the three sisters, What were they called? Quite escapes me. Still two were rather nasty types plotting, poisoning and the like. Reagan was one of them – no, no, – that was a president. I know, I know! While the third tried to look after her old dad...

AVANT: Yes indeed, now can I look after that pint that you so kindly brought over for me. [*Taking glass from* CYPHER.]

CYPHER: Be my guest. Lear that's the cove! [*Nods off.*]

DE COOPER: No it's the system. How do you achieve a high quality research result when you might be deployed on a Neolithic site one week and a Roman site the next. Your work is determined by the vagaries of modern development not by a research agenda.

EARNEST: Heard of EH Regional Research Frameworks?

NINA: Come on Earnest, let's not make the claim that we're living in a golden age, when you wouldn't allow De Cooper and Avant to make a similar claim earlier. How often have we sat in the site hut and discussed the problems with the brief, the time pressures and the standards of work?

EARNEST: [*Looking like he's been slapped across the face.*] I see you're supporting him now.

NINA: It's not a question of supporting anyone.

AVANT: We've heard a lot of sound and fury but what does it signify? Nothing! You haven't named a single great excavation derived from the world of developer funding because I don't think that you can!

EARNEST: Of course I could, but I'm trying to get across to you that it's not about great excavations, it's about great archaeology. We're at a point when the discipline has the potential to develop exponentially if it can break down the barriers that fragment and separate it.

DE COOPER: We must live in separate universes. I see a discipline with declining standards, shoddy research and poor publication, collapsing central government funding and local government services fighting for survival. It's been an interesting conversation, but I can't help but feel that we've been talking past rather than to each other.

EARNEST: The mantra of doom again! Why do I feel like I'm trapped in some form of ground-hog day for depressives. All summer it's been this dialogue of despair. Have you ever considered that it's our professional language that encourages this maudlin *Weltanschauung*? We talk constantly of destruction, loss and damage and it seems to seep into our very bones. Uncle [*Gently shakes* CYPHER.] would you like a lift? I think it's time I left. Another busy day tomorrow, in the sterile enterprise of modern archaeology.

CYPHER: Err, what? No thank you. I've had enough!

EARNEST: I wasn't offering you another drink; I think I'm suffocating here and it's time for me to go before I say something that I really will regret.

CYPHER: Of course, of course. Time to hit the road. Goodnight all, it's been... well... err... yes!

EARNEST: Nina are you coming?

NINA: Not just yet, I'll see you tomorrow

EARNEST: Fine [EARNEST and CYPHER *exit.*]

AMBROSE: For people who study humanity, you do seem to rather lack any sense of the accumulated wisdom of the human condition. Now perhaps that's a problem of how and what you study and what you think is the underlying purpose of the discipline. But as you can appreciate I am fortunate as I only have to deal with the lives of the living.

NINA: [To DE COOPER.] How about inviting me back for that cup of coffee?

DE COOPER: The most interesting idea I've heard all night.

CURTAIN

Commentary

by Søren Churchyard

I have scoured the hard-drive but unfortunately it would seem that the play remained unfinished. I have discovered some fragmentary notes indicating that the love interest between De Cooper, Nina and Earnest leads to a denouement, which involves either a ranging pole or sharpened trowel, but most frustratingly the archaeological argument does not seem to be concluded.

With regard to its author, I suspect that he is writing under a *nom de plume.* I have checked the global digital biography and the only Hank Covethon recorded in this period was a dental hygienist in Fort Worth, Texas – an unlikely candidate for a dramatic work on the vagaries of British archaeology in the twenty-first century. There are certainly no other works ascribed to him.

In terms of the archaeology, it is intriguing to see the articulation of a debate that led in the first half of the 21st century to the establishment of major spatial data banks; the development of cross-organisational research networks; and the explosion of research that was able to manipulate previously unimagined data sets. That stated, we can look back with the benefit of history and assert that the great excavations continued to occur and were ultimately recognised.

Clearly, some of the vagaries of the sector remained for a considerable time. The absence of sufficiently strict regulation and the variability of standards remained a concern, while the pressures of a market place continued to distort or at least accentuate certain stresses in the archaeological community. Many mark the major breakthrough in the protection of England's archaeology with the requirement for organisations to be registered with the Institute for Archaeologists, and the gradual movement towards a certified archaeologist status as a requirement to practice archaeology as a profession.

Much later, the development of cybernetics leading to avatars meant that quality assurance problems were largely resolved at a technical level, but the human need for people to explore the human condition, to understand the historical condition of *Dasein,* as Heidegger would put it, means that archaeology has proliferated as a leisure activity in which people directly engage with the contested nature of being. De Cooper's recognition of the existential value of archaeological activity was a trend that amplified throughout the 21st century.

Earnest's disdain for the senior figures of De Cooper and Avant is clearly driven by the frustrations and arrogance of youth. However, in the long term it is clear that the discipline developed more along the lines that he envisaged, as opposed to the dire predictions considered by De Cooper and Avant. That stated, their anxieties were driven by genuine concerns and their perspective was not without foundation.

As for the other characters, their roles seem rather more symbolic or perhaps are to be further developed in later Acts. I suspect that Cypher, in particular, is performing a different function in the dramatic structure. The clue is probably in the name, but literary criticism is not my strength and I have yet to understand his role beyond that of a comic character.

Covethon's work, therefore, provides us with a fascinating snapshot of the discipline in the early twenty-first century. For those that would like to see the Act reconstructed, my avatars have recreated a performance on my holoweb space. Comments and research links can also be found there.

Afterword

by David Jennings

The Nineteenth Century and After

> Though the great song return no more
> There's keen delight in what we have:
> The rattle of pebbles in the shore
> Under the receding wave.
>
> W. B. Yeats, 1929

Under deteriorating health, such that a pall is cast over much in *The Winding Stair and Other Poems,* Yeats feared that the last great period of poetry has passed (but suggests that there are substantial themes that might still be derived from this state of affairs). However, even a cursory examination of poetry in the 20th century, will reveal the unfounded nature of Yeats' primary fear. Similar sentiments expressed in archaeology will share a corresponding fate.

It is a truism that our personal condition colours our perspective. However, to quote one of Ambrose's favourite writers, La Rochefoucauld: 'As great minds have the ability to say much in few words, so, conversely, small minds have the gift of talking much and not saying anything'.

I am aware that Covethon, Churchyard and myself have taken up much of the allocation given to us, and I believe it is more appropriate and a fundamental purpose of a literary work that the author's work is a springboard for further personal reflection. On that basis I commend Covethon's work to you without further exploration or comment.

What the Dickens happened to the IFA?

Peter Hinton

The conference session from which this book stems looked at some 'great excavations', and the Dickensian allusion of the title was obvious to all. The session coincided with the twenty-fifth anniversary of the foundation of the IFA, and the session organiser and now editor, John Schofield, felt that it would also provide an opportunity for a review of the Institute's first quarter century.

This review does not claim to be a complete history of the Institute, and I doubt that all of it is accurate – in fact it is probably every bit as partisan and nostalgic as the other chapters included in this collection. A thorough account would require much more detailed examination of the relevant papers, of which surprisingly few survive in the IFA's offices from the early years, though rumours abound of a rich seam running through the archives of the CBA. But at a time when the IFA is going through a process of modernisation, it does provide an occasion to look at the early history and prehistory of the IFA, and to reflect on the aims of its founders, which seem more pertinent today than ever.

All professional institutes have to perform a balancing act between supporting their members' interests and ensuring consumer/public protection through the maintenance of professional standards. In a healthy profession it's relatively easy to manage, because transparently effective self-regulation is the best way of demonstrating and promoting professional service delivery. The other trick is to meet the great expectations of those members who want their institute to reform and advance professional practice and are prepared to put their time and money into that effort, as well as those who hope to receive material, a personal benefit in return for their membership subscription. In a profession where institute membership conveys the right to practise it may be possible to satisfy both demands, but elsewhere one should look very carefully at professional bodies that promote themselves to potential members on the basis of a raft of discounts and offers for financial, motoring, retail and leisure services – does the Institute still have the vision of its founders? Does it remember what it's for? I believe that the IFA has and does, and am pleased that during its first 25 years most of its efforts have gone into standard setting, professional development and advocacy rather than into negotiating 5 percent off your next (or first) meal in your local Beefeater.

Great expectations

Our founders were definitely of a similar view and set a clear course for the IFA because they believed that something should be done about archaeology, and had great expectations of a professional institute set up to do it. That course has been followed with determination and vigour; and along the way – what larks, Pip, what larks!

The origins of the Institute can be traced back to at least 1973, when the CBA established a Working Party on Professionalism in Archaeology. This came in the context of a rapid increase in the number of employed archaeologists, who faced new challenges; and resulted in the creation of a representative steering committee to draft a constitution for a professional institute 'to be responsible for the establishment and maintenance of professional standards in archaeology' (CBA 1974, 7). The vision was for a 'graduated series of qualifications', providing 'a sound basis for a career structure for professional archaeologists'. Clearly anti-institute propaganda and tensions between the higher education community and other archaeologists both predate the IFA, as 'contrary to ill-informed correspondence in the press, it will offer an avenue for mid-career entrants to the profession, since a university degree in archaeology will no longer be the main indication of professional qualification'.

The proposal was for a 'British Archaeological Institution' with three grades of membership: Licentiates admitted via an exam that had much in common with the CBA Diploma in Archaeological Practice; Associates entering with a degree and two years' experience and Fellows having an impressive track record (Cleere 1984, 13). Wrestling with the 'grandfather principle' that all new institutes face, it was proposed that a body of senior archaeologists would declare themselves the BAI and seek applications from others.

Henry Cleere (1984, 13) produced the first of what was intended, like the great novels of Dickens, to be a serial publication of short articles on the prehistory of the IFA. Sadly it was also the last, but it usefully sets out the nature of the opposition to these proposals:

- there was no need for another body and another set of subscriptions to be paid
- an institute would be divisive
- it would be financially non-viable
- archaeology was not a profession
- some archaeologists already belonged to other professional bodies
- money for archaeology would dry up and the number of archaeologists fall
- it wasn't clear what purpose the institute would serve
- there had been insufficient consultation
- the proposed process of establishment was undemocratic

The CBA Executive Board took the view that more work was needed, and the BAI never came into being. This was a setback for the professionalisation of archaeology, but no doubt a sensible pragmatic decision, faced with the need to do more spadework with the potential membership.

The old curiosity

Gestation continued, and in 1979 an Association for the Promotion of an Institute of Field Archaeologists (APIFA) was established (Addyman 1984). It is worth looking at the papers of APIFA in some detail as these old curiosities are relevant to current debates in the profession.

Significantly, field archaeology was defined in clause 2 (APIFA 1979) as 'including the study, recording and conservation of material evidence bearing upon the human past, below the ground and upon its surface'. This is pretty all encompassing stuff. Importantly it includes the stuff that pokes out of the ground – buildings for example – as well as that buried in it; and even more importantly it refers not only to recording and analysis but also to conservation of all of that material. This is significant today for two reasons. First it begins to give a comprehensive outline of all those elements of what we now call the historic environment. Secondly it undermines a recent argument that IFA involvement in conservation issues amounts to parking our tanks on the lawn of more recently established bodies – a little more attention during turf-laying might have revealed the pre-existing archaeological heavy armour.

Interestingly this useful definition was not carried forward into the primary constitutional documents of the IFA, the Memorandum and Articles of Association. This was a deliberate move 'since any errors or omissions would be difficult to rectify. Rather, it will be for the Institute itself to make known its intended coverage – a coverage which might well change or evolve with the passage of time' (APIFA 1980d). In fact this robust definition – supplemented only by reference to the maritime and intertidal resources – continues in the *Code of conduct*, current mission statement, its predecessors and other documents – but it has not always been remembered. By 1983 there was already talk in IFA Council about refusing membership to those that merely managed the archaeological resource, admitting only those whose job it was to destroy it (providing they did so with great excavations, not mediocre ones). Fortunately the sensible decision was taken and all were considered eligible – Brian Davison's apposite warning that he could do far more damage to archaeological sites sitting behind a desk at Fortress House than could be achieved by anyone with a shovel may have originated at this time.

But APIFA was clear on its definition of archaeology, and determined (APIFA 1979, clause 3) that the objects of the proposed IFA were to include 'the definition and maintenance of appropriate standards of

   a. training and education in field archaeology
   b. responsible and ethical conduct in the execution and supervision of work
   c. conservation of the archaeological heritage'

In this context, the discussion of eligibility for membership matches well with modern debate. 'Amateur status is not seen as incompatible with professional standards of work' (Davison 1979). A discussion paper (APIFA 1980a) picks up this point in more detail:

> The Oxford English Dictionary contains various definitions of the word profession… a vocation in which professed knowledge of some department of learning or science is used in its application to the affairs of others and in the practice of an art founded upon it. Only more recently has the word been applied more loosely to any calling or occupation by which a person habitually earns his living. It is this last meaning that has bedevilled past discussion of an archaeological Institute in Britain, where the contributions of part-time and full-time archaeologists are so closely mingled.

The bedevilment has continued intermittently since, and the preferred IFA definition of a profession as 'an occupation in which skilled practitioners undertake their duties impartially, according to a code of ethics, and are subject to the oversight of their fellow practitioners' still hasn't fully taken. It is important because it emphasises that to be considered a professional the practitioner must have skill (technical competence), behave impartially and according to the *Code of conduct* (ethical competence) and be prepared to have their actions investigated by peers and submit to any sanctions they impose (a disciplinary process to enforce the *Code of conduct*). Thus with membership of IFA standing at 2600 at the time of writing and of the Association of Archaeological Illustrators and Surveyors at *c.* 200 and the figures for archaeological employment in the UK in 2007 estimated as 6865 (Aitchison and Edwards 2008, 41), we can see that a small majority of paid archaeologists are not professionals. Closer examination of the IFA's membership reveals that a minority of unpaid archaeologists are professionals. So the inclusive vision of APIFA has been implemented by example, but not yet in volume. There are still some who enjoy claiming that paid archaeologists, and even the IFA, wish to suppress the activities of those in the voluntary sector. When I was an amateur – as we were happy to be called – I never encountered a paid archaeologist who wanted to prevent voluntary involvement, though I saw a few fairly toxic examples of the reverse; but I admit that since earning my living from this discipline I have met a few paid archaeologists who mistrust and lack respect for the voluntary sector. So that 1970s devil still requires some exorcism.

In May 1980 APIFA (1980b) published a draft *Code of practice* based closely on that of the US Society of Professional Archaeologists. It was discussed initially in Scotland and then at a series of meetings in England and Wales during June. A substantially revised *Code of conduct* (APIFA 1980c) and a draft Memorandum and Articles of Association were issued in October, and both form the core of today's documents. These were voted on at the November general meeting, great expectations reinforced, and the way forward agreed.

A Christmas cabal

Tribute has been rightly paid before to the progenitors of the IFA for their achievement. Less recognised is the speed and effectiveness with which a great deal of drafting, consulting, persuading and artful dodging was done during 1980, securing the rather shaky foundations described by Cleere (1982). Such deft footwork recurs in the IFA's history, but it has rarely managed to stick quite so rigidly to its self-imposed timetable – in this case a crafty sunset clause that was designed to dissolve APIFA at the end of April 1981, although it lingered on until January 1983.

As it was the election of the Institute's founding Council (Figure 20.1) took place without bloodshed, and the first meeting of IFA Council, in its best seasonal sweaters, was held on 21 December 1982.

Figure 20.1. The first IFA Council in December 1982. Left to right: Tim Tatton-Brown, Henry Cleere, Martin Carver, John Wacher, Brian Hobley, Phil Barker, Peter Fowler, Chris Musson, Brian Davison, Roger Mercer, Peter Addyman, Peter Reynolds, and Richard Bradley. In pre-Photoshop inserts, Michael Farley, David Baker and Carolyn Heighway; not manifest John Coles and Francis Pryor. Photo: Museum of London

A tale of two cities

Supported entirely by voluntary effort, the IFA was initially housed with the Museum of London's Department of Urban Archaeology in Basinghall Street. By early 1983 the first staffed office was set up with Birmingham University Field Archaeology Unit in the city of Birmingham with Joe Davies initially undertaking the duties of Assistant Secretary, to be replaced by long-serving stalwart Steve Walls in 1983, who was in turn succeeded by Kitty Sisson after a long handover in 1994–5. In 1995 the IFA moved to its second long-term staffed office in the city of Manchester, courtesy of the University. In 1997 it moved again to the University of Reading, thus making the story of the staffed office so far a tale of two cities and a town that has failed in its bids to become a city. The duty of running the essential administrative infrastructure passed from Kitty Sisson to Rachel Boning in 1998, and with additional corporate governance responsibility to Alex Llewellyn in 2001: Alex has kept IFA legal, solvent, organised and accounted for ever since. The longest serving member of staff – and sole survivor of the Birmingham era – is Lynne Bevan, who has run the Jobs Information Service since 1991.

A review of IFA (IFA 1993) revealed that membership had plateaued at just over 1000 members, provided a range of services (publications, training, jobs information) and groups, and had aspirations to introduce a registered organisations scheme. The review proposed that a three-year post of Director be created 'to ensure that we break the cycle of lack or resources and enable us to achieve our aims', as well as additional administrative support – and sought to secure additional funds as the annual turnover of *c.* £65,000 fell well short of what was required. By 1997 the concept of an Institute dividing its responsibilities between standards and outreach was established, funding was in place and I was lucky enough to be awarded the post of Director; at the same time Jenny Moore became Editor, a role that passed to Alison Taylor in 2000. Eventually sufficient resources were in place to appoint a Head of

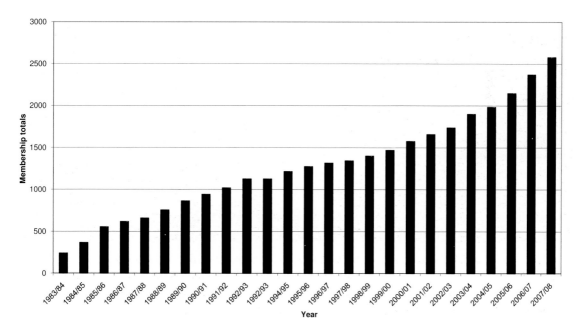

Figure 20.2. Histogram showing the growth in membership over the years: an encouraging start, the mid 1990s plateau, strategic development of the Institute from the late 1990s and a dedicated recruitment post from 2005.

Training and Standards (Kenneth Aitchison in 2001), and that side of IFA activities has grown ever since with an extensive portfolio of projects and increasing staff. More recent appointments have supported the Institute's administration, its recruitment and marketing (Tim Howard in 2005) and publicity (Kathryn Whittington in 2007).

One of my early roles as Director was to plan and fund the strategic development of the Institute, evolving into a ten-year strategic plan (IFA 2000). This confirmed the IFA's mission statement as: '[to] advance the practice of archaeology and allied disciplines by promoting professional standards and ethics for conserving, managing, understanding and promoting enjoyment of the heritage' (IFA 2000, 1), defining archaeology as 'the study of the human past through physical remains' (IFA 2000, 2) and placing more emphasis on partnership working than had previously been explicit. Six key objectives were set (four now fully, one largely and one partly achieved) across four strategy areas, with annual business plan targets monitored by Council.

DAMHB and Son

By 1983 the Institute's advocacy initiatives were underway, initially with information about IFA sent to the Division of Ancient Monuments and Historic Buildings (DAMHB) of the Department of the Environment followed by offers of advice to its English offspring, the Historic Buildings and Monuments Commission, now better known as English Heritage. With increasing devolution of historic environment matters the exclusively English focus of the early IFA has been moderated (Area Groups first emerged in 1983 with a proposal to set up a Scottish 'chapel', and a constitutional mechanism was established in 1986). IFA has throughout its life responded to government and agency consultations, but only in the last few years has it been lobbying in advance of consultation, seeking to set rather than respond to new policy directions.

Most of IFA's recent advocacy effort has been directed through The Archaeology Forum, an independent grouping of non-central government bodies concerned with archaeology. ALGAO UK, CBA, ICON, IHBC, IFA, National Trust, National Trust for Scotland, Rescue, SCAUM, Societies of Antiquaries of London and Scotland, SMA UK have worked well together, descending into acronymy but not acrimony, and it is clear that this partnership working has opened doors that would be closed to IFA or any of the other organisations lobbying alone.

It is also apparent that IFA's profile has increased: presence on the ministerial Christmas card lists is a reliable indicator of perceived importance if not value, and the attendance of the English Secretary of State for Culture, Media and Sport at the IFA's conference in 2005 showed recognition of IFA at cabinet minister level. Perhaps politicians and policy makers are just getting politer, but it does appear that what the IFA thinks matters.

Hard times

Low pay and poor job security in archaeology have been major problems throughout IFA's history. As early as 1985 a working party on archaeological contracts looked both at contracts for services to developers and of employment for archaeologists, but later subdividing. That group advising on employment conditions was in part reacting to a growing sense of dissatisfaction from the junior ranks of fieldwork employees who perceived that there were fundamental problems with the structure and funding of archaeology. As today, some saw IFA as a body that could address the problems while others considered the Institute to be complicit in them. A report of the Assistant Public Relations Officer on a meeting of 100 members of the short-lived federation Archaeologists, Communicate, Transform (ACT) in 1986 recognised the group as 'committed, concerned, caring…naïve' (I think the last one was me) and sought to capture that energy to work with the Institute – as most ACTivists went on to do, allowing the grouping to wither on the vine.

By its fourth meeting in August 1983, IFA Council had already discussed concerns about the archaeological product of the many Manpower Services Commission schemes involving archaeological work, and it is clear that – in parallel with ACT but partly in reaction to the voice of that constituency (playing a role equivalent to that of the Diggers' Forum today) – attempts to improve the lot of junior archaeologists increasingly featured on Council's agenda. Significantly at the fraught 1986 AGM a resolution was passed that the Institute 'regards the system of "paid volunteers" as directly contrary to the "highest standards of ethical and responsible behaviour" professed by the Institute' (IFA 1986), and this policy was reinforced over the following years, leading to resignation by a Council member expected by his employers to continue to employ excavators on 'fees and subs' – though that organisation subsequently abandoned this practice.

In 1996 Council adopted the report of the *Archaeological employment in Britain* working party (see Schaaf 1996). The report recommended that the IFA continue to take an interest in employment matters and career structures, introduced to the *Code of conduct* Principle 5 ('the archaeologist shall recognise the aspirations of employees, colleagues and helpers with regard to all matters relating to employment…') and accompanying rules, and proposed a set of minimum salary recommendations. Recently reformed, those salary recommendations appear now generally to be met and widespread employment abuses a thing of the past, but archaeological salaries still fail to reflect the skills and responsibilities of the sector, falling behind those of comparator disciplines by some margin (Price and Geary 2008).

It remains to be seen how much scope the IFA has for further improvement of archaeologists' pay and conditions without there being some barriers to entry to professional practice. Working towards those barriers has been one of the highest priorities for IFA during the early years of the 21st century, and it is pleasing at the time of writing to see signs of support from government and politicians.

In 1999 IFA launched its 'training vision' (Bishop *et al.* 1999) in Glasgow. It proposed to set out the roles that archaeologists fulfil (done, occupational mapping, Carter and Robertson 2002); the skills they require to fulfil those roles (done, national occupational standards in archaeological practice, Carter and Robertson 2002)); the training that provides those skills (ongoing – never ending – with partners in the sector); the qualifications that indicate the presence of those skills and competences (done, levels 3 and 4 NVQs in archaeological practice, Carter and Robertson 2002; Annex 2); professional membership grades that recognise those qualifications (done, just, at the time of writing, IFA 2008, 9); and remuneration that rewards the skills and responsibilities of holders of those IFA grades (done to the extent several employers link pay to IFA membership grades, manifestly not done in that pay does not match the qualities of an archaeologist). In short it laid out the plans for a professional career structure, and one that IFA has made good progress in establishing.

Bleak house

Of course the main reason for barriers to entry to professional practice and the greater powers for self-regulation that they would bring is not to improve archaeological remuneration, but to raise standards of archaeological work – to provide a better service to the public. With the publication of PPG 16

Table 20.1. Characteristics of a professional institute assessed at different stages of IFA: launch in 1982, at the beginning of planned investment and growth in 1997, and today. The quantitative measures are self-evident, the qualitative ones debatable.

	1982	1997	2008
Code of Conduct	yes	yes	yes
Standards	no	some	more
Membership entry proceedure	assertion and reference	rigourous, bureaucratic	rigorous, reforming
Professional qualification	no	no	yes
Disciplinary Measure	no	cumbersome	effective
Members	240	1300	2621
RAOs	0	12	61
Staff FTE	0	2.2	10.9
Turnover	£8k	£93k	£834k
Professional influence	some	growing	considerable
Political influence	none	none	significant

(DoE 1990) in England a long but far from uniform tradition of developer funding for archaeology was normalised, but with its publication (only days apart from Margaret Thatcher's resignation as Prime Minister) so too was archaeological competition normalised. Discussion of competitive tendering (apparently the only mechanism for competition that archaeologists could visualise) was the mainstay of several IFA conferences in the late 1980s and early 1990s, and fear that the cowboy archaeologists down the road were intent on undercutting local quality drove demands for greater regulation. Against this bleak assessment of a house in need of setting in order, IFA established a Standards in British Archaeology working party in 1991 (Hinton 1996), and the first five standards and guidance documents – primarily relating to fieldwork – were drafted for adoption at the 1993 and 1994 AGMs. Subsequently expanded, but still far from a complete set, the documents are widely specified and almost as widely observed.

At a similar time and for similar reasons, there were moves to introduce the registration of organisations as well as individuals. After a couple of false starts (Locock 2002), a workable scheme was introduced in 1996. It is interesting that the IFA initiative closest to the trade association end of the professional institute spectrum is perhaps its most successful enterprise, rigorously assessing organisations' compliance with the *Code of conduct* and expanding suite of standards. Peer inspection has been universally constructive. There have been numerous recommendations to registered organisations for improvement, most of which have been acted on. Several practices have had to be politely turned way, and sadly a couple of organisations formerly registered have had applications refused, but in both cases the applicant bodies committed themselves to programmes of improvement and worked diligently to build up evidence to persuade the Institute that they are eligible to be placed back on the Register. There can be little doubt that commitment by archaeologists to the scheme has led to a very significant general improvement in the quality of archaeological work.

In its first decade or so the Institute's legal advisors received a substantial proportion of IFA's resources. Though navigating through procedurally compromised AGMs formed part of the cost, investigating alleged poor practice with attendant scope for litigation made up the bulk of it. The need for a 'Professional Grievance' procedure was first raised in 1984 and rules were adopted at the 1986 AGM, where they were given the amended title of Disciplinary Regulations. Following a long-running and potentially viciously costly case in the late 1980s and early 1990s they were rewritten, but even in their revised form both bringing and investigating allegations involved a cumbersome process; thus most potential cases remained as pub grumbles that IFA could not act on, failing to satisfy popular hunger for a public execution. Following further reform in 2005 in line with best practice in other sectors, the regulations now seem to be working effectively, applying positive recommendations where useful but also resulting so far in one expulsion.

Notes and sketches

In 1984 Council first discussed the forthcoming (1986) World Archaeology Congress in Southampton and agreed to participate. At the beginning of 1986 the UK Executive committee of WAC decided to exclude participants from South Africa (as protest against the apartheid regime), and Council considered whether to withdraw the IFA's sponsorship (as a protest against this curtailment of academic freedom). The Chair, John Coles, proposed that IFA should withdraw, but the motion was defeated by eleven votes to five and the Chair resigned his post later that day. At the six-hour long 1986 AGM at Birmingham University a special resolution 'that the Institute should withdraw its sponsorship from the World Archaeological Congress… because of the exclusion

Figure 20.3. Somewhere between the end of the stuffy, formal institute and the consolidation of the non-sexist approach, this T-shirt design was a popular seller at the IFA conference in Brighton in 2000. IFA conferences began in 1987 and now regularly attract 400–500 delegates.

of South African and Namibian residents' was lost (IFA 1986). This was a difficult debate in which both sides had manifestly valid moral arguments: those proposing the resolution pointing out that many of the archaeologists excluded were amongst the bravest and most vocal opponents to apartheid, and those opposing it considering a position of principle on racial discrimination to be more important than one on academic freedom. The debate was complicated by some admitted constitutional confusion and potential irregularities under company law, which involved lengthy adjournments while the officers spoke to IFA's solicitors and the members went to the Gun Barrels pub in Edgbaston Road – both of which no doubt fuelled the vigour of the debate and the flamboyance with which some delegates walked out of the meeting in disgust. Harsh words were spoken but subsequently most of us were reconciled by our mutual friends and by reading thoughtful, conciliatory editorials in *The Field Archaeologist* that promoted the respect for both viewpoints that generally lasts to this day. But it was a troubling and dangerous time for the Institute, and it is a relief that there have not been more such potentially destructive schisms in the years that followed.

Justifiable expectations

Rapid and decisive though the Institute was at inception, even cursory study of Council minutes shows that by the mid 1980s the growth in the number of committees and working parties rapidly reduced the number of decisions made, no doubt normally to the benefit of greater levels of consultation and cross reference but to the detriment of rapid progress. At the same time a formal tone of IFA communications became entrenched as IFA quite rightly sought to convey an impression of authority and professionalism to the archaeological world and beyond, an impression that came across rather more as old-fashioned and bureaucratic.

The introduction of the strategic plan and the significantly increased resources that flowed from a more business-focussed approach seems to have shifted the Institute up a gear or two, with clearer divisions of responsibility between members, Council, committees and staff, a wider range of services, rising membership, effective advocacy and generally speedier operation.

Sexist language reduced as the 1980s progressed, and we gradually lost the full stops from 'I.F.A.' that must have been the bane of the Birmingham typists (budget: £200 pa) in the days before the Institute discovered word-processing. The policy on stuffy tone was reversed in the late 1990s in the interests of becoming a more responsive and engaging organisation, though in practice is has been hard to eradicate: only recently was a typical example of the Birmingham years – the years of the Office of Circumlocution – eradicated with the removal of 'Notice is hereby given' from the head of the AGM notice. Even now we occasionally still write to members as Ms S. Port, Mr A. Silt, Mr W. Table or Dr D. Diss-Audley instead of using their given names of Sally, Sandy, Walter and Duncan, and there are many members who refer to IFA in the third not the first person, not fully accepting that they *are* the Institute. Perhaps it is to be expected that as the organisation has grown that some of its members feel disengaged – in 1984 85% of eligible members participated in the ballot for Council members; in 2007 the figure was only 4% (Taylor 2007) – but it seems likely that reengagement will be high on the Institute's agenda for the rest of this decade. The creation of an IFA group on Facebook (http://www.facebook.com/home.php#/group.php?gid=8531366027) provides an example of contemporary social networking.

Table 20.2. The IFA in 2007: some statistics

Members:	2,510
MIFA	1,000
AIFA	596
PIFA	361
Affil	273
Student	265
RAOs:	57 employing 1,894 people in archaeology

Epilogue

This retrospective and partial (in every sense) history suggests that the Institute lost its way somewhere in mid-career. This may be an unfair criticism, as limited resources had to be applied where the demand was greatest, but the message about the greater non-fieldwork remit of the Institute was certainly unclear. In part the lack of clarity relates to the 'F-word'. Amongst our founders the voting was 8 to 7 for including 'Field' in our title (Henry Cleere, pers comm), and its presence has undoubtedly provided an excuse if not a reason for many in higher education and museums to feel excluded – though of course there are stalwart supporters in those areas. *The Field Archaeologist* became *The Archaeologist* in 1996, a resolution to change the name to Institute For Archaeologists was supported by a majority of members in 1999 but not the 75% required, yet a new Memorandum and Articles from which 'field' was dropped was voted in by more than 75% in 2002.

Our founders' beliefs and vision are firmly back in the ascendant. Central to the present plans for repositioning and modernising IFA are ensuring that

- the Institute is seen to be relevant to the work of a wide range of historic environment professionals
- archaeology is recognised as including conservation and future management as well as investigation, recording and dissemination
- archaeologists have responsibilities for landscapes, buried sites, upstanding structures and maritime heritage
- professionalism is about standards of competence and ethics and not about livelihood

The evolution of our institute will no doubt continue, and, whatever its future name and nature, great excavations will always be in its DNA.

References

Addyman, P. 1984. Chairman's Statement. *The Field Archaeologist*, 1, 2.

Aitchison, K. and Edwards, R. 2008. *Archaeology Labour Market Intelligence: Profiling the profession 2007/8*. Institute of Field Archaeologists.

APIFA 1979. *Association for the Promotion of an Institute of Field Archaeologists: constitution.*

APIFA 1980a. *A professional institute of field archaeologists?* (discussion paper prepared by the APIFA committee, May 1980).

APIFA 1980b. *Draft code of practice for field archaeologists.*

APIFA 1980c. *Proposed Institute of Field Archaeologists: draft code of conduct.*

APIFA 1980d. *Notes for the General Meeting of the Association to be held on Saturday 1st November 1980.*

Bishop, M., Collis, J. and Hinton, P. 1999. A future for archaeologists: professional training and a career structure in archaeology. *The Archaeologist*, 35, 14–16.

Carter, S. and Robertson, A. 2002. *Occupational and functional mapping of the archaeological profession.* www.archaeologists.net/modules/icontent/inPages/docs/training/occupational_and_functional_mapping.pdf.

CBA, 1974. *Annual Report no 24 for 1973–74.*

Cleere, H. 1984. The Origins of the Institute – 1. *The Field Archaeologist*, 2, 13–14.

Davison, B. 1979. *Association for the Promotion of an Institute of Field Archaeologists* (paper for the inaugural meeting of APIFA, 20 October 1979).

DoE 1990. *PPG16 – Archaeology and planning.*

Hinton, P. 1996. Good archaeology guaranteed: standards in British archaeology'. *The Field Archaeologist* 26, 7–11.

IFA, 1986. *Minutes of the third Annual General Meeting of the Institute of Field Archaeologists held at 11.00 am on Monday 7 July 1986.*

IFA, 1993. *Institute of Field Archaeologists: past, present and future.*

IFA, 2000. *Institute of Field Archaeologists: strategic and business plan July 2000.*

IFA, 2008. *The Applicants' Handbook (revised July 2008).*

Locock, M. 2002. The Registered Archaeological Organisation scheme. *The Archaeologist* 46, 12–13.

Price, F. and Geary, K. 2008. *Benchmarking Archaeological Salaries* www.archaeologists.net/modules/icontent/inPages/docs/Benchmarking%20report.doc.

Schaaf, L. 1996. Report and recommendations of the Archaeological employment in Britain working party. *The Field Archaeologist* 26, 12–18.

Taylor, A. 2007. *Scrutineer's Report of IFA Council elections.*

Great Excavations?

Geoffrey Wainwright

I sat in the outer ditch of the hill fort at Hod Hill on a peerless summer day in 1956 and ruefully contemplated my mint copy of *Archaeology from the Earth* which was stained by the yolk of a soft-boiled egg. Sir Ian Richmond, the director of the excavation on which I was working as a seconded undergraduate from Cardiff University, squatted nearby and grinned amiably. 'You need a high crotch and a country estate to be an archaeologist around here,' he remarked, eyeing a wire fence that surrounded the ramparts and the rolling downland beyond. I agreed companionably, both of us comfortable in the camaraderie of the excavation which had brought us together. Though still a teenager I reckoned myself an experienced hand. I had survived the traumas of Cardiff Bus Station at 9 a.m. on a Sunday morning in order to travel to Dinas Powys where my supervisor – the redoubtable Leslie Alcock – was conducting the Departmental Excavation. In between times I had been sent on loan to the top of a mountain in the Lleyn Peninsula, where my birthday was spent in thick fog excavating a round house in Tre'r Ceiri hill fort. I had excavated the stoke-hole of a Roman Bath House at Castell Collen in Radnorshire and drawn my first section (as a mirror image of course) under Chris Musson's merciless supervision. I was also comparatively well travelled amongst my peers, having gone to England earlier that year to excavate at Verulamium. Two subsequent weeks with Sir Ian had restored my faith in the subject and the bonding power of an archaeological dig and I wiped the egg-yolk off my book with a contented sigh.

Here I am over 50 years later and still digging, writing a chapter in a book on Great Excavations. What then makes an excavation great? Not the criteria proposed by Sir Ian I imagine. There must be more to a Great Excavation Director than agility and a private income. Everyone will have their own benchmarks but I was surprised to see that one of my personal criteria – that of immediacy – does not feature. It is rare indeed for an archaeologist to encounter a situation which brings the past up close and vivid. The Rose Theatre in London in 1990 was a pressure cooker. I walked onto the site of the excavation through the baying crowds of protestors and sorrowful luvvies – Nicholas Ridley's patrician contempt for both ringing in my ears. This was the first Tudor theatre in London to be excavated and passions were running high. 'Don't Doze the Rose' screamed one flame-haired thespian – if only that were possible I thought with longing. Then I felt something crunch beneath my shoe. I looked down and realised that the theatre floor was covered with hazel nuts dropped by the Tudor audience. The uproar around me dimmed into a background hum as I came to terms with the vivid immediacy of what I was standing in.

Fast forward a decade or so to Boxgrove on the south coast of England where Mark Roberts had uncovered the stone tools and animal bones of a 500,000 year old kill site, on what was then the shore of the English Channel. The remains were in a pristine condition just as they had been abandoned and encapsulated that elusive quality of immediacy. I glanced at my companion – Jocelyn Stevens the Chairman of English Heritage, not known for his soft imaginative side – and knew I had his whole attention. 'Give them what they need Geoffrey' he said. Then turning to his long-suffering but intensely loyal Press Officer – 'Stone Age Man wore mink coats' he barked triumphantly – certain in the knowledge that this would be the headline next day. Immediacy is a scarce and precious commodity for the person fortunate enough to encounter it, and the Rose Theatre and Boxgrove rank high on the greatness scale on this count alone. Similarly the book relates the story of the Coppergate Houses in York, dated with precision to 974–5 AD and could have included the prehistoric Sweet Track in Somerset where dendrochronology has shown that the main structure was built in the winter of 3807 BC and the spring of 3806 BC. Such accuracy adds colour and immediacy to these remote events. Immediacy of a different and special sort can be created by understanding and interpreting past events as at Danebury. The extent of these excavations and their interpretation by Barry Cunliffe enables us to understand the underlying purpose of the spatial lay-out of the hill fort interior, thus putting flesh on the mute evidence of bones, stones and pottery. Rarely has Wheeler's maxim of digging up people not things been so elegantly demonstrated.

The association with historic events is another criterion which makes an excavation great in the public mind. Wheeler was a master of this black art. Maiden Castle makes a deserved appearance in this volume, best known in the popular mind for its 'war cemetery' of plucky Brits who died defending their hearths and homes against a foreign invader. What a story for Britain in 1939! The unfortunate fact that the cemetery is of the wrong date matters not at all for the public perception of a good story. In a different element the excavation of the *Mary Rose* gives us a genuine and authenticated link with the past and deserved inclusion for that reason. The mass graves of the Black Death in London are gripping evidence of a link to historic events. The encampments of Venutius at Stanwick (Wheeler again!) or with King Arthur for South Cadbury and Tintagel are much more tenuous but nevertheless grip the public imagination. Archaeology is a science that must be seasoned with humanity for it to be touched with greatness.

Great excavations are also those which have a special place in the history of our subject through the application of innovative techniques. Of these, Mucking is special as being one of the largest projects in Europe at that time (18.2 hectares) excavated over 19 years. Wharram Percy (1953–1990) was the first and most extensive multidisciplinary project which was a key building block in the development of medieval studies. At Wroxeter, Phil Barker introduced open area excavation at a time when the process was regarded with deep suspicion by those raised in the Wheeler tradition of boxes and baulks. Haddenham saw the early application of phosphate, magnetic susceptibility and soil micromorphology techniques which justifies its inclusion in this short list of projects defined by innovation.

Some digs have proved to be a major influence in the thinking of a subsequent generation. The Somerset Levels Project and its directors John and Bryony Coles have been major influences on investigations of the wetlands in the United Kingdom. These have collectively been the most important investigations of the past century, shedding new light on the environment and material culture of our prehistoric past. The Danebury project has shown the advantages of working on a large scale over an extended period of time but it is Winchester which must take the prize for innovation. Martin Biddle's work between 1961 and 1971 represented a major departure in the study of our great cities. He integrated archaeological, historical, topographical and architectural evidence rather than dealing with them as separate disciplines as was done previously. He also introduced new approaches – open area excavation, metrication and the matrix approach to stratigraphical analyses. Before he began his work, the story of urban life after the Roman period was largely the prerogative of historians. Biddle changed all that by establishing archaeological evidence as the key to our understanding of cities in these later periods.

The main results from Winchester were disseminated extremely quickly but the more detailed publication has not yet appeared in full. Publication of the results of an excavation are essential for it to achieve greatness. Lack of a publication diminishes the sum of our knowledge and the professional reputation of those concerned. Owlesbury is not published and so has had no long-term impact. The full publication of Mucking also seems a distant prospect, although the generous legacy by Margaret Jones to the Society of Antiquaries may transform the situation and encourage others to do the same. Maiden Castle and Sutton Hoo are prime examples of good practice but Danebury has set the standard for others to emulate. Barry Cunliffe has published 40 years of excavation and survey in nine volumes – an exemplary feat of leadership, teamwork and endurance.

Danebury has also given us a massive data-base which awaits re-interpretation and reminds us that very often the most appropriate places to ask questions are on sites where we already know a great deal. There is always something more to be learned and no-one should be allowed to have the last word. Martin Carver describes how Sutton Hoo – pivotal to our understanding of the birth of the English nation – has been subjected to five excavation campaigns. Niall Sharples has reinterpreted Wheeler's seminal excavations at Maiden Castle by re-opening the great man's trenches. Repeated interventions at many sites – Stonehenge, Durrington Walls, Silchester, Chester and Hadrian's Wall have enhanced our understanding on each occasion and are to be welcomed. To a very large extent each generation of excavators stands on the shoulders of their predecessors – some more gently than others!

A constant theme throughout the book are excavations as a social experience – almost a form of therapy – and that is how they are graded for greatness by many authors. For some the excavations were clearly seen as a refuge in a counter-culture with its own codes of conduct and a palpable sense of bonding. Commercial companies pay big money to develop a comparable team spirit, and never make it. Nowhere else can one feel so much part of an enterprise.

The therapy can take many forms – serious late evening debates around the cocoa at the Breiddin, pretensions to gentility at the Howe, immersion in routine at Wharram Percy and self-conscious interaction with the local community at West Heslerton. The transient communities which form around excavation projects inspire great loyalty from the participants and the feelings of belonging are common to most excavations. This raises the leadership question – many participants relate and react in diverse and revealing ways to project Directors. The answer to the question does a great excavation require a great director must surely be in the affirmative. Directors come with various eccentricities and extremes of style. Chris Musson and I cannot be alone in having happily married members of our work-force! Phil Barker roamed the site according to this book as an interested and well-informed bystander asking awkward questions – which sounds absolutely infuriating. By contrast, anyone who dug at Mucking is marked out as having special qualities. Margaret Jones had a forceful manner and her sharp exchanges on site commanded respect. Barry Cunliffe comes across as reassuringly normal with a clear understanding of what the job is all about. Visibility on site, leading from the front, the continuity of a core team and the maintenance of a strict work ethic. That approach takes Danebury to the top in my estimation as the greatest of the great excavations in the book. I suspect, however, that for many of us, an excavation qualifies as great when one has been there as a youngster immersed in an experience that is incapable of replication.

Index